While My Guitar Gently Weeps

The Music of George Harrison

Simon Leng

HAL•LEONARD

Published by Hal Leonard Corporation

7777 Bluemound Road
P.O. Box 13819
Milwaukee, WI 53213

Trade Book Division Editorial Offices
19 West 21st Street
Suite 201
New York, New York 10010

Cover image © David Redfern/Redferns
Cover design by Bob Antler, Antler Designworks
Book interior by Lisa A. Jones

Library of Congress Cataloging-in-Publication Data
Leng, Simon.
  While my guitar gently weeps: the music of George Harrison/by Simon Leng—1st ed.
     p. cm.
  Includes discography (p. 325) and bibliographical references (p. 331).
  ISBN 1-4234-0609-5
  1. Harrison, George, 1943-2001—Criticism and interpretation. I. Title.
ML420.H167L46 2006
782.42166092—dc22
                                                    2006004098

Printed in the United States of America.

Hal Leonard books are available at your local bookstore, or you may order through Music Dispatch at 1-800-637-2852 or www.musicdispatch.com.

For Caitlín and Áedán, with love

Contents

8
Working from Home, England (1979–1982) *199*

9
On Holiday in the Armani Age (1985–1987) *239*

10
Good Times with Old Friends (1988–2001) *259*

11
And in the End (2001–2003) *289*

Preface

On April 6, 1992, George Harrison carried out the most unexpected decision of his career—he played a concert in London, England. It was the silent superstar playing for his forgotten audience, and the last full-length concert this uniquely misunderstood entertainer gave.

Moreover, it was entirely in keeping with the man's beliefs that he didn't pocket a single penny from this Albert Hall date. The show was a benefit in support of the Natural Law Party, the "political wing" of the followers of an Indian spiritual teacher, the Maharishi Mahesh Yogi. This was the man who, in 1967, brought centuries-old Indian meditation techniques to the attention of the Western world via Harrison and the Beatles. To some, he was a charlatan. George Harrison, then a part-time member of the Fab Four, had found in Hindu beliefs the answer to his feelings of dissatisfaction with his life. Some said that Harrison was a traitor to his culture for embracing Eastern philosophy; others said it was a fad. This 1992 date revealed it to be a twenty-five-year-old fashion.

Inevitably the concert was nostalgic, but it was not merely misty-eyed remembrance—it was a great performance by a great musician. Seeing George Harrison in the flesh, on a stage with a guitar strapped on, singing, was a strange experience, rather like waking up on the steps of the Taj Mahal. A double take was required when faced with the reality of such a famous image. After all the years of Beatles hype, here was George Harrison, finally: in person, a musician, playing in his home country.

And the reality of Harrison the musician was startling, as he reeled off one classic song after another: "Something," "Old Brown Shoe," "Isn't It a Pity," "My Sweet Lord," "Here Comes the Sun," "Give Me Love," "What Is Life," "Piggies," "Taxman," "While My Guitar Gently Weeps." How many songwriters would have given everything to have authored just one of these? Time did not allow for inclusion of "Beware of Darkness," "I'd Have You Anytime," "Far East Man," "Learning How to Love You," or "All Things Must Pass." But there was more than just a replay of the classics—strangely moving guitar notes introduced "Something," and a late 1980s rocker, "Cheer Down," rolled on burning slide guitar. This was clearly a man of many talents.

It was obvious that this man was a great songwriter and guitarist. Yet, away from the Albert Hall that spring evening, no one was shouting about it. That didn't add up.

At the climax of the concert, as the wild applause for a mesmerising "Isn't It a Pity" died down, the middle-aged, suited guitarist poured his heart out to the London crowd: "Thank you very much, it's really overwhelmed me, you know. I'm always really paranoid about whether people like me, I don't know."

A discomforting, uncompromising, naked honesty was always George Harrison's way, in his music and in his life—what you see is what you get. That honesty, and a pressing need to state what he felt, frequently brought him into conflict with the media and with the music business from which he ostensibly made his living. Harrison's tendency to challenge the popular myths about the Beatles made him the forgotten man, the one who never quite fitted the fantasy vision of the group.

Sadly, today, even after his death, his music is largely overlooked and passed over as unimportant when, as the London concert proved, he was a major artist. Wave after wave of Beatle-related trivia and canny marketing has kept the fans returning again and again to the Beatles, while Harrison is, by virtue of his lack of "Beatleness," a marginal figure.

When he died, the media was more interested in unearthing shocking revelations about the "weird" Hare Krishna rituals alleged to have accompanied his passing rather than pondering his music in any depth, if at all. His image, in life and death, was not defined by his personal musical output, considered less interesting than his Beatles image. At one time, it seemed that the cartoon George Harrison was more authentic than the real one.

This is perverse, as an artist's creation is his only true connection with his audience, and at the center of the debate about his worth. But the Beatles were the first victims of a trend that made it possible to speak about musicians without reference to their music.

This book is about George Harrison's musical journey of self-discovery, which became inextricably linked with his personal search for the truth of his own existence. Harrison's odyssey began in Hamburg 1960, when he took the first steps toward becoming a professional musician.

Acknowledgments

Most of the people who have helped with this book are musicians who gave freely of their time and insights into George Harrison "the musician." Some of them were talking about this for the first time, and often it was no light decision to do so. I hope this book manages to convey the admiration and affection they felt for George Harrison.

My thanks and debt to:

John Barham, Max Bennett (www.maxbennett.com), Delaney Bramlett (www.delaneybramlett.com and www.zanerecords.com), David Bromberg (http://www.geocities.com/SunsetStrip/Stage /2349/contents.html), Rosanne Cash for permission to adapt the article that first appeared on her Web site (www.rosannecash.com), Jim Horn (www.jimhorn.com), Larry Hosford (www.larryhosford.com), Joey Molland (www.joeymolland.com), Andy Newmark, Bob Purvis, Emil Richards, Tony Sheridan, the late Doris Troy (www.doristroy.com), and Klaus Voormann (www.voormann.com).

There are two special people who have been instrumental in making this new edition of the book happen—Frank de Falco and Anthony DeCurtis. I am lucky to have such wonderful, true friends.

Thanks also to John Cerullo, Belinda Yong, and Jenna Young at Hal Leonard for their tremendous help, Vickie de Falco, Rip Rense, Tony Kilbert, Phil and Dennis Shaw (WBA 4 EVER), the Lurgan stargazers (lens cap off, boys), Martin Magee, William Ncube (City 0), Rupert Snell, Dino Airali, Kathie Molland, Dave Mattacks, Wendy Farwell for introducing me to the Cello quote, Bruce Kay, Nigel Bell, Paul McSharry, Ray Marshall, Darcy Hepner, John Harris, Sean Body, Robert Sellers, Tomas Bonn, Danny Kahn, Stephen Bailey, and Walker Ed Amick.

Special thanks to Klaus Voormann for the artwork, and Patti Murawski and Kristen Tash of *The Harrison Alliance* magazine for the Dark Horse Tour reviews and invaluable advice.

And, always, all my love to Susan, Caitlín, and Áedán. Keep your head to the sky.

Simon Leng
County Armagh
March 2006

"'Technique' in its fullest sense, means discovering and developing the physical means for bringing into existence a piece of music. Thus it follows that technique *per se* cannot exist apart from the music it is meant to serve. This fanaticism about 'technique' as an end in itself severs the thread between the physical means and the music, and creates a separateness which is contrary to the nature of things."

—*Cello*, **William Pleeth, Kahn & Averil, London 1982**

1

The Beatles' Early Years

Incredibly, until the mid-1990s the full range of the Beatles' talents was largely unknown. Their official studio recordings told only part of the story. And after 1963, very few Beatles concerts were more than a circus of almost no musical merit—that this was a tight, versatile, compelling live band was lost in the mayhem. As a result, the real roles that the members played were limited in the public imagination.

The fog lifted in 1994 when *Live at the BBC* was released—a set that gave a glimpse of what the group was like as a live act before the madness of celebrity and fame took over. The *Anthology* series, which followed, captured video footage of the early band at work, and for the first time revealed how the Beatles worked in the studio. All of this presented a very different view of each Beatle's role in the whole, and in particular, the importance of George Harrison's contribution was inescapable.

The received wisdom about the group's accomplishments and their lead guitarist's part in it is summarized by Ray Connolly's introduction to the 1982 edition of *The Beatles Complete* songbook:

> George Harrison's contribution as a songwriter was slow to develop, and I always felt that his interest in all things Indian may have placed him in a kind of melodic straitjacket. Early in the careers of The Beatles Brian Epstein was widely quoted as saying that George was the most naturally musically gifted of the four. This may easily have been said to boost George's ego, since he must have often felt in danger of being swamped by the two heavyweights with whom he was working. But there is little doubt that many of the most instantly memorable facets of Beatles records were *little* acts of Harrison inspiration.

There are hints of insight into Harrison's contribution here, but ultimately Connolly cannot see beyond the supposed Lennon-McCartney oligarchy. So George's inspired efforts become deeply patronized "little acts," and, of course, Epstein stated that Harrison was the most naturally musically gifted not because it reflected a truth, but to boost his ego. It has been easier for commentators to believe that George Martin was a bigger influence on Beatle arrangements than their own lead guitarist was.

In the post-*Anthology* era, with the Beatles' recording methods available for all to hear, Harrison's part in developing the group's basic song ideas, just chords and melody, into a finished musical product can be recognized for what it was—fundamental. The Beatles' music as we know it simply could not have happened without George Harrison's input.

The nature of Harrison's role was shaped in the music sweat-shops of Hamburg, where many, many years ago, he was the guitar player in a Liverpool band called the Beatles. Hard to imagine, perhaps, that there was not yet a Harrison of popular imagination, not yet a cartoon Harrison; he was not yet "the quiet one," only one quarter of a package called "the Beatles." He was just a guy, playing the guitar in the vague hope that he might make a few quid for a year or two, and temporarily escape life as an apprentice electrician on Merseyside.

The time that George Harrison spent in Hamburg from 1960 to 1962 was effectively his apprenticeship as a professional musician, and the defining, formative period of the group. The pecking order and roles within the Beatles were forged in Germany, and many of the unique factors that led to their unprecedented success came together there. One of those factors, and one of the most overlooked since, was George Harrison's pivotal part in the architecture of the Beatles' sound.

Driven by the ambition of John Lennon and Paul McCartney, the Beatles arrived in Hamburg in August 1960 to join a host of Liverpool bands playing rock 'n' roll for people who fifteen years earlier had been "the enemy." It was a very strange setting indeed for musical peace talks. Tony Sheridan, another Englishman and an accomplished rock 'n' roll guitarist, was already there, plying his trade at the Kaiserkeller with his group, the Jets. Sheridan had backed Eddie Cochran, which only enhanced his standing with the Liverpool lads. The Beatles, however, initially struck him as just another band: "All the groups who came over from Liverpool had a similar sound, all the drummers sounded the same—at that stage none of them were much good at all. The Beatles had obvious talent, but they were copying people like Chuck Berry and there was no individual style."

By the time of the Beatles' second trip to Hamburg in April 1961, they and Sheridan were regularly playing together, hanging out. Crucially, the older guitarist had taken the role of teacher to Harrison's eager pupil, as he describes:

> The thing about George was that he was so young—he was just trying to feel his way into what it meant to be a guitar player. He wasn't sure if he was going to stick at it. When he came over he didn't know much apart from a few Carl Perkins things. I showed him stuff I learned from Eddie Cochran, who was a very good guitar player. But George was keen as hell, keen enough to sit down three or four hours a day and put it all together. He was a bit of fanatic when it came to learning—we would have breakfast, then come back and start practicing. We did it almost every day; there was nothing much else to do.[1]

This was primarily a time of survival—and for Harrison, that meant keeping his place in the band by being indispensable. In Hamburg, both Harrison and the group learned that the best way to do this was to be different. George, being no front man, had only the guitar and his music to help him stand out. But he also had Tony Sheridan to point the way.

> George used to say to me, "How did you play that, show us that chord, how come you can play a D up there with an E in the bass?" His way was to be different, do his own thing. In order to do that he had to have sufficient material, licks, chords, and rhythmic styles—he learned all that in Hamburg. I used to teach him weird chords, ninths, elevenths, flattened fifths, whatever sounded different, because at that time everyone was just playing straight chords. George was copying stuff like this as well—but he also started putting in some weird chords. No other group was doing that. At the start John didn't know what it was, he was more into playing straight chords.

So while the Beatles had to be different, they had to do it within the bounds of what was popular—they needed to make money. That was what they were there for, after all; no one thought that the rock 'n' roll fad would last long. "None of us seriously believed that rock 'n' roll was going to last more than a year—everyone was saying that," recalls Sheridan. "We didn't really expect to make it as rock 'n' roll players." And the imperative of financial survival meant that most of the Liverpool groups couldn't afford an interest in the blues, which would provide a parallel British music boom in the early 1960s. As

---

[1]Sheridan. Phone interview with author. August 2004.

Sheridan puts it: "Very few of us were into music deeply enough to be getting into blues—blues meant going towards jazz in a way, and it was not commercial. The Beatles wanted to make it, and the ambition made them shy away from getting into too deep waters like blues and jazz. The Beatles would have done anything to get their foot in the door. The ambition was John's and it was tremendous."

One of the key factors in Lennon and the Beatles' making it very big indeed was George Harrison, even if they never told him so. Amid the demands to *"mach schau"* for the locals, Tony Sheridan is clear that Harrison was keeping the music on an even keel:

> You had to have an anchor guy, making sure that everything stuck together—someone who was not bawling at the front and screaming. You had to have somebody like that in the group. It allowed Paul and John to do their theatrical thing at the front. Paul was not a guitar player, he definitely did not love it—he loved being in the front, in the limelight. John was not a good guitar player so George had to do it, even though he was just struggling to keep the job. George's thing was to embellish and be musical in any song. He was the only guy in their group who was able to do that.

In a sense, Hamburg was a music scene of extremes—extreme demands to put on a wild show, and for extreme hours. So while Lennon and McCartney had to be the front men, George Harrison had to learn to inject something musically different into a huge repertoire. "In Hamburg you arrived with 100 songs and you needed 200 to cope with the hours," recalls Sheridan, "so that meant that you had to grab songs from here and there, unlikely material as well. Filling the time also meant doing five- or ten-minute versions of three-minute songs, which meant getting away from the recording and discovering improvisation. So they rehearsed onstage and the arrangements happened onstage. People were improvising all the time and not playing the same solo twice. You could take chances because the public weren't listening—they were not playing to a listening audience."

Given this latitude, Harrison started developing the role of lead guitarist beyond the basic "riff and solo" model to that of a musical commentator, punctuating the tune with short statements developed from the melody, to add color and interest. He can clearly be heard doing this on "My Bonnie," one of the recordings the Beatles made with Tony Sheridan in Hamburg in June 1961.

Notably, this session captured a rare Harrison-Lennon composition in the shape of the instrumental "Cry for a Shadow"—a feature for Harrison's distinctly bluesy lead. The cut is an overlooked minor success that gives an early account of the synergy of the Lennon-

Harrison "rhythm-lead" pairing, a catchy melody built around precise bent notes and a fast-picking middle eight. The melody was all Harrison's, and as Pete Best later recalled, it was created spontaneously: "'Cry for a Shadow' was born during our first Hamburg tour, the result of trying to take the Mickey out of Rory Storm. It was put together by George in a few minutes after Rory had called in on us during a rehearsal at the Kaiserkeller. He was telling us how much he liked the Shadows' song 'Frightened City.' 'Can you play it?' he asked. 'It goes like this,' he added, starting to sing the opening bars. George intentionally began to play around the Shadows' melody in a sort of counterpoint—without Rory having the slightest suspicion he was being sent up. John joined in and I picked up the beat."[2]

At this stage of his development, Harrison had a relatively sophisticated guitarist's tool kit based on his expanding knowledge of non-standard chord voicings, Buddy Holly's crisp musicality, Carl Perkins's chord and note pick 'n' mix, and the basic Chuck Berry rock 'n' roll licks. But the limitations of the guitars of the time and the Beatles' avoidance of blues meant that aside from "Cry for a Shadow," exaggerated string bending played a limited role, as Harrison's original guitar mentor Tony Sheridan explains: "In those days there was only one type of guitar string, from Gibson, and they were heavy. Bending hadn't come in with a bang at that time—it was a blues idea, which wasn't our thing. It was physically exhausting to keep bending these heavy strings—we suffered from finger sores all the time, from playing for hours and hours." And, playing fast, the guitar obsession of the late 1960s and '70s, was not a Hamburg fixation. "Acrobatics was not what it was about for us," is Sheridan's memory; "a fast rock 'n' roll song was as fast as you could go."

Fortunately, the group's Hamburg sound was taped and later released on a 1977 set, *Live at the Star Club Hamburg*. The music is basic and potent, with Harrison prominently leading the songs. And his playing is full of energy and bravado—compare his raw, aggressive solos on "Little Queenie" with his Beatlemania sound. This is a very different Harrison lead voice from the supposedly diffident "quiet one." And the version of "Roll Over Beethoven" is evidence that George had mastered Chuck Berry and moved on—the extended solo finds him already emancipated from Berry's blues-scale shackles. Another, "Lend Me Your Comb," captures a visceral solo of the kind that EMI rarely did.

---

[2]Best, *Beatle! The Pete Best Story*.

On balance, Harrison's Hamburg years provide much of the context for understanding how and why he became the guitar player he did. The music was already enormously eclectic, demanding great versatility from the lead guitarist, whose overriding function was to hold the band together and be musical. Stylistically, the main factors were the lack of blues influence, which reduced the emphasis on bends and vibrato, and the relative unimportance of playing fast. It all added up to a picture where the lead guitarist was playing to support the song, not his ego.

Other than the Hamburg bootleg, the Beatles' pre-stardom live sound was a mere memory. Not until 1994 and the release of *Live at the BBC* did a proper document of the early Beatles as a live act appear. It offers invaluable insight into how the Beatles operated as a band, and casts new light on George Harrison's place in it. In fact, the two most prominent "voices" on the set are John Lennon's voice and Harrison's lead guitar, which is heavily featured on practically every song. *Live at the BBC* captures the Beatles playing large chunks of their Hamburg and Liverpool live set, mixed with a smattering of their own compositions.

The album shows them adept at arranging virtually any rock 'n' roll or R&B song for the guitar band format, while also documenting what it meant to be a "lead guitarist" in that era. As the name implies, it was akin to being the band's metronome, starting and closing each song, setting the tempo and essentially providing the framework for the "soloists," the singers. As Tony Sheridan pointed out, Harrison was the musical "anchor man" who kept the ship steady; he was also the main "soloist," notwithstanding Lennon's occasional harp or harmonica breaks. This does not diminish Lennon or McCartney's prime role in any way. Their part in the group was to be charismatic front men. Harrison would never have fulfilled that role and happily accepted in 1974 that he had the stage presence of "a wet sponge."[3] The point is that the set high-

---

[3]Murawski, "All Aboard the Hari's on Tour Express!" reported that after one of the Dark Horse Tour shows at Madison Square Garden in December 1974, a DJ, while praising the show, noted that Harrison had the stage presence of a "wet sponge." Harrison then apparently called the station, saying, "Hello, this is the wet sponge," but actually agreeing with the DJ's assessment.

lights the magical synergy and versatility of four musicians, and the critical part of George Harrison as the lead guitarist.

Live at the BBC has countless examples of this Harrison lead role, like his chord picking that opens "Don't Ever Change." This fine cover of the Crickets' 1961 hit is led by Harrison's opening riff, which runs throughout the verses and closes with a staccato coda signaled by the lead guitar changing the rhythm. "A Shot of Rhythm and Blues" is similarly accented. And, of course, all the Chuck Berry covers are based around Berry's one-dimensional licks, while the excellent "Soldier of Love" finds the Beatles mixing things up with an introductory riff played on lead and bass. This is just what lead guitarists did at the time, and in some ways, the Beatles stuck to the formula. Even if most of the music they covered did not feature extended guitar solos, Harrison was one of the most innovative guitarists in the country, fusing styles into his own new approach.

One of the highlights is his work on "Crying, Waiting, Hoping," a song Buddy Holly taped in his apartment shortly before he died. Holly played no solo on this demo cut, so Harrison's break on *Live at the BBC* is his own work, and he recaps Holly's chord-based style in the first half. In the second he mixes things up with single notes and a liquid, fast run. The net result is a development of the original. Harrison had studied his heroes' parts and was now moving onto his own ground. And when the original had no guitar showcase, as on Little Richard's "Ooh My Soul," the young guitarist plays in his nascent style, with rumbling bass-register notes rubbing up against chord-picking vamps and Berry bends. For the Beatles' take of "I've Got a Woman," a guitarless Ray Charles classic, Harrison calls on Carl Perkins's six-string phrase book.

Live at the BBC also captures some of Harrison's finest ever vocal performances, making obvious the fact that the Beatles originally had three lead singers. Notably, Harrison offers tremendous versions of "Glad All Over" and "Roll Over Beethoven," both driven by his powerful and committed singing. Here is a George very different from the reflective, contemplative vocalist of the 1970s—on these live cuts he's full of audacity and energy. Another highlight is "Youngblood," a relatively obscure Coasters B-side on which Harrison mimics the Southern drawl of the original, alongside John Lennon's now inconceivably offensive "spastic voice."

And while John Lennon takes the lion's share of the lead vocals on the cover versions, the set also showcases wonderful harmony singing and two duet vocals. Harrison is captured to good effect on "So How Come (No One Loves Me)" and "Don't Ever Change."[4]

The abiding impression is of Harrison as a fundamental part of a great working band, multitasking as lead guitarist, musical stabilizer, lead vocalist, and harmony vocalist. The first two Beatles albums followed this pattern.

---

[4]Of the more than fifty songs on the set, Lennon leads the vocals on nineteen, against McCartney's ten and Harrison's seven.

2

The Beatles' EMI Recordings

When George Martin first listened to the Beatles' acetates being hawked around London by Brian Epstein in February 1962, what about the music caught his ear and made him decide to give them a studio test? Contrary to accepted dogma about the strengths of the group, one of the critical factors was George Harrison's guitar playing. Beatles historian Mark Lewisohn notes that Martin "wasn't overly impressed, but was curious, commenting favourably upon George's guitar playing." One of the songs on the demo was "Till There Was You."[1]

The Beatles' recording trajectory confirmed the four possessed Darwinian powers of adaptability to new surroundings and demands. Lennon and McCartney developed classic songwriting skills at such a pace that the band's reliance on covers was over within little more than eighteen months after the release of *Please Please Me*. The band's live repertoire exposed them to a wider harmonic color wheel than most, at least partly the reason for the early sophistication of the Lennon-McCartney songbook. And for Harrison, complementing this œuvre on lead guitar required more than the standard Chuck Berry or Carl Perkins licks. It was a task for which Harrison was uniquely well qualified, but for which he has received little recognition, least of all public acknowledgment from John Lennon or Paul McCartney.

As the Beatles moved away from the basic twelve-bar structures of R&B and rock 'n' roll, led by the Lennon-McCartney compositions and guided by George Martin, Harrison developed the ability to perform a musical narrative as a counterpoint to the main melody. He created a seemingly endless stream of musical obbligatos—"a melody of some independence that accompanies another musical idea"—that was the initial expression of his innate musicality. This inherent

---

[1]Lewisohn, *The Complete Beatles Chronicle*, 53.

grounding in melody had its source in the British music halls, dramatic Irish folk songs, and lush Tin Pan Alley scores he'd grown up with. The strong melodic emphasis of country music that was uniquely popular in Liverpool and Ireland added to an intense melodic education.

And key influences on Harrison's lead guitar were Elvis Presley's legendary Sun recordings. While these had the force of a musical revolution in Liverpool, to many American ears the "Sun sound" was fundamentally "country"—home ground for a first-generation Irish Liverpudlian like Harrison, who'd grown up hearing Hank Williams's tuneful guitar motifs. Critically, those classic Presley Sun sessions also introduced Harrison to the lead guitar of Scotty Moore, whose playing drew on a wide range of influences, especially the blues-jazz fluidity of T-Bone Walker, evident in rapid runs and a broad melodic palette. In retrospect, Moore's approach to lead guitar is the one most clearly reflected in Harrison's, especially as Moore thought hard about what he was playing on the premise that the song, not his ego, was the focus. Reflecting on his time with Presley, this understated guitar legend told a journalist: "I tried to keep it simple—and simplicity, you know, that's something you have to work at. I listen to some of the things now and I think I could have played a lot more stuff there. But I'm glad I didn't. Like on 'Don't Be Cruel': I played the little intro on that and played a chord on the very end, and that's all I played during the whole song. But it didn't need anything else."[2] Just change the title of the song in this quote and it could be George Harrison talking about any number of classic Beatle tunes.

When the Beatles arrived in London to record their first LP, they were a hard-kicking, guitar-driven R&B setup. The music released on *Please Please Me* in March 1963 presented a vocal act that featured some guitar. Has there ever been a more dramatic metamorphosis in a band's sonic footprint?

The band had new concepts to grapple with, chief among them "the song" as a recorded product, rather than a one-off live performance. For the cover versions that made up more than half of their repertoire, they just repeated the live arrangements. But for the Lennon and McCartney material, they had to master the discipline of routing the song for the studio—taking it from the basic chords and

---

[2]Roberts, Michael. "The Sideman." *The Dallas Observer.* March 2000.

melody-writing stage to a completed recording. Without doubt, the songs came from John and Paul, but the arrangements were a matter for the band and George Martin.

In the earliest sessions, in 1962 and 1963, George Martin directed the group, as he was the one who had signed them and effectively underwritten their product. A number of changes were made, and Harrison's identity was the most affected. First, in the studio setting overblown amps and volume battles were no more—balancing and compression were prerequisites of recorded sound, so the group's live power was immediately weakened. The primal lead guitar tone George Harrison had in Hamburg at the turn of the year was literally castrated, almost turned into a weedy reverb whimper. It was for good reason that Harrison was initially unhappy with the sterile studio atmosphere.

And, whereas in the live set Harrison's lead was a dominant solo instrument, at Abbey Road George Martin hit on Lennon's harmonica as a tone to distinguish the band from the mass of guitar groups. So, on "Chains," "Love Me Do," and "There's a Place," it states the lead themes. And as *Anthology 1* reveals, the "Please Please Me" lead motif was originally played in octaves by Harrison only, rather than by the final harmonica-guitar duet. This was the stamp of Martin the musical director, the first they had worked with. He made the harmonic-guitar unison obbligatos a Beatle sound trademark, immediately reusing them on the follow-up single "From Me to You."

The net effect was a massive diminution in Harrison's guitar profile—compared to his live role, his earnest acoustic strumming on "Love Me Do" was quite a comedown. In fact, the song sounded unlike anything the Beatles had played live for years, when they were literally electric. Tellingly, only "Boys" and "I Saw Her Standing There" gave a glimpse of George's R&B guitar solos, but neither song quite takes off. On this album, Harrison the vocalist was more to the fore; aside from some prominent backup vocals, he had two lead slots, one good ("Chains"), and one not so good ("Do You Want to Know a Secret").

If Harrison wasn't half the man he used to be on *Please Please Me*, his musical personality was far more evident on the second wave of 1963 recordings completed by the release of *With the Beatles*. This was a revue, offering soul, R&B, country, and show tunes as well as a new George Harrison composition. The main impression is of a superbly honed vocal group, but there was more of George's guitar too, from the repeating rumbling Duane Eddy riff on "It Won't Be Long" to elegant Scotty Moore brushstrokes to open "Devil in Her

Heart.""Till There Was You" captured his first song-long guitar narrative highlighted by a sumptuous, fluid jazzy solo, while his uniquely origi- nal "All My Loving" break was a highlight of Paul McCartney's first clas- sic. His guitar parts weren't yet defining the songs, but they were essential colors.

Harrison was most prominent on his own song, "Don't Bother Me," and his guitar-vocal showcase, "Roll Over Beethoven." This driving performance gives the lie to the fable that Harrison barely managed to copy Chuck Berry's original solos, fluffing a few licks in the attempt. The reality is that Harrison matches Berry, and avoids an audible mis- take from the original 1956 recording. While Berry's Chicago style is obviously more blues-based, Harrison's is substantially more fluid. This is even more evident in a kicking October 1963 live performance of the song from Stockholm on *Anthology 1*. Here George forcefully *leads* the band and overhauls Berry's licks, taking them to a new level. "Don't Bother Me" was also distinctly fresh and had the hallmarks of a guitarist's composition—the main melody was firmly fixed around the five-note "blues scale" driven by a repeating R&B guitar riff. The ris- ing figure in the chorus was a pointer to the future, but the song is most renowned for the pseudo-grumpy, tell-it-like-it-is lyrics. In retro- spect, this is an early indicator that Harrison wasn't driven to please the audience. Even in 1963, it seems, he wanted to define his concept of being "an entertainer" rather than conform to a standard model. But even if he had dispensed with artifice, he had produced a song that was up to standard on his first attempt.

However, his main job was lead guitarist, and the most significant guitar part Harrison played in this period was his closing obbligato on the delightful "This Boy." In a four-note summation of the melody crowned with a slidelike musical sigh, Harrison creates a wonderfully understated moment of musical narration that encapsulates the entire song. It is a classic early example of his innate lyricism and his unerring ability to give the song "just what it needed." Indeed, Mark Lewisohn reports that Harrison was playing to order here, and at the end of the take sought reassurance that his customers were content with his work: "Something like that, you mean?"[3]

This sense of Lennon and McCartney as Harrison's customers says much about the insecurity that Harrison still felt in the band. In Hamburg, Tony Sheridan characterized Harrison as "this little guy from Liverpool who was being tolerated by the other two." That may be an

---

[3]Lewisohn, *The Complete Beatles Recording Sessions*, 40.

overstatement, but it is clear that Lennon always regarded the Beatles as *his* band and, even in 1969, did not hesitate to suggest replacing Harrison with Eric Clapton after Harrison walked out. Certainly, Ringo Starr felt insecure in the group—how could he not, after seeing Pete Best axed without a second thought? The unease was compounded when, due to illness, Starr himself was replaced by Jimmy Nichol to fulfill live dates in 1964. Notably, only Harrison objected to this move.

However, once Beatlemania kicked in, it became unthinkable to replace any of the four. But, good as this was for Harrison's and Starr's places in the band, the increasing sophistication of the arrangements was overlooked in the celebrity frenzy that accompanied the group. One result was that Harrison's musical skills were underestimated again. An example is the closing sixth chord for their epochal single "She Loves You"—this harmonic sophistication was Harrison's idea, but the kind of musical detail that was increasingly ignored in the media frenzy that began to report on the Beatles as a social phenomenon rather than a music group. John Barham, a close musical collaborator of Harrison's, offers this summary of the group's status in the 1960s: "The Beatles received continuous and relentless coverage by the media for what seemed like a very long time—nothing had previously been given such treatment in the memory of my generation. For the older generation, only the Second World War would have been comparable. For people of following generations, it would be difficult to imagine to what extent the Beatles were forced into the arena of public awareness. The coverage of Princess Diana by the media was far less intense!"[4]

This unrelenting media coverage, and Beatlemania itself, drew attention away from the Beatles' qualities as performers and placed more emphasis on their personalities. Harrison tended to let his guitar do the talking, so in the nascent celebrity-obsessed media world he barely got a look. For instance, the legend of the 1963 Royal Variety Performance centers on Lennon's acid class commentary to introduce a song rather than the song itself. Harrison's suave "Till There Was You" solo is never mentioned, and his innovative "All My Loving" break on the first *Ed Sullivan Show* appearance is similarly lost in the general uproar. The footage from Stockholm in 1963 released on *Anthology* gives a rare glimpse of the band's power in full flow. Fans in the United States soon reveled in the "Beatles Show" experience, but completely missed out on the group's potency as live musicians.

---

[4]Barham, John. Interview with author, spring 2002.

Once the Beatles had cracked the United States with "I Want to Hold Your Hand," the demand for "product, product, and more product" to feed the world's richest and biggest market was intense. This meant delivering a stream of new recordings while keeping up an almost inhuman touring, and now filming, schedule.

Fortunately, the Hamburg years had left the group with a vast repertoire of R&B covers on which they drew throughout 1964. Most famous is the *Long Tall Sally* EP released in June. There is the sense of a band treading water: while on "Long Tall Sally" McCartney and Harrison spark Hamburg fireworks, on "Slow Down" and "Matchbox" George misses the kick of live performance. This is apparent from the considerably more convincing solo he plays on the live "Slow Down" released on *Live at the BBC*. Far more interesting is the one original on the set, "I Call Your Name," which mixes things up rhythmically. Here George complements the mood with a staccato break that doesn't obviously draw on his roots. It seems that the new material was firing Harrison's musical imagination.

The recordings of 1964 contain the penultimate examples of the Beatles' alternation between new songs and cover versions. The catalyst for significant progress during this period of extreme pressure was their first foray into filmmaking. The music released on *A Hard Day's Night* showed John Lennon inspired, and Paul McCartney, while not as prolific, producing songs of daunting quality. The set was primarily "about" great songwriting and broader harmonic possibilities. At the same time, there was strong rhythmic emphasis based primarily on acoustic guitars. The lead guitarist had far fewer riffs on which to center his playing, and on this album Harrison explored the structure of chords to add shadow and light to the arrangements. His sympathetic arpeggios on "If I Fell" show this, while his almost zither-like flourishes during "Things We Said Today" are a lesson in playing essentially a second rhythm guitar part, yet not clashing with Lennon's rock-steady strokes.

The group members were clearly on a confidence high and asserting themselves in the studio as arrangers. And while Harrison didn't have a new song of his own, he was beginning to influence the arrangements, building on his "This Boy" coda. Most famous is the startling opening chord to "A Hard Day's Night," which introduced a new guitar sound to the world, the jangling resonance of his Rickenbacker twelve-string. And the origin of the fast twelve-string solo is revealed on *Anthology 1*—on the early take, George can be heard searching for the right combination of the core notes in a clear precursor of the final solo. And back on his main Gretsch guitar, Harrison served up a powerful performance for McCartney's swinging "Can't Buy Me Love," his natural empathy with the mood of the music drawing out a sassy break built around a blues-influenced bend. Harrison later told journalist Rip Rense that his Beatles solos "just happened": "I'd just play to the song...I got an idea of where to go, and I tended to blank out when I actually was doing the solo...I didn't really know what I'd done till afterward."[5]

But foremost among Harrison's arrangement contributions is the leitmotif he created for McCartney's excellent "And I Love Her." Again, *Anthology 1* reveals the development of the song's final arrangement by uncovering its initial *electric* setting. Not until the third day of work on the track, when George tried it out on his new Spanish guitar, did he conceive the opening theme, which is now so central to the piece that "And I Love Her" seems unimaginable without it. This was the first time a Harrison part had completely changed a song.[6]

The advancing sophistication of Harrison's playing was a function of the band's development in the studio, which was in marked contrast to the endless drag of worldwide live shows that became a circus. These tours were little more than a moneymaking chore, playing to people who weren't listening, just screaming. There was little point even playing in tune—who would have known the difference? In the midst of this, the clamor for more product raged, and the group scuttled into Abbey Road on days off to record new material. The results were "I Feel Fine/She's a Woman" and *Beatles for Sale*.

While the single was rapturously received, to many the new album signified a backward step, a retreat into covers masking a lack of new material. This is unkind to the original songs that were of good quality, including the closing sequence of new pieces—"Every Little Thing," "I Don't Want to Spoil the Party," and "What You're Doing." But the pressures of the road were beginning to tell. Harrison is largely subdued, tamed by the studio on a lackluster "Kansas City" solo, but the LP did gather a catalogue of his styles and influences. Together with his full-blown homage to Carl Perkins, "Everybody's Trying to Be My Baby," there are original rockabilly solos for "I'm a Loser" and "I

---

[5]Rense, Rip. "There Went the Sun: Reflections on the Passing on George Harrison." *The Rip Post* (web site): December 2001.

[6]He immediately reused this idea on "I'll Be Back."

Don't Want to Spoil the Party," and sweet Buddy Holly picking for "Words of Love." "Baby's in Black" offers an exploration of whammied bent notes that worried George Martin, while two of the unheralded originals gave notice of his increasingly focal role in the arrangements. John Lennon's fine "Every Little Thing" is enhanced by Harrison insights—a neat summation of the melody to open, and a lyrical solo capped with tumbling arpeggios that pointed toward "Help!" McCartney's equally estimable "What You're Doing" is partly defined by George's tuneful overture and intriguing break.

Notwithstanding the powerful bustle of the "I Feel Fine" riffing, the best of Harrison's playing from these sessions was not released until 1994. "Leave My Kitten Alone" is among the Beatles' greatest recordings. Driven with demonic power by an astonishing Lennon vocal, it rivals "Long Tall Sally" as the band's classic rock 'n' roll cover version, the vitality of the band transcending studio manners. It also captures the best rock guitar solo of George Harrison's recorded career—the flow of ideas is matched by true excitement and an inkling of blues passion.

While *Beatles for Sale* is a mix of retrospection and forward motion, it did herald the major developments in the group's music that began in earnest in 1965 with *Help!* Their core audience demanded songs of teenage angst, but they themselves were heavily influenced by the distinctly mature Bob Dylan. The revolution he'd sparked was pervasive—the Minnesota minstrel freed musicians from the grip of Tin Pan Alley and re-created popular music as a new artistic vehicle for free expression. David Bromberg, one of Dylan's favorite musicians, explains the effect: "Before Bob Dylan, music was 'Rock Around the Clock,' it was such simplistic tripe. It was all teeny love affairs and Dylan—he was able to convey things in his songs you couldn't get out of short stories. It was about a feeling you got out of those words strung together. He revolutionized songwriting completely and articulated the *inarticulable*."[7]

The Beatles were listening. In the throes of a grueling global touring schedule, they reached out for the freedom Dylan offered. Other changes were also afoot—John Lennon was seriously depressed just as Paul McCartney's lightning-quick musical mind had matured to a point where his songs came into his head almost fully arranged, a skill Lennon never mastered. George Harrison was beginning to write quality pop songs that could no longer be dismissed, and

---

[7]Bromberg, David. Telephone interview with author, December 2001.

one of his best friends, Eric Clapton, was in the vanguard of a new style of guitar playing—white blues virtuoso. It started as a fashion, but soon spawned a dogma that only long virtuoso solos have any merit. The Beatles were keen students of musical fashion, and McCartney in particular acutely aware of the need to compete and keep up.

Help! is very much the product of this year of change—in retrospect, it marked the moment when Paul McCartney started to "go solo" ("Yesterday") and demand more of his band mates in realizing the sounds in his head. Accordingly, on "Another Girl" and "Ticket to Ride" he cut blues-boom inflected lead licks and solos himself, not satisfied with Harrison's playing or ideas. In the case of "Another Girl," he actually wiped George's parts and replaced them with his own. This was a major change in the constitution and balance of the group—up to this point the guitar solo had been strictly Harrison's domain, the space for his ideas, his part of the collective "band product." And he felt the shift on two levels: his role in the band was beginning to be overlooked, and on McCartney's songs he had little space to be creative. But not until a 1977 interview with *Crawdaddy* did he express it: "I helped out such a lot in all the arrangements. What Paul would do, if he'd written a song, he'd learn all the parts for Paul and then come into the studio and say, 'do this.' He'd never give you the opportunity to come out with something."[8]

As Paul McCartney advanced as a composer and arranger, he inevitably became more self-sufficient and resolved in his vision, in a way that Lennon did not. The trend that started on *Help!* was repeated in numerous songs that were essentially Paul playing solo under the Beatles name. Paradoxically, this was also a period of development for George Harrison, and while his musical ideas didn't always satisfy McCartney, his influence on the arrangements was growing with each album. On *Help!* the fundamental shape of a number of songs, notably John Lennon's, came out of Harrison's head. Is it now possible to conceive of "Help!" without George's lead arpeggios, or "It's Only Love" without the guitarist's melodic hook that launches the cut? The demos of these songs on *Anthology 2* make clear that when Lennon brought the pieces to Abbey Road, they were "just" chords and melody. It wasn't until the twelfth take of "Help!" and the sixth run-through of "It's Only Love" that these parts appeared. Harrison developed them as the Beatles practiced the songs in the studio.

---

[8]Glazer, "The Harrison Interview." *Crawdaddy*: February 1997.

And having been introduced to serious electronics at Abbey Road, George maintained an interest in new guitar sounds, the latest being the volume pedal. It automated the effect he'd sought on "Baby's in Black" and gave the electric guitar another range of vocal nuances. Luckily John Lennon had just reproduced "This Boy" in a new song, "Yes It Is." This sublime Beatles nugget revels in breathtaking harmony singing from Lennon, McCartney, and Harrison, supplemented by a fourth voice, George's lead guitar, seeming to sing via the volume pedal. The pedal adds a comment at the end of each line and provides the final touch, a four-note chorus that seems to say, "Oh, yes it is."

Help! also documents Harrison's progress as a songwriter, even if the boy-girl lyrics of "I Need You" and "You Like Me Too Much" would soon be passé. Both tunes show George learning the craft of a pop writer, particularly "I Need You," with its saccharine, romantic melody. There were also signs of melodic idiosyncrasy as he worked on the guitar to resolve the musical puzzles of the song. This explains the unusual chord change from G major to D minor over the phrase "and never *leave you*," and the vaguely dissonant A7 to A minor variation with "I just can't *go on anymore*." These were the fruits of a guitar player's songwriting, and early signs of Harrison's tendency to unwrap the harmonies within chord changes. He was clearly learning fast, but the times had fundamentally changed for the Beatles. And Harrison was about to change himself and the world for good.

In a matter of a few months, the Beatles and George Harrison emerged transformed on *Rubber Soul,* well on their way to the final severance from the group's live act. The new album, released in December 1965, showcased increasingly subtle arrangements of a stunning collection of songs, driven by harder guitar tones that recaptured some of the power of the Hamburg sound. Harrison's role was becoming central, and he had taken a quantum leap forward as a songwriter. The metamorphosis from the teenage love angst of "I Need You" to his loose word association with "If I Needed Someone" spoke of a man coming to terms with new freedoms. And the Bob Dylan effect was unmistakable on "Think for Yourself," a jagged bout with an unknown enemy and a sonic forerunner to "Taxman." George obviously welcomed the mental emancipation, but, for now, his version of Dylan's adversarial satire consisted of wagging fingers. "I've got a word or two to say about the things you do" is more schoolteacher than poet, but in time

Harrison would learn to choose more effective vocabulary. With "If I Needed Someone," Harrison's first fully realized melody, he'd embraced a theoretical thought process. And this was clearly his best song to date, with a rapturous, keening melody, cast around the high timbre of the Rickenbacker twelve-string, played with a capo at the seventh fret.

In a period of unprecedented musical growth, Harrison had also become entranced with an Indian stringed instrument, the sitar. He first came across it on the set of *Help!*, where it added "local color" to ham-fisted handling of subcontinent culture. The sitar looked enough like a guitar to make it approachable, and Harrison had soon grasped the basics of tuning and eking a melody from its four main playing strings.[9] In his experimentation with new sounds, this one soon found its way onto tape—Harrison's sitar part on "Norwegian Wood" is simple enough, just restating the melody as another sonic tint with no hint of formal Indian technique. Nevertheless, the effect was volcanic and still reverberates nearly forty years later. In that one act of "giving the song just what it needed," Harrison sowed the seeds of "world music."

The remainder of his contribution to *Rubber Soul* was equally pivotal, if less dramatic in the aftershock. The opening salvo on "Drive My Car" is Harrison's soul-rock riff, which reappears in the middle eight of "The Word." Another Beatle classic, "Nowhere Man," is substantially defined by an archetypal George "chord solo," played in tandem with John Lennon. This is the logical, resonant end of his account of the Buddy Holly–Carl Perkins style. Perkins also gets a nod on the final rockabilly knockabout "What Goes On," the old giving way to the new with a sharp, high-register, blues-inflected break that gives "Run for Your Life" even more bite.

Rubber Soul is a document of the Beatles' rapidly increasing studio and arrangement skills—their organization of ideas and instruments had taken a huge leap forward. Other trends that had started with *Help!* were becoming more prominent. Critical among these was Paul McCartney's increasingly independent musical vision for his own songs. Key to realizing these ideas was George Martin. John Lennon seems to have relied more on his band mates for arrangement ideas. This meant that George Harrison's role tended to be more prominent on Lennon's songs—he provides the frameworks for "Girl," "Nowhere

---

[9]The number of playing strings on a sitar can range between two and four, and in many cases only the two strings farthest away from the sympathetic strings are actually used to play a raga.

Man," "Run for Your Life," "Norwegian Wood," and "In My Life." On Paul's songs he tends to play vignettes, such as the flashy lick at the end of each "I'm Looking Through You" verse and his rich solo for "Michelle." Notably, this fluid, mid-range jazzy performance was of notes dictated to him by Martin; legend has it that the guitarist's hackles were raised by this scholarly intervention.

If *Rubber Soul* was a major turning point, the release of *Revolver* in August 1966 completed the Beatles' journey from pop stars to cultural alchemists. It was a period of revelation for the band—LSD, new philosophical avenues, Dylan, and in Harrison's case, a complete embrace of Indian music. The Byrds' David Crosby gave the guitarist his first record by India's best-known sitar ambassador, Ravi Shankar. Harrison immediately related to this music as if he had been immersed in it from birth, and he took his sitar practice further, but still interpreted the instrument in guitar player's terms. He quickly grasped the basics of classical Indian music structure and instrumentation, particularly the drone instrument that underpins all performances, the *tamboura*. His strong identification with Indian music and instruments became pivotal to the Beatles' arrangements from *Revolver* until *The White Album* announced the end of the psychedelic adventure. For the first time, Harrison was one of the navigators of the group's musical direction.

The different approaches of the band's songwriters were also apparent. There is a marked distinction between Paul McCartney's *Revolver* songs and those penned by Lennon and Harrison, and, again, more evidence of McCartney's independent method. There is little suggestion of his fellow band members' input to most of his arrangements. In fact, his songs can generally be distinguished by the use of hired musicians playing parts developed by McCartney and George Martin. So the setting for "Eleanor Rigby" is a string quartet, "For No One" features a French horn, and, like "Good Day Sunshine," both entirely eschew guitars and use a piano backing. And "Got to Get You Into My Life" is driven by a horn section, limiting Harrison's function to a four-second burst at 1:52. Lennon's and Harrison's roles on these pieces were reduced to backup vocals or sundry percussion, apart from George's Mediterranean trilling to accompany "Here, There and Everywhere."

The two types of material are so distinct that in retrospect it sounds as if the Beatles were two bands—one that worked together on Lennon and Harrison's compositions, and another that acted as backup musicians to fulfill Paul McCartney's requirements for *his* songs. This is no criticism of McCartney—the implausible mix of styles reflected the epic skills of the band's songwriters.

The evidence is in the arrangements—Lennon and Harrison's pieces are guitar-led, and are collaborative efforts. McCartney's, being the product of a more versatile musical mind, were largely based on piano foundations. And characteristically, Harrison's role on Lennon's songs is considerable—he developed the thrilling major-scale lead parts for "And Your Bird Can Sing," and can clearly be heard "finding the notes" on the early take released on *Anthology 2*. Then there were the backward guitar solos he painstakingly created for "I'm Only Sleeping," a tune that arrived at Abbey Road with just acoustic guitar chords. Mark Lewisohn's *The Complete Beatles Recording Sessions* reports that the idea and execution of the parts for Lennon's drowsy classic were entirely George's. In an extraordinary act of dedication, Harrison worked for six hours first settling on a string of notes, then writing the sequence in reverse order and playing that part. *And* he double-tracked it. He also created a guitar coda tonally and rhythmically based on Indian forms. "I'm Only Sleeping" is a classic example of the massive influence Harrison had on arranging the band's songs in this period.

Another key song on the album for George was "She Said She Said," created in the first Abbey Road session during which a Beatle offered a general "fuck you" and stalked out. Perhaps surprisingly, this was Paul McCartney, who by his own account was dismayed that his input on the recording was minimal. The problem was that between them Lennon and Harrison had routined the tune, with Harrison helping Lennon fuse the "when I was a boy" segment to the main verse to complete the song. It had started out a completely different piece, as Harrison later commented: "I was at his house one day and he was struggling with some tunes. He had loads of bits, maybe three songs that were unfinished, and I made suggestions and helped him to work them together so that they became one finished song."[10]

And in the studio the lead guitarist's arranging skills were prominent in developing the song, which is driven and characterized by his powerful, distorted Gibson SG riffs. Harrison's licks give a response to each line of Lennon's vocal, providing a slightly different melodic twist while simultaneously offering rhythmic support with picked chords. In effect, George's lead becomes a second voice—entirely

---

[10]Beatles, *Anthology*, 97.

apposite for a piece that is about the relationship between tellers and listeners. After all, "She Said She Said" is a song about voices.

The best of the group's collective abilities was found on "Tomorrow Never Knows," a work that gathered the skills and inspiration of the whole band. Supporting Lennon's wondrous vocal are whirls of tape loops, telepathic bass-drum synergy from McCartney and Starr, and another precise backward guitar solo from Harrison. He also provided the first use of the classic Indian drone instrument, the tamboura, to the track—it introduces the song with a power it was not designed for in the Indian setting, but does underpin the philosophical substrata to the lyric.

If Harrison's solos for "I'm Only Sleeping" were an example of his guitar innovations, his three compositions for the album were evidence of his wider development. "Love You To" was the first attempt in the rock world to marry the structures of Indian music with a grinding rock rhythm. Here Harrison is still playing the sitar like a guitar player, using blues and rock 'n' roll bends rather than the intensely intricate Indian equivalents. The recurring motif first heard at 0:55 on the track was essentially an adaptation of a blues lick, and the melodic form of the sitar solos and commentary were the product of George's Western roots. However, the song was nothing less than a revolution, not only as the first mixture of pop-rock and Indian music but also in the sincerity and understanding of the music that Harrison displayed. While Harrison's achievements were of little interest to the rock press, Asian music commentators wrote with clarity about it: "One cannot emphasise how absolutely unprecedented this piece is in the history of popular music. For the first time an Asian music was not parodied utilising familiar stereotypes and misconceptions, but rather transferred in toto into a new environment with sympathy and rare understanding."[11]

The Indian influence is also present on "Taxman," one of the Beatles' great rockers that neatly presents the yin-yang concerns of an earthbound taxpaying musician with spiritual aspirations. The guitarist was writing fine songs, but was ever to be regarded as a junior partner. He later suggested that the price he paid for having "Taxman" on the album was Paul McCartney's dynamic guitar solo, and the structure of the song was agreed upon collectively— Lewisohn reports that "there was much discussion, caught on tape, about how the song might be best structured."[12] And his third song,

---

[11]Reck, "Beatles Orientalis."

[12]Lewisohn, *The Complete Beatles Recording Sessions*, 75.

"I Want to Tell You," fronted a stuttering guitar riff over Indian inflections. By this time, Harrison was matching the music to the theme—the offbeat guitar hook mirrored the song's preoccupation with finding the correct words. His work also showed signs of an increasingly fertile harmonic imagination, especially in a complex chord sequence around the line "it's only me, it's not my mind" (A major–B seventh–B–minor–D diminished). Harrison was absorbed in a phase of intense creativity and growth.

This album changed George Harrison's identity as a musician for good. Was he mainly a guitarist, a singer, a world music innovator, or a songwriter? The answer was that he was already all of these. His guitarist's version of sitar accompaniments to "Norwegian Wood" and "Love You To" proves his transformation almost overnight from the guitarist who sang "I'm Happy Just to Dance with You" to a leader of international musical fashion. George Harrison's musical and cultural leadership of the Beatles, and an entire generation, was focused in an Eastern direction. Unfortunately, he still had the annoyance of his day job to contend with.

With *Revolver* due for release in August, the Beatles continued their schizophrenic life by embarking on their final world tour in July, churning out a set that included only one current song, "Paperback Writer." Here they delivered "couldn't care less" versions of old songs they no longer identified with to audiences still playing out Beatlemania. The difference this time was that there was real mania and real danger—during a summer Far East jaunt, they managed to offend the Marcos dictatorship in the Philippines and were beaten up by paramilitary police in Manila. Next, during the last calamitous U.S. tour, they found themselves in the eye of a Christian fundamentalist storm whipped up by Lennon's observations on the relative popularity of the Fab Four and Christ. Immediately topping the Ku Klux Klan's key offenders list, the band received death threats, and a stray firecracker let off at a show in Memphis had the boys looking around to see which of them had been shot. The touring game was well and truly up.

The Beatles were beyond the breaking point, no longer in control of their own lives or even their identities. George Harrison, for one, was acutely aware of this distortion, and the question of identity became a critical theme of his music career and spiritual life. The product called the Beatles existed in the fantasy world of the media and the fans' imaginations. The fantasy was supplanting reality, and Harrison was on the lookout for something real, something he could believe in beyond all the nonsense that clung, limpet-like, to the Beatles. He found it in India.

In September 1966, when Harrison stepped into the confounding heat of the Bombay airport to meet Ravi Shankar, the strings attaching him to the Beatles had been loosened. More than once he'd felt his life was at risk as a result of the madness that attached itself to the group, and many, many times he'd realized that as musicians, they were not keeping up with the pace. Happily adopting the position of student at the feet of the master, a centuries-old tradition in India, Harrison effectively ditched the guitar for all but studio work until the spring of 1968. He put all his emotional energy into playing the sitar, and in the course of doing so was exposed to the philosophy of Indian music, which would set him on a spiritual path he traveled for the rest of his life.

At the climax of his autobiography, *Raga Mala*, Ravi Shankar simply states, "I believe in the age-old saying, 'Nada Brahma' — 'Sound is God.'" Those words encapsulate an attitude to musical expression that is alien to Western popular music, but one that George Harrison immediately understood. In fact, to the Hindu mind, music *is* God.

On his first visit to India in 1966, Harrison found a complete solution to life's mysteries, a one-stop shop. This was a universal answer in which music was embedded within a philosophical framework. Indian music was basically an extended hymn to God; the culture embraced spirituality as a natural part of life, and ostensibly eschewed the material obsessions of the West. Hindu practice offered a more direct experience of the divine than he would have encountered as a second-generation Irish Catholic, where the religion was as much about national identity as God. Hinduism promises a one-to-one connection with the Creator, and for a man who actually had a cartoon doppelganger, this was an appealing prospect.

Indian music's origins can be found as far back as 1000 B.C., when Aryan tribes used chants to accompany religious ceremonies. Music is believed to be a divine art, created by the holy trinity of Hindu gods and handed down to great sages who are considered saints. As part of this heritage, musicians often spoke in terms unknown to the Western mind: "Musical sound and the musical experience are steps to the realisation of the self. We view music as a kind of spiritual discipline that raises one's inner being to divine peacefulness and bliss. The highest aim of music is to reveal the essence of the universe it reflects, thus, through music, one can reach God."[13]

---

[13]Shankar, *My Music My Life*, 17.

This was some way away from jellybeans and mop-top haircuts, an art form that dealt with the "big questions," not popular myths. Indian music is a whole life package, inextricably linked to culture and religion; its subject matter is simple: life and death. Indian music is the fruit of cultural roots thousands of years old, and part of a society where songs of spiritual devotion are pop music.

Inspired by Shankar, Harrison embraced Hindu philosophy and led the Beatles into explorations of yoga techniques in the summer of 1967. When a sojourn to study meditation with the Maharishi Mahesh Yogi in Wales coincided with Brian Epstein's death in August, suspicion of Harrison's motives, and even sanity, filled the tabloids. And yet, in the ghetto of Indian music, it all fitted hand in glove, naturally. Music, spirituality, and God—there was no contradiction. This is how Ravi Shankar explained it: "I feel all the richness of India in our music. A raga reflects the spiritual hopes of our people, the constant struggle for life. It is drawn out of the prayers in our temples, life on our rivers, the Ganges in the holy city of Benares. Sound is everywhere. As a child I would spend hours filling myself with the vibrations of this place. Our music reveals to me the whole process of creation from the childbirth to the death."

Indian music itself is refined to a level unknown in the West, not least because it recognizes twenty-two microtones or *srutis* within an octave. Moreover, the time signatures are not limited to 4/4, waltz time, and march time of Western popular music. Some Indian drummers have constructed rhythmic patterns of up to 104 beats per bar! The *raga*, a series of notes within a predetermined scale, is the basis of melody and improvisation, through which the player reveals skill using the subtlest of nuances and inflections.

The basic training period for an Indian musician is five years of eight hours' daily practice, and a further fifteen years before a player is considered up to scratch. Harrison soon realized that the masters of Indian instruments had a complete identification with music, viewing their role as performer as a sacred task. The rigorous discipline involved in even beginning to approach an acceptable standard of expression contrasted sharply with the casual attitude in Western pop music. George Harrison's musical eyes had been prised open.

George Harrison had first met Ravi Shankar at Peter Sellers's house, after a Shankar concert, in June 1966—the maestro of the sitar coming face to face with a symbol of Western youth culture. Shankar agreed to teach Harrison the sitar and gave a number of informal concerts at his Esher home, as well as introducing him to the basic exercises and disciplines of Indian classical music. At one of these private recitals, Ravi brought along another of his English pupils, John Barham, a man destined to become a close musical and personal friend of Harrison's on his new musical journey.

John Barham had studied trumpet, piano, and composition at the Royal College of Music, and was already so deeply involved with Indian music that he'd written piano compositions based on Indian ragas. This was unprecedented for a classically trained English musician. By the mid-1960s, his work had been noticed by a group of observers who included a journalist with the *India Times* and the cultural attaché to the Indian High Commissioner in London. These well-connected contacts wrote to Ravi Shankar to introduce Barham, who soon found himself a student of the sitar master and was later described by his guru as "a brilliant young pianist." At a stroke, John Barham's life had changed forever.

Not only was Barham capable of producing shimmering piano interpretations of some of India's most famous ragas, he also made piano transcriptions of the slow movements of three Gustav Mahler symphonies and converted one of Shankar's famous sitar concertos into a piece for Western instruments.[14] His talent was very much to Ravi Shankar's liking, especially as Shankar was planning a collaboration with the violin master Yehudi Menuhin at the 1966 Bath music festival in the west of England. Menuhin had engaged a German composer, Peter Feuchtwanger, to write a duet piece for the occasion, but that interpretation of the evening "Raga Tilang" didn't capture enough Indian essence. Shankar's solution was to write his own piece based on the raga and have John Barham transcribe it into Western musical notation. This already taxing task was compounded by Barham's need to convey in notation for Menuhin the ornamental "effects" of the Indian sitar or *sarod* (a fretless, lutelike instrument with more than twenty strings) player, the *meend* (equivalent to Western glissando) and the *gamak* (varieties of infinitely subtle string bends or "wobbles"). The final results, and the triumph of all three musicians, are heard as "Swara-Kakali" on the legendary *West Meets East* album, for which Barham also provided liner notes explaining the concepts and structures of Indian music for a Western audience.

The week after their first meeting at the Esher sitar recital, Harrison invited John Barham back to Surrey to play and discuss Indian music, private sessions that marked out a shared musico-spiritual journey and a new friendship. Barham still has vivid memories of

---

[14]They were the adagios of Mahler's Fourth, Fifth, and Ninth symphonies.

these intimate occasions: "I remember playing some solo piano to George, who was fascinated by my playing ragas on the piano. George played sitar to me and we also tried combining sitar and piano. One of George's favorite ragas was 'Raga Marwa'—when we were first introduced by Ravi, I had just composed a piano piece based on this raga. George liked it a lot and played a recording of it to John Lennon, who also liked it. George also told me that his song 'Blue Jay Way' was influenced by this piece."[15]

"Raga Marwa" is a dark and dissonant affair, exploring powerfully intense emotions of struggle and unrelenting self-analysis. The music is characterized by a repeating, discordant figure that constantly disrupts any reprieve found by the soloist. This challenging harmonic structure clearly captured Harrison's attention and probably provided the template for his use of unstable diminished chords that entered his songs began in this period.

As George Harrison pursued his transcontinental study of the sitar with Ravi Shankar, John Barham was his closest confidant and fellow traveler. Despite Barham's significant accomplishments in Indian music, the pair continued to learn from Shankar, and each other, as equals. The pianist is well placed to comment on how the rockabilly guitarist grappled with one of the world's most sophisticated musics: "George was very quick and very focused, but his grasp wasn't only intuitive: he was given exercises by Ravi that he practiced regularly. I felt that as a sitar player he could have gone a long way if he had wanted to study seriously. With Ravi as a teacher, he could have gone as far as he was prepared to practice."

But the lessons this unlikely musical duo received from the sitar maestro were as much philosophical as musical. It was Shankar who introduced them both to the "Nada Brahma" concept, as John Barham recalls: "The first I had heard of this was from Ravi—George and I always discussed what Ravi was teaching us. George also believed that God was present everywhere—including in shit. I will never forget the time or place when he told me this. George was a very gentle guy physically, but he could grab you verbally and shock you into a receptive frame of mind."

Harrison had already concluded that his own guitar technique was being destroyed by farcical Beatles shows, where the music could not be heard above the crowd hysteria, but this work with Shankar really brought home the sheer indolence of the Western pop musi-

---

[15]Harrison's posthumous album *Brainwashed*, released in 2002, included a tune called "Marwa Blues."

cian. Only jazz and classical music demanded the virtuosity displayed by a Ravi Shankar or an Ali Akbar Khan. While George Harrison knew that his lifestyle would never permit him to become a true sitar player, his exposure to sitar study made him the best musician in the Beatles. It also gave him the basis of a new style that would only flourish when he discovered slide guitar.

Suddenly, through Harrison's interest in it, Indian music became the latest fad to obsess middle-class teenagers across the Atlantic— they all wanted a sitar and to learn to play it in two weeks. This Western propensity to trivialize and commercialize anything of value dismayed Shankar, who had dedicated twenty years to mastering his instrument. Some used the music as a sex aid or as an accompaniment to LSD experiments. When he arrived in the States to play the big rock festivals of the 1960s, Monterey and Woodstock, Shankar was aghast that people would so much as smoke during his performance. To the Western mind, his music was just another commodity. To Shankar, it was a sacred trust.

But George Harrison was no cultural tourist, and his embrace of Indian music changed the occidental view of it forever. And while rock orthodoxy might have ignored the facts, world-class musicians like the great guitarist John McLaughlin did not. This true "fusion" master stated in 2001: "The association of George Harrison with Ravi Shankar was itself a particularly important boost in the discovery by the Western world of the music and culture of India."[16] On a personal level, as John Barham notes, "Indian music did fulfill something that George needed. The meditative aspect of some Indian music touched George in a way that no other music did, and this did influence the development of his own identity in a profound way."

Back in London, Harrison was present at the EMI sessions in late November 1966 that started work on "Strawberry Fields Forever" and "When I'm Sixty-Four." Even though Lennon's song kicked things off, from late 1966 through *The White Album,* Paul McCartney became yet more dominant. That was just as well; left to Lennon or Harrison, the Beatles might well have just faded away. Now fully immersed in sitar study and Hindu philosophy, George was changed forever, and his view of music and fame fundamentally transformed. He had lost his

---

[16]Liner notes to *Remember Shakti* (Verve, 2001).

identification with the "musician as entertainer" Western model—the Indian musician is part educator, part keeper of a scared tradition, but primarily a worshipper. At its core, Indian music is a means to praise God, and by embracing this philosophy so absolutely, Harrison set himself on a collision course with the Western view of popular music. Time and again over the three decades that followed this epiphany Harrison clashed head-on with the occidental music press for whom the Hindu outlook was anathema.

This affected the Beatles in that Harrison was now filled with vision, if not yet confident enough to fully realize it. And while Indian music provided a temporary new diversion for the group, it was also the true start of the band's demise. Harrison no longer *needed* Lennon or McCartney to set a musical course for him; almost immediately he started to write songs that could not fit within the framework of the band. Both Lennon and McCartney were musical visionaries in their own right, who, like all artists, would be happy to use a vehicle to express their ideas, but only for as long as it served their purpose. If Harrison was no longer playing a role that supported the realization of their vision, what was he for? The evidence is readily available—after *Revolver,* John Lennon could hardly be bothered to play on any of Harrison's songs recorded by the Beatles.[17] And Paul McCartney had effectively been recording his own songs as a solo artist with the group as backup since 1965.

But by the time *Sgt. Pepper's Lonely Hearts Club Band* was revealed to an astonished and adoring public in the summer of 1967, the most apposite question about Harrison was whether his identity could be contained within the Beatles at all. *Revolver* had been the apogee of the Fab Four's collective creativity; *Sgt. Pepper* was made with George's input, and even interest, questionable. Paul McCartney's imagination and instinct to entertain gave the album life—his vision dealt in concepts for an entire LP, unlike Lennon's bursts of individual creativity. And the concept here was theatrical—the new album presented the group's songs in a "show biz" format, straying into pure theater with the band assuming costumed alter egos. It's hard to imagine a concept further from Harrison's.

As a work of studio alchemy, the record set new standards, but the songs are not as consistently good as those on *Rubber Soul* or *Revolver.* And as the group, in this case Lennon and McCartney, diverged from their standard arrangements, there was little for

---

[17]Lennon only appears on "The Inner Light," "While My Guitar Gently Weeps," and "For You Blues" among Harrison's post-*Revolver* songs.

Harrison to do. The fundamentals of the Beatles changed again, and he was reduced to shaking maracas on "A Day in the Life," and supplementing "Mr. Kite" with a harmonica part. On McCartney's songs Harrison barely had the status of sideman: "There used to be situations where we'd go in, pick up our guitars, all learn the tune and chords and start talking about arrangements," Harrison later stated. "But there came a time where Paul had fixed an idea in his brain as to how to record one of his songs. It was taken to the most ridiculous situations, where I'd open my guitar case and go to get my guitar out and he'd say, 'No, no, we're not doing that yet.' It got so there was very little to do, other than sit around and hear him going, 'Fixing a hole…,' with Ringo keeping the time."[18]

It was a very strange period for the temporarily ex-lead guitarist—he played one solo on the album, a rich throwback to his "Nowhere Man" break on "Fixing a Hole." McCartney added a characteristically flashy solo to "Good Morning Good Morning," usurping Harrison's place…if George was still interested in keeping it. He no longer thought of himself as the group's lead guitarist, because he thought of himself as a sitar student—in 1967 he only picked up the guitar for recording sessions. His primary input to the album was Indian instrumentation or techniques. The tamboura appeared on "Getting Better" and "Lucy in the Sky With Diamonds," the latter also featuring sitar and *swarmandal* (an autoharp). Here too he used the guitar to double the vocal line, a technique straight out of Indian music, where the "upright violin" family of bowed instruments (*dilruba, sarangi*) accompanies the singer. He would repeat this method on "Baby, You're a Rich Man," also from 1967.

His famous contribution to *Sgt. Pepper*, "Within You Without You," was completely out of kilter musically and thematically with the rest of the disc. Here was his statement of identity in the midst of a record on which he was a deliberately peripheral figure. "Within You Without You" was a bombshell in popular music and the first of Harrison's really daring songs. It was a seriously successful marriage of Indian music with the Western pop idiom, and showed a rare musical sophistication with its instrumental passage. This section not only proved that George had gone well beyond the basics of playing the sitar but also introduced the 5/4 time signature to the pop world.[19] In every respect it was innovation—evidence of how quickly and deeply

---

[18]Beatles, *Anthology*, 316.

[19]It was, however, known in jazz and classical music.

Harrison had understood Indian music. This was recognized by Gerry Farrell, an authority on Indian music: "The manner in which these music elements are manipulated in 'Within You Without You' is more sophisticated than it is in 'Love You To,' no doubt a reflection of Harrison's increasing knowledge of Indian musical forms and structures. The overall effect is of several disparate strands of Indian music being woven together to create a new form. It is a quintessential fusion of pop and Indian music." [20]

George had invited John Barham to the studio, making the pianist one of the few outsiders to be present at a Beatles session—Barham describes the occasion as "an afternoon that I will never forget." He noticed that George had the entire structure of the song mapped out in his head, with parts for all the Indian instruments, including the dilruba, the thick-toned bowed upright violin, which introduces the first theme of the song. Barham witnessed Harrison's technique for bringing his idea to life: "Everything played by the dilruba player was sung to him by George."

Lyrically too, "Within You Without You" was startling in the midst of pieces like "When I'm Sixty-Four" and "Lovely Rita." For those looking for a synergy between Hindu belief and the self-indulgence of the acid generation, "Within You Without You" may have appeared to provide it. The song was largely a series of rhetorical questions from Harrison; there seems no reason to doubt that the person being asked "Are you one of them?" was the singer himself.

Although "Within You Without You" was born in the psychedelic era, it does not sound like a period piece; in a sense, Harrison had freed himself from Western musical fashion, simply because Indian classical music transcended time. For while it's true that the song, and Harrison's leadership of the Beatles into Vedic philosophy, sparked the entire fashion for Indian music and a million backpackers' pilgrimages to Kashmir, it was fixed in its own centuries-old musical tradition. Ultimately George Harrison created a fashion that he was no part of.

And aside from that song, Harrison was minimally involved in *Sgt. Pepper*—if, as is often suggested, "A Day in the Life" is the group's ultimate creative work, then it rather sidelines Harrison, as he was barely on the track. Notably, Harrison was not alone in his distance from the Beatles' grandiose project—across the Atlantic in Woodstock, recuperating from a motorcycle accident, Bob Dylan heard self-

---

[20]Farrell, *Indian Music and the West*, 185.

indulgence on *Pepper's* corpulent arrangements. His response was an album from the opposite end of the Wall of Sound spectrum, *John Wesley Harding*. The set pointed the way to Harrison's later minimalist style and predicted the preeminence of Dylan's onetime backup group, the Band, and rejected the virtuoso ramblings of the guitar heroes who were just rumbling to life.

But thoughts of guitar hero status were far from George's mind in 1967—such was his immersion in sitar study that by December, he told an interviewer that he could barely remember guitar chord changes. Harrison had changed his identity in the group from lead guitarist to Indian stylist and thought leader; the others followed him on an exploration of Hindu philosophy in the form of meditation. And with Lennon frequently in another world altogether, it was left to McCartney to give the band professional direction after Brian Epstein's death—someone had to do something to keep the Beatle ship afloat. McCartney's vision was to take the vaudeville of *Pepper* to the next level with the wretched *Magical Mystery Tour* concept. It would be hard to conceive of greater polar opposites than McCartney's homespun do-it-yourself film and Harrison's spiritual search, but again Paul proceeded to go solo. He wrote and performed most of the material himself, and directed the film. George's role was extremely limited, and even when he did rouse himself to contribute a lead guitar part, it was often not to Paul's taste. And if the mood took him, McCartney would just wipe Harrison's parts for something else. Thus, a lead solo for "Hello, Goodbye" was obliterated for a McCartney vocal solo, just as an earlier lead part for "Penny Lane" had been similarly aborted.

On the face of it Harrison didn't care about his guitar parts, charged as he was with his own nascent musical vision. Indeed, his instrument of choice for composing in this period was the Hammond organ, probably because it could play a drone like the Indian harmonium. "Only a Northern Song" (a *Sgt. Pepper* outtake), "It's All Too Much" (cut during the *Magical Mystery Tour* sessions) and "Blue Jay Way" were all based on this concept. Other instruments added rhythmic color, and harmonic variation was kept to a minimum, mirroring the Indian concept he was trying to honor. The songs eventually appeared on *Magical Mystery Tour* and *Yellow Submarine* as one Beatles project melted into another.

Superficially, "Blue Jay Way" may sound like a soporific period piece. It actually documents Harrison's erudite embrace of Indian music theory and his ability to express it in a pop context. The sequence of notes he casts around "there's a fog upon L.A." imposes part of the scale from "Raga Marwa" onto a basic C major chord. He uses notes that are dissonant in the C-major setting (E-flat and F-sharp), pivoting them around a C diminished chord. Harrison was working at a sophisticated level of extrapolating Indian scales to the Western setting, something no one else had done. Along the way, he'd effectively rejected rock 'n' roll—something that the rock press has barely forgiven to this day. The problem was that the beauty of his work was now to be found in the details, not in an immediate impact. The net effect has been that another example of Harrison radically pushing the envelope is virtually forgotten. "Blue Jay Way" explores the structures of Indian music just as "Within You Without You" debates its philosophical roots.

Harrison was also pushing back at the Beatles as an organization he found wanting. He spelled it out in "Only a Northern Song," which, unsurprisingly the group decided to leave off *Sgt. Pepper*. It's far from being a great song, but the main angst was that it took the group apart piece by piece and declared the whole thing an overblown circus. "It's All Too Much" was a less confrontational commentary on spiritual aspiration delivered as a heavy, spaced-out, sub-Hendrix incantation that was probably conceived as a twin to "Tomorrow Never Knows," with its pseudo-Indian vocalizations and "We are dead!" moans.

With the filming and recording for *Magical Mystery Tour* complete by early November, George started work in London on his first solo project, the soundtrack for the *Wonderwall* film. This took him to India in January 1968, and there is potent symbolism in the fact that Harrison started the new year on a non-Beatles venture. There were now three Beatles who held firm artistic visions. The group was unraveling in earnest.

To the casual observer, the Beatles were as unified as ever in the early months of 1968. Prior to a "group" trip led by Harrison to India to study meditation in more depth, they worked on new material in February. The session produced "Lady Madonna," "Across the Universe," "Hey Bulldog," and "The Inner Light," and was the last time that the Beatles recorded together as a fully functional group. "Hey Bulldog" in particular was a great band track, filled with good-time rock riffing and humor. Harrison had also come up with a beautiful melody he added to Indian instrumentation—"The Inner Light" was created during the Bombay sessions for his *Wonderwall* soundtrack and, given an Abbey Road sarod overdub by young Ashish Khan, Harrison mixed in the moods of Indian music. He contrasts the leitmotif *esraj* and sarod ecstasy with the meditative peace of the richly melodic verses. The lilting euphony suggested that George had tapped a new source of inspiration.[21]

But notably, Harrison was still diffident about his vocals and had to be encouraged by Paul McCartney to actually take the microphone. Tape operator Jerry Boys said, "George had this big thing about not wanting to sing it because he didn't feel confident that he could do the song justice. I remember Paul saying, 'You must have a go, don't worry about it, it's good.'"[22]

With this task completed, the band set off for India. The meditation study trip to Rishikesh was the last time the four Beatles shared an adventure away from the studio or live stage. Ironically, it was the trek that broke them, partly because Harrison returned a prolific writer of very fine songs. Rishikesh also marked his return to the guitar as his main instrument—he never recorded with Indian instrumentation for the Beatles again. He wrote a number of new guitar pieces, including "Piggies," "Not Guilty," "Sour Milk Sea," and "Dehra Dhun." His days of exclusive sitar study were numbered. He truly had found a muse and was inching ever further away from the Beatles.

Back in London, work on a new album ran from May to October through torturous hours filled with bitterness and rancor. The reality of the Beatles as a group was all but over, and not even Harrison's mid-session American absence to work with Jackie Lomax and Ravi Shankar interrupted things. Why should it, when Ringo Starr's two-week August walkout didn't?

The Beatles (a.k.a. *The White Album*) is an album of separation and alienation. Paul McCartney continued his solo efforts, with five of his twelve songs recorded without other Beatles. Harrison barely had any role to play on Paul's songs—he made audible contributions to only "Birthday" and "Back in the U.S.S.R." And the last of these was cut in extremis after Starr's walkout, leaving McCartney

---

[21] The recording of "The Inner Light" has been greatly debated. The basic instrumentation taped in Bombay was harmonium, flute, *pakhavaj, tabla-tarang* (a range of tuned tabla drums) and esraj (a violinlike bowed instrument similar to a dilruba). Compare the sound of the esraj on the *Wonderwall* track "Crying." By his own testimony, Ashish Khan only recorded with Harrison at Abbey Road, so his sarod part must have been overdubbed at the same time as Harrison cut his vocals.

[22] Lewisohn, *The Complete Beatles Recording Sessions*, 133.

to pick up the drumsticks. Here Harrison's inventive fills are the sonic glue that holds the Beatle sound together, but barely. And while Harrison's guitar was prominent on "Back in the U.S.S.R," his ideas were not always welcome on Paul's material. "Hey Jude" is a case in point: Harrison was reduced to watching the recording from the control room with George Martin, after McCartney had rejected his idea for a lead guitar part. The symbolism of Harrison's physical separation from the group was captured by cameras rolling on a *Beatles in the Studio* documentary for the British Music Council. In this clash of visions Harrison was easily dispensed with, and such was McCartney's determination to do it his way that "Why Don't We Do It in the Road?" was a premonition of the *McCartney* album, with Paul playing virtually everything himself.

As ever, George made a significant contribution to Lennon's arrangements, adding the lead guitar framework that was noticeably absent from McCartney's songs. Notably, Harrison's lead gave structure to "Yer Blues," grumbling bent bass notes punctuating Lennon's litany of doom, while a jaunty R&B figure highlights the satirical melodrama of "if I ain't dead already." He provides a similarly telepathic performance to support the minidrama of "Dear Prudence." Here Harrison's lead forms a substratum of the arrangement, building on Lennon's picked rhythm figures but crucially driving the song emotionally, as Lennon's voice often did on other tunes. As Lennon urges "Prudence" to come out and play, Harrison builds the tension by stepping through a high-register D major scale, perhaps inspired by Jimi Hendrix's similarly climactic "All Along the Watchtower" solo.

If "Dear Prudence" offered a welcome return to *Revolver*-era Lennon-Harrison musical empathy, "Happiness Is a Warm Gun" found the two collaborating to turn inspired fragments into a finished product. The last time they had worked this closely on a song was on "She Said She Said." The *Anthology 3* set includes the first run-through at Harrison's Esher home at the end of May. On this acoustic demo Lennon is heard finding his way through the four parts of the song, and even looking for the correct chords to match the melody. At one point, in frustration with himself, he declares, "Oh shit, wrong chord!" Comparing this nascent scattershot exploration of ideas with the finished version gives a classic exposition of Harrison's critical role in developing Lennon's ideas. Initially Harrison's lead merely punctuates Lennon's picked chords with driving power chords, but his fuzzed lead later provides the bridge to the "I need a fix" section, by giving an elliptical version of the new melody. This is clearly a Harrison concept.

The combination of Lennon's spontaneous bursts of raw inspiration with Harrison's methodical, musically erudite precision was compelling, and equally audible on "Everybody's Got Something to Hide Except Me and My Monkey." Again, the Esher demo has none of the electric guitar structure of the release version, meaning that Harrison's part in the "creative act" was to "compose" the riffs and fills that provide the song's backbone.

Equally potent and noticeable on the album was Harrison's return to the guitar, and a new inflection in his lead playing—he had discovered what Carlos Santana calls the "cry" of the guitar. His breaks tend to have a fuller, fatter sound, not least as a result of his using a Gibson Les Paul guitar for the first time. This can be clearly heard on his "Everybody's Got Something to Hide Except Me and My Monkey" fills, throughout "Sexy Sadie," and on a short but screaming outburst on "Cry Baby Cry." This was more blues-fueled than anything Harrison had played before. His years of sitar study had given him far greater control over his instrument—notably in string bending and vibrato techniques, not to mention a unique harmonic sense.

The confluence of three events had drawn Harrison back to the guitar. First, midway through the *White Album* sessions in June, he flew to California to complete some work for a Ravi Shankar film eventually released as *Raga* in 1971. During the shooting he met other Shankar students and realized his lifestyle, and just being "George Harrison," would not give him the latitude to seriously study the instrument. His "sitar period" was at an end. Shortly after he'd reached this conclusion, his friend Eric Clapton presented him with a coveted cherry red Gibson Les Paul, a guitar with a distinctively broad tone that changed Harrison's "sound" completely. Finally, he had a chance meeting with Clapton *and* Jimi Hendrix in a New York hotel, something that reinforced his identity as a guitarist. Nevertheless, this encounter only served to emphasize that Harrison was not a blues-based player. And while a guitarist like Doc Watson has never been disparaged for not playing long, electric blues solos, George Harrison was never given the benefit of that particular doubt.

But history shows that no matter what the fashion was in 1968, the world did not need another Eric Clapton, Jeff Beck, Peter Green, or Jimmy Page clone. In any event, the critical backlash against "guitar heroes" was only a matter of months away—Eric Clapton himself and a fair proportion of critics soon tired of the long solos favored by

Cream, preferring the low-key approach of Bob Dylan's erstwhile backup group, The Band. Harrison's style was far more in keeping with theirs than the megasoloists', even though Harrison and Clapton were already close friends. It was a relationship that spanned decades and even transcended Eric's liaison—and eventual marriage—with George's wife.

Harrison's musicality would triumph in the end. But as journalist Rip Rense recounts, there was always a suspicion that George could have played hot licks that way if he'd wanted to: "Eric Clapton tells a little story about seeing Harrison smiling in the wings at a concert once, and realizing that George could have played anything he or Hendrix did, if he'd wanted to. Harrison touched on this, in reference to the guitar heroes of the '80s: 'There's a lot of players who are really good, but there's still not a lot of them who blow me away—and there's a lot of stuff that they do which I could do if I wanted to do that kind of thing.'"

What Harrison wanted to do was to play music, not play up his own ego. His ability to conjure memorable hooks revealed a musicality that would eventually surface in his songwriting. Other musicians already recognized the inventiveness of his guitar phrases and its place in the Beatles' sound. Someone listening hard was a Southern blues and soul singer, Delaney Bramlett[23]: "George was blanketed by John and Paul, he didn't get a chance to really show his true feelings for a long time in his music. But without his guitar playing, the Beatle thing would not have taken the turn it did, without those guitar hooks that basically tell a story. He always gave them a musical hook. You hear one of his riffs and you know what that song is before you even hear the first note."

But despite the unquenchable narcissism of Lennon and McCartney, *The White Album* did see Harrison blossom as a songwriter with four varied offerings. "Piggies" was his version of a Dylanish, finger-pointing protest against the establishment—its basic folk genealogy obscured by the satirical, drawing-room arrangement. "Savoy Truffle" was a gusty joke, and introduced the electric piano–baritone saxophone combination that would be found later in his solo work.[24] Far better was "Long, Long, Long," which marked a confluence of the Indian, folk, and spiritual influences the guitarist had been exploring since 1966. It provided a musical template for

---

[23]From an interview with the author, December 2001.

[24]"The Lord Loves the One That Loves the Lord."

George's internal dialogue that would see him through the remainder of his career. The song creates a deeply personal and spiritual mood that seems almost suspended in time; his dreamy vocal materializes from the ether, but also is deeply moving. Harrison was obviously not as powerful a singer as Lennon or McCartney, but he had the greater gift they shared: he could convey emotion. The peaceful mood of "Long, Long, Long" was the first time George managed to share the spiritual refuge he'd found.

And with "While My Guitar Gently Weeps" Harrison had crafted a bona fide classic. The main advance shown by this major work is the tension and drama throughout the song, the first time Harrison had achieved this. The track was also cleverly arranged, with rhythmic counterpoint a key feature—the descending bass and guitar pattern contrasting with McCartney's piano vamp, the basic guitar chords, and Harrison's eerie vocal. The song also demonstrates his tendency to seek pragmatic solutions to the group's problems—when given the chance. Frustrated with not being able to realize the "vision in his head" for the guitar solo, and alarmed at the increasing tension within the Beatles, Harrison hit on the idea of getting Eric Clapton to sit in and play the lead part. It was another master stroke of "giving the song just what it needed," and crucially proved again that Harrison was more interested in the song than in his image.

Nevertheless, his clear thinking about the group's predicament could be uncomfortably piercing. The band worked for hours on another Harrison song, "Not Guilty," which was well up to the standard set for the album. It was based around the same descending arpeggiated guitar as "While My Guitar Gently Weeps," but went further in exploring the harmonic construction of the song's root chord (E minor), examining the harmonies implied by the other notes that surround the triad. Musically challenging, "Not Guilty" was also lyrically replete with barbs about the Beatles, taking up where "Only a Northern Song" left off. Here Harrison makes pointed observations about "upsetting the Apple cart" and band mates determined to "steal the day." He also declares that he knows his place in the band and won't "get underneath your feet"—after all, he's "not trying to be smart." Maybe when the cut came, "Not Guilty" was just a little too candid in airing the band's dirty linen.

Even if "Wild Honey Pie" was preferred over "Not Guilty," Harrison had shown himself to be an emerging, distinctive voice as a songwriter. Unless his growth could be accommodated within the band's formula, tension was bound to increase. But, in spite of the stresses at these sessions, the core bond that set the Beatles apart from outsiders remained. This was witnessed by John Barham, who worked with George on his individual ventures from 1966 to 1969 and beyond: "Sometimes I would be working with George at Abbey Road in the afternoon when a Beatle session had been booked for the evening. After working very closely with George on his own productions, it was very noticeable that as soon as the other three appeared in the studio, he would suddenly become distant and unapproachable. His focus changed abruptly. It wasn't something unpleasant; in fact, musicians who experienced this admired the professional and creative focus that it showed."

By the time the group assembled in January 1969 in a West London wind tunnel for their next venture, George Harrison was writing brilliant songs as regularly as Lennon and McCartney had in 1963-64. In the course of the roughly three weeks spent on McCartney's *Get Back* project, Harrison offered more than ten songs to the group, many destined to become classics, like "All Things Must Pass." The tepid reception given songs like "Let It Down," "Isn't It a Pity," "Hear Me Lord," and "I Me Mine" added to the guitarist's alienation from the Beatles.

Ironically, the idea behind *Get Back* was to present the Beatles as a working, unified band. Perhaps in response to the obvious group ethic of the Band, Paul McCartney's vision was a film that would show the Beatles rehearsing and performing as a "real band," something they hadn't managed for years. Unfortunately, for a setting they chose a drafty edifice with the charm of an aircraft hangar, and the 9 a.m. starts were hardly conducive hours for musicians.

But it was also the Band who had unknowingly hammered one of the nails into the Beatles' coffin through the simple act of massively boosting Harrison's confidence. After the *White Album* sessions had terminated—almost literally—Harrison spent Thanksgiving in Woodstock, jamming with Bob Dylan and the Band. There he had enjoyed being treated as a peer, rather than the kid from the class below. He cowrote songs with Dylan, one of the very few ever to do so.

Harrison's feelings were hardly at the top of John Lennon's agenda, given his discussion with Paul McCartney in which he mused, "You try and make George play competently because you're a friend, but how he'll play won't be how you want him to play."[25] The tenor of these events was famously captured by the cameras for world consumption in the *Let It Be* film, in a scene where Paul and George are debating how to play the guitar. Some have interpreted Harrison's legendary "I'll play whatever you want me to play" remark as a response born of anger. Others who knew him suggest that it was perhaps reflective of the fact that he genuinely didn't want his ego to prevail and really would play whatever they wanted, if that would help the group. It all came to a head on January 10 when Harrison packed up and left, went back to Esher, and wrote "Wah-Wah."

When the music from these sessions finally emerged, no doubts about Harrison's competence seemed appropriate, as his guitar playing had improved from that heard on *The Beatles*. He delivers blues-inflected, string-bending solos that lift "Dig a Pony" and "One After 909." In retrospect, these emphasize Harrison's position as a bridge between the Carl Perkins and Scotty Moore rock 'n' roll guitar school and the white blues sounds of Eric Clapton and Mike Bloomfield. Had his fleet-footed "One After 909" solo been played on his red Les Paul, and remixed through a heavily overdriven, screaming valve amplifier, it might have been more highly lauded, but that wasn't Harrison's style. His job was to play an exciting break, to complement a rocking live performance in which the Beatles almost recaptured their original rock 'n' roll dream. Foremost among his lead parts, though, was the wonderfully musical, song-changing contribution he made to Lennon's "Don't Let Me Down." Here is a classic example of his instinctive lead playing, drawing out new melodic avenues from within the chord structure and providing a great series of low-register riffs in the middle eight.

Meanwhile, Harrison's own songs for the session partly reflected his American adventures, with the happy twelve-bar, "For You Blue," and his concerns with the egocentricities of world celebrities, "I Me Mine." Before Phil Spector got to work, this was just a fragment of a keening, minor-key melody, juxtaposed with an unusually heavy rock blowout that featured some of George's most aggressive rock playing. Nevertheless, on an album that featured such poor fare as "Dig It," Harrison's songs were a relief. But in general, as 1969 became 1970, *Let It Be* again showed the guitarist that he had perhaps outgrown his role in the group.

---

[25] This discussion was reportedly held on January 13, 1969.

As the *Get Back* sessions merged into *Abbey Road,* the Beatles' guitarist recorded evidence of his rapidly advancing arranging skills. On the occasion of his twenty-sixth birthday in February 1969, Harrison booked himself into Abbey Road and cut demos of three songs, "Something," "All Things Must Pass," and "Old Brown Shoe." The last of these was the most complete in conception—Harrison's demo includes the now familiar rolling piano figure, bubbling bass and guitar line, and multilayered lead guitars. "Something" revealed that George already had the chromatic link between the bridge and solo, as well as a countermelody in the space that would become his most famous guitar statement. Indeed, on this demo we hear Harrison scat singing in a gospel style that would find its way into his final solo.

The seismic shift in the life of George Harrison, the musician, was evident for all to hear with the September 1969 release of *Abbey Road.* As usual, he had two strings to his bow—one as a guitar player and the other as a singer-songwriter. The evidence showed that he'd reached a new peak in both areas.

The serene elegance of "Something" should secure George a place among the great songwriters—he appears to have discovered the spaces within chords and the ability to create a melody that ebbed and flowed. Harmonic interest comes with almost every line, initially with the softening of the C major chord to a major seventh emphasised by the B in the vocal line; this is immediately flattened to B-flat, leading the melody a half step further from the tonic and resolution. The second melodic phrase, over "Something in the way she woos me," finally resolves to the dominant G before the descending half-step pattern is repeated through a sadder A minor for the emotional crux of the verse, "I don't want to leave her now." A minor becomes A major for the purposeful chorus, in which the singer answers his internal doubts. With the final note, on the final "I don't know," the song returns to the C major tonic and home.

The power of the melody is that it's a musical and emotional search for perfection (i.e., resolution to the tonic) that winds around two verses, and two trips through the probing chorus. It gives a sense of a search, filled with bittersweet longing. Whether he did so consciously or not, George Harrison had created a complex circular journey up and down the musical ladder that expressed a real depth of emotion. His wistful, fragile voice is perfectly suited to delivering the song, which is about doubt and striving to attain an uncertain goal. This is why Joe Cocker's powerful, rock-soul voice doesn't convey as much of the song's true emotional vulnerability on his version. He sounds too sure of himself.

For his second *Abbey Road* blockbuster, "Here Comes the Sun," Harrison used nature as a spiritual metaphor for the first time. The positive, major-key setting is in contrast to the mood of "Something" and recycles a chord pattern he'd recently created with Eric Clapton.[26] The reason for the fresh musical mood is not the change of the seasons but rather the artist's internal awakening, achieved through spiritual revelation. From this point on, Harrison regularly used nature symbols to make his inner journey more explicable to the listening public.

In George's guitar journey, *Abbey Road* was a key moment. As the group knowingly breathed its last in the studio, the Beatles bowed out with a showcase guitar battle as the climax to "The End." It was their final statement of rock 'n' roll defiance meeting spiritual aspiration. The famously traded solos showcase Lennon's passion and McCartney's flash but, above all, Harrison's virtuosity. His final flurry has a sweeping level of expression, born of ripe vibrato and climatic blues bends, that the others never could have matched.

Then there was his near immortal playing on "Something," a performance that is widely regarded as one of the great guitar solos, and with good reason. In this testament to taste, craft, and expressiveness, Harrison's guitar tells a story for the first time in his career. His tone is especially rich. While reflecting the Clapton influence, his work also presages the talking slide-guitar style he would later develop, but also includes some Indian gamaks. The triumph of George's "Something" solo is that he says more with one note than most fret-freakers and other six-string madmen manage in their entire careers.

Harrison later reflected on the performance, telling journalist Rip Rense: "Now, that is an example of that kind of thing where I find roughly where I can go," he said. "In those days, I don't know if that was an eight-track or whatever, but I remember specifically that it wasn't a clean empty track to put that solo on. Ringo was overdubbing something, and Paul was overdubbing something at the same time I was doing my solo. So in order for me to practice, I'd say, 'Let's do it again, and again.' But they'd have to do their bits, too. Even in those days, there were times when we were also very cooperative, and we'd do that to help each other. And I think also I sort of smoked something, and I didn't really know what I was doing. I did that solo a number of times, and then we left and went on holiday, came back, put the

---

[26]"Badge."

tape back up, and I was very pleasantly surprised, because I did hit some right notes, and it did have a certain spontaneity to it."

Abbey Road may be the Beatles album that most heavily features Harrison's melodic signature, played on guitar or moog synthesizer (another Harrison innovation). Aside from "Oh! Darling," his is the most prominent musical voice on side one of the album; even the nauseating and bizarre "Maxwell's Silver Hammer" is lifted by a memorable Harrison guitar break. And the arrangement and execution of "Octopus's Garden" was clearly George's work—not least in his delightful country-blues licks and solos. A new factor on the sessions was that Lennon was absent for a fair portion of the recording, and only contributed one completely *new* song, "Come Together." Harrison's sweet licks are prominent here, as are his intensely lyrical fills on "Sun King" (echoes of "Till There Was You"), but critically, he worked tirelessly on the guitar parts for "I Want You" to help realize Lennon's vision. Harrison contributed the climactic opening lead salvo, and the main counterpoint riff that defines the lengthy coda. Notably, Lennon did not reciprocate with ideas for George's songs.

Paul McCartney continued to offer support for Harrison's work, and ironically, perhaps, there was plenty of room for George to contribute to Paul's songs, which dominate the album's second side. This was helped by the fact that the group actually played much of the material live in the studio, returning to their "traditional" roles in the band. That was just what Harrison wanted to do: "We got to play the whole medley. We put them in order, played the backing track and recorded it all in one take, going from one arrangement to the next. We did actually perform more like musicians again."[27]

The sequence of songs on side two of the album is partly held together by Harrison's guitar parts. The rolling Leslie guitar chord motif on "You Never Give Me Your Money," itself a development of similar parts on "Badge" and "Here Comes the Sun," provides the bridge between "Carry That Weight" and "The End." Also, his teasing solo for "Polythene Pam" runs over into an inventive guitar commentary throughout "She Came in Through the Bathroom Window." This is characteristic Harrison picking: single-note statements mixed with chord vamps. He replicated the tone and style of these passages years later, in 1974.[28]

---

[27]Beatles, *Anthology*, 338.

[28]Found on "Somebody's City" from Splinter's album *The Place I Love*.

The other Harrison song from this period is the excellent "Old Brown Shoe," which says much about George's dilemma as one of the Beatles. In any other band, this upbeat boogie that matched lyrical sophistication with another outstanding guitar break would have taken precedence over the rough, self-serving travelogue that was "The Ballad of John and Yoko." Harrison's song works on any level, in any context, while the Lennon piece could only have relevance within the Beatles' self-referential sphere. "The Ballad of John and Yoko" is noted for its part as a signpost only in the Beatles' story, not in their music. It is simply not particularly good, whereas "Old Brown Shoe" is. This kind of glaring anomaly forced George Harrison out of the Beatles.

In the course of his career as a Beatle, Harrison had continually used his considerable musical talents to work collectively for the band's "common good." He played a pivotal role in creating their "sonic signature," his guitar arrangements holding the group together. The evidence of his contribution is readily available, but like much of Harrison's music, it is heard in the detail, not the immediate impact, and has been too easily overlooked. His innovations weren't "little acts of inspiration" but critical, defining elements.

And as Harrison forged his own identity and drifted away from the Beatles, he became a world-class songwriter, musical pioneer, and single-handed catalyst for a generation's interest in Indian culture. It's a rarely mentioned truism that there would have been no New Age books, shops, courses of study, and other products around the cities of the globe without the strong influence of Harrison's intensely personal, but paradoxically public, quest for spiritual truth. The acceptance of Indian music into the mainstream was also primarily his achievement. George Harrison had, literally, changed the world, musically and culturally, between 1966 and 1969.

The irony was that having been eclipsed by two geniuses of rock song craft, Harrison finally emerged from their shadow without the ambition to match them. Although *Abbey Road* documents seismic developments in his songwriting and instrumental skills, Harrison's goal was not to be regarded as the equal of John Lennon or Paul McCartney, or as a great guitar hero. His deepest concept was of music as a channel to reach God, and it was of no consequence to him whether he was regarded as a "genius." The comparisons with Lennon and McCartney were all part of a general preoccupation with the Beatles, an obsession that made it hard for the world to accept that the band's relationship had run its natural course. Harrison wasn't the main catalyst for the group's demise—in fact, it was Lennon who decided to break up the band he had started. By the end of the *Abbey Road* sessions in August, there was no turning back and the Beatles were on their own.

3

George Harrison
Early Solo Work
(1968-1970)

Wonderwall
(recorded in Bombay and London, December 1967 to January 1968; released December 1968)

Both *Sgt. Pepper* and *Magical Mystery Tour* held only marginal interest for George Harrison. At the time, he was compelled to forge his own musical identity, and the perfect opportunity came when he heard of a low-budget film in search of a soundtrack. A left-field American director, Joe Massot, had shot it in London. When Harrison viewed *Wonderwall*, it literally blew his mind with its loose tale of isolation, failed relationships, and human dislocation, presented in splashes of vivid color and integrated animation. The lack of dialogue left acres of room for music to speak, and a soupçon of cosmic apotheosis also helped. Beneath all its glaring trippiness, *Wonderwall* touched on themes that would come to preoccupy George Harrison—critically, the objectification of celebrities and the shallowness of fame. The wafer-thin plot revolves around a *Vogue* cover girl, played by Jane Birkin, who is a mere object for two men, one she knows and one she doesn't. The first is her self-obsessed boyfriend, who quickly moves on when she becomes pregnant, and the other is her neighbor, an introverted scientist, who observes her through a hole in the wall. He thinks of her either as a beautiful specimen under his microscope or as an idealized damsel in distress. One of these male suitors eventually "saves" her, through an epiphany that reveals her to be a normal, frail human being, rather than an object.

The *Wonderwall* film and music were born in a period when musicians, and artists in general, genuinely believed they could change the world. It was a short era of bliss before Altamont and Charles Manson blew the dream to pieces. It was almost as if the Romantic age of classical music had been reborn in the minds of rock stars; they took themselves very seriously and felt they had a duty to enlighten the world. For many, the idea was a side effect of pseudo-spiritual revelations induced by trysts with LSD—by his own account, this was part of the route through which George Harrison concluded that there was a "cosmic purpose" to what he was doing. Although cynical twenty-first-century observers may scorn such fancies, they were sincerely held, and largely harmless, beliefs. John Barham remembers an era when nothing was ever quite what it seemed: "The period was very exciting and sometimes very confusing—there was a seductive mixture of glamor, girls, cannabis, and easy money. I don't think that artists in general believed that love could save the world— most artists were, as always, having a hard time making ends meet and saw that it was easy to be spiritually euphoric when you were making plenty of money, but not so easy when you weren't. There were plenty of wolves in sheep's clothing prowling around, although in the '60s they were often in Afghan goatskin."[1]

George Harrison and the other Beatles were at the forefront of this intensely creative period, and Harrison saw an opportunity with Wonderwall to present a brief encyclopedia of Indian music to the Western public. He'd tried to do this in a small way in "Within You Without You" and "Love You To," but now he wanted to go to the source and record the real thing. His commitment extended to personally bankrolling a ten-day recording session in Bombay for which he gathered the cream of Indian musicians. They included one of Ravi Shankar's sitar students, Shambu-Das, and the heir-apparent sarod master, Ashish Khan, the son of Usted Ali Akbar Khan, one of the foremost musicians of any era.[2]

Harrison clearly was keen to absorb and learn as much as possible about Indian music and culture. Soon he'd traced the career of Ravi Shankar and discovered the revolutionary music Shankar had produced for films like *Pather Panchali*, the internationally lauded

---

[1]Barham, John. Interview with author, December 2002.

[2]Many of the musicians on this session became close friends of the guitarist's, and three joined him later on the 1974 *Dark Horse* tour of North America; Shiv Kumar Sharma (santoor), Hari Prasad Chaurasia (*bansuri*/flute) and Rij Ram Desad (tabla/percussion).

work of Indian filmmaker Satyajit Ray. Ray turned his camera onto the lives of ordinary Indians living in rural villages, away from the ornate and choreographed urban set pieces of Bollywood. Shankar's haunting musical theme for the film is an evocative, atmospheric creation. Harrison didn't quite hit those heights with his score, but he had obviously learned well from the sitar master.

The shrill, celebratory cry of the classic Indian reed instrument, the *shenhai*, opens the LP ("Microbes") and sets the tone for *Wonderwall*, which presents a kaleidoscope of sounds from Indian music. These ranged from familiar sitars, juxtaposed with the wonderfully resonant Persian dulcimer, the *santoor* ("In the Park"), to the intensely human affectations of the esraj ("Crying"). Marshaling the Bombay session, stopwatch in hand, George presented the two mainstays of Indian percussion in tandem with "Tabla and Pakavaj" and a beautiful sequence of double-tracked sarod from Ashish Khan for "Love Scene."[3] This was a companion in spirit to the *Conversations with Myself* album by American jazz pianist Bill Evans, for which he recorded himself twice. The idea of double-tracking the sarod, to produce a call and response, was literally revolutionary in Indian music. It was part of the soundboard legacy Harrison had learned from George Martin and the other Beatles, through the hothouse 1966–67 period of intense creativity.

Back in England, Harrison booked Abbey Road to create balancing Western music for the soundtrack. The sessions were very much a product of their time and had a free-form spontaneity that let the music "create itself," using virtually any musician known to Harrison who happened to be around. So a visiting Monkee, Peter Tork, found himself playing guitar on one session; Eric Clapton dropped in to play lead on a track ("Ski-ing"); and renowned British harmonica virtuoso Tommy Reilly was summoned on the recommendation of George Martin. The guitarist also called on a Liverpudlian rock 'n' roll combo, the Remo 4, to join in. Colin Manley and Tony Ashton from the Remos were old friends of the Beatles, as they'd backed Lennon & Co. on British tours at the height of Beatlemania.

But the most important figure in Harrison's troupe was John Barham. *Wonderwall* was clearly George's project, one that he would manage his way and for which he would need musicians who empathized with his ideas. That was why only Barham could be the link between musical idea and musical notation, rather than George

---

[3]Unlike most of the Indian pieces, "Love Scene" was recorded in London.

Martin, who was the musical bridge for the Beatles. To produce the soundtrack, Barham trailed in Harrison's wake, scribbling his ideas onto staves, providing orchestral arrangements where needed, and helping the inspired Fab to organize his music.

The discipline of harvesting instrumental music changed George's modus, and the piano—rather than the guitar—became his tool for picking out melodies. He'd already composed some songs on keyboards ("Blue Jay Way" and "It's All Too Much"), but pieces like "Red Lady Too" and "On the Bed" were developed from fragments of ideas that George doodled on piano. On the latter, a Harrison piano vamp is met with spacey steel guitar and a fugue of flugelhorn counter-melodies, added by Barham. The best collective work came on the slight but hauntingly beautiful "Wonderwall to Be Here," a short stream-of-consciousness piano melody from Tony Ashton, enhanced by ethereal Barham strings and guitar details. This moving music was a close fit with the scene it covered—a mute passage in which the implied lust of the aging academic turns to compassion for Jane Birkin, whose suicide attempt he witnesses while secreted in her wardrobe, hoping to seduce her. Harrison's melody was strongly empathetic to the first appearance of human feeling in the film.

Another composition, "Singing Om," was a significant early pointer to Harrison's desire to fuse Vedic chants with Western harmonies, but the best mix of Indian and Western was created on "Dream Scene." This musical acid trip accompanies a whimsical sequence of a hallucinated duel and rivals anything on *Sgt. Pepper* for sheer freak-out effect. In five and a half minutes, Harrison fused hauntingly fragile male and female Indian voices in a love duet, with a charging John Barham piano vamp answered by a host of flutes. An abrupt white noise nightmare is interjected, tempered by an elegant trumpet solo, before the playful harmonica of Tommy Reilly swirls in unison with police sirens that give way to distended, decelerated voices. One of these seems to be preaching a sermon on the nature of existence. This juxtaposition of opposites ends with a peal of church bells. As this oddity was cut months before "Revolution #9," it points to Harrison's early grasp of studio power.

When Joe Massot received Harrison's finished tape, he was non-plussed that no editing was required. Harrison had produced a perfect fit to the visual images, but also added his gloss to them—the final scene has the pathologist observing a microbial Jane Birkin, freed into the cosmos and merging into a galaxy. This spoke to Harrison of Vedic promises of emancipated souls, merging with the universal conscious-ness. Thus his musical accompaniment was "Singing Om."

Although almost entirely a product of its time, the *Wonderwall* soundtrack was an important step for Harrison, because as a document of Indian music it predated the legendary '60s album *Call of the Valley*. This was one of the landmark recordings of Indian music to reach a mass Western audience, as an introduction to the rich and varied flavors of the art form. It suggested that Harrison was a pioneer in fusing global music.

Although *Wonderwall* was the best expression of Harrison's universal approach, it simultaneously marked a pause in his Indian experiments. Throughout his Carnatic sabbatical he remained an avid Bob Dylan buff and followed the 1966 controversy accompanying Dylan and his backing band, the Hawks, as they transformed folk into rock.

By 1968 the Hawks had emerged as a creative unit in their own right but, in deference to their past, they were known simply as the Band. Multi-instrumentalists and songwriters, the members comfortably covered all bases in American popular music, incorporating folk, bluegrass, and rock 'n' roll influences with consummate ease. The release of their first album, *Music from Big Pink*, in August 1968 had an influence normally carried only by a new Beatles or Dylan platter. David Bromberg explains: "They were very different and very good. How many pop albums start with a slow song? The interaction on that record between bass and drums is extremely different from what anyone else was doing. Another thing is the vocals, which were unlike any others I'd ever heard before. They weren't extremely schooled, they weren't blues, and they weren't Dylan. But they were very evocative."

Another attraction of the Band was their group ethic and camaraderie, something that Harrison experienced firsthand when he accepted their invitation to spend Thanksgiving 1968 with them in Woodstock. The easygoing mood was a far cry from the tensions at large during the *White Album* sessions. Where the guitarist would always be "our kid," the younger brother in the Beatles, with the Band he was an equal.

More than that, Bob Dylan regarded him as a potential musical partner. Harrison stayed for a few days at his house in Woodstock. The idyllic setting gave Dylan not only a place to recuperate after his 1966 motorcycle accident but also a much-needed refuge from his own celebrity and the pressures of stardom. In fact, the bucolic tranquility of Bearsville, surrounded by woods, waterfalls, and natural swimming pools, provided the same rustic haven for Dylan that Harrison was to find at Friar Park within two years. And Dylan's life-affirming immersion in family at this time was also something George would later find at Friar Park. Despite the good vibes, both Dylan and Harrison were awkward during the visit, until the guitars appeared on the third day. The mix of Harrison's harmonic knowledge and Dylan's linguistic mastery fused to produce "I'd Have You Anytime" and "When Everybody Comes to Town." Dylan also showed George a new song, "I Don't Want to Do It," which neatly captured the American's reflective mood. This opened a channel of collaboration for Dylan that spanned thirty years.

But why did Dylan collaborate only with this particular Beatle? What did George Harrison offer that John Lennon or Paul McCartney didn't? In 1968, George had no illusions about his skills, and no pretensions to be considered a genius. He wasn't competitive at all and was happy to share his harmonic knowledge. By all accounts, this is what Bob was most interested in: Harrison's knowledge of harmony and chords, which, objectively, exceeded Dylan's at this time. Harrison was also a lead guitarist, something Dylan didn't have time to be![4]

In the meantime, George's ears were awash with the sounds of the Band's *Music from Big Pink* and its 1969 successor, simply titled *The Band*. These discs were a major influence on the emerging Harrison solo sound—they sounded fresh and infinitely lighter than the overblown psychedelia that the Beatles themselves had gone a long way to invent. The Band were not dissimilar to the Beatles: they were all versatile, if not virtuoso musicians; they too were steeped in the history of black music; they were accomplished songwriters; and they used tight vocal harmonies to great effect. Their approach to instrumental solos was that, if they were needed at all, their purpose was to complement, not overwhelm, the song. In the era of Hendrix, Clapton, et al, Robbie Robertson and George Harrison stood out as two players who made economy of expression a virtue. Their styles were similar, and Harrison could easily have played Robertson's sparse notes on "Jemima Surrender."

The Band's two classic albums were clearly part of the musical atmosphere that Harrison absorbed, not so much in direct influence as in general approach. Numerous elements of *Music from Big Pink* either show a Beatles influence or find echoes in the Beatles' and Harrison's music: "In a Station" features distended slide guitar and

---

[4]Harrison's licks were to appear uncredited on Dylan's *New Morning*.

"Tears of Rage" has the Leslie-toned guitars that immediately appeared on *Abbey Road*; "The Weight" has an acoustic guitar introduction that would be heard again.[5] Their version of Dylan's "I Shall Be Released" was a model for later Harrison ballads, with its solemnly strummed acoustics and raindrop piano cascade, although the imitation tamboura drone must be indicative of the reverse influence. Later efforts, "Whispering Pines" and "The Unfaithful Servant," were in the same mellow mold, and their tempo is found on numerous Harrisongs.

But there were clear differences: for one thing, Harrison's music was far more emotive and revelatory than the Band's. But George's basic musical template was minimalist in the style of *The Band*—fingerpicked acoustic guitars, supported by piano and organ, topped with horns. Nevertheless, "The Unfaithful Servant" has the strongest suggestion of George Harrison: the medium tempo, the tension of the second theme, and the eccentric chord structure. The passionate climactic singing has the hint of being just at the edge of the singer's range and, above all, the sweet-and-sour horn arrangement on this track was recycled by Harrison.[6] Moreover, Robbie Robertson's melody-tracking guitar solo is in keeping with George's style. But beyond these specifics, the mood of the song suggests Harrison. It sounds reverent.

The Band's music set the scene for George Harrison's first solo composition proper, created with the man he came to call his "guitarist-in-law."

[1] **Badge (2:43)** (Harrison–Clapton) *(recorded by Cream)*
Harrison guitar; **Eric Clapton** vocal, guitar; **Jack Bruce** bass;
Ginger Baker drums; **Felix Pappalardi** piano, mellotron

Music from Big Pink skimmed the U.S. Top 30 and missed the British album charts completely when it appeared in September 1968. But if the sales weren't volcanic, the effect on the musical fraternity was. The album's impact was almost that of a *Sgt. Pepper* or *Pet Sounds*. For one thing, it sounded the death knell for Cream, who had brought unprecedented levels of instrumental virtuosity

---

[5]"All Things Must Pass."

[6]See *All Things Must Pass*, especially "Run of the Mill," which uses the closing lilting clarinet legatos.

to the fore in their two-year run between 1966 and 1968. The focus of attention was Eric Clapton, who temporarily reveled in the "Clapton is God" tag. But the English guitar master soon tired of the genre he'd virtually invented, and The Band's album suggested new possibilities to him: "I got the tapes of *Music from Big Pink* and I thought, well, this is what I want to play—not extended solos and maestro bullshit, but just good funky songs."[7]

George Harrison felt the same, even though he had no extended solos or maestro bullshit to excise, and he was well placed to help Clapton's metamorphosis. The pair had been friends since Christmas 1964, when the Yardbirds opened a Beatles Christmas show; paradoxically, when Clapton took Harrison's place on "While My Guitar Gently Weeps," he helped Harrison establish his own musical identity. The return favor George offered was to help the guitar god on a track for the final Cream album, which was cut over Christmas 1968.

"Badge" certainly had more in common with The Band's work than it did with "Toad" or other Cream archetypes, but it also recalled the first Harrison-Clapton collaboration. Its similarity to "While My Guitar Gently Weeps" is unsurprising, given that it has the same A-minor setting and jangling piano track. It also matches its progenitor for tension and a stirring Clapton solo, while Harrison's spare, driving licks were later described by Cream's virtuoso bass man Jack Bruce as "wonderful rhythm guitar work." "Badge" introduced one of rock's more enduring arpeggio chord sequences: the D-C-G-D chord riff introducing the song's climax formed the basis of "Here Comes the Sun" and the coda to "You Never Give Me Your Money," as well as a hundred lesser efforts.[8]

"Badge" was more than a rare example of superstar synergy: it was a new type of rock-pop song. It was less blues and more pop than Clapton's trademark style, and more "rock" than Harrison's. Clocking in at less than three minutes, "Badge" is a model of clarity and incision. It also marked the start, in earnest, of George Harrison's slow drift away from the Beatles.

---

[7] Quoted in Turner, Steve. "Eric Clapton Interview."

[8] Just one "B list" example would be Boston's 1970s hit "More Than a Feeling."

One offshoot of the interminable sessions for *The White Album* was the acceptance into the Beatles' fold of a generally unknown Liverpool rocker who'd also found his way to Germany in the early 1960s. Jackie Lomax sang backup on "Dear Prudence" and had the same background as the group. Before trying his luck in Germany, he worked as a wages clerk on Liverpool docks. Without music, his future prospects had been as bleak as George Harrison's when he faced life as an apprentice electrician. Lomax had a powerful, if nasal, singing voice and plenty of songs ready to be recorded.

Musically, the Beatles were a restriction to Harrison, but their Apple Records label was an emancipating force. It offered him the chance to test his skills as an arranger and producer for Lomax, in sessions that were split between London and Los Angeles. Harrison did all he could to help Lomax, enlisting McCartney, Starr, Eric Clapton, John Barham, Klaus Voormann from Manfred Mann's Earth Band, and Rolling Stones session pianist Nicky Hopkins. He went so far as to donate a new composition of his own to the cause, another from his Beatles scrap heap, "Sour Milk Sea."

The album was called *Is This What You Want?* The public's answer was generally an apathetic "no." Lomax's songs were formulaic rock-pop, which Harrison loaded with all the studio trickery he had at his disposal. Pared-down "Glass Onion" cellos appear on the opening cut, "Speak to Me," while the title piece is almost a rerun of "I Am the Walrus." Some of the arrangements touched on the Big Band sounds that all these war babies would have heard on their radios ("Sunset" and "Little Yellow Pills"). But Harrison also had the newest musical technology to bring to the session: with the help of an American engineer, Bernie Krause, "Take My Word" includes a short passage played on a synthesizer. It was definitely a more pleasing exercise than Harrison and Krause would concoct for their follow-up synthesizer project, *Electronic Sound*. The more familiar strains of Harrison's guitar are all over the disc, from inventive supporting riffs for "The Eagle Laughs at You" to his sharp, Steve Cropper rhythm licks on "You've Got Me Thinking."

The Lomax LP exemplifies why Apple was only half a good idea and why most of the artists signed to the label achieved minimal success. For the Beatles, any association they had with a record was virtually a guarantee—most of their albums automatically hit number one, and they didn't tour to promote them. This was the model they applied to the artists they signed: record the album, find a hit single, and success would follow. Apple simply did not employ the tough marketing tactics of the majors like Columbia, but only the Beatles were sufficiently shrouded in artificial mystique to need no promotion. As most of the acts signed to Apple could testify, the model worked less often than it failed, unless the act were powerful writers, like Badfinger. The problem for Jackie Lomax was that "Sour Milk Sea" wasn't catchy enough to make the charts and, as a result, the album died. One of the Fab Four's oldest friends, Klaus Voormann, who knew the band from their pre-fame, early 1960s Hamburg days, took time out from his Manfred Mann duties to play on this album and the other Harrison productions that followed. He offers a sobering view of why so few of the Apple acts prospered: "I think the Beatles didn't know how hard it was for a new act to be successful in the business. They did what they could to help them, but most of the time it wasn't necessarily what was best for those people."[9]

But John Barham, who provided orchestral arrangements, wonders if sales were Harrison's main goal for this album: "I don't know if George thought that he would have a hit. Jackie was an old friend who George liked and respected as a musician. At that time, George was just beginning to take an interest in record production and, in some sense, it may be that these productions were his preparatory training for his production of *All Things Must Pass.*" The project included the first song George Harrison "gave away:"

[2] **Sour Milk Sea (3:52)** *(Harrison) (recorded by Jackie Lomax)*
Harrison guitar, second guitar solo; **Eric Clapton** guitar, first guitar solo; **Jackie Lomax** vocals; **Paul McCartney** bass; **Ringo Starr** drums; **Nicky Hopkins** piano

This song about the benefits of meditation was recorded in the heavy rock style of the period, a repeating blues guitar riff battling with Starr's booming drums and Hopkins's "Revolution" honky-tonk piano. As with most Harrison songs, it was evident that "Sour Milk Sea" was written on acoustic guitar—the electric riffs and, therefore, the mood of the finished product were created in the studio. Though not a particularly memorable melody, "Sour Milk Sea" does capture the first recorded example of Clapton and Harrison exchanging guitar solos.

---

[9]Voorman, Klaus. Telephone interview with author, March 2002.

What Jackie Lomax made of the lyrical content is unknown. The song's writer assumed the role of advertising executive to push the benefits of meditation to the public, outlining the problem—"Looking for release from limitation?" ("Problem dandruff?")—and offering the solution, "There's nothing much without illumination" ("Try 'Scalp and Shoulders'"). At the time, it was the enlightened artist's job to share their insights with "the people," which makes "Sour Milk Sea" an obvious companion to "Within You Without You."

A superior, if unfinished, version of the song was taped by the Beatles during the May 1968 Esher session to run through potential *White Album* material. Played with real enthusiasm, and reveling in a fine Harrison vocal, this garage rendition is more exciting and convincing than the Lomax recording.

Electronic Sound
(recorded in Los Angeles, November 1968 and at Esher, February 1969; released May 1969)

The term "genius" is flung around with such abandon in the rock world that it has become meaningless. It also has no reference point. When a rock star is described as a "genius," does this rank him with the likes of Beethoven, Mahler, and Stravinsky?

The problem multiplies when the media manage to convince the artist, as well as the public, that they are worthy of the term. Then, as Ian MacDonald points out,[10] the musician assumes that anything they do is part of the artistic process and therefore of import. John Lennon and Yoko Ono were the doyens of such preposterous self-indulgence and sadly, with *Electronic Sound*, George Harrison showed himself susceptible too. Forty minutes' evidence that a Beatle had no idea how to play a new electronic keyboard is at least thirty-nine minutes too much.

This "event" was born from Harrison's delight at witnessing the birth of the electronic synthesizer in Los Angeles during the Jackie Lomax sessions. The father was Bernie Krause, who showed Harrison more. There has always been a hint of a dispute about whether *Electronic Sound* was Krause's work or Harrison's. It's a marvel that anyone cared, given the results. Whatever its genesis, releasing this unlistenable mess on an experimental label dedicated to the avant-garde (whatever that is) perhaps softens the blow, but

---

[10]MacDonald, *Revolution in the Head,* 277.

there is no excuse for the album, certainly one of the worst records of all time. Had the European Court of Human Rights existed in 1969, *Electronic Sound* would surely have been charged with unnatural cruelty. At least Harrison stopped the nonsense at one release—Lennon and Ono simply went on and on and on, until Lennon's member became as highly regarded in his own mind as the collected works of James Joyce.

Electronic Sound excepted, George Harrison was immersed in music. His day job at the *Abbey Road* sessions continued. His guitar was also heard in exalted musical company: on Jack Bruce's most successful solo work, *Songs for a Tailor*,[11] but also, more tellingly, on two dates that set the mood for *All Things Must Pass*. Even as overdubs were being applied to "Something" and "Here Comes the Sun," Harrison was introducing an unlikely group of hit makers to Abbey Road. The Hare Krishna movement, sometimes referred to as a "cult," is also actually a strand of Hinduism—it is based on the same philosophical and textual roots. As he remained until he died, Harrison was interested in "God-realisation for a change."[12] The Krishna sect offered it through the chanting of a simple mantra. Harrison's experiences through this practice were obviously seismic and, far from being a fad, it became his spiritual mainstay for the rest of his life.

Being part owner of his own label, George could record anything that took his fancy. So he simply assembled his new friends from the local Krishna temple at Abbey Road to record a three-minute, chart-friendly version of the centuries-old "Hare Krishna Mantra." The sounds of harmonium and Harrison's Leslie-toned guitar (straight out of the Band's "Tears of Rage") introduce the naggingly catchy theme, spiced with drums and hand cymbals. It builds to a dervishlike climax that took it into the British Top 10 a matter of months after another spiritual, Edwin Hawkins's "Oh Happy Day," had cracked the charts. Harrison would soon bring these two varieties of spiritual expression together.

More than the Maharishi, "Within You Without You," or *Wonderwall*, the guitarist's involvement with the Krishna movement was the most daring of his exploits. It wasn't just that the media thought the move-

---

[11] "Never Tell Your Mother She's Out of Tune," recorded May 11, 1969.

[12] From "Brainwashed."

ment bizarre: they were certain it was a dangerous subversion of Western values and, for all the supposed challenges to society posed by rock 'n' roll, Harrison's "Hare Krishna Mantra" was the most revolutionary. The single marked the start of his deep interest in the Krishnas, and later in 1969, both he and John Lennon came face to face with A. C. Bhaktivedanta Swami Prabhupaba. This unassuming man, founder of the modern Krishna creed, was considered a saint by his devotees. For George, this was getting very close to the source, and it inspired his attachment to the Krishna belief system.

George Harrison was immersed in an incredible phase of creativity throughout 1969. Even if the *Let It Be* escapade was more a chore than a joy, it gave him the chance to work with a first-class American musician, the electrifying gospel organist Billy Preston. His appearance at the splintering sessions put a stop to the Beatles' bickering, just because he was an outsider. Working with Preston cemented Harrison's interest in soul music and gave him firsthand experience of gospel power, which seemed a natural partner to Krishna power.

The Beatles decided that the amiable Texan should be signed to Apple, and a grand scheme was hatched to produce a major album. Billy Preston reflects on how the plan didn't quite work out: "They asked me would I like to be on Apple Records. I was with Capitol at the time. The next day I went to the studio and they said, 'You're on Apple.' Which was great, as it gave me a chance to produce for the first time and also be able to sing, because most of my albums before that were just instrumental. George Harrison did most of the coproducing with me—originally, it was supposed to be all four Beatles producing a couple songs for me, but that's when all the disturbances came up. So everybody kind of split up. But me and George hung in there."

Left to his own devices, Harrison wasn't slow to enlist help for Billy: he recruited Eric Clapton and Keith Richards to work on *That's the Way God Planned It*. Including them almost resulted in a fatal clash of styles, as Preston's gospel sensibilities collided with period Cream heaviness. The album survived almost unscathed because Preston's compositions were generally strong. Some, like "I Want to Thank You," are full of the modulating gospel sevenths that would partly define *All Things Must Pass*. Others reflect the rock influence, including an obvious "Hey Joe" cash-in ("Hey Brother") and a Dylan cover ("She Belongs to Me") that retains a gospel character through a phalanx of backup vocalists. It was George Harrison's first session working with a gospel choir, but the concept became a fixture in his music right through to *Extra Texture*. The highlight of the album is the climactic title track, one of the more successful fusions of gospel with rock; its theme was close to Harrison's emerging musical vision. All the music Harrison was involved with touched on the spiritual, from the Krishna temple to Preston's rocked-up gospel to the would-be maxim of "The End."

Harrison was also developing his studio skills. His production for Preston almost totally eschewed the psychedelic filters and wild panning of *Wonderwall* and the Jackie Lomax album (those effects make a last stand to close "Let Us All Get Together Now"), but was still locked in the heavily phased placement of instruments on the soundstage. Even in the field of sound engineering and production, Harrison was slowly leaving the past behind.

The Preston album was Harrison's earliest soul project and gave him firsthand exposure to the gospel backup vocals the Beatles recycled and made their own. During the session, a New York soul diva, now based in London, was drafted to add her gravitas to the proceedings. Doris Troy well remembers her first encounter with Harrison in 1969: "I was called to do a session for Billy Preston and, when I got to the studio, it was George producing Billy. So when I walked in, George gave me a great big smile, picked up his guitar, and started playing 'Just One Look.' I said, 'Wow, you know my song!' and he said, 'I know everything you ever did.' We got along real good."[13]

The uplifting "Just One Look" had been a major hit for Doris during her stint on Atlantic in 1963. The Hollies' cover version almost topped the U.K. chart the following year, the same year as another Troy hit, "What'cha Gonna Do About It?" It wasn't just George Harrison who admired Doris Troy: she was being courted by the Rolling Stones, who used her to organize the backup vocals for their 1969 hit, "You Can't Always Get What You Want."

Like most of the soul divas, Doris Troy got her singing background in church, intoning gospel music. This was an everyday fact of life for a girl whose father was a Pentecostal minister: "I was brought up in the church—until I was sixteen, I was totally involved in church songs and church music. Then I wanted to get out in the world. In those days, gospel was only in the church, not like it is today. There were no gospel charts." Troy's taste for "the gospel music that gives

---

[13]Troy, Doris. Telephone interview with author, December 2001.

you good news" was perfect for "That's the Way God Planned It," and perfect for George Harrison's emerging philosophy of music.

As the Preston session drew to a close, Harrison wanted to know if Doris was signed to any label. Not a man to waste time, when he found that Troy was unattached, he offered her an Apple contract on the spot. Within days, Doris was signed "as writer, singer, and producer. They gave me my own office, and I was in business."

As autumn approached, Harrison decided it was time to start work on a Doris Troy set. It was going to be a collaborative effort between the Beatle and the preacher's daughter. They first decided who they wanted to play on the album—Ringo Starr would handle drumming chores with the Plastic Ono Band's Alan White, and Billy Preston would play too. By the time the sessions started, the album was mutating into an all-star affair, with Leon Russell, Delaney Bramlett, Stephen Stills, Klaus Voormann, Jackie Lomax, Eric Clapton, and a young Peter Frampton dropping by.

As Doris only had two fully arranged pieces in mind, most of the album was written in the studio or at George's Esher home. The work at Kinfauns was mostly limited to a trio of Preston, Harrison, and Troy, and to one room of the house, as the rest was too cold! Despite the Surrey frostbite, the music flowed and the New York pianist soon realized the depth of the Fab Four's knowledge of black music: "I think he had been involved in soul music for years—he listened to it, he loved it, and that's what made him want to do it. I wasn't actually introducing him to the stuff, he already knew it. The Beatles as a whole listened to black music, a lot of their soul and feelings came from American music."

Two of the cowritten tunes, "Ain't That Cute" and "You Give Me Joy Joy," tap into a spirited soul vein. Others, notably "Give Me Back My Dynamite," almost run aground on period heaviness. The power and panache of Doris Troy's vocals transcends any rock overkill, but the album works best when she sticks to her soul roots. At their best, Troy's compositions sparkle. "I've Got to Be Strong" sounds like a long-lost Motown hit that the Beatles might have covered on *With the Beatles*, while "So Far" is the songwriting highlight of the disc. Cowritten with Klaus Voormann, it is overrun with harmonically sophisticated chord patterns, a powerful vocal, and immaculate Stax rhythm guitar from the resident Beatle. The observant Harrison could not have failed to learn from the construction of this song, and others like the jazzy "Exactly Like You," notably how to make subtle use of a horn section to enhance rather than dominate.

Aside from "So Far," the pivotal *Doris Troy* track for George Harrison's career was a version of the gospel standard "Jacob's Ladder," arranged by Harrison and Troy. The straightforward piano-led arrangement conveys the "up" gospel mood of Troy's choice. Other than a characteristically concise Harrison guitar break, the main points of interest were the call-and-response backup vocals and a sense that this was essentially a chant, something it shared with the great "Oh Happy Day." As such, it was an unlikely companion piece to the "Hare Krishna Mantra" and a pointer to "My Sweet Lord."

By the time the album was ready for release, hard-nosed American businessman Allen Klein had taken the reins at Apple, and the marketing of non-Beatle product left much to be desired, even though *Doris Troy* was generally well received by the critics. Despite the disappointing sales, the artist's encounter with George Harrison was positive. She was left with warm feelings toward a man in the midst of a spiritual quest: "He was into his spiritual life—that was who he was, he wasn't a partying person. He always appeared to be really cool and really calm, he never cursed nobody. He was just a good guy—the child was serious."

In a small way, Harrison's work with Billy Preston and Doris Troy was his soul version of the British blues revival, an attempt to gain some recognition for greatly talented songwriters and musicians. Simultaneously, the Liverpudlian was learning plenty. Harrison was in effect taking a songwriting master class from the New York soul diva as he fought his way back from self-imposed raga exile.

Traveling to Los Angeles in late 1968 to deliver the master tapes of *The Beatles* to Capitol, George Harrison met a man who proved to be one the biggest influences on his early solo career. Delaney Bramlett was raised the hard way in Pontotoc County, Mississippi. As a teenager he broke his back as a sharecropper, a cotton picker, way down South where there was no guarantee of the next meal. The homes had no electricity or running water. The experience was the same for blacks and whites, who also shared a musical language called the blues.

When Harrison first heard him play in Los Angeles, Bramlett had already been through the navy to escape life in the fields and had made a name for himself as one of the Shindogs, the regular band on the ratings favorite *Shindig*. Besides earning his living in the television studio, Delaney kept musical and social company with other local players, Leon Russell and J. J. Cale. He was also cutting tracks with the soul fraternity, among them Booker T. Jones, Bobby Womack, Aretha Franklin, and Billy Preston. After he married "Ikette" Bonnie O'Farrell in 1967, following a five-day romance, a new act, Delaney & Bonnie, was conceived and signed to the classic Stax label, the home of soul. Their breakthrough came with a 1969 platter, *Accept No Substitute*, which featured a drummer called Jim Keltner; the couple was soon hot news in the transatlantic music world. And Keltner's talents had been noticed, as well as logged for future reference, by Harrison.

There was an honesty and energy to Delaney & Bonnie's music that grabbed George's attention. His first impulse was to sign them to Apple. The more lasting effect was that he made a new friend. Conversely, hanging out with these English musicians, Delaney realized that they were playing the same music he was and shared his passion for it. Howlin' Wolf's language was universal, and London was the natural place to be.

The chain of events that brought Delaney and his band to England in the late summer of 1969 touches on rock history. The years 1968 and 1969 saw British music turn itself inside out—the Beatles were on their last legs and two other leading English bands, Cream and Traffic, were also no more. The world's inaugural power trio bowed out just before the *Wonderwall* album hit the racks; Traffic fell apart when the multitalented Steve Winwood moved on to join Eric Clapton and Ginger Baker in a new venture aptly called Blind Faith. A fine, eponymous album was a number one smash by September 1969. Meanwhile, Traffic's guitar picker, Dave Mason, had also taken off for California, where newly airborne Byrd Gram Parsons introduced him to Delaney. Mason was added to the ever-growing Delaney & Bonnie backup roster.

The classic Delaney & Bonnie lineup included drummers Jim Gordon and Jim Keltner, bassist Carl Radle, and Bobby Whitlock, who doubled on organ and guitar. This basic unit was reinforced by a pulsating horn section of Bobby Keys (sax) and Jim Price (trumpet), and a backup singer, Rita Coolidge. Vocals were split between Delaney and Mrs. Bramlett, who, on an earlier gig, had been the first white singer to back Ike and Tina Turner.

The Delaney musicians weren't quite virtuosi, but neither were they prone to the occasional sloppiness for which the Beatles were known. They were just professional working musicians, and their sound was *big*. The music mixed the showmanship of black R&B reviews with a brash boogie shuffle, underpinned by pounding bass lines and Stax horn charts. The vocals were powerful testimony to the grinding poverty of a Southern upbringing, and this honesty caught the ear of English blues purists. Their music was a more direct version of Cream's ultraheaviness. There were solos, but they weren't measured in days' duration. The tunes had catchy riffs, but weren't reliant on them. In 1969, compared with the power trios' instrumental navel-gazing, Delaney & Bonnie's powerful, raucous soul-blues was refreshing.

One of the rockers in need of Southern comfort was Eric Clapton, who was finding that his collaboration with Steve Winwood was not the panacea for his superstar afflictions. After a single, huge concert at London's Hyde Park in June, Blind Faith jetted off to the U.S. Eastern Seaboard for a tour that killed the band dead. The support act was Delaney & Bonnie, whose balls-out rock 'n' soul was far more to the taste of the crowds than the efforts of Messieurs Winwood and Clapton. The Blind Faith spectacle at Madison Square Garden in July was more about a rioting crowd than about musical fireworks. But the band itself was highly combustible, as Delaney Bramlett observed: "We opened for Blind Faith. They were getting terrible write-ups in the papers—they didn't get along. Eric asked me, 'Can I come up and jam with you?' and I said 'Sure.' A little later he was saying, 'Can I ride the bus with you?' You see, they were flying, but they wouldn't fly together. They flew separate, they just could not get along. In the end, he was onstage with us all the time, and they were getting pissed. The next thing I knew, Eric asked: 'Can I just join your band?'"

Eric Clapton wound up playing guitar or just tambourine in Delaney & Bonnie's set, as well as on his own *Blind Faith* success, "Presence of the Lord." He preferred the hillbilly camaraderie of the Delaney troupe to the overexercised egos of his own band, and arranged for the Southern boys and gals to hit Europe for a November tour. He'd be free to play after joining John Lennon for September's *Live Peace in Toronto*.

A week late and back in London, work started on sessions for another Dixie singer and Phil Spector alumnus, Leon Russell. The collective toil of Russell, Harrison, Clapton, Bramlett, Bill Wyman, and Charlie Watts produced the fine *Leon Russell* album, a swirling soup of Southern rock, folk, and ballads. Of the many guitar licks on the session, it was Delaney Bramlett's simple, harmonized slide part to open "Delta Lady" that became most firmly lodged in George Harrison's musical brain.

But Harrison didn't have too long to dwell on this bottleneck revelation, as he was soon cutting a session with another Blind Faith outcast. With unexpected time on his hands, bass and violin man Rick Grech had plans for a solo album. Sessions with George were held in October 1969. They lumped Harrison in with two parts of a fluid band who gloried in the name Balls: future Wings accomplice Denny Laine and ex-Move bass man Trevor Burton.[14]

The music taped was not release quality:[15] a loose blues jam, "Exchange and Mart," and a half-finished busking song, "Spending All My Days," that was light-years behind "Sea of Joy." Although it was classically poor outtake material, the session was all part of Harrison's musical emancipation. It was as if he had opened the hidden back door to the Beatles' house and discovered an entire parallel universe of musicians out there.

He made up his mind to step over the threshold on December 1, when he witnessed Delaney & Bonnie's tumultuously received first U.K. date amid the brushed velvet of London's Royal Albert Hall. Harrison was so impressed by what he saw that he popped the question backstage: "Would you mind if I joined the band? Would there be too many guitars?" When Delaney & Bonnie's bus pulled up to the Harrisons' Esher bungalow next morning, Harrison's guitar and amp were on the pavement outside, plus a present for the troupe's leader: "When I picked him up the next morning at his house, he said, 'I've got something I want to give you for what you did for me last night.' He gave me a handmade guitar from Leo Fender, a Rosewood Telecaster. It was one of a kind."[16]

George Harrison's return to the English concert stage followed, at the Colston Hall in Bristol the next day, December 2. It would have been easy to overlook his presence entirely. Harrison was satisfied to lurk at the back of the stage, virtually masked by the stacks of amplifiers, playing rhythm to Clapton's lead. By December 6, the tour had hit the Liverpool Empire—it would be the last live appearance Harrison ever made in his own city. In Liverpool, Harrison finally succumbed to Delaney's perpetual demands that he should sing. The natural choice was his own Southern signature tune, "Everybody's Trying to Be My Baby."

The carefree mood of Delaney & Bonnie was in sharp contrast

---

[14]Other groups of Balls included Jackie Lomax, Mike Kellie (later of Spooky Tooth), Richard Tandy (who played on the late 1980s "Poor Little Girl" Harrison sessions), and Alan White.

[15]The tracks were issued as bonus cuts on the 1986 German CD reissue of the *Blind Faith* album.

[16]This is the guitar Harrison played during *Let It Be*.

to the doubts and hang-ups that plagued both Harrison and Clapton. Delaney Bramlett was a man devoid of complexes—he didn't have to satisfy the demands of fans or media to be a cultural icon or guitar god. He just told the nervy pair to get on with it, have fun, and start singing. But the time Delaney and George spent together as the tour rolled on was more than simply a reality check; it changed Harrison's music forever. Harrison was fascinated by Bramlett's colorful past, his slide guitar, and his knowledge of gospel music. The pair sat for hours, talking and playing: "He was a very inquisitive person. He wanted to know something about everything. One time he asked me, 'How did you feel when you were out there picking that cotton?' We would sit for hours, and I would show him different tunings, and what kind of atmosphere it would cause. If you listen to 'My Sweet Lord,' well, we had that guitar part worked out before he ever thought of it in the studio."

Legend sometimes has it that Delaney Bramlett taught George to play slide guitar. The man himself disagrees: "One time he asked me if I would teach him how to play slide, and later, George said I'd taught him how to play it. Well, he did make that statement—but I didn't teach him anything, George already knew how to play guitar, he just wanted to know my technique, what I thought about it and what I did. All I did was teach him my style of playing."

Included in the Delaney & Bonnie set was a tune Delaney and Eric Clapton had written together during the Blind Faith jaunt. "Coming Home" was a compulsive, major-key boogie, based around a growling, rhythmic guitar riff, relentless bass, and stabbing horns. Against this huge sound canvas, "Coming Home" introduced a short, ostinato slide guitar statement, which Dave Mason was handling. As the tour hit Scandinavia, Mason suggested to George Harrison that he play the lick himself, which he did. It was the birth of one of the most recognizable guitar signatures in popular music.

But besides learning, there was time for rock 'n' roll games, for George to let his hair down and live up to his prankster reputation. His victim, Delaney Bramlett, explains: "We were in this pub, the bar was all locked up with the grille. George said, 'I'll just break it, we'll just pay for the trouble.' The cops came in and called the landlord. He just laughed and said: 'Let them have it, as long as they pay for it.' So we had a party. Tony Ashton was playing piano and we were singing, running in circles, and throwing pies, you know, food fights. It was the damnedest thing you've ever seen. George's security guy came in and said it was time to go. I was heading for the door when George said,

'Wait a second, I think you've got something on your pants.' I turned around, and *he tore my pants off of my body*. I didn't have any underwear on, I was naked as a jaybird. They all set off running and laughing, jumped on the bus, and took off. I was running up the street after them, naked. George stuck his head out the bus window shouting, 'You'll never catch us.' I finally caught them and jumped on, and just as I caught them, the bus stopped at the hotel." The good times George remembered from the Beatles' early days had returned, and he liked being part of a tight-knit group of friends.

With the tour reaching its climax in Copenhagen, George's attention was turning to gospel music. He was in good hands—Billy Preston was on the tour—and Bramlett also had deep roots in gospel; he'd started out playing and singing in Pentecostal churches down South. It was in his blood. "George loved gospel so much, we spent more time talking about gospel music than playing the slide. One time he asked me, 'Where do you get the thoughts when you play those gospel songs?'" The template for "My Sweet Lord" came with a simple inquiry: "He said, 'Say you were going to write a gospel song, how would you start it?'" Delaney started scatting on "Oh My Lord," Bonnie and Rita Coolidge chorusing "alleluia." Harrison had his concept.

With "My Sweet Lord" all but written, the happy group returned to London for a mid-month encounter with the unknown—a blind date with the Plastic Ono Band on December 15. The Lyceum Ballroom happening was billed as a "Peace for Christmas Concert," and never was a less appropriate notice posted. A huge band was gathered on the small London stage—Alan White and Klaus Voormann from Lennon's new band, most of Delaney's original crew, plus Harrison, Clapton, Billy Preston, and Legs Larry Smith. Ex-Remo Tony Ashton was also at the scene of the crime: his new crew, Ashton, Gardner and Dyke, had played support on the Delaney tour. Delaney Bramlett could not make out why there was a sack on the stage, or even what to play: "That was the craziest thing I ever went through. George was the one who talked me into it. He said to me, 'You guys want to be in the Plastic Ono Band tonight?' I said, 'I don't know any of those songs.' He said, 'You don't have to. Don't worry about it.' We started playing and there was this sack on the floor out there, and I kept poking George, saying, 'What's in the sack?' All he'd say was, 'You'll see in a minute.' Next I asked, 'What key is the first one in?' and he said, 'It don't matter.' I thought he was pulling my leg again, then all of a sudden Yoko was like a snake coming out of that sack, and she was going 'woo-oo,' shrieking. George was laughing his ass off at me—

we were playing so loud that we blew all those old Orange amps up. I blew mine first and he said, 'Just plug it into mine.'"

The result was the most excruciating, ear-splitting trauma inflicted on humanity since Harrison himself unleashed *Electronic Sound*, but also the last time Lennon and Harrison would appear together on the same stage. The results are preserved in aspic on Lennon's *Some Time in New York City*.

Ominously, the Ono Band's tortured clamor was generally reflective of the times. The new decade had kicked off with the Biafran war, riots in Derry, riots and the killing of four students at Kent State in Ohio, and the death throes of racial segregation in the Southern states. If the Beatles were the saviors of world consciousness and music the cleansing catalyst, there was clearly some room for improvement.

As the counter-revolution dream seemed to fade into the black hole of the 1970s, George Harrison was almost ready to emerge from his musician's cocoon. The previous year had brought a plethora of new sounds and influences that would be on his own debut album of songs: Krishna chants, gospel ecstasy, Southern blues-rock, slide guitar, spiritual revelation, Billy Preston, Delaney Bramlett, Bob Dylan, and the Band. Clearly, no one person could save the world; Harrison had decided that the best anyone could do was to save themselves.

4

All Things Must Pass

Ringo Starr was the man most unlikely to be found jamming with Yoko Ono—he preferred country music and the Band. Many feared for the amiable drummer's career prospects when the Fab Four imploded: he'd produced only two songs of his own, and his vocals tended toward cameos. His most recent work, "Octopus's Garden," would probably never have surfaced from the seabed had George Harrison not been at hand. Ever one to help a friend, the guitarist made his first session of the new decade another shot of "Ringo Aid." The work of February 18, 1970 was to cut a single for Starr. It will probably never be known if the pleasing "It Don't Come Easy" was the product of Harrison's muse or Ringo's. The previous eight years hadn't really suggested that the man who wrote "Don't Pass Me By" was on the verge of producing a well-rounded piece like this. Nevertheless, when it was finally released in 1971, Starr had a major hit with what remains his best song. The fact that the stamp of George Harrison as tunesmith and guitarist is all over it is probably not wholly coincidental.

Another "Liverpool scene" friend who found George a willing compañero was Tony Ashton, last seen in a studio with Harrison for *Wonderwall*. As the Remo 4 were now The Remo Zero, Ashton had started afresh with the sadly overlooked Ashton, Gardner and Dyke, who managed one modest hit with "Resurrection Shuffle." They also had "I'm Your Spiritual Breadman," a witty commentary on the rent-a-guru times that featured both Harrison and Clapton, captured at a March session. Harrison saw no contradiction in performing on a tune that exhorted the listener to "take a slice" of the Spiritual Breadman's wisdom—he had as little time for the sham gurus as anyone else. As the remainder of 1970 would prove, he was looking for the real thing. In musical terms, it started to come together with Billy Preston and Phil Spector.

After completing the final Beatles session to round off *Let It Be,*[1] and noting the work of Phil Spector to resurrect the shoddy originals, Harrison came face to face with the American's mixing-desk genius when he worked on a John Lennon single. "Instant Karma" was written and recorded in one late January day and had a powerfully gripping sound full of urgency and sheer excitement. Klaus Voormann, who played bass on the session, speaks of the Spector wizardry he witnessed at first hand: "We cut the song and it was great, but there was this little guy walking around with 'PS' on his shirt, and I was thinking, 'Who is this guy?' I had no idea who he was. One minute he would say, 'Can you put the cymbal a little higher,' the next it was 'No, no, take it off, take it off.' We were just going through the song and it sounded great, and we felt confident. When it was finished, this mystery guy said, 'Come in and listen,' so we went into the control room. It was filled up with equipment—every tape recorder from EMI was rolled into that studio. When he turned on the playback, it was just incredible. First, it was ridiculously loud, but also there was the ringing of all these instruments and the way the song had such motion. As a first experience of the difference from the way you played it to the sound in the control room, it was overwhelming. And I knew immediately who he was…Phil Spector."

Harrison would not forget this production master class, even while he was honing his own control-room talents throughout April to complete a second Billy Preston album for Apple. *Encouraging Words* was a significant signpost on the road to *All Things Must Pass*.

Preston's new album was a different affair from his first Apple work. The heavy rock guitar arrangements were mostly dropped—this was a soul workout rather than a rock session. Preston's enraptured Hammond organ eruptions were far more prominent, and he delivered real soul passion on a driving solo during "The Same Thing Again." For all that, some of the Delaney & Bonnie flavors were used, especially the Stax horn sections and backup vocals. Harrison was also much more prominent in the mix. He leads the backup vocals on the funky opener, "Right Now," and brought a then unreleased Beatles tune ("I've Got a Feeling") and two of his new songs to the session.

---

[1] A roaring second guitar solo for "Let It Be" and the finished "I Me Mine."

One was the piece that would become the title of his own solo album, which he gave an orchestral setting—indeed, the first recording of "All Things Must Pass" speaks of Ray Charles and Las Vegas.

The other was "My Sweet Lord," written during the Delaney & Bonnie jaunt. As if to emphasize the song's genesis, the visiting Edwin Hawkins Singers were enlisted to add the backup vocals to what was a pure gospel groove. Their presence on the version may make this the definitive "roots" take of "My Sweet Lord," especially as Harrison just about coaxed the gospelers into intoning the Krishna mantra. Edwin would certainly have recognized the chord changes on this new song from "Oh Happy Day"—the dominant-seventh chord that shifts the tension of the song on the line "but it takes so long" was straight out of the Hawkins single. Here was George Harrison's dream realized—a gospel incantation mixed with a Vedic chant in a musical setting that was drawn from the gospel-soul heritage. It was all an attempt to show that the sectarian divisions of world religions were irrelevant to his search for enlightenment. The mood was also evident on another Harrisong produced with a friend.

[3] Sing One for the Lord (3:37)(*Harrison–Preston*) (*recorded by Billy Preston*)
Harrison guitar; **Billy Preston** organ, piano, lead vocals;
Edwin Hawkins Singers chorus; *uncredited bass and drums*

This rolling, lilting evocation of African-American spirituality, penned with Preston, is the unsung companion piece to "My Sweet Lord." It's another important milestone in George Harrison's career. Unlike its predecessor, it is cast in an authentic church-preaching mode, with Preston leading the congregation with his own revelations about the power of "singing one for the Lord." The Edwin Hawkins Singers reappear to deliver the simple hook in circular lines of rising ecstasy, driven by Preston's piano and Hammond, all anchored by familiar descending Harrison guitar arpeggios. A simple but intoxicating confection, "Sing One for the Lord" is effectively the manifesto for George Harrison's solo career. Within a few weeks, Harrison had written the gospel-drenched "Awaiting on You All" with its exhortation to "chant the names of the Lord." Without doubt, Billy Preston and Edwin Hawkins were the catalysts.

Encouraging Words was a far better release than *That's the Way God Planned It*, more redolent of Preston's soul roots than the rock-swamped first Apple disc. Although rarely spoken of, it is one of the key albums in George Harrison's musical story for what it taught him about the structure of gospel music and how that music is used to express spirituality.

But Preston's gospel wasn't quite the end of Harrison's warm-up to *All Things Must Pass*. Late April saw the guitar man in New York City, viewing Apple's new office on Broadway, proclaiming he had enough songs in the can to fill four albums. Before returning to London, he visited Columbia Studio B in the Big Apple, where Bob Dylan had just started work on *New Morning*.

Reports of the twelve-hour May 1 session soon made the music press. By the time they'd finished, the talk was of a "sensational" collaborative album in the pipeline. The date did bear worthy fruit; two of the finished *New Morning* tracks, "Went to See the Gypsy" and "Day of the Locusts," were obviously cut on this day—Harrison's guitar can be clearly heard. "Went to See the Gypsy" fades out to a short, country-rock solo that is unmistakably George, although uncredited. Aside from this, and the release of an alternative "If Not for You" on the *Bootleg Series Vol. 1–3*, years later, nothing was known of what was taped.

However, the bootleggers had been vigilant as ever, and eventually pirated CDs made the full session available to collectors. It's clear that, apart from "If Not for You" and the finished *New Morning* pieces, the results were far from sensational. The bootleggers had stumbled on a break from serious recording: Dylan knocking off a few tunes for fun with Harrison on lead guitar. The other musicians who happened to be there were bass player Charlie Daniels, drummer Russ Kunkel, and, taking an occasional turn on the piano, Bob Johnston, who was engineering the "event." To call the session loose would be an insult to looseness. What is documented is a happier version of the opening section of the *Let It Be* film, a busman's holiday for Dylan and Harrison. They sound like they're having fun. For some fans, the chance to hear Bob and George smirking their way through "Yesterday" will be a life-changing event. As the truly awful rendition comes to a stuttering end, Harrison is heard sardonically suggesting that they "dub some cellos on."

This was a comfortable setting for Harrison. Most of the songs were folk- or blues-based, there was none of the Lennon–McCartney competitiveness, and it was a real band, playing live, with no studio trickery. It is interesting to hear George Harrison in such a friendly environment: improvising a fine, extended rockabilly-blues solo on a decent "Mama, You've Been on My Mind" and coloring this harmonically simple music with inventive rhythm playing.

Unlike the Woodstock session, this meeting created no new songs, and there were no collaborations of the "I'd Have You Anytime" variety. It was, after all, Dylan's studio time they were using. The session was more evidence that Dylan viewed Harrison as a musical peer. But ultimately the collaboration underlined the one certain truth in the music business: there is a good reason most outtakes aren't released to the public—embarrassment.[2]

But the outtake that counted was "If Not for You," as it includes the first recording of George Harrison playing slide guitar. Although obviously still finding his voice, he had unearthed a technique for realizing his melodic gifts on the guitar. *New Morning* also features the work of another unsung guitarist, David Bromberg, the East Coast's Ry Cooder, a living musicologist of American guitar techniques. Bromberg's own slide is prominent on "One More Weekend." He was also known for his dexterity on the dobro, an instrument that soon became a Harrison favorite. The dobro and its louder cousin, the National Steel guitar, both had resonators (the "pie pan") built into their bodies. The dobro was made of wood, while the National Steel was built along the same lines out of metal. Invented by two Eastern European brothers in response to a 1920s craze for Hawaiian slack-key music, the National Steel was a favorite among black street musicians for its enhanced volume. With it, they could make the blues heard for blocks around. These two instruments were picked up by folk musicians and given interesting double lives as key blues and folk guitars. Musicians like David Bromberg knew both traditions well and, having been exposed to these unique members of the guitar family, George Harrison began featuring them on his songs.

David Bromberg first met Harrison during final sessions for Dylan's *Self Portrait* album and was surprised by the star's knowl-

---

[2]The songs played at the session included: "Song to Woody," "True Love," "Matchbox," "Mama, You've Been on My Mind," "Don't Think Twice, It's Alright," "Yesterday," "Just Like Tom Thumb's Blues," "Da Do Ron Ron," and "One Too Many Mornings."

edge of his music: "I met him at Columbia Studios, and he sang me a song I wrote, and told me that Bob taught it to him. It floored me." He later discovered that all the Beatles were interested in his music, particularly "Sammy's Song," a barrier-breaking tale of a young man's sexual encounter with a prostitute. As one of Bob Dylan's favorite musicians, Bromberg is well placed to comment on why Dylan struck up a partnership with Harrison: "Bob is a very sensitive guy, with big ears. He has this strange image, but he's good man, a man of great integrity. I'm sure he had a lot of respect for the things George did beautifully—for one thing, he asked him to play on his records! He didn't tie himself to George because he was famous. He and George met at a certain level of sincerity." But David Bromberg was also struck by the superstar's diffidence: "My impression of George when I first met him was that he wasn't really extremely confident, didn't understand what all the fuss was about and felt like maybe people were mistaking him, or making a mistake, or seeing something that wasn't there. That was the feeling I got from him." It was a picture of a man who felt he couldn't offer what the mores of the day demanded: "Everyone was into hot licks, but he didn't have any. So I feel he didn't have a glimpse of how really wonderful a musician he was.... He was very conscious that he couldn't read music and that he couldn't play searing solos off the top of his head. What he could do was worth more to me. He was a beautiful musician, extremely musical. The 'Moonlight Sonata' is a very simple thing to play on the piano, but it's beautiful. And beauty is not about technique."

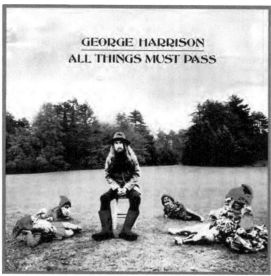

All Things Must Pass
(recorded in London, May–October 1970;
released November 1970)

By the time George Harrison came to record *All Things Must Pass*, he was an unwitting symbol of a new phenomenon, which came to be known as pop culture. The general belief was that the radical social change witnessed in the 1960s was at least partly catalyzed by popular music. As pop became rock, it temporarily ceased to be mere entertainment and was reborn as the force that held the counterculture together and the fuel that lit the fire. As they were the most popular group in the world, the Beatles' music appeared to be at the heart of everything that the 1960s stood for. The overtly political stances taken by Dylan on his early 1960s albums and by John Lennon from 1968 onward established an unshakeable critical paradigm that rock 'n' roll should at least partly be concerned with challenging authority and highlighting state-sponsored injustices.

To some extent, George Harrison believed this, but he also knew that Beatles news was rarely about their music. The cult of celebrity that grew up around the group meant that anything they touched, ate, said, or sat on became the subject of headlines in the tabloid press. Whatever he did, it was impossible to escape. One of the many contradictions of *All Things Must Pass* is that Harrison's attempt to assert his own musical identity and burst his pop culture image only fueled it.

Thus *All Things Must Pass* is a paradox of an album. While it was obviously Harrison's attempt to break free from his Beatles identity, the whole venture was framed by the mythologized history of the group. At this point in 1970, the Beatles were Harrison's context, and he was immersed in it. The entire album is concerned with the group and Harrison's experiences in it. The themes—the nature of friendship, failed relationships, the search for spiritual peace, and escape to a safe haven—all result from the distortion of his life through his years within the Beatles.

All Things Must Pass, like all of Harrison's albums, charts the feelings of a man living his life in public, as one of the few people in the world whose uneaten, soggy toast could generate column inches and auctions. It's hardly surprising that the album is itself a contradiction—private thoughts shared with millions, a collection that shot a man who wanted to free himself from his own myth to even greater heights of celebrity. Like most of Harrison's musical career, there was no master plan involved—for him it was just a question of getting his music out to the public. The fact that the effort spawned an international megahit and was itself a blockbuster, multimillion seller was accidental. He didn't appear to crave attention like some of his fellow rock stars.

George Harrison's psychological needs were at the opposite end of the spectrum, because his desire was to escape from attention. The album finds Harrison in the space between entropy and certainty. Those who characterize it as being the work of a religious obsessive have not listened closely enough. The two key spiritual songs on the album are works of longing for certainty, not zealous proselytizing. Part of this insecurity resulted from his place within the Beatles. Harrison still retained the old diffidence that his status within the group engendered, even though he had recently enjoyed being treated as a musical peer by Dylan, the Band, and Leon Russell. So he presented his new songs with reticence, almost with a Pavlovian expectation of their being rejected. To Delaney Bramlett, Harrison's flowering was no surprise: "He knew he had something special there and he wasn't covered with a blanket anymore. You see, George played me a bunch of songs when he was with me, and I kept saying, 'Why aren't some of these on those Beatle records, George?' He said, 'They let me do one, maybe two, on an album.' I didn't think he had much to develop—he was ready. How much development does a man need?"

Fundamentally, Harrison was still primarily interested in being a musician, whereas Lennon, at least, had realized that his place in pop culture was such that he didn't actually have to make music to get his message through. Hence, *Two Virgins*, *Life with the Lions,* and *The Wedding Album*, which took up the sound collage concept where "Revolution 9" left off. Part of what *All Things Must Pass* achieves is to magnify the general oversight of Harrison's abilities. As a work of professional, high-quality songwriting, musicianship, and production, the album eclipses much of the Beatles' latter output. The record was received in some quarters as an affirmation that "the dream" was still alive. Of course, in the same way that Lennon did on "God," Harrison's record clearly told the Beatles-obsessed media and public that it had always been a delusion.

George Harrison had no time for delusions. Suddenly, after the three-year busman's holiday with Indian music, the Krishnas, Bob Dylan, the Band, Leon Russell, Billy Preston, Doris Troy, Delaney & Bonnie, and Eric Clapton, on May 27, 1970 he was at Apple, playing his stock of songs to Phil Spector, whom he'd enlisted to co-produce the set. He ran through a seemingly endless catalogue of polished melodies on acoustic guitar to see what the steely producer thought of them.

Stepping out as a solo artist meant a major change of identity for Harrison. Eight years earlier, he'd been "the guitarist" who occasionally took a turn at the microphone. Now, as a fully fledged singer-songwriter, he had to change his priorities and, as he had done on "While My Guitar Gently Weeps," he entrusted his role as lead guitarist for half the album to Clapton. With *All Things Must Pass*, the spotlight would be on his voice for every track, and both he and Phil Spector seem to have been ambivalent about how to handle it. The issue of Harrison's vocals has always been a source of debate. Clearly not as strong a singer as Lennon or McCartney, he was hampered by a fear that his throat could give way at any moment: it did this in spectacular fashion just as he was about to hit the road in 1974. Harrison had been plagued by sore throats since childhood, and there was always a nagging doubt in his mind. When the first *All Things Must Pass* mixes were completed, Spector detected typical Harrison diffidence, and he told the guitarist as much: "I think you should spend whatever time you are going to on performances so that they are the very best you can do and that will make the remixing of the album that much easier. I really feel that your voice has got to be heard throughout the album so that the greatness of the songs can really come through. We can't cover you up too much (and there really is no need to) although, as I said, I'm sure excellent mixes can be obtained with just the proper amount of time spent on each one."[3]

Harrison had enlisted his old friend, John Barham, to create the orchestrations for the album. Barham produced arrangements for some of the album's pivotal songs, among them "Isn't It a Pity (Version 1)," "My Sweet Lord," "Beware of Darkness," and "All Things Must Pass." "I stayed at Friar Park while we did the preparatory work for the orchestrations of *All Things Must Pass*," recalls Barham. "We discussed arrangement details, as George wanted them to be finalized before the session. George didn't want any surprises at the last moment in the studio—he didn't like last-minute changes, and preferred things to be well thought out in advance. He conveyed his musical ideas to me by singing, playing guitar or piano, and I would make my suggestions at these sessions. I was surprised by the songs' originality, but not by their spiritual feeling. By this time, I was convinced that George was a genuine spiritual seeker, one of the very few that I have ever known."

Back in London, as the sessions took shape, Harrison's stock of songs seemed to grow exponentially. There were early versions of future hits and misses like "When Every Song Is Sung," "You," and "Beautiful Girl." Others that missed the cut were "Gopala Krishna," a rocking companion to "Awaiting on You All," and the 1968 throwback "Dehradun." Other also-rans had titles like "Mother Divine" and "Cosmic Empire," while another Dylan song, "I Don't Want to Do It," was tried out and left unrecorded until 1985!

The backing tracks were cut by Harrison, Klaus Voorman, Bobby Whitlock, Spooky Tooth's Gary Wright, Billy Preston, Carl Radle, Jim Gordon, Eric Clapton, Ringo Starr, Bobby Keys, Jim Price, and Badfinger, with additional keyboards from Gary Brooker of Procol Harum. The luxuriant backup vocals, a feature of the album, were basically Harrison overdubbed multiple times, along with Clapton and Bobby Whitlock. The movement of people in and out of the sessions was equally fluid. In keeping with the looseness of the time, musicians like Dave Mason swapped places with Krishna devotees—performances by Tony Ashton, Peter Frampton, and Phil Collins have only just been acknowledged.[4] Delaney Bramlett was there observ-

---

[3]An extract from a letter from Spector to Harrison dated August 19, 1970.

[4]Ashton played on both versions of "Isn't It a Pity"—Frampton had played on "Ain't That Cute" on the *Doris Troy* album. Harrison was not even aware that Collins had played on *All Things Must Pass* until years later.

ing George's studio demeanor:"He was very businesslike in the studio—sure, he got tired sometimes and always had a joke, but when it came back to the '1, 2, 3' he was very businesslike. He was a very good producer and very well mannered in the studio. People respected him for that."

Among the other recruits to the session were Apple's most successful "discoveries," the potential heirs to the 1960s melodic, power-pop crown: Badfinger. Signed to Apple by Paul McCartney, Badfinger had already cracked the charts with the McCartney-penned "Come and Get It" when George Harrison invited Pete Ham and Tom Evans to sing backup on a demo of "It Don't Come Easy." With the four-piece band recording at Apple throughout the early summer of 1970, Harrison had an in-house rhythm guitar section on his doorstep. Two digits of Badfinger were Liverpudlians like the Beatles, and guitarist-singer Joey Molland thinks this natural affinity with the superstar may have been part of the reason they were invited to the session:"We'd seen George at Apple, like, and he was always very friendly to us. I think he wanted to try us, and decided to ask us to come and do it. Once he found out that we could learn the songs quickly, and not kind of be enthralled with him being a Beatle, he decided that he would use us. It would save him a lot of time and effort."[5]

Despite the album's eventual "classic" status, there was a straightforward simplicity to how Harrison got what he wanted from Badfinger, as Molland explains:"He'd come over to us, bring the guitar over and say, 'Okay, this is "Isn't It a Pity."' He'd go through the song with us once or twice, and show us the changes; you know George used all those diminished chords. We'd learn it as he went along, and generally after two times through the song we had a really good idea of how it went. And basically, that was how we did it. We just brought acoustic guitars to the session. He set us all in a box in the studio, and that's basically what we did on the entire record—play acoustic rhythm guitars. We had three guitar players playing the same part on our bit and Mike Gibbins played percussion."

The album's sessions were long, large, and complex, with a plethora of huge personalities locking horns on Harrison's behalf, although Joey Molland was surprised by the lack of ego-antics on display: "They weren't big stars in the sense that they arrived with entourages—George would come by himself or with Mal, Eric Clapton would drive himself up there and carry his own guitars in. It

---

[5]Molland, Joey. Telephone interview with the author, March 2002.

surprised me that everyone was so nice—if Eric broke a string, he usually didn't have a spare with him, so he was going around the studio borrowing strings!"

There was a sense of risk too, as if they were stepping into the unknown. "He had all those songs in his drawer and just started," recalls Klaus Voormann. "George didn't know what was going to happen because he'd never done a record by himself. But he had the help of Phil Spector, which gave him the confidence to do it. He had great songs and great musicians." Spector, with his taste for the grandiose, demanded banks of acoustic guitars or pianos all playing the same chord pattern or theme in unison to create his wall of sound. It was a new experience for Voormann. "Phil was in full control of this whole bunch of musicians playing. We played all at the same time—we didn't record one on top of the other; it was six people playing acoustic guitars and five keyboard players playing the piano all at once. It was crazy!"

Nothing about the album was modest in scale, and this was a change for Harrison, as John Barham observes: "George liked me to be present at all of the sessions, even if I wasn't playing or conducting. His approach to recording backing tracks was of course much freer and less structured than the orchestral arrangements—the instrumental lineups for the sessions were very large, which contributed to a less personal feeling in the studio."

The difference in Harrison's and Spector's working methods could hardly have been greater and it didn't pass unnoticed by the musicians: "Up until the time of *All Things Must Pass*, all the sessions that I had worked on with George had an intimate, friendly atmosphere," recalls Barham. "Phil Spector's presence changed this. Phil was respected by the musicians, but he didn't connect to us as a colleague. He remained distant and authoritarian—he was a complex guy who went everywhere with a bodyguard. There were times when George sat back and let Phil Spector take control. Once Phil gave me a conducting lesson in front of the string players, whereas George's approach was to coax musicians into giving him what he wanted. He was very practical and would not persist if something wasn't happening—instead he would try another approach until something worked."

Despite the support, the pressures on Harrison were great: he had to juggle the roles of songwriter, singer, guitarist, and producer, a full load that few of his contemporaries ever managed. Having Eric Clapton to share guitar duties obviously helped, as Spector was not always available, or reliable. In the end, Harrison had to do the job himself: "George was in control of *All Things Must Pass* too—Phil was an incredible guy, a genius, but he is uncontrollable," Klaus Voormann remembers. "I think he broke his arm in the Apple control room—George was doing some overdubs, Phil came in and was completely drunk and just fell over backwards. And in the end George got irritated by it, and Phil sort of disappeared. So George finished the album."

From Joey Molland's perspective, the producer's eccentricities didn't detract from his greatness at all: "Phil Spector was always in the control room, I never saw him come into the studio, but as far as I knew he was very drunk. When we did 'Wah-Wah,' it was the one time that he invited us all into the control room—there were about fifteen musicians in there. He played us a two-track mix back and it sounded wonderful, even though I know that at that time he was hitting the Courvoisier pretty hard, and this was, like, early afternoon! He was still Phil Spector as far as I was concerned—the sound was incredible."

Apart from the control room antics, Harrison also had problems with EMI, which was beginning to look hard at the time he was taking on the album, and its cost. Harrison's old Hamburg friend observed this too: "George was pissed off with EMI, you know, 'What are they saying that I'm taking too much time?' EMI was on his back because he'd been in the studio so long and it was so expensive." For all these reasons and because it was George Harrison coming out of the shadows to make a record, the whole *All Things Must Pass* episode is surrounded by an air of risk and boldness. This edge can be heard on the final product, and that is partly what makes it compelling. The fundamental reason for the album's success was the quality of the songs. Despite all the pressures and madness in the studio, the players, like Klaus Voormann, knew that George was creating something special: "You could feel after the first few sessions that it was going to be a great album."

[4] I'd Have You Anytime (2:57) *(Harrison–Dylan)*
Harrison guitar, vocals; **Eric Clapton** lead guitar; **Klaus Voormann**
bass; **Alan White** drums[6]; **John Barham** string arrangement;
uncredited xylophone[7]

All Things Must Pass unfolds with this strangely neutral song, which
captures a mood of open, laid-back warmth rather than offering narrative insights. A product of Harrison's 1968 visit to the bucolic family
cocoon of Bob Dylan's home in Woodstock, "I'd Have You Anytime"
radiates a sense of simple contentment. The lyrics are a stream of
sound, where "let me say it, let me play it, let me lay it on you" are
essentially meaningless linguistic, rather than emotional, connections.
If anything, the piece is a partner to Dylan's "I'll Be Your Baby Tonight,"
which has a similarly understated arrangement and is also concerned
with reflecting a mood of emotional intimacy.

Evidently, Harrison's harmonic palette was broader than Dylan's
at this time, as the song is set in lush major sevenths, which creates
the idyllic mood. The gently undulating melody heard here was
already a Harrison trademark, previously encountered on "If I Needed
Someone" and "I Me Mine," while its sparse guitar-dominated arrangement suggests the Band's country and western style. George was also
following the Band's lead by defying rock orthodoxy and kicking off
an album with such mellowness.[8]

If Harrison was interested in making statements about his gravitas in the music industry, he couldn't have done much more than
introduce his first solo album with a song cowritten with Bob Dylan
and featuring Eric Clapton all but mimicking his "Something" guitar

---

[6]*General note regarding player annotations:* No track-by-track details of who played on
All Things Must Pass have ever been officially released. The annotations should be taken as
largely accurate but by no means faultless. They are based on various interview sources, the recollections of some of the musicians involved, and obvious stylistic differences: i.e., Ringo Starr
has a unique approach that is evidently distinct from Jim Gordon's. This, coupled with Klaus
Voormann's assistance, means that the listings for the rhythm sections are 99% accurate. Also,
both Klaus Voormann and John Barham have identified Gary Wright and Bobby Whitlock as the
core keyboard players on the sessions; therefore, the annotations for keyboards are based on that
assumption. However, ultimately they are more indicative than authoritative. The author would
welcome definitive information or additions.

[7]The xylophone parts were played by either John Barham or Alan White.

[8]The Band's *Music from Big Pink* was noted for its slow opening cut, "Tears of Rage."
Music business dogma was that rock albums should kick off with attention-grabbing rockers,
like "Back in the U.S.S.R."

style. But even if Harrison was not trying to impress, "I'd Have You Anytime" was evidence that "Something" was no fluke. Beautifully sung, it's a product that reeks of quality. Paradoxically, it is a calm opening to an occasionally tumultuous album.

[5] My Sweet Lord (4:37) *(Harrison)*
Harrison slide guitar, vocals, backup vocals; **Eric Clapton** guitar; **Billy Preston** piano; **Klaus Voormann** bass; **Gary Wright** electric piano; **Badfinger**[9] acoustic rhythm guitars; **John Barham** string arrangement; **Ringo Starr** drums; **Jim Gordon** drums; **Mike Gibbins** tambourine; *uncredited harmonium*[10]

"My Sweet Lord" was among the boldest steps in the history of popular music, with the added *frisson* of having the potential to be a fatal career move. Here was a man popularly conceived as a cheeky, happy-go-lucky, 1964 mop top, singing a direct appeal to God with the passion of a gospel incantation.

It was a triumph because it was obviously genuine. Just as a nonbeliever can be moved by the spirit of Edwin Hawkins's "Oh Happy Day" because it is clearly free of affectation, so "My Sweet Lord" rings true, in spite of the plagiarism case that later overshadowed its success.[11]

The song was in essence the final fruit of the guitarist's labors with the Radha Krishna Temple and his gospel sideline with Billy Preston. "My Sweet Lord" marries Krishna chants with gospel rapture on an exquisitely painted tableau of chiming twelve-string chords and painstakingly crafted backup vocals that went beyond even the multi-part harmonies of the Beatles. Harrison and Spector recorded several drum tracks and chose the ones they felt best suited the song. They also worked hard to create a resonant soundscape, from the batteries of ringing guitars to the swarmandal-like flourish that introduces the guitar solo and other key changes in the song. This is a subtle but clear attempt to re-create the sympathetic strings of the sitar that are similarly used in Indian music.[12]

---

[9]Pete Ham, Tom Evans, and Joey Molland; the band's drummer, Mike Gibbins, played percussion.

[10]The harmonium part was most likely played by John Barham.

[11]Harrison was successfully sued over similarities between his song and the Chiffons' early 1960s track "He's So Fine," in a case that focused on two three-note phrases.

[12]The swarmandal is a type of small Indian harp.

For all of Harrison's work in the studio, the power of the song comes from the naked emotion it transmits. The chance Harrison took in releasing such a piece made him vulnerable, and the track itself candidly reveals his feelings. Above all, this is the work of a man who really needs to believe and, more, to know. It's clear from his passionate vocals that this is George's tilt to reach higher; it's his grasp for the infinite, condensed into a four-minute power packet. In a small way, it was also the musician's attempt to put a little dent in religious sectarianism—his call to "God" ranges from the Christian "Alleluia" to the entire text of an ancient Vedic prayer.[13]

The Sanskrit text may have passed most listeners by, but what didn't was a new guitar sound that Harrison created for this song. The slide guitar tone he developed for "My Sweet Lord" would become his trademark and as much part of his musical identity as his voice. It became the perfect tool for him to create short melodic vignettes that were akin to songs within the song. His Beatles instinct was to multitrack these guitar parts, playing harmonies and counterpoint melodies. They became his guitar version of the vocal harmonies on *Abbey Road*'s "Because."

Harrison's slide guitar sound had no real ancestor, other than Delaney Bramlett and the contemporary style used by Jeremy Spencer of Fleetwood Mac on their major hit "Albatross." Spencer was a master at re-creating and updating the style of bluesman Elmore James, the godfather of modern slide guitar. George Harrison's style was not blues-based at its inception. In fact, slide guitar suited the guitarist because he could find his own sound that was not limited by his lack of blues roots. One of its attractions was the ability that it gave him to produce the sounds of his beloved Indian instruments on a guitar. The free movement of the bottleneck, and its micro-vibrato, made it easy to mimic the sounds of Indian instruments like the sarangi.[14] By 1969 and his classic solo on "Something," George was incorporating Indian gamaks into his technique. When he chanced upon slide guitar in 1969, he had found his own way to honor the Indian idiom in his playing.

---

[13]The prayer is:

> Gururbrahmaa Gururvisnuh, Gururdevo Mahesvarah.
> Gurussaakshaat Param Brahma
> Tasmai Shri Gurave Namhah.

[14]The sarangi is a stringed Indian instrument that is bowed rather than plucked—akin to an upright violin, but larger. Its continuous tone is thought to come closest to the human voice of any Indian instrument.

As his short passages on "My Sweet Lord" show, he soon developed his own voice with slide guitar. He created a sound that, like the Indian dilruba, mimicked the cry of a human voice. His tone was beguilingly sweet, but also wistfully sad. Even though the guitarist later suggested that one of his reasons for recording "My Sweet Lord 2000" was to "play a better slide guitar solo," this remains among the best-known guitar passages in popular music. The memorable solo added to the many attractions of what became an international megahit.[15]

[6] **Wah-Wah** (5:35) *(Harrison)*
Harrison guitar, vocals, backup vocals; **Eric Clapton** wah-wah guitar; **Klaus Voormann** bass; **Billy Preston** keyboards; **Gary Wright** keyboards; **Badfinger** acoustic rhythm guitars; **Ringo Starr** drums; **Jim Price** trumpet; **Bobby Keys** saxophone; **Mike Gibbins** tambourine

This unusually heavy chunk of rock was born of two bands. The lyrics are part of Harrison's Beatles hangover, but the main guitar part and overall arrangement speak of Delaney & Bonnie. "Wah-Wah" was written during the *Let It Be* fiasco, on the January 1969 day Harrison "left" the Beatles. But by the time *All Things Must Pass* was recorded, Harrison had been exposed to Southern soul-rock. The result was a strong, snarling guitar riff, developed from Clapton's "Coming Home" lick, with a virtually identical use of Bobby Keys and Jim Price's horns. Undoubtedly, the rollicking horn chart that lifts the middle eight would not have happened without "Coming Home." This foundation gave Phil Spector room to unleash his full armory of reverb-flooded production values, while the libretto was pure Beatles angst. In retrospect, Harrison concluded that songs like "Wah-Wah" had been overcooked, a view Klaus Voormann shared: "He knew it was overproduced. If you have all those acoustic guitars on top of each other, it clutters the sound. He knew that."

The self-referential nature of many of the solo Beatles' songs is unique in pop music. It's as if "the Beatles" were an everyday fact of life, as much a natural subject for a song as the weather or walking the dog. Such celebrity status was attached to the group that the public and media longed for these further installments of "the Beatles soap opera." For the record, "Wah-Wah" trashes the roseate memory of the

---

[15]It also returned to #1 on the British charts when it was re-released in 2002.

Beatles, who, its third man says, were "there at the right time" and "cheaper than a dime." "Wah-Wah" in this context means "pain in the butt" and is about rejecting the Beatles, the artifice and the pretense. It's a song of anger and alienation, redolent of betrayal and hostility. To that extent, it's a good-time number to rival Delaney & Bonnie, with a heart of pure stone.

[7] Isn't It a Pity (7:08) *(Harrison)*
Harrison slide guitar, vocals, backup vocals; **Tony Ashton** piano; **Gary Wright** keyboards; **Billy Preston** keyboards; **Klaus Voormann** bass; **Badfinger** acoustic rhythm guitars; **Ringo Starr** drums; **John Barham** orchestral arrangement; **Mike Gibbins** tambourine

A simple, two-note pedal opens George Harrison's magnum opus, which captures the album's struggle between gospel ecstasy and the failure of human relationships. Floating grace notes combine with the "Hey Jude" piano drone to create a hypnotic, eerie vista, seemingly lost in the "now time" of meditation.

Harrison's world-weary vocal is delivered with utter candor, the surprising diminished chord on the word "pain" emphasizing dissonance. George remains in character at all times; there is no hint of a third-person projection here. This is his very personal reaction to emotional stress, but it also reveals a depth of personal awareness and self-criticism. "We" clearly includes "me" for Harrison—it's a rare burst of humility for a rock star. Not for the first time, his private revelation has a universal application—the listener identifies with where he's been in this song. The phrase "Isn't it a pity" conveys no sense of an observer sitting in judgment; rather, it's a shared sigh. Unlike Bob Dylan's general sense of emotional detachment in his songs, with "Isn't It a Pity," Harrison adopts the paradoxical position of the neutral observer who *is* involved.

In what is ultimately a yin-yang comparison of light and darkness, illumination comes with a balmy guitar solo—a soothing melody within a melody. The guitar is Harrison's alter ego; its sweeping, soaring cry empathizes with his human struggle but also transcends it to find fulfillment. The bottleneck conversation flows on as the song's pseudo-symphonic tension bursts with the "what a pity" mantra, where Harrison's vision of human failure is swept up in Beatle grandeur. It's an emotional projection as the star's personal pain becomes part of the universal search for peace.

Musically, the track is sumptuous, with filigree minor six voicings shuffling along with easier busker's fare. The use of the G diminished chord emphasizes the inventive melody and Harrison's unique use of notes beyond the key signature. This harkens back to the minute divisions of Indian music, while John Barham's evocative, suspended orchestration recalls the shifting realities of *Wonderwall*. More than any other song except "Wonderwall to Be Here," this magnificent piece captures the depth of the musical understanding between George Harrison and John Barham. The fruits of those prerecording meetings at Friar Park include a rising string statement that merges seamlessly into the first notes of Harrison's falling guitar solo, producing an exquisite musical synthesis. This rising and falling statement is similar to one of the key elements of form that comprise an Indian raga, which include at least five *swara*s (tones) in both ascending (*aroha*) and descending (*avaroha*) scales.

As the music develops, Barham's arrangement provides a yearning counterpoint to Harrison's euphoric slide guitar melodies—a falling three-note horn figure emphasizes the mournful chord pattern. Musically, the song becomes a balancing act between a celebration of life (slide guitar and choir) and introspection (the orchestra and underlying harmony).

"Isn't It a Pity" is the essence of *All Things Must Pass*—the singer's personal epiphany, appearing momentarily to be all-embracing. It survived Spector's bombast and is ultimately a work of hope, and one of Harrison's best—a song whose majestic sweep he would never recapture. Ever bittersweet, "Isn't It a Pity" records the last dying echoes of the Beatles.

[8] What Is Life (4:22) *(Harrison)*
Harrison guitar, vocalss; **Eric Clapton** guitar; **Bobby Whitlock** piano; **Carl Radle** bass; **Badfinger** acoustic rhythm guitars; **Jim Gordon** drums; **Jim Price** trumpet; **Bobby Keys** saxophone; **John Barham** string arrangement; **Mike Gibbins** tambourine

George Harrison never overestimated the significance of his skills as a songwriter: "There's no comparison between me and someone who sits and writes music. What I do is really simple."[16] While never fully reconciled to his day job as an entertainer, he occasionally embraced

---

[16]Harrison interview in the video *Hare Krishna Tribute to George Harrison*, 2002.

this role and maximized his innate ability to write very fine pop-rock songs. "What Is Life" is one of those.

Had "My Sweet Lord" not been a huge world-beater, this Motown-spiced offering would probably have exceeded its number 10 ranking on *Billboard*. Harrison had always been a follower of American soul, and "What Is Life" emerged from a period where he had been working closely with Billy Preston and Doris Troy, both genuine R&B heavyweights. Phil Spector, too, knew well how to record this genre. With another stirring rock guitar riff, Stax horns, and a rock-steady Northern soul backbeat, "What Is Life" was as innovative an exercise in rock-soul as The Temptations' "Cloud Nine."[17]

[9] If Not for You (3:29) *(Bob Dylan)*
Harrison guitar, harmonica, vocals; **Klaus Voormann** bass;
Gary Wright piano; **Billy Preston** organ; **Alan White** drums; **Ringo Starr** tambourine

As the Beatles became moribund, George Harrison was involved in the sessions for Dylan's *New Morning* when he passed through New York in the spring of 1970. "If Not for You" was the opening cut on that LP. The transition from Dylan to Harrison emphasizes the difference in approach between the two performers. The *New Morning* version has a slightly offbeat, left-field mood. The sound space is filled with busy instrumentation. Dylan's deliberately lazy vocal hints at a melody without fully realizing it. A second, slower version of the song was recorded with Harrison on guitar; this one eschews the quirky arrangement and emphasizes the tune more firmly. A riff emerges from the chord pattern to provide a slide guitar hook, becoming the first recorded Harrison slide part. Although obviously this version was used as the basis for *All Things Must Pass*, the track that emerged decades after the event on Dylan's *Bootleg Series Vol. 1–3* was not a polished effort by any means.

The other comparison the versions of "If Not for You" draw out is how Dylan and Harrison viewed their product at this stage in their respective careers. Dylan appeared to be aiming for spontaneity rather than polish on *New Morning*, while the final *All Things Must Pass* version is a gleaming pop creation. The sound is seductive, soft and light, with multiple guitars and George's sweet vocals floating on a sea of soothing slide guitars (drummer Alan White has stated that

---

[17]Harrison originally wrote "What Is Life" for Billy Preston.

one of the rhythm guitarists on the track is John Lennon).The song is organized into firm sections, with a stronger emphasis on melody and instrumental embellishments. It's obvious that, with his version of "If Not for You," Harrison was aiming for aural pleasure. He certainly succeeds.

Placing "If Not for You" amid the highly personal songs that make up this album neatly illuminates the differences between the two songwriters.At face value, "If Not for You" is an exercise in neutrality, where the songwriter imagines a situation and a response to it.There is no real sense that the song conveys Robert Zimmerman's feelings about an actual event. By contrast, "My Sweet Lord," "Wah-Wah," and "Isn't It a Pity" are exact documents of George Harrison's emotions. Most of Harrison's songs directly convey his personal feelings.While he assumes a neutral position as narrator on certain songs ("Teardrops"), they tend to be his least effective.

[10] Behind That Locked Door (3:05) *(Harrison)*
Harrison guitar, vocals; **Pete Drake** pedal steel guitar; **Gary Wright** piano; **Klaus Voormann** bass; **Alan White** drums; **Billy Preston** organ

Having already served up a menu of Krishna-meets-gospel, Southern rock, Motown, Dylan, and pure Harrison ("Isn't It a Pity"), *All Things Must Pass* moves to country and western, a style that was musical bread and butter in the Irish diaspora of 1950s Liverpool. In Dylan's rendition, "Behind That Locked Door" is redolent of *Nashville Skyline* and The Band, the introduction of Pete Drake's pedal steel emphasizing the point (Drake had played on Dylan's *John Wesley Harding* and *Nashville Skyline*). In keeping with these albums, Harrison manages to temper Phil Spector's taste for the extreme, and a light production touch is used for the piece. No wall of sound is employed.There is a simple blend of acoustic guitars, piano, and drums—and, contrary to the usual expectation, Harrison's voice holds up very well without the mask of a big arrangement.

Music and lyrics work in tandem here, with the opening line of each couplet outlining Dylan's problem with a rising figure ("Why are you still crying?") and the second providing the solution with a falling melodic consolation ("Your pain is now through"). It is one of Harrison's more attractive efforts. Ironically, the counseling he gives Dylan here prophesies the slough of despond into which George himself would fall in 1973. Nevertheless, it is refreshing to hear Harrison singing about another's pain, suggesting that, unlike some of his contemporaries, he was able to displace himself as the center of his universe for a moment or two at least.

[11] Let It Down (4:57) *(Harrison)*
Harrison guitar, vocals, backup vocal; **Eric Clapton** guitar, backup vocal; **Bobby Whitlock** backup vocal; **Carl Radle** bass; **Badfinger** acoustic rhythm guitars; **Jim Gordon** drums; **Jim Price** trumpet; **Bobby Keys** saxophone; **Gary Wright** organ; **Gary Brooker** piano; **John Barham** string arrangement

While much of George Harrison's music has sought to express spiritual concerns, "Let It Down" provides a brief sensory interlude, cataloguing an unusual combination of sexual passion, paranoia, and hidden emotion. Singing to an unnamed lover, he seems to take his marriage vow again ("I do, I do") and praises his partner's physical glories. The verses are languid takes on self-indulgent indolence, reveling in the kind of sensory luxury any Krishna devotee is required to reject. The chorus has clear climactic overtones.

As usual for Harrison, his contentment is framed by contradiction—he seems to be struggling with the demands of his life and his desire to be with his lover. Hence he is "wasting away" potentially "heavenly moments" with her, distracted by business. As ever, his feelings about this are not positive and, in a foretaste of the scalded-cat reaction of "The Light That Has Lighted the World," he ponders that he's "wondering what it is they're expecting to see" and "should someone be looking at me?" This is one of the early appearances of George's own nemesis, the unnamed "them" or "they." As he reveals in later songs ("Grey Cloudy Lies," "Who Can See It"), Harrison seems to have occasionally viewed his life as a battle with an unseen enemy waiting to pounce and divert him from his quest for reality. At this stage, on "Let It Down," it passes almost unnoticed. Later, it verges on paranoia.

Fittingly, one of George's most tactile lyrics, full of images of sight and touch, is contained within a dynamic musical frame. The track opens with Harrison's heaviest-ever intro, a shattering concoction of wild slide guitars, sledgehammer drums, and Gary Wright's roaring Hammond organ. Without warning, it slips into the cool waters of a balmy, smooth sensuality, using warm major sevenths. But the passion returns with the George O'Hara Smith singers (including Clapton and Whitlock) again turning on the gospel style in the chorus, backed by multiple guitars and horns.

The "big sound" of "Let It Down" was mostly the result of Phil Spector's grandiose vision. In fact, he had plans for even more than was finally used: "The vocal group on the 'Let it Down' parts sounded okay. The 'Moonlight Bay' horn parts should be out the first time and very, very low the second time they play that riff, I think. Perhaps at the end, near the fade, a wailing sax (old rock and roll style) played by Bobby Keys would possibly add some highlight to the ending and make it totally different from the rest of the song. It's hard to explain, but some kind of a screaming saxophone mixed in with all that madness at the end might be an idea."[18]

Although George Harrison's music is rarely associated with hard rock, "Let It Down" does fit comfortably in the emerging British rock movement. Although the song's main riff is partly based on a Billy Preston hook ("It Doesn't Matter"), the grinding Hammond organ has more to do with late 1960s rockers Spooky Tooth than Preston's gospel instincts.[19] Admittedly, it is impossible to imagine Harrison duetting with his namesake, Mike, on a take of "Evil Woman," but lurking in the 1969 grooves of the almost-seminal *Spooky Two* was an American pianist-composer named Gary Wright. George Harrison was a fan of the Spooky Tooth album and invited Wright to play on *All Things Must Pass*. It was the start of a thirty-year friendship.

[12] Run of the Mill (2:51) *(Harrison)*
Harrison guitar, vocals; **Carl Radle** bass; **Jim Gordon** drums;
Jim Price trumpet; **Bobby Keys** saxophone; **Gary Wright** piano;
Bobby Whitlock organ

Relationships and the nature of friendship loom large on *All Things Must Pass*, once again as a function of the Beatles drama. The demise of the group had been a minibereavement for Harrison—after all, he had been friends with Lennon and McCartney since his school days. Through the Hamburg and the touring years, they had been constant companions. Now they had gone their separate ways. It was inevitable that Harrison should reflect on this. "Run of the Mill" is the first Harrisong to catalogue a failed or betrayed friendship. It presents his realization that he has to walk away and carry on with his own life. George Harrison is not his Beatle brothers' keeper.

---

[18]From the August 17, 1970 letter to Harrison in which Spector set out his views on the first mix of the album.

[19]It also recalls the Band's "Chest Fever," which was founded on similarly heavy-duty Hammond sounds.

Fortunately, he sets out these observations in a universal language that doesn't exclude anyone from sharing the experience, unlike the distinctly onanistic "The Lovely Linda" or "Oh Yoko."[20] Harrison's acute observations flow in a stream of thought, barely pausing for breath. Aside from the instrumental introduction and coda, the song is a continuum. Musically, Harrison's developing sophistication is on display—he switches from a minor to a major chord to emphasize the psychological stress of "No-one around you can carry the blame for *you.*" The arrangement reveals how much he had been listening to the Band. In keeping with much of that album, it has no instrumental solos, is cast in an acoustic setting, and has prominent horn sections mirroring the jaunty, swinging, brass parts of the Canadians' "Across the Great Divide."

That the twenty-seven-year-old Harrison should write "Run of the Mill" shows the distorting effects of the Beatles' story. The song is not an abstract musing on the nature of friendship and individual responsibility. Clearly, as usual with this songwriter, these thoughts arise as the direct result of his experience. "Run of the Mill" is also at the other end of the *All Things Must Pass* intellectual spectrum in its collective rejection of celebrity myth and attachment to its trappings. Songs like "My Sweet Lord" and "Hear Me Lord" strive for a spiritual answer, while "Run of the Mill" and "Isn't It a Pity" conclude that human relationships are the other side of the coin. In doing so, this is one of his most successful songs.

[13] Beware of Darkness (3:48) *(Harrison)*
Harrison guitar, vocals; **Eric Clapton** guitar; **Dave Mason** guitar; **Bobby Whitlock** piano[21]; **Gary Wright** organ; **Carl Radle** bass; **Ringo Starr** drums; **John Barham** string arrangement; *uncredited xylophone*[22]

Even though overt Indian elements in George Harrison's music had temporarily faded with "It's All Too Much,"[23] his exposure to the music had expanded his harmonic sensibility to the point where he could create a complex and highly original melody like "Beware of Darkness." It ranges from a G major pedal through a thorny shift to G-

---

[20]Post-Beatles tributes to their respective wives penned by Paul McCartney and John Lennon.

[21]Bobby Whitlock later told an interviewer that "Beware of Darkness" was the first song he'd ever played piano on in a recording studio.

[22]The xylophone parts were played by either John Barham or Alan White.

[23]They'd return in his bottleneck playing as it advanced technically.

sharp minor that simply should not work in harmonic terms. It's the musical equivalent of counting, "one, two, *six...*" The musical twists and turns make this an ethereal highlight of *All Things Must Pass*, a curious enigma that has our hero conjuring dreams and shadows, warning about the same "Within You Without You" "wall of illusion."

The music takes George on a walk down dimly lit streets in the dead of night. He is still immersed in the "them" and "us" finger-pointing of the counterculture, hence his concerns about "greedy leaders" out to corrupt the innocent souls who might have bought *All Things Must Pass*. In one of the stranger examples of reverse anthropomorphism, Harrison likens people to "Weeping Atlas Cedars," evergreens whose natural inclination is to head for the light. Only the negative earthly influences distract them from this natural quest. Harrison's mistrust of politicians and businessmen was in keeping with what was a virtual article of faith in the 1960s and 1970s. It's something he never lost.

A highly original song that sets a course between an almost chromatic harmonic sense and a straightforward rock middle eight, "Beware of Darkness" is one of the thematic keys to *All Things Must Pass*. It draws together Harrison's caution to himself not to become distracted by the illusion ("maya") of the rock life and a more generalized despair at the corruption that often follows political power. Ultimately, though, it frames his desperate desire not to end his days as another soft-shoe shuffler, just another "unconscious sufferer."

[14] Apple Scruffs (3:04) *(Harrison)*
Harrison guitars, harmonica, vocals

Part of the unique phenomenon of rock music is that the fans are not content to be mere consumers but need to be a part of the experience. As with so much pop culture, this was virtually invented by the whole Beatles saga. The cynical view is that the cult of "fandom" is just another device through which the industry fools the unsuspecting listener into buying more product. It's notoriously difficult to keep the public interested in a musical act for more than five years. However, if they feel loyalty to the artist, they will provide a core audience for years to come. The dissonance comes with fans unable to draw a line between reality and illusion.

"Apple Scruffs" records a more innocent period, when real feeling could be established between the musician and the audience. The Scruffs were a self-named group of fans who maintained a vigil outside the recording studio in support of the guitarist. When Harrison sings "How I love you" to his fans, the reality of his feeling is indu-bitable. After Lennon's murder and the 1999 attempt on his own life by a crazed fan, Beatlemania all seems a long, long, long way removed from today's distorted reality. The song really feels like an echo from a distant, carefree age.

It also echoes the influence of Bob Dylan, except that it's impos-sible to imagine Dylan intoning a heartfelt tribute to *his* fans. The sim-plest arrangement on the album centers around Harrison's sturdy busker's chords and reasonable harmonica efforts, but the real inter-est comes with the inventiveness of the backup vocals, the best on the album. The star's increasingly confident bottleneck parts add another voice to the proceedings. Ultimately, if "Apple Scruffs" con-veys even a hint of a true picture of the relationship this star once had with some of his fans, it shows how much has been lost.

[15] The Ballad of Sir Frankie Crisp (3:46) *(Harrison)*
Harrison guitars, vocals; **Pete Drake** pedal steel guitar;
Bobby Whitlock piano; **Billy Preston** organ; **Gary Wright** electric piano; **Klaus Voormann** bass; **Alan White** drums

Never the most enthusiastic participant in the Beatles' cinematic ven-tures, George Harrison later surprised observers by entering the film business with vigor. Maybe the clues were there all along in "The Ballad of Sir Frankie Crisp," a rolling, filmic snapshot of his Friar Park home built by the eponymous Victorian eccentric. The song reads like a movie script: scene one rolls through the house and pans out into the garden; scene two finds the star among the trees and the garden maze; scene three is a trip through eerie caves and cooling, shady woods. The final scene is of the illusions within the illusion, the real people who live in the house, the housekeepers and the spiritually awakened Lord and Lady. The shot rolls off into the unknown beyond.[24]

The soundtrack to this slice of Harrison's new bucolic life in sleepy Henley-on-Thames is an ethereal and echoey version of the Band's minimalist melodicism. The ectoplasmic Sir Crisp floats around this tour of Harrison's Friar Park home in the shape of Pete Drake's pedal steel. The current owner sounds like he's recorded his vocal track in one of the park's legendary caves.

---

[24]The song also featured Harrison's first clear reference to Monty Python's Flying Circus, who had just released their *Matching Tie and Handkerchief* album.

It might have been a different story. In May, when George ran through his songs for Phil Spector, the tune was called "Everybody Nobody," and was a semiformed series of word games and puns that used motoring as a metaphor for the cycles of life. It would have been an interesting first "motoring" song for Harrison. As it was, "Let It Roll" is the true musical companion piece to the album's cover. It conjures an allegorical dream world, populated by smirking gnomes (stone versions of the Fab Four), a disembodied Victorian lawyer, and, in George Harrison, a refugee from the world's attention. Sadly, in 1999, Harrison's sanctuary at Friar Park almost became his tomb rather than his refuge. "The Ballad of Sir Frankie Crisp" comes from a more hopeful era.

[16] Awaiting on You All (2:45) *(Harrison)*
Harrison guitar, vocals; **Carl Radle** bass; **Klaus Voormann** bass; **Jim Gordon** drums; **Eric Clapton** guitar; **Jim Price** trumpet; **Bobby Keys** saxophone

Chanting the names of the Lord has never been *de rigueur* in rock circles, but it has long been at the heart of gospel, Indian, and Jamaican music. When Bob Marley emerged in the mid-1970s, his constant refrain was "Jah, Rastafari." So it's possible that George Harrison was anticipating events when he recorded this hot gospel stomper, even though he left himself open to attack once again with its bold lyrical assertions.

"Awaiting on You All" is about George Harrison's quest for direct spiritual experience rather than the trappings of organized religion. It also catalogues his rejection of all political-cum-intellectual musings— hence the opening tongue-lashing for John and Yoko. The song includes another stab at the sectarianism of which anyone raised in Liverpool would surely have been aware. Badfinger's Joey Molland was from the same side of that city as Harrison and remembers how much could be told just from where you lived in the divided metropolis. "'What neighborhood are you from?'—that was a really scary question in Liverpool," he says. "You had to get it right first time." And Harrison once reported that his family had tried to raise him as a Catholic: the rebellious streak the Church often engenders in its unwilling members certainly surfaces in the guitarist's barbed attack on the pope. So awe-inspiring was it that EMI decided to omit it from the lyric sheet, lest Christendom collapse.[25]

---

[25] "While the Pope owns 51% of General Motors, the stock exchange is the only thing he's qualified to quote us," was the offending savagery.

The music matches these full-throttle word games as Harrison once again shows off his grasp of gospel power. A sweeping arrangement is driven by a virtual guitar orchestra, floating on Spector's patented wall of sound, which works, for once. It's the most successful example of Spector's work on the album. But Klaus Voormann's memory is of Harrison adding the slide army after Spector's premature departure from the sessions: "All those slide parts were done after Phil had left. They're worked out, note-by-note parts, sometimes four or five slides on top of each other. I wished he'd had a little less slide. I like his solos, but I think there's too much on the record."

[17] All Things Must Pass (3:44) *(Harrison)*
Harrison guitars, vocals; **Pete Drake** pedal steel guitar; **Eric Clapton** guitar, backup vocals; **Bobby Whitlock** piano, backup vocals; **Klaus Voormann** bass; **Ringo Starr** drums; **Jim Gordon** drums; **John Barham** string arrangement

This song is one of George Harrison's most famous, and its renown is fully justified. Harrison tried to interest the Beatles in a dreamy electric guitar demo way back in 1969. Failing, he reproduced it for himself with an acoustic arrangement that again invokes The Band, with its horn charts and country overtones. The music rises and falls like the natural images he conjures, the horn section playing the bittersweet lines usually reserved for Harrison's slide guitar. John Barham returns to confirm his sensitive understanding of George's music with a subtle orchestration that doesn't impinge on the simplicity of the song. Phil Spector's grand schemes had been thwarted. The reason was his outright admiration for the track: "This particular song is so good that any honest performance by you will be acceptable as far as I'm concerned, but if you wish to concentrate on doing another then you should do that." [26]

The song is best known for its lyrics. Although it is a work of incredible maturity and insight for a man in his early twenties, there is also much ambiguity. At one level, Harrison uses natural images (sunrise, sunset, cloudburst) as a metaphor for life's ephemeral character. But he also attaches the withdrawal or failure of his love to the image. Love is also transitory, it seems.

Ultimately, the cycle of nature is a consolation: a new day always dawns. Crucially, the singer has to face the new day on his own—with-

---

[26]Another quote from the August 1970 Spector letter to Harrison, which gave his view of the album's first mix.

out a partner: "I must be on my way and face another day." The song asks more questions than it answers: Does an acceptance that "none of life's strings can last" mean that human love is futile, or is he abstracted from his love? "All Things Must Pass" is a classic of Harrison's lyrical ambiguity, in essence a hopeful song, without sounding so. It's one of George's most moving compositions, and one of his lyrics that approaches Bob Dylan's standard.

[18] I Dig Love (4:54) *(Harrison)*
Harrison guitar, vocals; **Eric Clapton** guitar; **Dave Mason** guitar; **Gary Wright** electric piano; **Billy Preston** organ; **Bobby Whitlock** piano; **Klaus Voormann** bass; **Ringo Starr** drums; **Jim Gordon** drums

The most notorious manifestation of the 1960s social revolution was the loosening of social taboos about sex and sexuality that reached its zenith with the advent of "free love," as celebrated by Stephen Stills's hymn to hedonism, "Love the One You're With." For once the humble music fan could enjoy the same indulgences that rock stars considered their birthright! In the midst of Harrison's self-doubting quest for spiritual certainty, "I Dig Love," a paean to free love, is an unusually libidinous detour for *All Things Must Pass*. It now sounds like a period piece.

A hackneyed, falling-and-rising chromatic chord pattern is colored by a fecund drum section; the song's lyrics are probably the weakest of Harrison's career. Pseudo-Dylanesque wordplay vies with George's schoolboy jokes ("small love, big love") for sheer silliness. It's a brief throwback to the latter days of the Beatles, when the group appeared to assume that any free-form drivel they uttered would be of interest as art.

This is one of the few songs in Harrison's canon not covered in his autobiography or the *Songs by George Harrison* volumes, which perhaps suggests what its writer ultimately thought of it. A sassy guitar solo and particularly strong vocal performance almost save the day for a song that lacks the expressive clout of the rest of the disc.

[19] The Art of Dying (3:37) *(Harrison)*
Harrison guitar, vocals; **Eric Clapton** lead guitar; **Bobby Whitlock** piano; **Gary Wright** electric piano; **Billy Preston** organ; **Carl Radle** bass; **Jim Gordon** drums; **Phil Collins** percussion; **Jim Price** trumpet; **Bobby Keys** saxophone

Had George Harrison pursued his trade as an electrician in Liverpool, there would've been a slim chance he *might* have become aware of the timeless message of Hinduism. Given the journey he traveled as a musician, there is nothing out of place about him recording a track concerned with reincarnation for a popular rock album. Written as early as 1966 under the influence of *The Tibetan Book of the Dead* and the Leary-Alpert acid-trip guidebook version of it, "The Art of Dying" candidly sets out some of the basic tenets of Hindu beliefs with a little humor, but a deadly earnest purpose. If ever a song challenged the one-eyed nature of the rock world, this is it. Nothing could be further from superficial pop culture.

Attentive Beatles fans shouldn't really have been surprised. "The Art of Dying" merely picks up where "Tomorrow Never Knows" and "Within You Without You" paused. This time Harrison eschews the wild experimentation of the *Revolver* classic and the Indian setting of his own *Sgt. Pepper* showstopper; instead, he picks the hard rock idiom. Derek and his Dominoes deliver a pounding accompaniment to the singer's "man in the street" essay on the finer points of Hindu philosophy.

The line between Harrison and Clapton blurs as the latter, presumably, handles the wah-wah duties. If so, he manages to re-create one of Harrison's licks from "The End." This had been a track on which Harrison was lauded for sounding like Clapton. Reincarnation indeed.

[20] Isn't It a Pity (Version 2) (4:45) *(Harrison)*
Harrison guitar, vocals; **Eric Clapton** guitar; **Tony Ashton** piano; **Bobby Whitlock** organ; **Carl Radle** bass; **Ringo Starr** drums; **Badfinger** rhythm guitars; **Mike Gibbins** tambourine

In a sedate restatement of the album's pivotal song, George goes for a solemn, pensive mood. Although it uses the heavily echoed piano sound first heard on the *Wonderwall* soundtrack, this version lacks the uplifting gospel sway of the first. There is no saving epiphany. Ringo Starr does not achieve liftoff.

When viewed in the context of Harrison's later travails with the record industry,[27] the fact that he could record two versions of the same song for one album speaks volumes for the man's status at the time. Fortunately, "Isn't It a Pity" is close to his masterwork, but such license in the studio for ex-Beatles could lead to hideous self-indulgence (George's *Electronic Sound* and "Bye Bye Love"; McCartney's

---

[27]The 1980/81 *Somewhere in England* saga, when Harrison became the first Beatle to have an album rejected by his record company.

Wild Life; Lennon's *The Wedding Album*; Starr's *Sentimental Journey*). And as bootleggers and purchasers of the thirtieth-anniversary reissue of the album know, there were other fine songs that didn't make the final cut of *All Things Must Pass*—"I Live for You," for one, would probably have been preferable to this.

[21] Hear Me Lord (5:48) *(Harrison)*
Harrison guitar, vocals; **Eric Clapton** guitar; **Carl Radle** bass; **Jim Gordon** drums; **Gary Wright** piano; **Bobby Whitlock** organ; **Billy Preston** keyboards; **Jim Price** trumpet; **Bobby Keys** saxophone

There is little room for doubt that much of *All Things Must Pass* is autobiographical. But even against that background, there is something almost inconceivable about "Hear Me Lord"—the self-revelation is unprecedented.

How many millionaire rock stars use a song to beg forgiveness from God, or anyone else, as Harrison does with the opening line of the piece? Is it humbug or humility? Honesty or artifice? Is he playing games with his audience, or does he really mean it?

Simply reading the lyrics off the printed page, it is possible to consider the message falsely pious. But hearing the music makes the man's sincerity clear. Even more than "My Sweet Lord," the closer to the album proper is the most emotionally compelling piece on an emotionally naked compilation. This is a true outpouring of feeling, with the singer virtually begging God to be heard. After the eight-year Beatles roller coaster, the guitarist sounds utterly lost and desperate for an answer. The effect is of hearing someone reduced to a childlike state of pleading. To reveal this to three million album buyers is candor of a different class.

The song's anchors are the phrases "forgive me," "help me," and "hear me," and the mood of purging atonement is matched by the slow-cooking, gospel rock that contrasts with the "Let It Down" bombast, with sweet slide guitar licks and a rolling Gary Wright piano commentary. A movingly impassioned vocal completes a picture that is as cathartic as anything on Lennon's *Plastic Ono Band* album.

[22] I Remember Jeep (8:05) *(Harrison)*
Harrison guitar; **Eric Clapton** lead guitar; **Ginger Baker** drums; **Billy Preston** organ; **Klaus Voormann** bass

Debate about the purpose of the *Apple Jam* set that came with Harrison's album has raged for years. The simple fact is that George decided to include the extra album in the *All Things Must Pass* package purely because he liked the songs. Klaus Voormann recalls: "Those jams happened all the time. You know, we were very relaxed; there was no pressure and we had time to jam as we warmed up, or after we did a track. It was never organized—somebody would just start playing something, we'd all join in and started jamming around. In the end, George had a whole tape full of this stuff—he knew from all the past sessions that so many things were just forgotten, so this time he thought he'd just keep the machine on."

Anyone familiar with the endless bootlegs of the Beatles' 1969 *Get Back* sessions will know that jamming tended to stretch the limits of the Fab Four's instrumental skills. Those borders had also been highlighted by the 1966 birth of the San Francisco jamming scene, which took blues improvisation to new levels. The focus was on guitarists and very long solos. At the heart of this movement were the Paul Butterfield Blues Band and Cream, with guitar heroes Mike Bloomfield and, of course, Eric Clapton, respectively. Harrison, who at the time was immersed in studying the sitar, was acutely aware that he would never match these blues-based players for flashy technique. He was more than happy to take a back seat. So the jams here are largely showcases for Eric Clapton, who unleashes one of his best performances for "I Remember Jeep." It says something about George Harrison's neglect of his own ego that he gave over six minutes of his album to celebrate the talents of another guitarist. Klaus Voormann is adamant that Harrison had no illusions about his guitar skills: "Well, George told me, 'I was never a real guitarist—I can't improvise like Eric.'"

[23] Thanks for the Pepperoni (5:32) *(Harrison)*
Harrison guitar; **Eric Clapton** guitar; **Dave Mason** guitar; **Bobby Whitlock** piano; **Carl Radle** bass; **Jim Gordon** drums

This six-minute vamp on Chuck Berry's "Roll Over Beethoven" presents the longest sequence of Harrison rock guitar on record. No longer restricted by the country-inflected tone of his early 1960s Gretsch guitars and relatively weedy amplifiers, his rock 'n' roll salvos here sound uncannily like Eric Clapton. In fact, Clapton yields center stage to George and Dave Mason on the cut—Harrison solos for the first minute or so, and closes the track. Mason is heard in the middle section. These *Apple Jams* are often dismissed as valueless, but for those who care about them, "Thanks for the Pepperoni" contains George Harrison's "hottest licks" since "The End."[28]

[24] Plug Me In (3:18) *(Harrison)*
Harrison guitar; **Eric Clapton** guitar; **Dave Mason** guitar;
Bobby Whitlock piano; **Carl Radle** bass; **Jim Gordon** drums

The main point of interest about this hard rock excerpt is that it came from a session that saw the creation of Derek and the Dominoes. A single day, close to the album's completion, produced "Plug Me In," "Thanks for the Pepperoni," and the first Dominoes cuts, "Tell the Truth" and "Roll It Over."[29] Spector originally produced these rocking, Southern-spiced numbers for release as a single, which was put out but soon withdrawn, the band apparently unhappy with his work. Both tracks are upbeat, rocking roller-coaster rides, but they also highlight the originality of Harrison's compositions on the rest of the LP: he seems to have broken free from standard rock forms.[30]

[25] It's Johnny's Birthday (0:49) *(Harrison)*
Harrison vocal; **Mal Evans** vocal; **Eddie Klein** vocal

A thirtieth-birthday tribute to John Lennon, "It's Johnny's Birthday" is a throwback to the generic, left-field antics that the Beatles occasionally served up ("You Know My Name," "Wild Honey Pie"), and could only have been contained within the *Apple Jam* disc. It's hard to imagine it following subtle fare like "Beware of Darkness."

[26] Out of the Blue (11:13) *(Harrison)*
Harrison guitar; **Klaus Voormann** guitar; **Carl Radle** bass; **Jim Gordon** drums; **Bobby Keys** saxophone; **Gary Wright** organ; **Bobby Whitlock** piano; **Jim Price** trumpet; **Al Aronowitz** *unspecified instrument*

While the title suggests a completely improvised effort, "Out of the Blue" itself tends to point to a more organized session—it's the only one of the *Apple Jam* tracks that might have been turned into a song. It's very much in the mold of the long and winding jams much favored in late-'60s San Francisco, with ostinato guitar riffs and shifting dynam-

---

[28]The sequence of solos is: Harrison 0–1:30; Mason 1:40–3:00; Harrison 3:00–3:17; Clapton 3:18–4:46; Harrison 4:47–5:52.

[29]The date is usually given as August 5.

[30]Having virtually brought Derek and the Dominoes together, Harrison could not have known that the group's classic "Layla" was a tortured lament of unrequited love from Clapton to Harrison's own wife, Patti.

ics. Indeed, many a San Francisco band of 1970 vintage would have released this as an album track proper. Overall, with its extended Bobby Keys solo and moody guitar jabs, the piece is quite evocative, even if it was a Harrison–Voormann guitar team rather than Clapton–Harrison, as the liner notes suggest.[31]

Despite its instant transatlantic number one status, the vagaries of fashion have not been kind to *All Things Must Pass*. Only since its 2001 reissue has the album been positively reappraised.

In retrospect, *All Things Must Pass* has a split personality, being divided between a small number of big production efforts ("Wah-Wah," "Isn't It a Pity," "Let It Down," "Awaiting on You All," and "Hear Me Lord") and songs produced in the minimalist tradition of the Band and Bob Dylan ("I'd Have You Anytime," "Behind That Locked Door," "Run of the Mill" and "Apple Scruffs"). Harrison's inherited Beatles instinct was for a big sound, but most of the songs were conceived with simplicity. Bootlegs of the album's acetates confirm this. That the final product covers gospel, hard rock, country and western, Motown, and everything in between serves as a reminder of his versatility as a musician and producer.

Harrison's instinctive instrumental aesthetic was also low key. He didn't have the blues-derived technique of Clapton or Bloomfield, but in the context of his music, that was a good thing. Only short guitar statements were needed, and with the exception of "Isn't It a Pity," that is what he provides. Harrison always played songs rather than solos—the point is the song, not the guitarist's technique. When that balance tipped too far the other way, many tired of the guitar hero idiom. While George turned over many of the guitar parts to Eric Clapton, he was quietly developing his own unique voice on the guitar, which found expression on "Isn't It a Pity," "My Sweet Lord," "Apple Scruffs," and "Let It Down." First heard on *All Things Must Pass* in its nascent form, Harrison's bottleneck guitar style would become his signature, as instantly recognizable as Dylan's harmonica playing or Stevie Wonder's. In time, he would be acknowledged as a slide guitar virtuoso. For John Barham, these solos were just one aspect of Harrison's musical personality revealed by *All Things Must Pass*:

---

[31]Klaus Voormann: "On that track they said Eric played the guitar, but it was me. He thought it was Eric, because I was playing a little thing like Eric."

"George had his own recognizable style in everything he did—song-writing, singing, guitar playing—and I would even recognize his piano playing. His guitar solos were like variations on the song and sounded like an essential part of the song. They were outstanding for their economy, simplicity, and memorability."

At its core, *All Things Must Pass* is a classic collection of very high-quality songs. More than that, however, it is one of the most remarkable self-revelations ever released by a major artist. In the same way as Joni Mitchell's *Blue*, it catalogues a moment in time, events within a specific context and the performer's relationship to them. The background, of course, is the Beatles phenomenon. *All Things Must Pass* is the first installment of the inside story about being caught in that Kafkaesque chain of events. The *real* man it reveals is private, sensitive, and deeply confused by the whole affair; the album documents his search for his own space and peace of mind. That he made this search public merely deepens the paradox. On *All Things Must Pass*, George Harrison stands emotionally naked in front of his audience, and his God. For this compelling emotional power, the record will always be a bona fide classic.

5

Working for Bangladesh

By the end of January 1971, *All Things Must Pass* and "My Sweet Lord" were sitting proudly atop the American and British charts, but George Harrison seemed to be taking it in stride and getting on with being a musician. The album and single had given notice that he had developed a new and unique guitar style; from 1971 on, it was in great demand. Harrison was the only ex-Beatle modest or gifted enough to have taken up a second career as a session musician.

As early as February he was back in the studio with Phil Spector, for a session that represented self-indulgence for them both. The increasingly eccentric producer wanted to record his wife, Ronnie Spector, and Harrison provided songs, a studio, and a label as evidence of his admiration for the Ronettes' leader. The guitarist had two new songs for her, a grandiose showcase number, "Try Some Buy Some," and a retro 1960s pastiche, "You." "Try Some Buy Some" was obviously not right for Ronnie and, although her vocal range was far better suited to it than Harrison's would later prove, the entire venture seems misguided. As the session progressed, another piece, "Tandoori Chicken," was hatched for a B-side.

[27] **Tandoori Chicken (2:15)** *(Harrison–Spector) (recorded by Ronnie Spector)*
Harrison guitar, dobro, backup vocal; **Ronnie Spector** vocal;
Carl Radle bass; **Jim Gordon** drums; **Leon Russell** piano;
Pete Ham guitar

This take-away, rockabilly session was Harrison's first and last straight Carl Perkins pastiche. He often reported that he wanted to write more rock 'n' roll tunes, but tended to get lost in chords and melodies. There are no such problems with this good-time paean to the glories of tandoori chicken and a bottle of wine, spiced with a little dobro. Obviously knocked together in a matter of minutes, "Tandoori Chicken" would certainly have challenged Harrison's serious image, had anyone bought the single.

Indeed, the good times rolled throughout this session. A recently excavated Apple acetate captures Harrison and Spector enjoying a boisterous jam. Clearly studio and engineer time came cheap to ex-Beatles in 1971, as the pair had license to record half an hour's worth of shared memories, bashed out on acoustic guitars, with Ronnie Spector adding the occasional vocal embellishment.[1]

Like a couple of teenagers sitting in the garage, playing any song they can think of, the duo pick out the chords to "I'll Be Your Baby Tonight," "The Great Pretender," and "That'll Be the Day." They roar with laughter as each tune takes well-soaked shape. Harrison's encyclopedic knowledge of 1960s pop music is well in evidence—when the first line of an Arthur Alexander song occurs to Spector it's George who identifies the artist and title, "You Better Move On."[2] In this relaxed mood, Harrison sings the "Hokey Cokey" over the chords of "Let It Down," and a run-through of two old '60s chestnuts, "Baby Let's Play House" and "Blue Bird Over the Mountain," prompts Harrison to poke fun at "Ob-La-Di, Ob-La-Da." He even treats Phil to a version of the George Formby song, "Leaning on a Lamppost," an echo from Harrison's childhood that Spector doesn't know. Playing music for fun, in good company, set the mood for George's next collaboration.

[28] The Hold Up (2:55) (*Harrison–Bromberg*) (*recorded by David Bromberg*)

Harrison slide guitar; **David Bromberg** guitar, vocal; **Steve Mosley** drums; **Willow Scarlett** harmonica; **Steve Burgh** bass; **Jody Stecher** mandolin

In this period, George Harrison was virtually a transatlantic commuter. This had its benefits, including the creation of a song with David Bromberg, the gifted guitarist who played in a plethora of traditional American styles, being equally at home with blues and Appalachian roots.

"The Hold Up" was the result of an evening meal arranged by Al Aronowitz, a New York journalist who was also Bromberg's manager. Aronowitz had written a column about the making of *All Things Must*

---

[1]In the days when vinyl LPs ruled, record companies produced metal master plate pressings (covered in acetate material) to test engineering quality—it was the step before a test pressing was made. They could only be played a few times and were fragile, very expensive to produce and, hence, made in very small numbers. In the days before cassettes or digital audio tape (DAT), well-heeled musicians also used them to preserve one-off sessions.

[2]The Beatles covered Alexander's "Anna (Go to Him)."

Pass and was even featured on "Out of the Blue." Songwriting was not on the dinner party menu, but a gut-string guitar was in the room. David Bromberg picked it up and started playing a vaguely Hispanic chord pattern that became "The Hold Up." As Bromberg recalls, Harrison couldn't resist getting involved and "the song came out of us in about thirty minutes. We weren't trying to do anything—least of all to write a song. It just came out."

The finished product appeared on the *David Bromberg* album, and is redolent of the two men's celebrated senses of humor. The track was a quirky, jokey version of "Taxman," the "holdup" in question being one perpetrated by the IRS. The writing was shared, but vernacular abounds, and it's not hard to pinpoint who wrote which lines. The witty piece still tickles Bromberg: "Some of the best lines are his—the phrase 'getting the nose wet,' that's very English. Also, it was also in his head to say, 'I'll put a bullet right through your best liver.' That's very funny."

Harrison was true to form when a session was held to overdub his slide guitar onto Bromberg's live recording of the song. The multi-skilled Bromberg appreciated his thorough approach: "He was a very thoughtful player; I never saw him do any improvisation at all. In our interactions, with me, he worked in a way I've never seen anyone else work. He worked on the solo in the studio, he sat in the control booth, plugged the guitar into the board, and had the tape played over and over. He worked out exactly what he was going to play, and laid it down."

The outcome was a classic Harrison guitar vignette, displaying a skill admired by other musicians rather than critics, as David Bromberg explains: "He could develop an instrumental hook, and that is much harder than playing a hot solo. He could develop a simple little melodic idea that would be repeated in the course of a song, so that you would never be able to hear the song without hearing this hook. He was really good at that. That's not something that people often discuss."

The essential ingredients that he detected in a Harrison solo were tone and musicality:

> The thing about what he did, to me, is that he was intensely musical, without ever being technical, in terms of finger technique. But he certainly had great technique with the electric guitar. There is definitely technique in setting up the instrument, the guitar and all the effects, to produce a sound. I would compare it to a trumpeter—all you have is the lips and the horn, and you develop different sounds by the way you use those lips. Well, a guitar player turns knobs in order to do all this, but this is technique. The machines don't do it for you.

To an accomplished player like Bromberg, the fact that George Harrison, the guitarist, played songs rather than performing Olympian feats of muscle-flexing was reason to respect the man. Harrison had equal respect for Bromberg's wide-ranging talents and, although Bromberg himself would demur, George was strongly influenced by his dobro revels.

In fact, the dobro was becoming something of a party piece for Harrison, and he brought it out to support Billy Preston on the title track of his first A&M album, _I Wrote a Simple Song_.[3] Another friend who benefited from Harrison's spare time was Gary Wright, who had temporarily left Spooky Tooth. Launching his own career on A&M, he put out two albums in quick succession. The second, _Footprint_, was cut in London with half the cast of _All Things Must Pass_, including Klaus Voormann, Jim Keltner, Alan White, Bobby Keys, Jim Gordon, and Jim Price. Although _Footprint_ saw no chart action, it provided evidence of Wright's songwriting talents. One of the highlights was the rousing "Stand for Our Rights." This track was improved by Harrison's arrangement suggestions, as Wright points out: "I showed the song to George, and he suggested adding gospel singers over the chorus to get the right vibe."[4] John Barham was also on hand to offer more rich orchestrations, especially on a strong ballad that influenced Harrison's writing style. "I still find his song 'Love to Survive' deeply moving," says Barham. "It's one of the most emotionally powerful love songs that I have ever worked on. I know that at that time, Gary and George were close friends. They were similar in temperament, quiet and gentle. George introduced me to Gary. I think that musically there was a strong rapport among the three of us."

By the time Wright's album hit the stores in May, plans were advancing for a new John Lennon album and, after an informal jam in New York, Lennon invited Harrison to play on it. The result is best remembered for Lennon's most famous solo song, "Imagine," but also for some of the finest guitar performances from the Beatles' original lead man. Harrison's old versatility abounds on _Imagine_, from the jaunty dobro solo on "Crippled Inside" to the sensitivity of his support for "Oh My Love." Most impressive are a devastating volley of

---

[3] The album is best remembered for Preston's first major U.S. hit, "Outta Space."

[4] Liner note from Gary Wright's CD _The Best of the Dream Weaver_, 1998.

angry slide riffs for "Gimme Some Truth" and a rightly famed solo on "How Do You Sleep?" Despite the ultra self-indulgent lyrics and the inevitable "Who cares?" reaction they provoke, this slab of paranoid vitriol features one of Harrison's greatest guitar statements. In the midst of Lennon warning McCartney that "a pretty face may last a year or two, but pretty soon they'll see what you can do," Harrison's Fender stabs, the syntax of the notes sneering, laughing at its prey. At the climax of the passage, the bottleneck drops to the lowest register of the guitar, before a sledging two-note right hook is thrown from two octaves higher. This was the polar opposite of the sweet soloist of "Something," and a new departure for Harrison, as Lennon's working method gave him little time to create his usual guitar mosaic: "George played really good on that," Klaus Voormann recollects. "He didn't have much time because John was so eager to get out of the studio—he wanted to get things over with. So George didn't have that much time to prepare that solo, so it was very raw and he really had to concentrate. It was improvised, which is why it's so different from his other solos."

Lennon was impressed, but also exasperated by his old colleague's incipient perfectionism: "Do you know that George wanted to redo his guitar solos on 'Gimme Some Truth' and 'How Do You Sleep'? That's the best he's ever fucking played in his life! He'd never get that feeling again. He'd go on forever if you let him."[5] Voormann concurs, but identifies another reason for the guitarist's changed modus: "Normally George would have said, 'No, no, let's do it again,' and then it's another five hours to get the solo together. It takes someone like Spector to say, 'This is great, John, leave it.' Phil had a knack of getting the best out of people."

The *Imagine* sessions were ringers for Beatles dates, in that musicians were summoned with regal confidence. And so, just before Badfinger started work on a new album, *Straight Up*, with George Harrison in the control room, the group was invited to Tittenhurst Park. "John's driver called us and said, 'John would like you to come down and play some acoustics, if you wouldn't mind,'" recalls Joey Molland. "Only Tommy Evans and I were in the house, so we went down there, it was about 10 o'clock at night. George was there, Klaus, and Nicky Hopkins. They had the keyboard player of the Moody Blues stuck in the toilet there with his keyboard! So John came down, and the first song he played was 'Jealous Guy.' We actually played on that,

---

[5]Badman, Keith. *The Beatles after the Breakup, 1970–2000.* London: Omnibus, 1999.

but they didn't use the tracks we did in the end. I think John just wanted us on that, because when it was finished he said to us, 'You guys can fuck off now if you like.' But we decided to hang around, and did 'I Don't Want to Be a Soldier.' George was in the control room; he didn't play with us, he overdubbed his parts later."

Little more than a week after this, Harrison and Badfinger were at Abbey Road working on the Badfinger album, after Apple had rejected work produced by famed Dylan sideman Al Kooper. Throughout June, Harrison committed himself to Badfinger, and an album that would produce two huge global hits, "Day After Day" and "Baby Blue." But, as a virtual premonition of the 1973-74 sessions with the band Splinter, Joey Molland found that Harrison was very much a hands-on producer: "He kind of joined the band in a sense—he brought his Strat with him; we were in the big studio in Abbey Road. He'd come in there and plug his guitar in, so it was like he was with us."

George's slide guitar is prominent on "Day After Day," in joint solos (played in unison) that he cut with Pete Ham after asking the band's permission to play! "Pete and I had done the backing track, and George came in the studio and asked if we'd mind if he played," says Molland. "It took hours, and hours, and hours to get those two guitars in sync. Because they did it live—George liked to do it together, live. He and Pete sat out there for hours trying different riffs."

This mix of perfectionism and enthusiasm is also found on one of Molland's tracks on the album, as he will never forget: "I had a song on there called 'I'd Die Babe,' and I wasn't really going to do the song, but George got really excited about it, he liked it a lot. He actually made up all the out-of-sync guitar lines for it. We were playing through the song one day, and because of the way the rhythm flowed, you were playing on the off-beat a lot of the time. One time George screwed it up, and I looked at him and I kinda laughed. Well, he didn't like that, 'cause the next time I screwed up he made a big deal of it, it was so funny."

And having George Harrison as your producer meant that Badfinger never knew which of his "heavy friends" would drop by and be invited to play. "We were in the control room and George was dancing around to 'I'd Die Babe,' doing that kinda shuffle thing he does, and in walks Leon Russell," Molland remembers. "And Leon was like an iceberg, very cool. So George got all chilled out too and just asked Leon to play a piano part on 'Day After Day'—they just played it to him three times and he cut it." Being associated with the guitarist also meant that Molland and his wife Kathie could join Harrison for some backstage schmoozing with The Band when George's favorites played at London's Royal Albert Hall. Harrison was such a fan of the group that he even went to the Kensington venue's box office himself to pick up his tickets. At this stage in his life Harrison could occasionally lead a normal existence, but it wasn't to last—his international status was about to take another exponential leap.

Even as the sessions for *Straight Up* were progressing, Harrison's attention was turning to the Indian subcontinent, and he had to leave the nascent power-pop classic unfinished. The idea of staging a concert to support the millions of refugees displaced by the sundering of East Pakistan from the rest of the Pakistani state was finalized in June, during a Los Angeles meeting with Ravi Shankar. But, as Klaus Voormann tells it, the idea had originated back in Henley: "Well, I was present when they first talked about it, because I was living in Friar Park at the time. I first heard him talk about it in the evening when we were eating together—he'd talked to Ravi and the idea came about of doing this show."

George Harrison's *Concert for Bangla Desh* was ultimately framed by one emotion—passion: passion to right a wrong and passion to help a friend. The musical content of the concert, album, and film was not top-notch, but the sense of urgent commitment still bursts through, thirty years later. In the twenty-first century, the armchair observer is punch-drunk from the immediately comprehensive intrusiveness of CNN. War, famine, and death are instantly available, if not inescapable, twenty-four hours a day. In 1971, it was little harder to get the full picture of international events; that meant that the chaos in East Pakistan (soon to become the state Bangladesh) was something that people read about in the papers if they chose to. By the time George Harrison had finished, Bangladesh was part of everyday vocabulary.

After Ravi Shankar had approached the guitarist for help in organizing a slightly bigger concert than usual, Harrison set about demonstrating his status within the music business by booking Madison Square Garden. He also lined up Eric Clapton, Leon Russell, Badfinger, Billy Preston, Ringo Starr, and above all, Bob Dylan to perform. The unavoidable fact was that not even Lennon or McCartney had the relationship with Dylan to pull *that* off. It seemed that Harrison had contacts everywhere in music circles—a call to Southern rocker-

cum-producer Don Nix, another Leon Russell associate, provided a full-sized gospel choir, featuring Claudia Linnear, the original "Brown Sugar." And for the art-music aficionado, the meeting of Ravi Shankar, Ali Akbar Khan, and Alla Rakha on one stage was the equivalent of finding Yehudi Menuhin, Glenn Gould, and Kathleen Ferrier together at Carnegie Hall.

By July, George had relocated to California with Klaus Voormann, who recalls the guitarist's frame of mind: "We flew over together to Los Angeles—George had a very serious urge that he had to do the concert and he wanted it to be successful. And he really worked at it in a very professional way and did everything possible to make it a success. It was very difficult for him with all the copyright stuff that came later. He put a lot of energy into it."

Step one was to record new singles by Harrison and Ravi Shankar to set the scene. Shankar produced a diverse EP that matched two vocal pieces with "Raga Mishra Jhinjhoti," a stirring six-minute duet with Ali Akbar Khan. This masterful performance offered a taste of the recital the two maestros would give at the concert, while one of the songs, "Oh Bhaugowan," was an impassioned and moving appeal for divine assistance. In contrast, George Harrison's sights were set on enlisting strictly earthly aid.

[29] Bangla Desh (3:52) *(Harrison) (recorded July 4–5, 1971, Los Angeles)*
Harrison guitar, vocal; **Klaus Voormann** bass; **Jim Keltner** drums; **Ringo Starr** drums; **Jim Horn** saxophone; **Leon Russell** piano; **Billy Preston** organ

The first-ever rock charity single predated "We Are the World" and "Do They Know It's Christmas?" by fourteen years, and found George Harrison working under extreme pressure. Recorded one July day, "Bangla Desh" retains an urgent "live" mood. The piece is driven by two drummers, Leon Russell's piano, and a horn section, led by a new face in the Harrison firmament, Jim Horn. He was to become one of Harrison's closest musical allies, a ready-made replacement for Bobby Keys, who'd eloped with the Stones. Horn soon discovered that playing with Harrison on "Bangla Desh" was more than just another studio date:

> I first met George in Los Angeles in 1971. He wanted to put some horns on a song he was going to release to raise money for his friend Ravi Shankar. He called Leon Russell and asked him who he could get to write the horn parts, and Leon told him to call me. So I went down to the studio—I walked in and I knew I was going to meet one of the Beatles. At that time, I was more or

less jaded because I had already worked with so many artists in the music business, but I was still meeting one of the Beatles, and I was excited about it. George was very, very gracious, very businesslike, and wanted to get all this stuff done properly. He asked me if I was aware of what was going on over there and explained the whole story to me about Bangladesh and Ravi his friend. It was a real turning point for me, because we were doing something for a cause through one of the Beatles.[6]

Klaus Voormann also noted a different atmosphere: "From the moment people knew that whatever we did for Bangladesh was for nothing [unpaid], there was a different attitude, because the people didn't feel they were there to earn money. They were there to have fun and do something good for a good cause."

In deference to the Shankar context, Harrison introduces the Bangladesh appeal with a rock version of Indian music's *alap*—a slow introductory statement of the main ideas. The music calls on the "While My Guitar Gently Weeps" formula, with the bass note stepping down a semitone in each of the first six bars.

The chord sequence at the song's heart is another exercise in the gospel-flavored rock of *All Things Must Pass* and, like much of that album, "Bangla Desh" demonstrates the appeal of Harrison's vocal style. It's obvious that Lennon or McCartney would have ripped through the chart with far more power than Harrison could muster, but George persuades with the conviction in his performance. The power of feeling that he conveys in the line "Won't you give some bread, get the starving fed" is tangible. This was a man on a mission. There is no sense that "Bangla Desh" is a song about the singer rather than the cause. This storming, urgent single has as much raw energy as anything the Plastic Ono Band ever offered.

[30] Deep Blue (3:39) *(Harrison) (recorded July 4–5, 1971, Los Angeles)*
Harrison guitar, dobro, vocal; **Klaus Voormann** bass; **Jim Keltner** drums

Created in response to his mother's death from cancer, midway through the *All Things Must Pass* sessions, this is a Harrison B-side to rival "The Inner Light" and "Old Brown Shoe." Harrison offers Band simplicity, coupled with David Bromberg fingerpicking. This is more advanced than the thumb-plucked bass lines of "While My Guitar Gently Weeps" and "For You Blue"—it was the first time Harrison picked the melody within the chord structure.

---

[6]Horn, Jim. E-mail interview, November 2001.

The rare Harrison folk-blues piece is delivered with unnerving intimacy, made possible by the sparse instrumentation and light-touch production. The obvious sources for "Deep Blue" are Dylan and Bromberg. But George was developing an interest in blues styles, as shown by "Sue Me, Sue You Blues," also from this period. Both songs feature resonant dobro inflections that aren't bound to folk or blues models—even when Harrison plays within the classic pentatonic blues scale, his musicality imprints his own distinct identity.

As Harrison continues the catharsis of *All Things Must Pass*, his unerring honesty does not waver, despite the deeply personal subject matter. Unlike in later material, here his pain does not spill over into bitterness. "Deep Blue" is one of the great forgotten Harrison recordings, a worthy companion to *New Morning* and the future work of Ry Cooder and David Bromberg, and a candidate for the "last great B-side" accolade.

With the singles in the can, preparations for the concert were finalized. Harrison played both administrator and musician, while Klaus Voormann headed south for a break. "We recorded the single and I stayed in George's house in Nicholl's Canyon. Then George went to New York and I went with Don Nix and George's father to Nashville. Don took us around in his Rolls Royce; they showed us the Stax and Muscle Shoals studios. But there was no air conditioning in the car and we were like wet blankets. From there, we flew to New York City for the shows."

Waiting in the Big Apple were Badfinger, who had temporarily halted work on their own album to help Harrison. Joey Molland sets the scene: "We were doing the *Straight Up* album when the Bangladesh thing happened. George had to leave in the middle of the album to set it up; then he called everybody up who played on his record and asked would they go to New York and do the concert. Everybody said 'Yes,' of course. We knew we weren't going to play a set, we only ever had the intention of playing like we had on *All Things Must Pass.*"

The Concert for Bangla Desh
(recorded in New York City, August 1, 1971; released January 1972)

The concert stage was not a comfortable venue for Harrison, the prime instigator of the Beatles' retirement from live performance in 1966. That move had broken the hitherto unshakeable music business dogma that dictated that a new album must be supported by a tour. It took Harrison three years to recover his appetite and join the Delaney & Bonnie troupe as the man in the shadows. The concert at Madison Square Garden was a different affair and marked his return to the mainstream of the business. This time there could be no hiding away behind the amps: George Harrison was the headline artist in his first-ever live solo show. Close allies like Klaus Voormann knew how hard this was for him: "George was very nervous, but he got this strength through his friends and his religion. His view was 'It's my gig, I have to do this. I don't like it, but I'd better do it.' It was very hard for him, it wasn't like Mick Jagger getting up there, who loves it. George didn't like to be on stage doing the monkey—he never liked that. He was happy because it was for a good cause. If it wasn't for the cause, he wouldn't have done it. For George, being on stage was definitely a case of 'I'm happy it's over.'"

New York was, perhaps, an incongruous city to host the world's first benefit rock concert—the epicenter of international banking and corporate power, as far from the famine-ravaged wastelands of Bangladesh as it was possible to be. But it was no fluke that Harrison chose the home of the business end of popular music to host his show. Where better than the dragon's lair to plan an assault on the contracts, exclusive distribution deals, and copyrights that had turned making music into a lucrative chore for lawyers? Harrison didn't want to be a star, but since he had no say in the matter, he was determined to use this unsolicited status to deliver the goods for Bangladesh. The end would justify the means. This single-mindedness drove one of the world's most reluctant live performers onto the stage at Madison Square Garden on August 1, 1971.

In the midst of dealing with record companies, lawyers, and accountants, Harrison had little time to rehearse his huge band, but the mood was so positive that that wasn't a problem. "We only did two rehearsals, but I knew all the songs, there were only a few Beatle songs I didn't know," recalls Klaus Voormann. "I mean everyone knew the songs, Ringo *certainly* knew them, and Eric too. All the Badfinger people worked like crazy to be able to play—Jim Horn and the horn players had all the music written down, and it was just a cinch for them. It was just like an easy jam session." Nevertheless, there were a few stragglers to deal with at the last minute: "Jesse Ed Davis came late, and he didn't know all the songs. I had to show him the chords in a hotel room because he missed the rehearsals." Davis was a Californian session guitarist brought in by Harrison to provide cover for Eric Clapton, who was in a methadone-enhanced haze; his appearance was very much touch and go.

When the album finally appeared, the main issue wasn't the performance but the sound quality. Originally a three-record set, *The Concert for Bangla Desh* is probably one of the poorest-sounding live albums ever made, with the exception of the awful *The Beatles at the Hollywood Bowl*. Its purpose was to document an extraordinary event in popular culture. Paradoxically, the world's first major charity concert was simultaneously the high point of countercultural altruism and the end of an era. After *Bangla Desh*, the 1970s succumbed to the greed and business ethos that had been kept under wraps in the politically sensitive '60s.[7]

As time passed, Bob Dylan's performance became the focus of attention as Harrison became critically passé, but the fact is that the Liverpudlian dominates the album. First, as a musical event, it provides a neat summation of George Harrison's evolution, with its nods to Indian music (Ravi Shankar), Dylan and the Band (Dylan), blues (Clapton), gospel-soul (Billy Preston), Southern rock (Leon Russell), and melodic British pop-rock (Badfinger). Second, Harrison's energy and drive were what made the concert happen at all, and their power dominates. This is a man who is a leader, not a follower for as long as required. "Everyone knew they were working for a cause, everyone was smiling all the way through," recalls bassist Voormann. "There were jokes, fun, and at the same time, concentrated work. Everybody was excited, but everyone was in their place, nobody overdid it. George was definitely in charge. It was part of his job and he did it." One of the best laughs of all was the result of Pete Ham's clothing

---

[7]The 2005 remastered version did improve matters sonically.

choice: "The only thing we were nervous about was that George and Pete both had white suits on," says Joey Molland. "We thought Pete had a lot of balls to do that!"

The Concert for Bangla Desh was more of a statement than a polished musical event—the only virtuoso display was the opening duet between Ravi Shankar and Ali Akbar Khan. The two masters, who were also friends, offered the perfect balance of technique and expression, where extravagant dexterity is only an aid for narrating complex emotions. Their stunning performance spoke of the deep cultural roots of a centuries-old musical tradition.

Similarly, the rock music in the concert worked best when passionate commitment rather than flashy power was the foundation. Leon Russell's consciously extreme hollerin' and classic rock star lecherous slavering ("Youngblood") weren't as effective as the unaffected naïveté of Billy Preston's "That's the Way God Planned It." The main foci of the show, Harrison and Dylan, eschewed any hint of histrionics and, as a result, delivered stirring simplicity.

Harrison-the-rock-star's entrance proper with "Wah-Wah" sets the tone for the stadium rock that came to dominate the decade. The huge band, thrown together that New York Sunday afternoon, replicated the cast of thousands who cut *All Things Must Pass*—there were three electric guitars, a whole band of acoustic guitars, two keyboards, two drummers, a gospel choir, and a full horn section.

Obviously, the gremlins that haunt live recordings were trotting about unimpeded, as Harrison's fervent vocals virtually disappear from his opening three numbers. The album is a full document of the poor sound delivered at concert venues designed for sports events. The mix changes as the songs progress, suggesting that the recordings were cobbled together from various sources—this is especially noticeable on the film version, where edits more brutal than the Beatles' "butcher cover" cut hard.

The recordings actually reveal George Harrison adjusting to his new status as a superstar in his own right. Hence, his nervous renditions of "Wah-Wah" and "My Sweet Lord" eventually give way to confidence, with a moody take of "Beware of Darkness" that marries his own Scouse tremelo with Leon Russell's mad-dog Southern growl. After all, this was a show about both George Harrison the singer and a man happy to share the spotlight.

George also shows himself prepared to live with his Beatles doppelganger, for the first-ever live rendition of "While My Guitar Gently Weeps." Speeded up a notch or two, Harrison's voice sweeps its upper ranges in a powerful, if not classic version. In a high-emotion coda,

Clapton and Harrison gently duel with solos that show no signs of degenerating into the macho showdowns that blazed a trail of boredom through the 1970s.

The real highlights are a tumultuous reading of "Bangla Desh" that outdoes the original for sheer balls, and "Something." This is the only song to truly showcase Harrison's guitar, his elegant break justifying Delaney Bramlett's praise: "He's not a speed demon, but makes up for that with taste. Anyone can learn to play fast, and it's pretty good for show. But when you hear 'Something,' you're hearing something beautiful. I just thought he was an absolutely wonderful, tasteful player."

However, for one of the *Bangla Desh* ensemble, playing Beatles songs was almost an out-of-body experience. Klaus Voormann had been a close friend of the band's for nearly ten years, but knew that the group was defined by the four members and no one else: "It was strange to play those Beatles songs, because I'd always refused to play with them when the Beatles were together. They asked me several times to play with them. One time, just for fun, Paul said, 'Come on, Klaus, you can play the bass and I'll play the piano.' But I said, 'No, I can't do it,' and just ran out of the studio. The Beatles were the Beatles. So, this was the first time I'd actually played a Beatles song for George, and it was strange."

Bob Dylan's appearance at the concert was headline-grabbing— it was his first major live show in years, and found him evoking the urgent, probing spirit of the folk age. The apocalyptic imagery of "A Hard Rain's A-Gonna Fall" still resonated loud and clear. At the start of a new decade, the dying embers of the Vietnam War crackled and famine gripped Bangladesh. And the search for freedom documented in "Blowin' in the Wind" was still just an aspiration.

Only Dylan, it seemed, was able to match Harrison's and Shankar's knife-edge emotions. One reason is that Dylan was nervous about participating in the concert—Harrison didn't know if he would actually play until the moment he strode on to the stage. At the previous night's sound check at the Garden, Dylan suddenly lost his nerve and made for the exit. Harrison always played it straight with Bob and pointed out in no uncertain terms that it was he, Harrison, who had never played solo in public before, whereas Dylan had been doing it for years. Clearly, George Harrison on a mission was an irresistible force. Klaus Voormann confirms that none of the musicians knew for sure that Dylan would show up: "It wasn't certain that Dylan was going to play. In a way, it didn't matter—of course it was amazing that he played, but the concert would still have been fantastic if he didn't come. I don't know exactly what frame of mind Dylan was in at the time, but I do know that he loves George and George adored him."

Joey Molland recalls the moment when the denim-clad Bob appeared: "By the Saturday, we had the show together and went to Madison Square for a dress rehearsal. So we were there waiting to go back to the hotel when Bob Dylan just walks on the stage. He simply starts playing—it was like a little private concert. We're all just sitting in the hall, and it was really hard to believe that this was going on. No one expected Dylan to come, and Eric Clapton only came on that Saturday."

Dylan's performance was purposeful, because the song was all-important, not the singer's appearance or voice, or the musicians. It was a scenario that George Harrison loved, giving service to the song. He reassumed his role as supporting lead guitarist with relish, giving his first public slide guitar performance. Harrison had no "hot licks," but he didn't need any; Dylan's songs were powerful enough without them.

There was a strong sense in which the concert was a potent political statement, with Harrison stepping into turbulent diplomatic waters by adopting a stance at odds with the stated American and British government positions. One Bangladeshi academic recently recalled that "to the utter consternation of Nixon and Kissinger, George Harrison's 'Bangladesh' hit the chart. It was a thrilling moment in the midst of all the sad news emanating from the battlefront. Even the Western journalists covering the civil war in East Pakistan were not yet using the word 'Bangladesh'. The warmth, care and goodwill expressed at the *Concert for Bangladesh* were echoed all over the world."[8]

This made Dylan's appearance all the more apposite, as it took him back to the strongly activist songs of *The Times They Are A-Changin'* and *The Freewheelin' Bob Dylan*. On these albums Dylan was a kind of troubadour by appointment to the forgotten underclass, whose oppressors he damned with words. The *Bangladesh* package was the closest Harrison ever approached to Dylan's political era, and all the songs performed had some resonance with the cause, except Russell's and Starr's. And Harrison's simple rendition of "Here Comes the Sun," played just on two acoustic guitars, found him performing in the classic folk tradition, with another of his songs seeking an inner solution to external conflict.

---

[8]Professor Farida Majid writing for *News from Bangladesh*.

The 2005 DVD release of the concert was an opportunity for reevaluation. Some of the concert's most striking features are how tangible its power remains, as well as a strong sense of how politically significant it was. Most remarkable is Harrison's performance as band leader and performer, confirmed by a new sound mix that that pushes his vocal and guitar to the forefront (albeit at the expense of the gospel choir's spirited interjections and Jesse Ed Davis's guitar licks). His vocal is astonishingly powerful and utterly committed, challenging his reputation as a "weak" vocalist. His potent singing on "Bangla Desh" is a pure act of zeal.

This song is obviously pivotal to the event, not least because it encompasses the two key themes—the cause and friendship. Its opening phrase, "My friend came to me," is about Ravi Shankar's initial approach to Harrison, but in a way Harrison is the subject. Indeed, both Dylan and Clapton could have recited this line about Harrison approaching them to appear at the Garden. The DVD makes clear that the appeal of "George the friend" was what made this groundbreaking concert happen.

Harrison's ability to generate great friendships frames the whole event. Clapton was in desperate shape, but he still hauled himself over to New York to help out. And their joint solo on "While My Guitar Gently Weeps" is about friendship, not six-string ego battles. Another indication is new film of a happy, relaxed Harrison having fun rehearsing "Come on in My Kitchen" with friends Leon Russell and Clapton. Here, to help Clapton, Harrison is so relaxed that he takes the main guitar solo and plays convincing blues.

And Bob Dylan was unnerved by the whole "scene" when he showed up for rehearsals, but Harrison talked him into making the show. The remarkable new sound check footage of Harrison and Dylan running through "If Not for You" shows why. It is an intimate glimpse of the warm friendship between two major cultural figures at a point when both were emotionally vulnerable. They don't hit every note precisely or even remember every line, but they are evidently relishing each other's company. This is support group material—neither was comfortable in this environment. They were just helping each other, as close friends do. It's a rare glimpse of "the real George Harrison."

But that's the point of *The Concert for Bangla Desh*—George Harrison only ever played for real.

With *The Concert for Bangla Desh*, Harrison's status reached giddy heights. But there's no sense of self-aggrandizement on the album. No ego junkie would give half his band a turn in the spotlight and engineer a coup (Dylan's appearance) that could have upstaged him. The paradox was that George had made use of the fame and status he felt so uncomfortable with "to get something done." It was the work of a man frustrated by political inertia and the apathy of the world establishment. As ever, he could not play politics and reacted with raw emotion to a crisis.

The event was born of altruism and the iconoclastic spirit of the '60s, but soon the harsh realities of the '70s hit. Harrison had a fire in his belly and wanted to release the concert album and film as soon as possible, knowing that they were what would bring in the revenue. He'd negotiated with all the artists and labels concerned and produced the accompanying lavish color brochure with Apple funds. But he hadn't bargained for Capitol Records wanting a cut for distributing the album. Later, his old enemy, the Taxman, would want his share too. The rounds of table-thumping with Capitol delayed the set's release by months.

The star's frustration grew, and during an appearance on a major U.S. talk show in November, he made an extraordinary challenge to Bhaskar Menon, the head of Capitol Records: "Sue me, Bhaskar!" Having virtually accused Menon of profiteering on the backs of famine victims, Harrison was shrewd enough to know that despite his barroom language,[9] the studio executive would not risk the bad press a public denial of the spirit of *Bangla Desh* would bring. Eventually, the product came out, but the experience left a bad taste in Harrison's mouth. It showed him that the countercultural revolution had had little impact on the motivations of the profit-driven record industry. In truth, the idealism of *The Concert for Bangla Desh* was almost torpedoed by boardroom balance sheets. To some, the concert was a manifestation of the *All Things Must Pass* vision—the era's last stand. By the time the rock charity show was reborn in the 1980s, it had assumed a puffed-up, self-serving air of mutual congratulation. Harrison's concert was a one of a kind, from a different age, and brought the curtain down on the 1960s dream.

---

[9]He called Mr. Menon a "bastard," before a panicking Dick Cavett intervened.

6

A Gelding
in the Material World

All Things Must Pass was hailed as a major musical-philosophical statement and seemed to light the way for the new decade—it was the start of George Harrison's personal melodic manifesto. Whether solo or supported by other like-minded individuals, Harrison was going to continue to "Sing One for the Lord" on his next album, which was just taking shape. Preoccupied with getting the *Concert for Bangla Desh* album and film released, and also working on the Ravi Shankar biography movie *Raga*, Harrison prepared for his next studio date by helping out old friends. After the success of "It Don't Come Easy," Ringo Starr had fallen in with new teen idol Marc Bolan and, under the "glam" influence, produced a strong follow-up single, "Back Off Boogaloo." This was a rocking, soccer crowd chant that suited Starr's talents well, aided and abetted by a roaring series of Harrison slide breaks that brought to mind Duane Allman.

Starr was doing well, which was more than could be said for John Lennon, who was at a "cause politics" dead end, or Eric Clapton, who was facing the long haul out of heroin addiction. Two of Clapton's Dominoes managed to squeeze solo albums from their record labels; both Harrison and Clapton are reputed to appear on *Bobby Keys* and *Bobby Whitlock*, sets that were too cool to include credits.[1] There's little sign of George on the Keys disc, but Whitlock's "Back in My Life Again" is curiously similar in parts to the *All Things Must Pass* jam, "Out of the Blue." The "Little Wing" riffs that filled "Hear Me Lord" are heard again here. Once a Harry Nilsson session was dispatched (George is heard on the thoroughly nasty "You're Breaking My Heart"), work began on a new Harrison offering, one of the most keenly anticipated discs of the decade.

---

[1]The press release to promote the Whitlock album identifies George, Eric Clapton, Carl Radle, Jim Gordon, Jim Keltner, Delaney Bramlett, and Klaus Voorman as being among the players.

Living in the Material World
(recorded in London and Friar Park, October
1972–January 1973; released May 1973)

In the category of "difficult second albums," *Living in the Material World* has a unique place, given the almost impossible task of following *All Things Must Pass*. Remarkably, this very high-quality release also has the status of a forgotten blockbuster, a million-plus seller that gets nary a mention. Energized from the overwhelming success of *All Things Must Pass* and *Bangla Desh*, Harrison produced a record that fully exposed his spiritual vision, further emphasized his melodic skills, and provided the best evidence of his claims to guitar greatness. This was a seemingly superconfident George Harrison, and a man positively pregnant with vision. He wasn't looking back: none of the leftovers from *All Things Must Pass* were revived. All these songs were written after 1970.

A number of key events provide the background to the disc's first session in autumn 1972. First, Harrison had made another trip to India that reinforced his spiritual convictions; he was later to receive another personal visit from Swami Prabhupada. By that time, his Krishna devotion was unparalleled, even by 1969 standards. Gary

Wright, who had experienced the same kind of spiritual revelations earlier, joined him on the India trip. Wright was part of the small core group that Harrison chose to record his new LP, along with Jim Keltner, Klaus Voorman, and Nicky Hopkins. Harrison wanted to play in a band again, rather than direct another *All Things Must Pass* cast of thousands.

The recording of *Living in the Material World*, which included his final sessions at Apple's London studios, was actually a tale of two LPs. During the week, Harrison's band worked on his album; on the weekend, attention turned to sessions for a pianist who'd played on *The White Album*, Nicky Hopkins. An important figure in the history of British popular music, Hopkins had a well-documented influence on the Rolling Stones. The slight Londoner had been on the scene for years, hanging around the blues clubs where Alexis Korner was king, before getting a break with Screaming Lord Sutch. The London rock world was tightly knit, and most of the session players who hung around one band knew one another. There was a circuit of studio musicians that flowed around the Beatles, the Stones, Traffic, and Cream.

So the other LP to emerge from this period was Hopkins's sadly forgotten *The Tin Man Was a Dreamer*. It is a fine collection of idiosyncratic pop songs and Southern hoedowns that finds Harrison launching his bottleneck to some effect. "Banana Anna" is a classic— or *the* classic—of English interpretations of Louisiana boogie, while "Sundown in Mexico" is a captivating moodscape. Even though "Lawyer's Lament" almost speaks of the Austrian masters of Romanticism—and it would surely have been hailed as a classic if Lennon and the boys had cut it—the real highlight fuses virtuosity with blazing blues dynamics. The irresistible "Edward" compelled Harrison to produce passionate, rocking slide guitar of the sort that would grace the title track of his new album. Hopkins was a classically trained musician who'd found the perfect synergy between technique and expression. There wasn't a chart that could have thrown him, but he had the blues touch vital for creating rolling and tumbling piano lines that elegantly drove songs rhythmically. An exciting soloist and a supportive but not overwhelming note painter, Nicky Hopkins had it all—he understood the piano's rhythmic as well as melodic potency. Aside from George's bottleneck, Hopkins's is the most prominent instrumental voice on *Living in the Material World*.

One little-known aspect of the album's creation is that the sleeve's assertion that it was a Saville Row recording may not give the full picture. Bassist Klaus Voormann has a clear idea of where most of the taping took place:"*Living in the Material World* was done at his house. On the record it says it was cut at Apple, but it was done at his house."

[31] Give Me Love (Give Me Peace on Earth) (3:36) *(Harrison)*
Harrison vocal, guitars; **Gary Wright** organ; **Nicky Hopkins** piano; **Jim Keltner** drums; **Klaus Voormann** bass

Living in the Material World could hardly have reveled in a stronger opening song than this #1 hit. A gorgeous ballad, awash with marvelously expressive guitar statements, "Give Me Love" retains the emotional power of *All Things Must Pass* in a compelling three minutes. The arrangement and production were considerably pared down: Spector's booming echoes, massed guitars, and grand gestures were excised. "Give Me Love" has a more plaintive, Dylanesque sound: single acoustic guitar, simply supported by bass, drums, and Nicky Hopkins's summer-stream piano lines. On top of this sit the two voices of George Harrison—his singing voice and his slide guitar, now resounding with greater clarity and eloquence. The harmonized guitar parts are almost too euphonious to be true.

Borrowing a melodic motif from Dylan's "I Want You," and based on the "My Sweet Lord" semichanted formula, the lyrics are like a stream of consciousness, effectively a plea for the "peace and love" idealism of the 1960s. The idealists needed help because the dream seemed to be in tatters in the selfish '70s. Again, as on "Hear Me Lord," Harrison calls out for help in a childlike way, as if all the success of the previous three years had left him shell-shocked. In that sense, the song was the start of Harrison's inner journey that would leave little room for the outside world. But for now he had proven again that his outstanding ability to create attractive melodies would satisfy the record-buying public, if not the critics.

[32] Sue Me, Sue You Blues (4:48) *(Harrison)*
Harrison vocal, guitars, dobro; **Gary Wright** electric piano; **Nicky Hopkins** piano; **Jim Keltner** drums; **Klaus Voormann** bass

A fair proportion of the album is given over to George's observations on his Beatles years. His reputation as the most level-headed of the group, with the least-colored memory, is supported by the stinging satire of "Sue Me, Sue You Blues." Less paranoiac than "How Do You Sleep?" and not as roseate as Starr's "Early 1970," the song takes a nearly impersonal overview of the Beatles' self-inflicted legal wounds. It revels in the certainty that lawyers are an easy target for general scorn and a quick way of securing a common denominator—"in the end we just pay those lawyers their bills." Way down the line in the 1990s, Joni Mitchell would revive the theme: "Lawyers haven't been this popular since Robespierre slaughtered half of France."

By 1973, George Harrison had had more encounters with the legal profession than is generally felt to be wise. Fortunately for him, he reacted with humor. He used a rhythm that faintly echoed the "do-si-do" of square dancing. Maybe the movement's cycle of two dancers approaching, circling back to back, then returning to where they started reminded him of the Beatles' seemingly endless, and pointless, legal orbits around one another.

Slightly strange then that this slice of Beatles soap opera was originally given by Harrison to American guitarist Jesse Ed Davis. Perhaps all musicians face this particular strand of the blues sooner or later. However, the demo that George sent Davis was astonishing, featuring just the guitarist and electric slide. Here Harrison sounds like a lost bluesman, bootlegged in Chicago. On this remarkable take, his spare bottleneck is a double for Elmore James's. In the verses, he sings over the slide in the old blues style revived in the 1970s by top players Johnny Winter and Rory Gallagher. If there is ever a *George Harrison Anthology*, this simple demo is a must, as it shows the depth of his understanding of blues styles.

On *Living in the Material World*, "Sue Me, Sue You Blues" is less rough and ready but still one of Harrison's most accomplished pieces. It speaks of a very confident, classy musician near the height of his powers. Four years earlier, his playing had been the subject of sibling jibes from Lennon and McCartney. Now here he was leading a session with top-quality players like Nicky Hopkins, Gary Wright, and Jim Keltner, and matching them. Keltner, in particular, performs superbly, but then so does Harrison on dobro and vocals. This George Harrison was a long way removed from the resigned figure of *Let It Be*.

[33] **The Light That Has Lighted the World (3:30)** *(Harrison)*
Harrison vocal, guitars; **Gary Wright** organ; **Nicky Hopkins** piano; **Jim Keltner** drums; **Klaus Voormann** bass

It is a testament to the sheer psychological pressure of the Beatles' individual experiences that George Harrison wrote this song in his twenties. *All Things Must Pass* suggests a man in search of a refuge from his public life. This desire is documented in an alarmingly direct fashion on the first of two *Living in the Material World* ballads. "The Light That Has Lighted the World" is lyrically disturbing—in the first verse, Harrison attacks people who make judgments about him, who he is and who he was. He clearly feels the force of public scrutiny; the song is really asking, "What right do you have to inspect me, just because I made a few records?" Indeed, it's stronger than that—his detractors are filled with "hate" and their negativity is sending him "down in a hole," because they can't accept that he's no longer a "Fab Four Mop Top." His goal seems to be freedom from this scrutiny as he pursues his spiritual quest.

The song is melodically strong but not quite fully realized, as there is no chorus and no hook to fix the piece in the mind. The tempo is set at the solemn pace of the Band's classics, "Tears of Rage" and "I Shall Be Released," and that wasn't fast enough for many critics. *Rolling Stone* called it "pretty leaden stuff."

The highlight of the track is the instrumental break, a rolling, lilting passage from Nicky Hopkins, topped by one of Harrison's finest performances. In the closing bars of the statement, repeated as the song's coda, the guitar vocalizes a series of six-string sobs. George finally made his guitar gently weep.

In the 1970s many performers explored the same ground as Harrison's "The Light That Has Lighted the World." A case in point is Joni Mitchell's "Ludwig's Song," for which she suffered some brickbats, and later, in response to that criticism, "Shadows and Light," on which she sings of "critics of all expression" and "judges in black and white." The fourth estate remains all-powerful in the music business. Artists hitting back usually pay a price. George Harrison's payback was due in 1974.

[34] **Don't Let Me Wait Too Long (2:56)** *(Harrison)*
Harrison vocal, guitars; **Ringo Starr** drums; **Gary Wright** keyboards; **Nicky Hopkins** piano; **Jim Keltner** drums; **Klaus Voormann** bass

One of the more anomalous features of George's career is that this certain #1 was never put out as a single. Maybe it was too similar to "Give Me Love," but the catchy tune, sweet guitar riffs, and chugging rhythm surely would have been a big chart success.

Like all great pop songs, "Don't Let Me Wait Too Long" sticks in the mind through melodic tension, found between the opening half of the melodic couplet ("How I love you") and the response line of the verse ("Only you *know how to* dry up all of the tears"). Harrison implies dissonance by singing a middle F, modulating the F major chord to D-flat major. These musical elements are often found in the pop-soul music that is the obvious root of this song, even though the arrangement suggests English pop. The construction and Motown "orchestration" signify that Harrison had learned well from Phil Spector. Although there are still echoes of Spector reverb, multiple drums, and over-the-top tympani, the song actually points the way to a new generation of British pop music in the shape of the Electric Light Orchestra. The similarity between the style of "Don't Let Me Wait Too Long" and the early ELO hit "Livin' Thing" is quite obvious.

The mystery of why this was not a single may never be solved,[2] but the hit potential shines on what remains one of George Harrison's most perfect pop confections.

[35] **Who Can See It (3:51)** *(Harrison)*
Harrison vocal, guitars; **Gary Wright** organ; **Nicky Hopkins** piano; **Jim Keltner** drums; **Klaus Voormann** bass; **John Barham** string arrangement

Harrison offered a new type of ballad with this track, one that was rhythmically complex, with the verses shifting through a bar of 6/4 time into a single 5/8 measure, on either side of more usual 4/4 sections. The melody has a new dramatic edge, full of sweepingly large chromatic intervals. This tension first appears on the line "I can see quite clearly now," where the word "clearly" swoops from C to E, a step of four semitones. It is a partial adaptation of the rising melismas of Indian music, whereas the song's instrumentation recalls the Beatles.

Perhaps the opening Leslie-toned guitar, circa *Abbey Road*, should be a clue that this is a song documenting Harrison's feelings about his Beatles years. The prevailing emotions are bitterness and anger. The overwhelming impression is of a man deeply traumatized by the whole experience. If any Beatles fan was laboring under the misapprehension that George had enjoyed the episode as much as they had, this song tells the exact opposite story. Whether or not the listener thinks such a reaction is justified, there's no doubting the intensity of sentiment. Notably, Harrison liked the song enough to initially include it in the set of his one and only U.S. tour a year later.

---

[2]In their book *Eight Arms to Hold You*, Madinger and Easter note that Apple planned to release the song as a single, but it was withdrawn at the last minute.

The second "Who Can See It" verse also reflects the general tendency of Harrisongs toward internalization of world events. So the negative reflections about the Beatles are projected onto the wider world that, as in "The Light That Has Lighted the World," is filled with hate, conflict, and strife. In many ways a companion piece to that song, this plea for his due features one of George's best vocal performances that positively bursts with passion. Never an especially strong singer, he had the ability to deliver the hidden power of a song. David Bromberg felt this when he heard George sing: "There's a couple of different ways to talk about this. Some people have wonderful voices, their instrument is great. Others have voices that are not as good, but that's their voice, not what kind of singer they are. There are people with mediocre instruments who are very fine singers, and George was certainly one of those who was a fine singer. He was evocative, which meant he really could sing the damn song. Was his virtuosity in the use of the vocal instrument? Not a bit of it, but he could sing the song. That's the importance of singing."

[36] **Living in the Material World (5:30)** *(Harrison)*
Harrison vocal, guitars; **Ringo Starr** drums; **Gary Wright** keyboards; **Nicky Hopkins** piano; **Jim Keltner** drums; **Klaus Voormann** bass; **Jim Horn** saxophone; **Zakir Hussein** tabla

This musical Roman Candle is the one time in his career that Harrison deliberately set out to create a big, showpiece rock number. Almost the full panoply of the Spector sound is thrown at it: two drummers, multiple keyboards, and tabla courtesy of Zakir Hussein,[3] a young man who would be a world music celebrity within two years for his work with guitarist John McLaughlin. "Living in the Material World" is as close as Harrison ever got to playing "rock star" music.

The song reviews his story with laconic humor and, with the insertion of an incense-imbued Indian interlude, looks back to the days of "Within You Without You." The use of Indian instruments in this low-key middle eight was a last-minute decision—the acetates of the backing tracks reveal plodding bass and drums where tabla and tamboura would eventually sit.

The cut is one of Harrison's best production efforts, as it uses the same genre of shifting musical dynamics that the Beatles did on "Happiness Is a Warm Gun." So the hard-rocking chugging core, based on George's favorite "Get Back" rhythm, effortlessly transforms itself to

---

[3] Hussein is the son of the late Alla Rakah, the legendary tabla player who was Ravi Shankar's best-known foil.

the spiritual sky, before an exultant instrumental section pits wailing guitar against Jim Horn's powerful sax. It's all intended to wow the listener with musical virtuosity and show-stopping flashiness. The model for the song may have been a cut from Billy Preston's *That's the Way God Planned It* album: "She Belongs to Me" has a similar R&B rhythm and big Las Vegas ending.

The lyrics find Harrison still caught in the yin-yang of his Beatles identity and his desire to shake it off. So he sings in jest about how the group emerged from their chrysalis, but simultaneously rues that these chance events cast him into the material world. The added layer of irony is that it was through his Beatles life that he was introduced to metaphysics, his "salvation." So the Beatles were both his nemesis and his saviors. It's this kind of cosmic mix-up that makes "Living in the Material World" part joke, part document of self-mocking serendipity. Essentially, like "Sue Me, Sue You Blues," this highly effective track is the work of a very confident musician.

[37] **The Lord Loves the One (That Loves the Lord) (4:34)**
(Harrison)
Harrison vocal, guitars; **Nicky Hopkins** electric piano;
Jim Keltner drums; **Klaus Voormann** bass; **Jim Horn** saxophones

An overlooked aspect of the Beatles' social impact was that it showed that people from working-class backgrounds could gain the three advantages of the social elite—power, wealth, and status. In the course of this achievement, they sacrificed their freedom, but they were the first raw northern English entertainers of their generation to take their regional accents onto global airwaves. Part of the group's appeal was their novelty: an international audience suddenly discovered that there were English people who didn't speak as though they had obligatory, medium-sized fruit in their mouths.

After ten years of fame, Harrison looked back on his experiences with "The Lord Loves the One (That Loves the Lord)," a song that prompted some despair and outrage in critical circles, hastening his demotion to the ranks of the unfashionable. Actually, this was one of the most overt challenges to the rock circus imaginable. The obvious Krishna overtones are a mere "philosophical" framework for the song's main thrust, which is that the pursuit of power, wealth, status, and fame is pointless and, worse, destructive.

Here is George Harrison, the most successful rock star of the day, reviewing the *Brave New World* of the "rock life" and declaring it bankrupt—the *soma* of fame and rock glory was a fantasy. The weak point of the music business, like all other sleights of hand, was that everyone pretended its exponents were great; of course, all the acolytes who fed off the musicians—the publicists, media men, and roadies—had to believe it too. It was their livelihood. In 1973, no one dared point out that the emperor had no clothes on—except Harrison. While he was still attracted to "the rock life," the theme of its basic falseness recurs again and again in his music.

The lyrics of the bridges are the singer's inner conversation— George is pointing out to himself that he's been running about looking for fame and fortune, when it's all a waste of time. Even the apparent religious theme has a more parochial context. "The Lord Loves the One That Loves the Lord" conveys the same basic message as "what you put in is what you get out," so, at one level, it's more a matter of common sense than divine revelation.

But the lyric is symptomatic of the difficulty some critics had in deciding whether the singer was preaching at them—or to himself. Harrison's verbal ambiguities left the door open for observers to accuse him of sanctimony when it suited them. Doubtless, George was addressing himself and his internal struggle to harmonize his spiritual aspirations with the omnipresent temptations of the rock life. Strong feelings and honesty characterized Harrison's approach and, to many, his appeal. But as David Bromberg observes, that approach tended to create dissonance: "I do know that the press was lambasting some of his tunes as being preachy. If he was preachy, he was preaching to himself. The worst songs come out of, really, the most sincere feelings—sometimes, when you feel something very strongly, the problem is relating it in a way that everyone is able to access. Sometimes when you have some deeply held feeling, it just comes out the way it is, and sometimes it's not great songwriting."

The musical accompaniment to this most uncompromising lyric is mean, dirty blues—funky and low-down. The heavily echoed vocal is a trick borrowed from Lennon's Plastic Ono Band cuts, and Jim Horn's sax charts are a straight lift from Harrison's favorite "Savoy Truffle" model. The most effective feature is the star's guitar playing, on an album that showcases Harrison's six-string talents to great effect. *Living in the Material World* was the first LP he'd made without the shadow of Eric Clapton looming over it. Anyone who listens can hear some standard-setting solos. One of them appears on "The Lord Loves the One," and it ranks as one of the best of his career.

[38] **Be Here Now (4:09)** *(Harrison)*
Harrison vocal, guitars; **Gary Wright** organ; **Nicky Hopkins** piano;
Klaus Voormann acoustic bass

Professor Stephen Hawking has done more for the image of time than any man before or since. He turned highly abstract cosmology into a mass-market paperback and got people on buses chatting about "imaginary time" and black holes. Hindu philosophy also has plenty to say about the nature of time, basically contending that only the "present moment" exists—the past is long gone, and the future may not happen at all. George Harrison was well versed in that universal view, but he also had a keen personal interest in not living in the past.[4]

"Be Here Now" is partly concerned with the rare phenomenon of "Beatles Time." George's only objective is to escape it by living in the present, not in a Fab Four prehistory that so obsessed the media and his fans. He had a compelling need to leave the Beatles' bandwagon firmly behind him. No doubt he related to Arthur "Two Sheds" Jackson, a character from a Monty Python sketch. The gag is simply that Jackson is a composer of modern symphonies, but the interviewer only wants to know how he acquired his nickname, and whether he actually has two sheds. No matter what, the sheds remain the only point of interest. The result is madness. In Harrison's case, the sheds were full of Beatles.

His answer is not the psychosis of Arthur "Two Sheds" Jackson, but a total public rejection of the past. He is going to move on, even if his public doesn't want him to. Harrison had no intention of living a life that "isn't real no how," and he proved it in 1974.

But, as Klaus Voormann reveals, the recording of a serious piece like "Be Here Now" still left room for low-level mayhem: "I love that song—it's so great. I remember we were playing it and I said, 'I'd love to play the upright bass on that.' And it was difficult to record, so I went into the bathroom at Friar Park and the microphone was put in there. What happened was that Mal Evans came and flushed the toilet while I was playing the bass! I did a drawing of that, and it was still there at Friar Park in that bathroom the last time I was there."

[39] **Try Some Buy Some (4:08)** *(Harrison)*
Harrison vocal, guitars; **Gary Wright** keyboards; **Klaus Voormann** bass; **John Barham** string arrangement; **Jim Gordon** drums

Releasing "Try Some Buy Some" in 1973 achieved nothing, except to prove that Spector's Wall of Sound was an anachronism. An obvious filler track, this is a rehash of the 1971 Ronnie Spector recording, with

---

[4]Notably, the song shared a title with the 1971 spiritual classic by Ram Dass, "Be Here Now."

Harrison's straining vocal substituted for hers. Phil Spector's characteristically lush production is out of step with the rest of the set—the banks of trilling "Long and Winding Road" mandolins sit uncomfortably with the album's pared-down mood.

The work itself is the most extreme example of Harrison's circular melodic style, seeming to snake through an unending series of harmonic steps. The highly unusual musical content was a result of its having been composed on the piano, an instrument Harrison was far from mastering. In fact, Klaus Voormann recalls that he had to step in so that Harrison could hear the entire piece played through: "He played the song on the piano with his right hand, just with three fingers. He couldn't play with five fingers and he couldn't play the whole song with two hands on the piano. I had to play the left-hand part so he could hear how the whole song sounded."

[40] **The Day the World Gets 'Round (2:52)** *(Harrison)*
Harrison vocal, guitars; **Ringo Starr** drums; **Gary Wright** organ;
Nicky Hopkins piano; **Jim Keltner** drums; **Klaus Voormann** bass;
John Barham string arrangement

The protest songs of the 1960s inspired a movement for radical political reform. In the summer of 1971, the final protest event of the counterculture era was held—*The Concert for Bangla Desh*. It was presided over by an unwilling symbol of the generation and featured a star turn by the man regarded as its spokesman. Bob Dylan's rallying songs had been the catalyst that turned the Beatles from boy-meets-girls popsters into "rock artists." Harrison's own "Think for Yourself" and "Piggies" were the direct result.

By the time *Living in the Material World* was released, protest songs lived only in the memories of the baby boomers, while the new generation was sunk in an ennui that lasted until the pseudo-rebellion of punk. This might explain why "The Day the World Gets 'Round" is not acknowledged for what it is—a classic 1960s protest song. Paradoxically, the composition is objecting to the need for events like *The Concert for Bangla Desh*. Tellingly, it was written the day after the two concerts.

In one sense, the *Bangla Desh* episode was a testament to altruism, but in another, the very fact that it was needed at all was a damning indictment of people and politics. "The Day the World Gets 'Round" is a reaction to the failure of the 1960s revolution to change anything. In "It's All Too Much," Harrison had asked to be shown his universal soul, but also to be delivered home for tea. The new piece reveals that what he found when he got there was that people were still destroying each other in the names of nationality and religion. Politicians fanned the flames for their own objectives.

Bangla Desh was a clarion call for an end to the Western self-indulgence of the 1960s. While the middle-class youth of America and Britain were busy finding themselves, conflict and despair were endemic in the nonwhite world. With the *Bangla Desh* concert, Harrison was partly saying "we've got to do something" rather than contemplating our own navels with typically Western self-satisfaction.

Undoubtedly, George's choice of language dissatisfied his critics because it was ambiguous and appeared to preach, they assumed, to them. The line "But Lord there are just a few who bow before you" is a case in point. This could be taken as Harrison's statement of his own spiritual superiority, or it might be his metaphor for a rejection of conceit. If ego-driven politicians and self-serving military leaders were able to bow before anything, even a "concept" like God, the world would be a better place. "The Day the World Gets 'Round" laments human nature and calls for a little humility. It's an idea Harrison used in a number of his songs[5] and is identical to the thrust of Dylan's epoch-making "Masters of War" from 1963. The political essence of this cut was overlooked because he couched it in a framework of spiritual redemption, even though on "Masters of War" Dylan had asked his targets if their money could save their souls. On this and many other offerings, Harrison and Dylan were circling in parallel orbits.

[41] **That Is All (3:43)** *(Harrison)*
Harrison vocal, guitars; **Gary Wright** harpsichord; **Nicky Hopkins** piano; **Jim Keltner** drums; **Klaus Voormann** bass; **John Barham** string arrangement

The Beatles were experts at creating a compelling sound, and George Harrison had learned well. He also took after-hours classes with Phil Spector. Similar in arrangement to the Spector take of "The Long and Winding Road," this song is his attempt to re-create some of that grandeur with stately keyboards (a return of the "Piggies" harpsichord), lush strings from John Barham, and a full choir.

As a piece of music, it was a development of his "Something" ballad style, also absorbing influence from Gary Wright, whose *Footprint* album had featured a very similar tune, "Love to Survive." Some of George's most characteristic musical devices are found here, along

---

[5] "Beware of Darkness" and "Tears of the World."

with some development. The melody takes a half step up with each line—the A minor is sharpened to an augmented chord to create drama. The middle eight is set in 3/8 time that gives a stuttering, hesitant syntax, exactly matching the message in the lyrics, "Times, I find it, hard to say." This is the same tongue-tied difficulty that Harrison documented with "I Want to Tell You," but he goes further, stating that words are "useless." The failure of language to express his deepest feelings is a recurring theme in Harrison's music.

Single (B-side, 1973)

[42] **Miss O'Dell** *(Harrison)*
Harrison guitar, vocal, harmonica; **Klaus Voormann** bass;
Jim Keltner drums, percussion

In the late 1970s, Eric Idle's Beatles spoof "The Rutles" lanced the boil of self-inflating pomposity that had attached itself to the group. George Harrison had showed the way some years earlier. This jaunty, Dylanesque flip side, complete with harmonica, shows the lack of seriousness with which Harrison takes himself. In great contrast to the strong emotion of "Give Me Love," "Miss O'Dell" is a short musical postcard to one of his office team, Chris O'Dell. Sent off to rock star exile in Los Angeles, George reports back on the boredom of being rich and famous: "I can tell you, nothing new has happened since I last called you."

The song is a glimpse into the minutiae of life as a superstar refugee. No ex-Beatle would fix a broken record player for himself: he'd have someone called Ben around to do it for him.[6] While he's preoccupied with the disappearance in transit of rice for refugees, he spends his time with musicians who have ambitions to fill the Fillmore, Bill Graham's legendary San Francisco venue.

Cast against everyday reality, it all seems like a very unglamorous joke—so much so that Harrison, earnestly strumming in his "Apple Scruffs" busking mode, bursts into uncontrollable laughter at key points in the session. It was all very deliberate, given that this version was released in preference to a polished, giggle-free take that has surfaced through yet another stray acetate.

---

[6]"The record player's broken on the floor, and Ben he can't restore it."

Living in the Material World was the work of a confident guitarist, songwriter, and singer. It aimed to please with a generally well-paced platter of rockers, ballads, and pop. The album is characterized as being overladen with Krishna paeans, but in fact only "The Lord Loves the One" and "Give Me Love" actually espouse philosophy in a direct way. Klaus Voormann, for one, felt that the album contained many gems: "Those songs are really fantastic. *All Things Must Pass* might be better, but those songs are incredible. I love it. But you can hear from the LP what his aim was; he definitely had a message he wanted to get across."

Nevertheless, despite its musical coherence, the record revealed more about George Harrison's internal conflict than a cursory listen might suggest. Those who knew him well quickly spotted his strained emotional state: "George was under stress during *Living in the Material World*," notes John Barham. "I felt that he was going through some kind of a crisis. I think it may have been spiritual, but I cannot be sure. I felt an austere quality was entering his songs."

Barham is right. The album emerged from a highly emotional period for Harrison in which he'd left the Beatles, been hailed as a superstar in his own right for *All Things Must Pass,* and produced the monumental *Concert for Bangla Desh.* It was also a period of personal crisis, as his marriage was ending, and the pressure resulted in a highly uncharacteristic temper tantrum in the studio. The record was a work of massive inner conflict. If it was preachy, Harrison was preaching to himself, desperate to reconcile his spiritual aspirations with the temptations and traumas of his own making—"How I'll pray, yes I'll pray, that I won't get lost or go astray."

As a man who wrote, without sham, about the feelings of the moment, Harrison was bound to produce an album that reflected his character. The retrospective title cut is a mischievous attempt to rationalize his Beatles years and discovery of Indian philosophy, while "The Day the World Gets 'Round" is a knee-jerk reaction to the political failings that created the Bangla Desh problem in the first place. Songs like "The Light That Has Lighted the World" and "Who Can See It" are childlike pleas for understanding from a private man living his life in public. Going beyond them, "Be Here Now" and "The Lord Loves the One" reveal doubts about the value of his professional life and the entire rock 'n' roll circus that he helped to create. Even "Give Me Love" contains a large hint that the uncertainty of "Hear Me Lord" still frames his search for peace.

So while George Harrison was bursting with musical confidence, *Living in the Material World* found him in roughly the same place that John Lennon was when he wrote "Help!"—shocked by the rush of overwhelming success and desperately wondering where it left him. Despite the critical tomato-hurling, as far as George's career was concerned, it left him where he'd started in 1971—at the top of the heap, with a million-selling, #1 album and single.

With *Living in the Material World* in the can, the guitarist hot-footed it to Los Angeles in March 1973 to start work on a LP for Ravi Shankar that he planned to release on his own record label. Talks had already started with A&M to host Harrison's nascent company and the Shankar sessions were held at Herb Alpert's Los Angeles studios. It was the first salvo in Harrison's most ambitious two-year campaign to date. The inventive *Shankar Family and Friends* mixed a side of Krishna *bhajans* with a flip of adventurous ensemble compositions, improvised on the spot in two days. These charts mixed Western styles and instruments with Indian inflections, and jazz was a constant thread. This effort was marshalled by young Tom Scott, a saxophonist well known for his work with Joni Mitchell on the groundbreaking *Court and Spark*. Harrison was deeply impressed with Scott's obvious talent and his gentlemanly demeanor. Another favorite player was David Bromberg, whom George summoned from New York to make an uncredited bow.

The most striking fusion on the album is in a pop version of a Shankar bhajan, "I Am Missing You," with Billy Preston, Harrison, Scott, and Ringo Starr all prominent. It must have been a case of déjà vu for Starr when, only weeks later, George hewed an identical production for his own "Photograph." The main difference was that the Shankar piece featured a better vocalist, the sublime Lakshmi Shankar, whose voice soared through three octaves with ease.

Almost as soon as George arrived on Sunset Boulevard, word reached him that Ringo Starr was in the studio cutting tracks with John Lennon. The guitar man soon added himself to the session, and the result was the drummer's famous *Ringo* album, to which Harrison contributed no fewer than three songs, including a blockbuster single. Joining Lennon, Harrison, and Starr for "I'm the Greatest" was bass man Klaus Voormann, who detected a small-scale revival of the

Bangla Desh spirit: "That album was fantastic—all those sessions were great because you had this feeling that Ringo needed a little help. And that was how that whole thing came about."

[43] **Photograph** *(Starkey-Harrison) (recorded by Ringo Starr)*
Harrison guitar, backup vocal; **Ringo Starr** lead vocal, drums;
Jim Keltner drums; **Nicky Hopkins** piano; **Klaus Voormann** bass;
Vini Poncia rhythm guitar; **Jimmy Calvert** rhythm guitar;
Bobby Keys saxophone; **Lon Van Eaton** percussion;
Derek Van Eaton percussion

Not until 1987 and *Cloud Nine* did Harrison put together a piece more redolent of the Beatles' effortless pop craft than "Photograph." A sweeping melody, an archetypal Beatle-George guitar hook, and a resonant arrangement serve Mr. Starr very well indeed, to the point where the drummer declared that Harrison's efforts made him "sound like a genius." Not quite, perhaps, but "Photograph" does underline what a consummate crafter of pop classics the guitarist had become—it was a sure-fire American #1, one of two Harrison compositions to hit the top slot in 1973.

[44] **Sunshine Life for Me (Sail Away Raymond)** *(Harrison)*
(recorded by Ringo Starr)
Harrison guitar, backup vocal; **Ringo Starr** lead vocal, drums;
Robbie Robertson guitar; **Levon Helm** mandolin; **Rick Danko**
fiddle; **David Bromberg** fiddle, banjo; **Garth Hudson** accordion;
Klaus Voormann acoustic bass; **Vini Poncia** backup vocal

A session that assembled two Beatles, most of the Band, and David Bromberg offers the kind of "fun" that Harrison would re-create decades later with the Traveling Wilburys. This simple song is arranged for multiple guitars, banjos, and fiddles, and, like much of the later Wilburys material, revels in the multiple vocal harmonies that were the shared inheritance of the Beatles and the Band. The paradox is that even when George seems most relaxed, the theme of "Sunshine Life for Me" is escape from people, pressure, and society. While musically an homage to the spirit of the Band's "Rag Mama Rag," lyrically the song touches on Harrison's natural introspection.

[45] **You and Me (Babe)** *(Harrison-Evans) (recorded by Ringo Starr)*
Harrison lead guitar; **Ringo Starr** lead vocal, drums;

Klaus Voormann bass; **Nicky Hopkins** electric piano;
Milt Holland marimba; **Tom Scott** horns; **Chuck Findley** horns;
Vini Poncia rhythm guitar

This corny effort is cut from the same cloth as the cameo tunes the
Beatles used to write for Ringo, like "Good Night" and "Yellow
Submarine." It trades on Starr's chummy stage persona, which to some
makes his delivery of the string of clichés packed into this song
charming. Here Harrison was writing with a specific singer in mind,
and the song reveals nothing other than his ability to write to order.
Only Ringo Starr could get away with the embarrassing cabaret-style
name checking that serves as the album's coda.

Even as the Starr sessions were winding down in May, *Living in the
Material World* had started its ascent to the #1 slot on *Billboard*, as
had "Give Me Love." But George Harrison was not one to rest on his
laurels. Before he left L.A., the so-called "mystical one" served up
some riffs for the pot smokers' own original comedy duo, Cheech
and Chong. While Harrison's own album was lavishly packaged with
opulent lyric sheets, Cheech Marin's garbled gaga was concealed
within a sleeve that folded open to reveal stashes of the weed. The
laughter was almost as great as that induced by the rib-tickling
"Basketball Jones," which unsurprisingly likened a basketball obsession to being a junkie.

Living in the Material World* was the last of George Harrison's
1970s albums to be seen as a major event. The critics turned up their
noses, however; this marked the start of his decline in their eyes.

In retrospect, this record was more than the end of Harrison's
media honeymoon: it signaled the close of an age, the last offering of
the Beatles' London era. As the first, and last, solo Beatle set recorded
partly at Saville Row, it hammered the final nail in the Apple coffin—
the idealism of the concept was in its death throes. The golden epoch,
when Jackie Lomax, James Taylor, Billy Preston, Doris Troy, Badfinger,
and Mary Hopkins found open arms at the Beatles' label, was all but
over. The Nicky Hopkins album really was the last throw of the Apple
dice, the final bow of the easygoing, collective dream. The harsh realities of the U.S. music business beckoned.

Nevertheless, friends were still dropping by to cut a track. While
Living in the Material World was emerging, *Bangla Desh* choirmas-
ter Don Nix recorded a track for *Hobos, Heroes and Street Corner
Clowns* with George for early 1973 release. As if in honor of Harrison,

the tune was called "I Need You." It was not a pastiche of the guitarist's *Help!* ditty of the same name, but George's final nod to the Southern country rock he'd been immersed in for three years. And unconsciously, Nix's album title predicted Harrison's imminent, critical tumble from hero to clown.

The Beatles' London years had been attended by a procession of American musicians heading east across the Atlantic, among them Leon Russell and Delaney Bramlett, who catalyzed bands for Harrison, Clapton, and Joe Cocker. In 1973, the drift was in the other direction—John Lennon had shifted to New York for good, Ringo Starr was a jet-setting tax exile, and Eric Clapton would eventually revive his life in Florida. The rest of Derek's Dominoes would either follow him or try their luck at solo success—but they were usually unlucky. Another Delaney sideman and *All Things Must Pass* player, Dave Mason, was also a permanent fixture in California, where he recorded *It's Like You Never Left*, another session for Harrison's bottleneck.

Living in the Material World didn't just mark the passing of Apple's Swinging London, it also represented the end of rock's grand statements and the final fading of the 1960s dream into middle-age contentment and fiscal luxury. The LP was still cast from a state of mind that said, "With our love, we could save the world, if they only knew." Despite the unraveling of idealism in the late 1960s, *All Things Must Pass*, the *Concert for Bangla Desh*, and Lennon's "Imagine" and "Happy Xmas (War Is Over)" seemed to revive it. As 1974 loomed, industrial strife, strikes, and power cuts were a daily fact of British life, and the mood was turning against wealthy rock stars musing on the nature of existence.

Living in the Material World marked the close of a golden era, when anything seemed possible and music was the rallying call for a generation now settling into middle-class family life. The great rock festivals of the late 1960s were long forgotten; the stars looked for tax havens and beaches. The world would never look so rosy again, and everyone knew it. In that sense, *Living in the Material World* was the elegy for a dream.

As 1973 turned to 1974, "people in the know," the inside crowd, were in awe of George Harrison's power in the music business. *All Things Must Pass*, *Bangla Desh,* and *Living in the Material World* had all been multimillion-selling blockbusters. In the course of three years, Harrison, now the leading ex-Beatle, had also written three U.S. #1 singles ("My Sweet Lord," "Give Me Love," and "Photograph"). Fresh-faced rock circus wannabes were told that if they crossed Harrison, they were finished in the industry. Even though Harrison was clearly no Godfather, that was the message that reached two jobbing musicians from the far northeast of England, as he temporarily took over their careers.

Singer-songwriter Bob Purvis and singer Billy Elliot had a stack of sweet melodies and harmonies that were strong enough to tempt a Beatle. After plying the Newcastle music scene with Half Breed, they were in London to work with their manager Mal Evans on an Apple film, *Little Malcolm and His Struggle Against the Eunuchs*. Elliot had already been given a glimpse of Beatleland when he was summoned to cut a vocal on a Lennon-inspired throwaway, "Do the Oz," while Purvis had an attractive piece he called "Another Chance I Let Go" with outstanding vocals. It became the film's main musical anchor, which meant Evans and Purvis had to come up with a new title. "Lonely Man" was born.[7]

George Harrison's vision of his own record label was also in gestation at the time. When Mal Evans played him a demo of "Lonely Man," Harrison had heard his first group signing to the label—Splinter. The duo's sound was close to the fashionable "soft rock" of the time, typified by The Strawbs, Lindisfarne, Steeleye Span, and their U.S. counterparts James Taylor, the Eagles, and America. The original plan was to make "Lonely Man" a fat hit single to accompany the film. When Purvis and Elliot sang the guitarist through the swathes of songs Purvis had written, George decided to cut a full-scale album. He would produce it, just as he had with albums for Jackie Lomax, Doris Troy, and Billy Preston. The quality of Purvis's melodies, coupled with Elliot's powerful vocals, and the pair's lush harmonies, must have made the slide impresario think he had another Badfinger on his hands—especially as he considered them "really good writers."[8]Splinter had all the qualities that Harrison admired in abundance; the way he went about directing the creation of *The Place I Love*—the first release on Dark Horse Records—offers a glimpse into his skills as a producer, guitarist, and arranger.

---

[7]This Splinter song was prepared for release as an Apple single, but though it was assigned a catalogue number, it was never released.

[8]From a taped message Harrison sent to a music biz exec in the U.S. in 1974. It is not officially published document, but has been released on bootleg CDs, the best known being "The Harri-Spector Show."

The disc took over seventeen months to record, in the midst of Harrison's own early *Dark Horse* demos and various trips to India and the United States. First, Splinter and Harrison, along with Pete Ham and Tom Evans from Badfinger, assembled at Apple Studios to try out some of the songs. Focusing initially on "Lonely Man," they soon expanded to demos that wouldn't see the light of day for years, among them "Love Is Not Enough." After these early sessions, the action moved to Henley, where Harrison had his own studio. When Bob Purvis and Bill Elliot arrived at Friar Park, any doubts they may have harbored about George Harrison's commitment to their music evaporated. Harrison had lined up a crack squad of his musical regulars—Jim Keltner, Gary Wright, Billy Preston, Klaus Voormann, Willie Weeks, and drummer Mike Kellie, late of Spooky Tooth.[9]

Summarily pitched headfirst into Harrison's musical world, Splinter were put on salary, and they holed up in London's Earl's Court. When George wanted them at Friar Park, he would send a limo. The duo soon learned not to flinch if Peter Sellers showed up during a photo shoot, or to make too obvious a beeline for Harrison's psychedelic *Magical Mystery Tour* Stratocaster—just one of the guitars lying around the studio.

For all these signs of past glories, they discovered that Harrison was an unassuming character: when Purvis arrived with his wife to meet the superstar, George appeared in the garb pictured on the *Dark Horse* back cover. Purvis's wife assumed he was the gardener. For the most part, of course, she was right, and not just in the horticultural sense.

Settling down to business amid the studio's Krishna iconography and incense, Harrison organized his team into a circle to run through Purvis's tunes on acoustic guitars. As they worked through the songs, the guitarist's musical mind went to work and he made suggestions for reworking them. What Splinter had thought of as finished songs were to Harrison good possibilities. By February 1974 he sent out a working demo of the album to a music industry colleague, enthusing about the quality of the music and the arrangements.

George himself directed the album, and he pieced it together as if he were creating a mosaic. Once the basic rhythm tracks were down, the pattern was painstakingly constructed over a period of months—built from a blending of Splinter's voices, Harrison's multi-

---

[9]The Splinter recordings coincided with the re-formation of Spooky Tooth for the album *The Mirror*. Purvis and Elliot cowrote the track "Kyle" from this LP with Gary Wright.

tracked guitars, and well-targeted horn charts. The guitarist worked relentlessly to get the music right—he worked himself hard and he worked Splinter hard. Hearing Elliot and Purvis harmonizing reminded Harrison of the days when he shared a microphone with Lennon or McCartney. One of the first tricks he taught the pair was how to use the studio to record multipart harmonies—up to that point, they had only worked in two parts. The duo soon found out that meeting Harrison's standard meant working into the night, until they thought their voices were going to give way. There was method to this madness, though; George Harrison was training them to use their voices as instruments.

Harrison assumed responsibility for the arrangements. Gary Wright acted as a sounding board and musical amanuensis. As Purvis and Elliot were still in awe of George as one of their music heroes, it would have been easy for him to take over completely and eclipse Splinter's identity. On the contrary, Bob Purvis's recollection is that the guitarist "bent over backwards to make us happy"[10] with the finished product, and that his focus was on music, not pampering his own ego. And Splinter's stamp as vocalists and songwriters is all over the disc. The songs of *The Place I Love* introduced a cast of northern English characters that were quite unlike anything Harrison would have recorded.

The final product, which Harrison played to fans entering the arena of every one of his Dark Horse Tour shows, was the best album George Harrison was involved with between *Material World* and *Thirty-three & 1/3*. In the admittedly myopic purview of Beatles-related music, it is an overlooked classic. By any standards, it is a fine album. *The Place I Love* is framed by two strong melodic rockers, driven by tight Harrison horn arrangements, George's spare rhythm guitars (echoes of "Get Back" on "Gravy Train"), and a little dose of Ten Years After flash from Alvin Lee. Splinter's vocals reproduced superbly on disc, and the effect was occasionally akin to an acid flashback, as Purvis's voice recalled John Lennon's on pieces like "Haven't Got Time," a virtual Plastic Ono Band out-take. "China Light" is a pretty ballad, enhanced by "Give Me Love" slide glissandos, while "The Place I Love" finds Harrison duetting with himself on dobro and electric slide. The most Beatle-esque moment came with an early reflection on northern unemployment, "Situation Vacant." The Leslie-toned gui-

---

[10]Purvis, Bob. Interview with author, Durham, England, November 2001.

tar chords take the long and winding road back to *Abbey Road* and the phased backup vocals are pure Beatles, especially as Harrison himself took the microphone. The sweeping background vocals accompanying another tuneful Harrison guitar break come straight from "Because."

Here was evidence that, much in the style of his hero, Ravi Shankar, Harrison was working as if he were the conductor of a pop orchestra. In some respects he assumed the role of teacher to two music business toddlers—merely by switching a chord voicing on "Drink All Day," he softened its mood. He also steered Purvis away from a third verse for "Costafine Town," substituting a climatic modulation that raised the song's natural drama a notch or two and helped it into the Top 20.

Inevitably, some of his suggestions weren't to the group's taste, but they still worked. One example is the backup vocals for Purvis's folksy "Elly May," embellished with "Here Comes the Sun" synthesizer flourishes. Bob Purvis had in mind a recurring refrain that was a staccato "early, early, early in the morning, I'll be, I'll be, I'll be on my way." The producer's preference was for a dreamy "early in the morning" phrase that drifted gently. Purvis's more intense part only appears once in the song, a switch that actually increases its impact. Clearly, George Harrison was using all he knew to lavish care on the album.

The record is also evidence of George's growing skills as a producer. Having seen Phil Spector almost drown *All Things Must Pass* in a sea of reverb and over-instrumentation, Harrison had used a pared-down approach for *Living in the Material World*. Made a year later, *The Place I Love* is one of his best soundboard efforts. Maybe the quality of Elliot and Purvis's vocals forced a spare mix on Harrison. The voices had to be given room to shine, and they do.

However, George's greatest contribution was the rich musical tableau he created with the many faces of his guitar playing. It was a throwback to his days as the Beatles' lead guitarist, when he seemed to be able to play a part in any style the song demanded. After all, this was the man who produced memorable, but wildly contrasting, parts as early as 1963 on *With the Beatles*. It is easy to forget that the same musician played the consistently excellent guitar breaks on "All My Loving," "Till There Was You," and "Roll Over Beethoven." For *The Place I Love*, Harrison embellished the songs with a feast of guitar, from the metronomic time keeping of his rhythm ("Gravy Train") to sweeping slide vignettes ("China Light"). There are Leslie-toned riffs from "Don't Let Me Down" ("Situation Vacant"), dobro country snippets

("Drink All Day"), and strong rock licks ("Somebody's City"). The album is an emperor's banquet for aficionados of this greatly underrated guitar stylist.

The meticulous perfectionism Harrison demanded of Splinter as vocalists was the standard that he set himself as a guitarist. As Splinter ran through the songs in the studio, he would watch proceedings from the control room, guitar in hand as he jammed along, picking out possible parts. As they came to cut the overdubbed guitar solos, Harrison's intense concentration required solitude. Kumar Shankar, Harrison's avuncular assistant, would gently usher Purvis and Elliot out of the studio: "George needs to be alone now." When they returned—perhaps days later—Harrison would roll the tape to another perfect guitar part and ask, "What do you think of this?" There were no complaints.

Both musically and from a guitarist's viewpoint, the album's highlight is the powerful "Somebody's City," Bob Purvis's prophetic lament for city life and the environment. Like all the songs on *The Place I Love*, it was conceived as an acoustic workout, but George Harrison electrified it in more ways than one. He added a stinging guitar introduction and an unusually flamboyant closing solo, which revived the sound and style of his section on "Polythene Pam," which is sometimes mistakenly attributed to Paul McCartney.[11] The song, and the entire album, was created in an unusually happy atmosphere, so much so that the entire ensemble burst into spontaneous choruses of "Hey Jude" as "Somebody's City" closed.

The Place I Love is probably the best Beatles-offshoot album of them all. With the exception of Badfinger, Splinter were the greatest "find," surpassing other solo Beatles' follies like Elephant's Memory, Mike McGear, Jiva, and David Hentschel by some distance. That aside, Splinter's first set is certainly a crucial recording in the career of George Harrison.

---

[11]MacDonald, *Revolution in the Head,* 291.

7

The Dark Horse Years
(1974-1976)

Dark Horse
(recorded at Friar Park, winter 1973 and
August–September 1974; final recordings in Los Angeles,
October 1974; released December 1974)

The view from "the top" can be daunting. This lofty lookout was George Harrison's place in 1974. As the purveyor of two #1 albums, two #1 singles, and the concert event of the decade, he was hot. The difficulty is: when you're that hot, the audience just wants more, and the only way to deliver it is to play the game.

Events conspired to push Harrison to the limit in 1974. As Apple had all but disintegrated, he wanted to launch his own record label; he'd agreed to a distribution deal with Herb Alpert's A&M and had two albums ready for release. He worked tirelessly on the Splinter and Ravi

147

Shankar albums, and financed a European excursion for Shankar. The Music Festival from India tour presented more than twenty musicians, making Shankar's ensemble concept a reality for the first time. In effect, this was the first Indian orchestra to appear in Europe. Immediately afterward, in September, Harrison recorded the music from this jaunt in the studio at Friar Park for a second Dark Horse LP under Ravi Shankar's name. This *Music Festival from India* album was held back until late 1975 in deference to the *Shankar Family and Friends* set, which was slated for a 1974 release.

Another positive circumstance was that Harrison's recent U.S. visa problems were resolved and he was free to work there again. He and Ravi Shankar had agreed to tour together when Harrison visited India in February 1974; the way was now clear. It would also be the biggest splash possible for launching Dark Horse Records. When the dates were scheduled for November and December, the only ingredient missing was a George Harrison product to promote. It would have been music business heresy for him to tour with nothing new on the market. The other angle was that Harrison probably wanted to complete his Apple/Capitol contract as soon as he could. After all, he wouldn't have started his own label if he were happy. The chewed apple cores that graced the cover of *Extra Texture* (another album released in a hurry) in 1975 made his feelings clear.

Had George not come down with laryngitis in late summer, he might have pulled the whole thing off. The truth was he needed a sabbatical to recover from a bad domestic year. He'd immersed himself in frantic work as a response to the end of his marriage, and taken one drink too many, too frequently. Against this turbulent background, he set to work on *Dark Horse*. It shows.

Where *All Things Must Pass, Living in the Material World,* and, for that matter, *The Place I Love* had a coherent "sound," *Dark Horse* was a sonic patchwork. Three or four sets of musicians recorded cuts at different times, during various stages of his voice's rabbit-style disappearances. One significant factor was the creation of Friar Park Studios, Henley on Thames (FPSHOT). With recording gear in his mansion, Harrison no longer had to trek to London to record. Critically, as he didn't have to pay for studio time in his own house, the discipline of working on a schedule flew out the ornate windows. The result was that the quality control went awry, because there was no coproducer, no sounding board, no one to gently comment on a duff vocal. Klaus Voormann's memory is that George saw the creation of the Friar Park studio as a blessed relief: "He never wanted to be in that London music scene, that's why he had a studio in his house! The scene never came into his house—all the musicians who came to the house, they were friends. They were all gentle, very tolerant guys—there was always a great atmosphere."

Being an ex-Beatle also gave George license to act on whims and fancies—if he saw a band he liked, he could invite them to Friar Park for a session, whether he had any songs or not. A case in point was the L.A. Express. In April 1974, Joni Mitchell played a series of dates at the New Victoria Theatre in London. Her backup band at the time was a group of jazz musicians, the L.A. Express, an accomplished troupe led by reeds man Tom Scott. Scott, or bass player Max Bennett, a veteran of sessions with Dizzy Gillespie, Miles Davis, and Charlie "Bird" Parker, wrote most of their material. Bennett suggested to Scott that they add a guitar player to the band, the sweet-toned Robben Ford. In 1974 the L.A. Express was one of the hottest properties in rock.

Also present at the New Victoria was George Harrison, checking out this ultrasophisticated chanteuse and her top-rated backup band. He was impressed. Backstage, he impulsively invited them to record the next day at Friar Park. Max Bennett recalls: "We were all invited out to his castle and spent the afternoon recording with him. I think we were handy and he thought it would be a good idea—he had developed a rapport with Tom Scott at that time, and Joni also. He sent the limos to pick us up, and when we drove up to the gate of the mansion, there was a lovely house on the left-hand side, but that was for the caretaker! He didn't come off as an arrogant superstar at all; he was very cordial, very hospitable—he took us through all the tunnels, we had the complete tour, it was like a mini-Disneyland."[1]

Musically, as Bennett describes, George had completely ditched his meticulous approach: "We took our instruments, started playing, and it developed into something. We worked it out, there was nothing on paper—he had an idea and we just latched onto it. There wasn't anything arranged, we just sort of ambled down the musical path until we came to someplace where we felt it sounded good. I wasn't sure that we had accomplished all that much musically. We just laid down rhythm tracks, and after that, I don't know what happened." After spending the night at Friar Park, Max Bennett and the rest of the L.A. Express made for Heathrow Airport and a date in Denver. Thus, the taping of "Hari's on Tour (Express)" and "Simply Shady" was a one-night stand. George Harrison was generally a painstaking craftsman; spontaneity was not his musical gift. The results on *Dark Horse* prove that.

---

[1] Bennett, Max. Telephone interview with author, February 2002.

[46] **Hari's on Tour (Express) (4:44)** *(Harrison)*
Harrison guitars; **Tom Scott** saxophone; **Roger Kellaway** piano;
John Guerin drums; **Max Bennett** bass; **Robben Ford** guitar

This neat instrumental sounds like a collaborative effort between Harrison and Tom Scott—the opening phrase is part guitarist's cliché and part horn player's syncopation. It unfolds with Harrison's Stratocaster roaring into action with the tougher "How Do You Sleep?" tone on the call-and-response riff. The reply is provided by Tom Scott's soprano sax. Set in major chords, the main melodic interest comes with the shift to a C-sharp minor seventh, a moment of softening sweetness.

It couldn't have sounded more different from the opulence of *Living in the Material World*. Here were no musical wings to carry the listener to the spiritual sky; the endeavor was far more earthbound. This was a working, rocking band, and George just wanted to be one of the boys, not a spotlight-grabbing philosopher. Some reviewers suggested that by cutting an instrumental, Harrison was revealing a creative crisis. This could also be considered a logical step for a man who started his career as a guitarist and cherished the virtuoso guitar singles of Chet Atkins.

As plans for the U.S. tour became firm, the title for this rare Harrison instrumental reflected its opening number status. Ultimately, this good-time guitar showcase is as relevant as Dylan's "Nashville Skyline Rag."

[47] **Simply Shady (4:38)** *(Harrison)*
Harrison guitars, vocal; **Tom Scott** saxophone; **Roger Kellaway** piano; **John Guerin** drums; **Max Bennett** bass; **Robben Ford** guitar

There are close parallels between this much-maligned effort and contemporary albums from fellow 1960s survivor Neil Young. Essentially, "Simply Shady" finds George Harrison at the same impasse reached by Young on *Time Fades Away* and *On the Beach*—decadence, dependency, and despair. Young's songs are full of allusions to drugs, drink, paranoia, and self-doubt, to the extent that he concludes on "Ambulance Blues" that he is "just pissing in the wind." The effects of superstar indulgence were also taking their toll on Young's performance, as his straining "Yonder Stands the Sinner" vocal from *Time Fades Away* testifies. In fact, "Simply Shady" could have been based on that Young rocker, not only because of the slightly ragged, gruff vocals and earthy arrangement but also because of the decidedly no-frills production.

Unfortunately for George, the world was not ready for his reincarnation as Neil Young, and the song was panned. Set in a country-rock mode, this stark-sounding cut, with Harrison's wobbly vocals, scared off many.[2] Here George sounds like a confessional Young declaring his duty-free goods at the airport: a few brandy binges and woman trouble—hence the return of Sexy Sadie. "Simply Shady" neatly shatters the "Beatle George" image and reveals the uncomfortable truths of life. Too much drink and failed relationships are hardly uncommon experiences but, for fans readying their *Sgt. Pepper* costumes for the Dark Horse Tour, it was all too much. Harrison had grown up, but was his audience able to?

[48] **So Sad (5:00)** *(Harrison)*
Harrison vocal, guitars; **Ringo Starr** drums; **Nicky Hopkins** piano; **Jim Keltner** drums; **Willie Weeks** bass

This plaintive *lied* illustrates the difficulty of being George Harrison in 1974. The subject of scorn when released, "So Sad" had slipped out a year earlier on an album by Harrison's new friend, Alvin Lee, and an American singer, Mylon Le Fevre.[3] On their *On the Road to Freedom* collection, "So Sad" was a country tune with a running Harrison dobro commentary. Le Fevre's country-gospel vocals emphasize the heartbreak aspects, so the song becomes a companion to "Jolene" and other country tearjerkers. The picture is of the lonely male partygoer, the only guy without a girl, staring into space. And as *On the Road to Freedom* wasn't a Harrison disc, the tune merited not a single critical sneer.

By the time Harrison recorded his own minimalist version, it was cast as another dose of self-pitying self-indulgence. The truth was that it was a harrowing encounter, a far more savage affair than the Alvin Lee take. The instrumentation is sparse—just acoustic guitars, a touch of Nicky Hopkins, and heavy Ringo Starr drums. Harrison's failing voice creates a pained mood, and as he laments that "he feels so alone," the musical tension takes shape with a beautiful rising augmented chord sequence. Cathartic release comes with weeping slide guitar riffs and the "So Sad" lament.

---

[2]Madinger and Easter, *Eight Arms to Hold You*, 443, note that Harrison is said to have taped five or more songs at A&M studios session for "Dark Horse" just prior to the Dark Horse Tour. It's possible that he recut some vocals already recorded at Friar Park, which would explain the condition of his voice on "Simply Shady."

[3]Le Fevre began a career as a church/gospel singer when he was twelve.

What passed for Southern melodrama from Le Fevre is plain mental suffering and self-doubt from Harrison, and there is no mistaking the personal nature of the revelation. The lyrics partly fudge the issue by changing the reference point from "I" to "he." Lyrically, "So Sad" is the flip side of "Here Comes the Sun": hope replaced with tiredness, sunshine supplanted by gloom, and confidence by self-doubt and despair. It's the same catharsis as Lennon catalogued on *John Lennon/Plastic Ono Band,* although it was less sympathetically received. It also reflects the temporary death of George's Krishna dream, as he finds that the spiritual comfort of *Living in the Material World* is not enough to soothe the human pain of separation.

[49] **Bye Bye, Love (4:08)** *(F & B Bryant)*
Harrison vocal, guitars, drums, bass, electric piano[4]

Doubtless intended as a barbed joke, this is the one track on *Dark Horse* that seriously fails the quality-control tests, sounding as if it were slapped together in a few hours. Harrison plays all the instruments on a desperately bad offering.

Almost thirty years later, the Harrison-Patti-Clapton love triangle is no more than an interesting footnote, and that is exactly why the song should not have been released. For once using his music as a vehicle to grind his axe in public, George rewrites the Everlys' teenage love lyrics, adding his own, none-too-subtle swipes at the pair. His imitation of the siblings' harmonies sounds ridiculously distended and, not content with naming Clapton as the cuckolder, he imitates his guitar sound throughout. A record company mixup led to Eric being named as a participant on the track. That would have been a bridge too far.

This is one example of artistic self-indulgence that the listening public could have done without. "So Sad" neatly encapsulates the pain of marital strife; we don't need to know the gory details. In its own way, "Bye Bye, Love" is a classic 1970s period piece, from the era when rock stars used music to settle their own personal scores. Thankfully, George Harrison only made that mistake once.

[50] **Maya Love (4:24)** *(Harrison)*
Harrison vocal, guitars; **Billy Preston** keyboards; **Tom Scott** saxophone; **Willie Weeks** bass; **Andy Newmark** drums

---

[4]Harrison was later adamant that Eric Clapton had not played on the track. His credit in jest to the guitarist had been misunderstood by a record company administrator.

This fine album cut presents the fourth style in as many tracks on *Dark Horse;* it finds George Harrison moving with the times, into the burgeoning world of funk. This should hardly have been a surprise, especially as George had been avidly following soul music for years. Aside from Bob Dylan, his favorite Western artists were still Smokey Robinson and Stevie Wonder. "Maya Love" isn't quite his ascent into George Clinton's Mothership, but the backing track of a tight, funky rhythm section, underpinned by Preston's skittering electric piano and Scott's snappy horn charts, was a new groove for Harrison.

The arrangement is chock full of R&B hooks, starting with Preston's loose "Ray Charles" Fender Rhodes but taken up through the horn section and Harrison's massed guitar tracks. The fine instrumental breaks compensate for a melody that is another in Harrison's long line of three-syllable chants,[5] but "Maya Love" is a showcase for his bottleneck technique and a tight band. The whole piece is full of the stabbing syncopations that characterized 1970s R&B. Well played and arranged, "Maya Love" was an effective live track.

[51] **Ding Dong, Ding Dong (3:40)** *(Harrison)*
Harrison vocal, guitars; **Ringo Starr** drums; **Gary Wright** piano; **Jim Keltner** drums; **Klaus Voormann** bass; **Mick Jones** guitar; **Alvin Lee** guitar; **Tom Scott** saxophone

The Beatles were known for checking out the competition and striving to produce something better. So when the Beach Boys recorded *Pet Sounds* in 1966, the Liverpudlians' response was *Sgt. Pepper.* George Harrison still kept an ear to the radio in 1973 and would have been very much aware of two major Christmas hits that were riding at the top of the British singles chart. As part of the glam rock fad, Slade and Wizzard both scored their biggest, and recurring, U.K. hits with respective Christmas party songs, "Merry Christmas Everybody" and "I Wish It Could Be Christmas Every Day."[6]

By the end of November 1973, Harrison had completed the basic backing track for "Ding Dong, Ding Dong," a rough acoustic guitar mix with just drums, bass, and piano. George was certain that he had a chartbuster on his hands to rival Lennon's recent "Happy Xmas (War Is Over)." His vision for the final mix was a version of the Spector wall of sound, updated to reflect the glam rock mood of the day. He sent

---

[5]"My Sweet Lord," "Give Me Love," "My-a-Love."

[6]In the U.K., the issue of which single will be #1 on the Christmas chart keeps people awake at night and is covered in the national newspapers.

one of his business associates this demo early in 1974, saying, "It's one of them repetitious numbers which is gonna have 20 million people, with the Phil Spector nymphomaniacs, all doing backing vocals by the end of the day, and it's gonna be wonderful. But I'd appreciate it if you don't let anybody steal it, 'cause I want the hit myself."[7]

Clearly thinking he was onto something, Harrison created a massive arrangement for "Ding Dong, Ding Dong" that included a revived "Awaiting on You All" guitar orchestra (this time including Alvin Lee and Mick Jones), chiming bells, and an unnamed army of backup singers intoning the cheerleader chorus. Some of the ideas on this growled party tune were lifted from those 1973 Christmas smashes. The double drums and heavy baritone sax charts sounded exactly like Wizzard, as did the grandiose tubular bells. The heavily distorted fuzz guitars spoke directly of Slade. The bad news was that Harrison's voice was on the road to oblivion, and the critics didn't get the joke at all. One called it a "raspy stab at 'Auld Lang Syne.'"

For this intermittently amusing rocker, Harrison shot a sporadically amusing home-produced film clip that has rarely seen the light of day. As the audiences at the Dark Horse Tour concerts were about to discover, the only "old" that he wanted to "ring out" was the Beatles. So he appears donning and discarding various Beatles outfits, before reaching his own, new identity, which looks like Jethro Tull's *Aqualung*. He also steps into a pirate outfit, as he is joined by a variety of dwarfs, gnomes, and other Pythonesque characters for a New Year's "knees-up." "Ding Dong, Ding Dong" is still occasionally heard at New Year's parties, but like the rest of *Dark Horse*, it would have been better hibernating another winter.

[52] **Dark Horse (3:54)** *(Harrison)*
Harrison vocal, guitars; **Billy Preston** keyboards; **Tom Scott** flute; **Jim Horn** flute; **Chuck Findley** flute; **Willie Weeks** bass; **Andy Newmark** drums; **Emil Richards** percussion; **Jim Keltner** hi-hats; **Robben Ford** guitar; **Lon Van Eaton** backup vocal; **Derek Van Eaton** backup vocal

This jaunty and pleasing hit exposes the confusion in the heart of a superstar. It finds George Harrison acknowledging that he has a double, his "media self," who is a music star. In what appears to be a reaction to the reviews of *Living in the Material World*, he attempts to balance the suggestion that he was a reclusive, religious obsessive by

---

[7]From "The Harri-Spector Show."

creating a new persona, the "Dark Horse." This "George" is a man one step ahead of his detractors, triumphing with quicker feet and better gags. Commentators try to pin his character down at peril, for he is likely to change and take the least expected course. The effect verges on schizophrenia: here was a man who seemed desperate to shave away celebrity imagery and artifice, engaging with his media image. He seems to want to project an image of his choice, but it would still be just an image—the real George will remain hidden.

Apart from the ambiguous psychology, the production also had the most chequered history of any Harrison single. George was working on "Dark Horse" as early as winter 1973 when he cut a scruffy demo at Friar Park with just bass, perfunctory drumming, and guitar— at this stage he was a "blue moon" ever since he "picked up his broom," rather than "my first spoon." A second, faster, guitar-only demo reveals a bluesy intention, emphasising the strong seventh chords that propel the tune—in this version, it was clear that "Dark Horse" had potential to be one of his best. However, the pressure of finishing work with Ravi Shankar, work with Splinter, and his own album's sessions in time to hit the road in November meant that the product was not finished as he set up his tour camp in Los Angeles that October. The other small factor was that he'd contracted laryngitis by this time and had almost no voice left.

With the tour bandwagon rolling, and with seventeen Indian master musicians already en route to L.A., Harrison had to keep going. He could hardly ditch the song that was the motif for the entire venture. The result was a decision to cut a new version live in the studio with the full *Dark Horse* band. Anyone wondering what Harrison's voice sounded like on the Dark Horse Tour need look no further: this track was cut only days before the first date in Vancouver. Although the band sounded good, his voice was in shreds and a fine crack at the charts was ignored in the clamor about his vocals. Some considered it an insult for such a product to be unleashed on the public—Harrison just thought he sounded like Louis Armstrong! He even agreed to a cut a video clip showing a live performance of the song. It gives a candid glimpse of the pain Harrison's need to sing was inflicting on him.

Released as a single mid-tour, "Dark Horse" might have achieved more than its #15 placing on *Billboard*,[8] had George's voice not sounded like the torments of a man swallowing razor blades. If he had just substituted the vocal from the second demo on the Los Angeles

---

[8] "Dark Horse" did not chart at all in the U.K.

backing tape, he would have had a bigger hit and a well-regarded recording.

[53] Far East Man (5:52) *(Harrison–Wood)*
Harrison vocal, guitars; **Billy Preston** keyboards; **Tom Scott** saxophone; **Willie Weeks** bass; **Andy Newmark** drums

In November 2001, shortly before George Harrison's death, a leading British Sunday broadsheet ran a feature article on a famed guitar veteran, a longtime member of one of rock's most famous outfits, the Rolling Stones. Nearing his sixth decade, Ronnie Wood did not disappoint 1970s orthodoxy, with his tales of rock-life debauchery. Along with accomplice Keith Richards, Ronnie is unchallenged as the Jack Daniels-sponsored granddaddy of rock 'n' roll.

Ron Wood and George Harrison may seem unlikely musical comrades. Yet, in October 1973, Reckless Ronnie was a houseguest at Friar Park, where he attempted to seduce Patti Harrison in time-honored rock 'n' roll fashion. He even boasted of the attempt to the drooling press. Still, tradition also dictated that guitar players could get a sex-eclipsing thrill through probing new and seductive chord patterns. In the case of George and Ronnie, the result was "Far East Man," the first Harrisong to tap into 1970s soul, and one of its writer's most beguiling pieces.

The chord sequence is a grin-making exploration of major and minor sevenths that oozes smoochy soul, matched by positive lyrics. "Far East Man" is a hopeful song, some distance from the bitterness of "The Light That Has Lighted the World" and "Who Can See It" and the despair of "So Sad." It's a musical acceptance of life as an unfathomable riddle, where the basic relationships of love and friendship can't be relied on, a wistful shrug of the shoulder set to music.

The middle eight is especially attractive musically, but it sums up Harrison's confusion. Critically and tellingly, his answer is to follow his instinct, his heart. This is the solution to the very real danger of falling into alienation and general mistrust. In this emollient work, Harrison counteracts the pain of "So Sad" and counsels himself on the need to rise above the trouble and carry on. He surveys the problems of love, social strife, and disconnection from spiritual values, but decides that taking his own advice is a good enough start.

"Far East Man" was first heard in September 1974, well before *Dark Horse* left the starting gate, on Ron Wood's *I've Got My Own Album to Do*; Harrison can clearly be heard harmonizing. More importantly, the session introduced Harrison to the newly wedded, crack rhythm section of Andy Newmark and Willie Weeks. Both had supreme soul credentials—Newmark from work with Sly Stone, and Weeks from work with just about everyone, including Stevie Wonder and Aretha Franklin. Newmark had suggested Weeks to a receptive Ronnie Wood for the date—the bass man's performance on a 1972 classic, *Donny Hathaway Live*, had been the talk of rock circles since its release. Harrison was equally impressed, and immediately invited the pair to Friar Park to cut his own take. Even though he'd just vacated the drum stool in Sly and the Family Stone, Andy Newmark had never expected this: "We were so happy to be a part of it, this was like a big thing to all of us. We were completely thrilled to be asked to play on his record, to be invited to his home and experience the hospitality. It was the most exciting thing to happen to me. I had to keep pinching myself to remember it was real."[9]

[54] It Is He (Jai Sri Krishna) (4:50) *(Harrison)*
Harrison vocal, guitars, gubgubbi, moog synthesizer; **Billy Preston** keyboards; **Tom Scott** flute; **Jim Horn** flute; **Chuck Findley** flute; **Willie Weeks** bass; **Andy Newmark** drums; **Emil Richards** percussion

With his life and marriage close to falling apart at the end of 1973, George Harrison found solace in another trip to India the following February. "It Is He" is the direct result. The journey was ostensibly to be present at a ceremony in honor of Ravi Shankar's new house, an event that required the chanting of Vedic hymns for over an hour and a half. There was more chanting as the pair visited Vrindavan, the traditional home of the young Krishna. The whole expedition seems to have been a spiritual epiphany for Harrison, who returned to England enthused again about the concept of "chanting the names of the Lord."

The key to "It Is He" is the bhajan, a Hindu devotional song. These are known and sung by "ordinary" people all over India. With "My Sweet Lord" and "Give Me Love," George had already mixed the bhajan concept with the gospel tradition, and found a place for it in Western pop music. The formula had delivered two #1 hit singles, and it was logical for Harrison to record another pop-bhajan, complete with Tom Scott playing Krishna's flute, for the 1970s.[10] George liked it so much

---

[9]Newmark, Andy. Telephone interview with the author, December 2001.

[10]In Hindu philosophy, the flute is the musical instrument most closely associated with Krishna.

that, at one 1974 session, he recorded a version with Splinter handling the backing vocals.

His problem was that the media were sick of the formula, and this was one Krishna paean too many. Nevertheless, the passage of time has revealed "It Is He" as a charming, upbeat pseudo-calypso that predicts the South Seas mood of another much-maligned Harrison album, *Gone Troppo*. As the guitarist moved between cultures, he naturally reflected both traditions. So while "It Is He" was greeted in some Western quarters with outright hostility, it was entirely in keeping with Indian customs.

It was hardly noticed at the time that this Krishna skiffle revealed Harrison's ability to tackle unorthodox instruments—he played the Bengali *khomok* throughout. This stringed drum, also known as the *gubgubbi* (although Harrison spelled it "gub-gubi" in his handwritten liner notes), originates from the Baul people of Bengal, sometimes considered a religious sect. Their music is another form of bhajan, so it was fitting that Harrison played the khomok on his chant, creating the banjo-meets-vocal sound heard throughout. Here, Harrison was virtually operating as an ethnomusicologist, preserving little-known instrumental traditions that predicted the world music trend of the late 1980s.[11]

Single (B-side, 1974)

[55] **I Don't Care Anymore (2:38)** *(Harrison)*
Harrison guitar, vocal, Jew's harp

Another throwaway Harrison flip side, in the mold of "Miss O'Dell," backed the slow march of "Ding Dong, Ding Dong" into the middle reaches of the singles charts.

Whether intentionally or not, on "I Don't Care Anymore" Harrison sounds in danger of coming off the dark racecourse completely. The subject matter of this Dylanish upmarket busking is a virtual regression to the teenage preoccupations of "Don't Bother Me" and "I Need You." The difference is that this time there's a menacing undercurrent of aggression and just a hint of one drink too many. The growled gibberish that opens this sad music was probably intended as a joke—the

---

[11]The khomok, khammak, or gubgubbi is a small drum with two strings attached to a small cup and stretched from within the skin to the drum head. The player places the drum under his arm, pulls the cup, and plucks the strings. In the 1990s, contemporary Indian fusion musicians, notably Jai Uttal, revived the instrument. Curiously, two Baul musicians are on the cover of *John Wesley Harding*.

real gag was that it mirrored exactly what his voice would sound like on the Dark Horse Tour. "I Don't Care Anymore" is hard to stomach.

Dark Horse is another remarkably revealing album from Harrison, and the disclosures are personal. It's a musical soap opera, cataloguing rock-life antics, marital strife, lost friendships, and self-doubt. For someone who didn't like living his life in public, Harrison was doing it with a vengeance here. Any voyeur who wanted to know the intimate details of his personal life didn't need to buy *National Enquirer*, they just needed to hear this disc.

One of the most interesting leaks from the LP was that, in the midst of personal turmoil, Harrison was experiencing a crisis of faith too. The spiritual certainties of *Living in the Material World* are absent and, although hopeful, "It Is He" is almost a reminder to himself of golden days in India, when he felt comforted by belief. Interestingly, for all his public chanting on the 1974 Dark Horse Tour, George told interviewers that he hadn't meditated regularly for years. On *Dark Horse* he sounds at sea and lacking purpose. This insecurity infected his next year's music too.

For all the problems, the quality of the songs remained quite high—"Dark Horse" and "Far East Man" are among his best. But the vocal performances were a problem. Had there not been a need to release an album to cash in on the tour, it would probably have been better not to put the record out. As an ex-Beatle, he was just about able to call his own tune and manage his own quality control—not many other artists would have been given such leeway. It was a hollow victory, as Harrison was too high profile and successful at the time to be given any margin for error, especially as some of his contemporaries sounded more like him than he did. Both John Lennon and Eric Clapton produced well-received discs in 1974, *Walls and Bridges* and *461 Ocean Boulevard*, sets that featured more of what the marketing men would have recognized as the archetypal George Harrison sound than *Dark Horse*. For his major hit "#9 Dream," Lennon had Jesse Ed Davis replicate George's signature bottleneck. Even Clapton was beginning to sound like Harrison, with his subtle dobro licks on "Please Be with Me." "Let It Grow" from Clapton's album was a virtual pastiche of "Something," doubling Harrison's descending chord sequences, guitar arpeggios, and simple bottleneck style. It was more a classic Harrisong than anything on George's LP.

Dark Horse was received by some as an affront to their dignity. *Rolling Stone* let George have it with both barrels, declaring him a failure as singer, songwriter, and guitarist; the record was "embarrassingly bad." It took the music press over a decade to recover their patience for Harrison—some never did.

The Dark Horse Tour

Klaus Voormann: "I was actually amazed that he did the 1974 tour, but he had a great feeling about the tour and the people, so he did it."

The Reviews

Vancouver: The audience was made up mostly of long-haired, jeans clad youths and many of them left grumbling. If they were looking for some magical, mysterious return to Beatle music, what they got was a lot of gospel and soul rock, interspersed with an occasional Harrison tune.... But the show was far from a disappointment in a musical sense. Harrison was backed by a heavyweight band, in fact he was more of a guest in the group than a member of it. It was in the first 45-minute set that the crowd began to realize that Harrison's role was to be mostly that of an emcee.... It was a sheer delight to listen to the varied sounds from sitar, tabla, flute and other stringed instruments. Harrison brought back Shankar's orchestra for a valid, viable marriage of musical cultures. The show concluded with a Krishna musical prayer, but the clamor for an encore resulted in the small group returning to play Harrison's "My Sweet Lord."

—John Wenderborn (*The Oregonian*)

In the press box at the PNE Coliseum in Vancouver, one reporter is guessing that the Sanskrit letter for OM is actually the Indian dollar sign. Another insists it means "No Smoking."... Harrison meantime is hoarse from the beginning and strains through each song. Billy Preston eventually perks up the show with two numbers in the second half, but the night sputters to a conclusion with more Indian music, more cries for rock and roll, and in the end, Harrison receiving a perfunctory encore call. He performs "My Sweet Lord" and out of the silence comes the silence—a still and seated audience with only the front section clapping along.

—Ben Fong-Torres (*Rolling Stone*)

Seattle: Harrison's opening instrumental piece was beautiful: the fullest, finest explosion of rock 'n' roll that I think I have ever heard.

Harrison's voice was at best raspy. "While My Guitar Gently Weeps" developed into a hectic jam session that thundered through the audience. Tragically, Shankar's beautiful music was wasted on a noisy minority of meatheads.... George Harrison's concert tour will be a successful, well-remembered entry in rock history.

—D. P. Bond (*Seattle Post Intelligencer*)

Oakland: Harrison's 6 p.m. Oakland show was a bona fide high but not quite a knockout. The star's voice was noticeably raspy, the band was superb. The most admirable trait of the show was its pacing, with energy constantly being built and relaxed. Harrison's band opened with a zingy and classically melodic instrumental, "Hari's on Tour," that was a touchstone of the Harrison style. The Shankar segment of the show was a genuine bauble of musical curiosity. Preston did in fact steal the show when he did "Nothing from Nothing," but it was an ego-less steal and it is to Harrison's credit that he gave him his head so totally.... There are potential troubles that could plague this tour. Harrison's presence is not so strong as might be anticipated, given that it is an ex-Beatle up there.

—Jack McDonough (*Pacific Sun*)

Los Angeles: Bad news travels so fast in LA that even the telegraph company are envious. By Tuesday George Harrison had performed three concerts in the Los Angeles area and the word circulating around the music industry was that the show was a "disaster." ...But for me the George Harrison concert was a complete delight: incredibly good tight music, played by people who were not on ego trips and who were enjoying their time on stage. Harrison's voice was gone, but there was so much music to cover the rough spots that it really didn't matter. The band has got to be one of the finest assembled anywhere.... Harrison still enjoys being part of a band, he still does not want to take center stage. This is a difficult philosophy for Americans to accept: we thrive on stardom, charisma. Harrison wore no glitter, pranced no prances, displayed no ego. If you wanted a superstar he was a disappointment: if you wanted good music, he was perfect.... The concert was enjoyable without being pretentious; dazzling in its skill without being theatrical in its presentation. Harrison should be very proud of himself. George Harrison is the first former Beatle to tour America. It's going to be very difficult for people to accept one of them as simply an excellent musician.

—Jacoba Atlas (*Melody Maker*, London)

Opening with "While My Guitar Gently Weeps" the band was cooking so fast and hard that Harrison's vocal shortcomings were easily overlooked. But as he tore into "Something," shouting the lyrics of a most tender ballad like a demented Bob Dylan on an off night, you realized the voice was almost gone.

—Robert Kemnitz (*Los Angeles Herald*)

Tucson: In his two sold-out concerts at the Tucson Community Center Arena last night we were treated to a concert of wondrous proportions. There was a special feeling, a very different type of excitement surrounding his show last night, much different from the sort of thing you often get at a rock concert. The worth of a Harrison is the fact that they are the creators. They are the ones who do it every time; they are the ones who do it with class.

—Larry Fleischmann (*Tucson Citizen*)

Salt Lake City: One of the most interesting, most entertaining and most memorable shows ever put on in Utah. His whole show was fantastic. He treated the screaming, frantic patrons like they were joining him in a religious experience. Shankar and his orchestra created a sound which sent the imagination running wild. Just before the intermission the two bands combined to blend the music of Western and Eastern cultures. It was unbelievable.

—Paul Rolly (*Salt Lake Tribune*)

St. Louis: The concert of former Beatle George Harrison at the Arena last night was full of surprises. It was an excellent show, in which the musicians all performed as if eager to please. But it was Harrison himself who set the tone; he had the charm of an artist who seems slightly astonished by his own success.

—Dick Richmond (*St. Louis Post-Dispatch*)

Fort Worth: George Harrison arrived at Fort Worth last night for a powerful three-hour concert. It was a concert of music: music full and pleasant, lively and nostalgic. It was a happy concert with first a quiet attentive crowd, then a cheering energetic crowd brought to its feet with Preston and "Nothing from Nothing," and one that was ecstatic with "My Sweet Lord" and "Give Me Love." Harrison is good. He always was and he is proving that he still is.

—Lorraine Haacke (*Dallas Times Herald*)

Memphis: Last night's show before a capacity crowd of 11,600 gave no evidence of any raggedness. From the start it was great, simply great. They throw the word "great" around a lot in the music world, but it was certainly deserved by Harrison and his friends last night. Musically, vocally and as an experience to be shared, the concert was successfully done. There have been few concerts as moving as last night's.

—Walter Dawson (*The Commercial Appeal*)

Baton Rouge: George Harrison, Ravi Shankar and Billy Preston put on a masterful show Tuesday night in Baton Rouge, and even if the show wasn't as electrifying as most hoped, none left untouched by the event. For there was Harrison singing "While My Guitar Gently Weeps." His throat was sore, but the guitar was the same magnificent lead he offered with the Beatles, and with sheer gut effort the singing came through....After a short intermission, the show, which had still lagged overall, came to life. Harrison moved from electric to acoustic guitars and played incredibly on each. And he began moving. The show had seemed too much like a mouthing of an album before, but the stage and the crowd began to move the way everyone was hoping it would.

—Richard E. Hart (Morning Advocate)

Detroit: The Harrison concerts are an international smorgasbord, featuring a mixture of Indian and jazz influences, a bit of the old Liverpool sound and the jazz-pop rock of Preston and Scott. Shankar's musicians, along with Harrison and his band, performed several well-received numbers, jazzy things that seemed to please. Although Detroiters didn't award him the constant, maniacal screams that greeted the Beatles way back in '66, their clamor for an encore indicated they liked him solo in the Motor City.

—Christine Brown (Detroit Free Press)

Boston: His first of two shows at the Boston Garden triumphed over dismal reports filtering ahead of his tour. What the crowd saw was a show where the featured attraction was sometimes the star, but most times just a guitarist in the band. But the essence of the night was summed up in his R&B styled "My Sweet Lord," where he urged the crowd to chant "Christ, Krishna, Allah, Buddha." This gesture suddenly interrupted the crowd's ecstasy.

—Peter Gelzinis (Boston Herald American)

Chicago: It finally came together for the George Harrison tour in a huge ice hockey arena in the middle of Chicago's Westside ghetto. He tried an experiment in front of 18,000 listeners. It meant putting his personal prestige on the line and already the arrows of the critics in other cities had drawn blood....The spotlight turned to Billy Preston who led the band into a rousing version of "Will It Go Round In Circles." George underwent a striking transformation. He had looked nervous and stiff during the previous numbers, but now it was as if a burden was lifted from his shoulders. He became carefree and animated, and was really enjoying himself.... George is now the shy ex-Beatle. He is still basically the lead guitar player who prefers to pick out delicious licks from the back of the stage. The Indian part was dazzling and the whole musical ensemble left the stage for intermission to wild cheers.... Finishing the set with a rousing "What Is Life," the audience went crazy with happy screams at the conclusion. George, too, looked high as the band rocked out "My Sweet Lord." The building almost rose several feet in the air from the combined happiness of singing audience and rocking musicians.

—Don Leyland (Sounds, London)

"Hallelujah!" The joyful worshippers repeated it again and again, dancing on their seats. It was a moving conclusion to a splendid concert Saturday by George Harrison and friends in the Chicago Stadium.

—Al Rudis (*Chicago Sun Times*)

Long Island: The young Long Island crowd seemed almost fraught with anticipation... The lights flashed on, the band roared into the instrumental "Hari's on Tour," and the crowd went wild. Until they heard George's hoarse voice straining through "While My Guitar Gently Weeps." After that the audience remained appreciative but largely uninspired. Harrison looked tired, the rigors of the road etched into his sallow, craggy face. In fact the Nassau concerts were salvaged only by the lighting maneuvers of promoter Bill Graham.

—Larry Sloman (*Rolling Stone*)

Philadelphia: Preceded by reams of negative reviews, George Harrison pulled off a surprisingly pleasant victory at The Spectrum. This concert was not the disorganized, self-serving venture portrayed by the national music press on the occasion of the tour's opening Nov. 2 in Vancouver.... Though reluctant to dwell on past glories, the former Beatle now deigns to throw us a bone or four from the halcyon days, including a curiously suitable, jazzed-up rendering of "In My Life." Harrison makes most points with his sweetly weeping guitars, riding the high end of the neck in a glissando of spare, single notes or bluesy, staccato attacks.

—Jonathan Takiff (*Philadelphia Daily News*)

Washington: Harrison had been preceded on the road by Eric Clapton, Bob Dylan, and Crosby, Stills, Nash and Young, but there is something different about the excitement surrounding this tour. Nearly 11 years after the Beatles' first appearance in the United States, it is obvious that anything associated with the most popular of all '60s rock groups still has a very special aura. In performance he has done everything possible to break with it [the past]. His two-hour show included only one Lennon-McCartney composition, "In My Life," which, like Harrison's own compositions of his Beatles days, has been radically restructured.... The lyrics of songs like "Something" have been changed to make the number sexier and less mellow, but even more noticeable are the new arrangements. Throughout the evening the audience, puzzled by unfamiliar beginnings to familiar songs, would give cheers of recognition only after Harrison started to sing.... Harrison obviously has clout, artistic and economic. So when he entered to the tune of Monty Python's "Lumberjack Song," it all seemed a bit too coy. Harrison may think that he is only a speck in the scheme of things, but his audiences know better. He's got the power, and what's more, he knows how to use it.

—Larry Rohter (*Washington*)

New York: A few pleasantries and a bit of excitement at the end aside, it can only be called eccentric and boring. The boredom derived from the nature of Mr. Harrison's music, his vocal estate and his onstage manner. His music making is increasingly homogenous and smooth; sometimes it can take on a restful, gentle swayingness, but more often it plods soberly along weighed down by homiletic verse and deliberately simple, sentimental melody. His on-stage manner was curious—petulant as he hectored the crown to buy albums and programs, cross as he scolded about marijuana.... Mr. Shankar's appearance at pop concerts in the late 1960s and early '70s, when he played whole ragas with the traditional classical Indian instrumentation were surely a better way to present Indian music to a young Western audience than last night's lame popularizations.... During Mr. Preston's solo turn Mr. Harrison reverted to the role of the vocally silent, different lead guitarist, flashing quick smiles to his fellow players and playing his part in the larger whole. It was a role that suited him. He has had his hits and he has deserved them. But one couldn't help but think that last night that was suited him best was the role that he longed so fervently to escape— that of the "silent Beatle," humbly taking second billing to those more charismatic than himself.

—John Rockwell (*New York Times*)

The band blistered through "Hari's on Tour," then George grabbed the mike, "I'd like to continue with one of my comedy numbers"—and he turned "Something" into a moving diary of his love life.

—Larry Sloman (*Rolling Stone*)

George Harrison's decision to embark on a major tour of North America in the winter of 1974 was the most peculiar of his career. By even considering taking to the road he created the most irresistible pressure on himself, especially as the past year had been the nadir of his personal life. The events surrounding the whole venture have an almost Pythonesque hue in retrospect, even putting aside for a moment the fact that Harrison almost certainly hated touring.

The tour was conceived on a February 1974 trip to India with Ravi Shankar, itself an escape from the disintegration of his marriage, and many nights spent nursing a bottle of brandy, as documented in "Simply Shady" and "Can't Stop Thinking About You." The laudable artistic decision to take Shankar on the road created more pressure, as it was impossible to predict how rock audiences in huge arenas would react to an hour's presentation of Indian music.

The paradox of the tour was immense—here was one of the world's most famous musicians telling a leading writer from *Rolling Stone* that he'd "gladly kiss it all good-bye" and pursue his utterly sincere spiritual quest. He said this at the very moment when he was launching a multimillion-dollar tour in support of a new album and record label. He seemed to have forgotten the Apple debacle and jumped into bed with A&M, who would surely require something back for their $10 million investment in Dark Horse Records. He'd also run out of time to finish his new LP and get it out for the first show.

As if the pressure of getting a return on investment for A&M wasn't enough, the tour would be the first of North America by an ex-Beatle, in a territory where the group had a status way beyond that of mere icons. The dates were scrutinized with media and critical attention beyond that focused on Dylan, and were crowned with the sheer impossibility of forever being Beatle George. The word "Beatles" was on everyone's lips, even if Harrison later pleaded in a state of bemusement that "a lot of people came and wanted to see the Beatles. I don't know why, because I'm not the Beatles," and, "I'm certainly not going to go out there doing Beatles tunes, it's just that *I'm not the Beatles.*"

Surely Harrison could not have been as naïve about the situation as those quotes suggest; perhaps he was temporarily imbued with his old boldness. But, once again, he found himself at the epicenter of a whirlwind of pent-up Beatlemania, which had been brewing since 1966. The expectations of the fans were insanely high, and the United States was hardly the place to slip onto the road unnoticed.

So the tour was framed by a massive mismatch of fans' expectations and artist's self-image. It was driven by immense pressure from A&M to be a business success, topped with the pressure of being "the leader" for the first time. It was the summation, and crowning paradox, of George Harrison's "Pisces Fish" musical life, a head-on collision between hundreds of thousands of American Beatle fans and one of the Fab Four themselves desperate to slash and burn that rosy image and assert his own identity. While Robert Zimmerman had created a stage persona called Bob Dylan, Harrison was not creating a new stage act: he was merely presenting himself as he was, as opposed to what the fans and media chose to believe he was. But by refusing to play the part of Beatle George, he caused bereavement for many.

And finally, on the eve of the tour, he contracted laryngitis and lost his voice.

All the musicians assembled for the Dark Horse Tour were top-notch. Harrison's all-American band had passed muster on *Dark Horse* and were the leading performers of the period—Billy Preston, Tom Scott, Willie Weeks, Emil Richards, Andy Newmark, Chuck Findley, Jim Horn, and Robben Ford. In time, Jim Keltner supplemented the percussion arsenal, bringing this band almost up to the size of the *Concert for Bangla Desh* ensemble. According to drummer Andy Newmark, the rehearsals at A&M studios in Los Angeles were fairly relaxed: "It was just a case of coming in, listening to the songs, and picking it up. At that point we were imitating records that had been made of a song, so the parts were dictated by the recording of the song. It was all very ad lib." The happy mood was largely the result of Harrison's worldview: "He just wanted to be in a band; he hated being a leader and wasn't comfortable being the leader—he hated giving orders, he wasn't at all a pushy superstar or egotistical. He was totally the opposite of all that."

Despite his natural diffidence, George Harrison did present himself as a very different musician on these dates—for one thing, his guitar playing was powerful and prominent. He showcased his excellent slide breaks throughout, even having the confidence to take a solo during one of Shankar's pieces ("Zoom, Zoom, Zoom"). But he also played some strong nonslide solos, notably on "While My Guitar Gently Weeps"—a piece that was expanded to over eight minutes by the end of the tour. At Madison Square Garden during the final show, Harrison received a standing ovation for an especially burning solo that supports the thinking that if he'd wanted to play guitar hero licks, he would have done so.

But while his guitar playing was in great shape, by rehearsal time it was already obvious to Newmark and everyone else concerned that the star's voice was well on the road to oblivion. This preyed on George's mind, even though his enthusiasm for the dates was high: "He was up for it, and quite concerned about how it would all be accepted. My vision at the time was, how could George Harrison ever be concerned about how he'll be received? He was really upset that his voice went—he didn't know whether to go on or to cancel the dates. He thought it wasn't cool to accept people's money when his voice was shot—it was very upsetting to him. I could hear he was hoarse. We all felt really bad for him. Having to go out in front of 20,000 people with no voice, it's got to be tougher on him than anyone. He was very worried about the product he was delivering."

Part of the package was the greatest collection of Indian musicians ever to tour America, thrown into the most alien setting imaginable for what was essentially a form of chamber music. Along with Shankar and Allah Rakha, the tabla genius, came the relatively unknown L. Subranamiam, a South Indian violin master who went on to jazz fame, and the sarangi virtuoso Sultan Khan. Two of the other players were known to rock fans through the seminal 1968 album *Call of the Valley*. This wonderful collection of impressionistic suites was one of the keys to bringing Indian classical music to the rock audience. The Dark Horse Tour brought Shivkumar Sharma and Hariprasad Chaurasia from *Call Of The Valley* onto the concert stage. Both musicians are now widely regarded as among the greatest to have emerged from the subcontinent. They are the acknowledged masters of their respective instruments: Sharma plays the santoor, a dulcimer-style device of Persian genesis; Chaurasia is the foremost bansuri flute player of his generation. All this happened a decade before the term "world music" was coined. In 1974, George Harrison and Ravi Shankar were leading the pack in fusing Indian and Western music.

The Indian contingent of the Dark Horse Tour was a musical tiara, and the Western musicians faced a steep learning curve to play with them. For drummer Andy Newmark, it was especially interesting, given the complex rhythmic structures: "We joined them for one or two things at the end of their show. It was music we weren't used to. They were all a very high caliber of musician and all seemed very disciplined. They were quite inspirational people and we sort of admired the way they lived, the way they behaved—they seemed spiritual, but kind of disciplined. It was very controlled, and their playing seemed to be very important. The music was very complex. You need to be clear and focused just to count through that stuff. So when we played some of those pieces, it was quite challenging and intimidating. It kept us on our toes." Reeds man Jim Horn emphasizes the wider significance of the tour and Harrison's status as a world music pioneer: "The Dark Horse Tour was one of the best I've been on. Ravi Shankar played with seventeen musicians from India—what a sound! George introduced Indian music to the world."

On paper, the mostly static set list for the Dark Horse Tour looked like a winning recipe. Harrison would play his three big hits ("Give Me Love," "What Is Life," and "My Sweet Lord") and some

Beatles classics ("While My Guitar Gently Weeps," "Something," "For You Blue," and "In My Life"). Unsurprisingly, he would introduce music from his new album in the shape of "Hari's on Tour," "Dark Horse," and "Maya Love." From his previous album, he pulled "Sue Me, Sue You Blues," "The Lord Loves the One," and "Who Can See It." In a show that featured no fewer than five #1 hits, Billy Preston alternated between his recent smashes, "Outta Space," "Will It Go Round in Circles," and "Nothing from Nothing." Between these hits, Tom Scott delivered his pop-jazz "Tom Cat," and there was "Sound Stage of Mind," a loose band jam. The Indian music was presented in one half-hour segment of music customized for the rock audience, or "continuously shrieking young rock fans," as Ravi Shankar called them. This showcased new work and music from *Shankar Family & Friends*, including the pop version of "I Am Missing You."

In theory, it looked good. The reality was slightly different but clearly no "disaster." The bad points were blindingly obvious—Harrison's voice was destroyed at the start of the tour, and he actually sounded in pain. He was in a catch-22: his voice wasn't good enough for the tour but plans, musicians and finances were too heavily committed to pull out. He would have to suffer the criticisms—and there were plenty, some self-inflicted. Aside from his vocal strife, the main tension was that the crowds wanted him to do "I Want to Hold Your Hand" and revive the Liverpool Leg. The man rebelled, sick of being asked when the Beatles were going to reform, and sick of Beatle George, the alter ego who followed him around uninvited.

The rebellion was none too subtle, the main victim being his classic "Something," which was denuded of all melody as the star ditched "Something in the way she moves" for a shouted "If there's something in the way, we move it." This was a little bit of English humor that the American audience didn't get. The hideously distorted mangling of a great love song was the nadir of the whole business and consciously provocative on the singer's part. Harrison wasn't the only artist known for doing this—as the years progressed Bob Dylan would often challenge his audience by rearranging songs past all recognition. At the time, Harrison seemed to view the song's status as a curse, but the "hit albatross" was a demon he'd previously warned Badfinger about. Joey Molland explains: "George once said to us, '"Come and Get It" is a big hit for you guys, isn't it? You know you'll have to play that song every day for the rest of your life!'"

In February 1975, talking about the shows, Harrison seemed deter-mined to release the music: "The proof of the pudding is in the tape. This year I'll mix the tape and put out the record, and the record will be pretty decent, the band was one of the hottest bands I'd ever... I mean, maybe I was the worst one in the band. It was a fantastic band and the tape is a rocking show." [12] Unfortunately, that never happened, so for years after the event the music of the Dark Horse Tour only lived through bootlegs sought out by the dedicated. They provide doc-uments of the shows that allow the listener to reach their own con-clusions about the performance and the crowd reaction. And when Harrison finally released two songs from the tour on his *Songs by George Harrison* sets, "Hari's on Tour" and "For You Blue," they did not suggest a calamity. The testimony of the musicians was also at odds with the "given" view. Witness this observation from the drummer's chair: "It was all good—I thought it was happening, musically, on stage. It seemed like everyone who came enjoyed themselves totally. I thought the response couldn't have been warmer and more enthusi-astic; people were thrilled to see him on stage."

The concept of the tour was certainly ambitious: the ultra-eclectic mix of Indian, pop-jazz, funk, and Harrison's own radically altered style was some potpourri. Some of the early shows were dam-aged by the severe state of Harrison's voice—the first night in Vancouver quickly established that he could not carry a song like "Who Can See It," so it was dropped. "The Lord Loves the One" was also played in Vancouver and never heard again, a fate the heavy-funky arrangement did not deserve. The shows in San Francisco seemed to be the worst for Harrison vocally and they were the poorest of the trip, but by the time the tour reached Long Beach the crowd was buzzing. This set the tone for the show as it moved into the Southern states, where it was very well received.

One of the best nights came in the heart of Billy Preston's Texan homeland at the 11,000-seat Fort Worth Convention Center. The bootlegs of this show capture the whole set, including the Indian sec-tion, and give a great overview of the performance. Although not good by any means, the condition of his voice had improved by this point, and the first two numbers ("Hari's on Tour" and "While My Guitar Gently Weeps") both storm through to a hot finish. Harrison's signa-

---

[12] An interview on the LBC radio station in London, interviewer Sarah Dickinson.

ture piece found him trading rock star licks with Robben Ford. Even his little joke does not offend: "I look at the floor and it looks quite tidy." Following a bemused reaction to the disemboweled "Something," the ever painfully honest Harrison introduces Billy Preston as "someone I would never have come on the road without, because I love him so much and need him so bad." Here's evidence, if it were needed, of the personal toll playing live took on Harrison. At the end of the opening segment, "Sue Me, Sue You Blues" is reborn as horn-driven funk with many doses of snakey bottleneck and a good new gag, "bring your lawyer, and I'll bring Klein."

Harrison's good humor grew exponentially as the audience ripped it up during the Indian music section. The guitarist was the Master of Ceremonies for the *Shankar, Family & Friends* segment, which was well paced and accessible. Two of the pieces were contemporary fusions of Indian themes and jazz, with Harrison, Scott, Preston, and Robben Ford taking solos. The Krishna pop of "I Am Missing You" was beautifully sung by Lakshmi Shankar. On the purely Indian selections applause broke out, jazz club style, after solo instrumental passages, but the biggest reaction was reserved for a collection of folk pieces called "Chepratee." These were whipped up with rhythmic scat singing and exciting drum exchanges between Allah Rakah's tabla and the barrel-shaped *mridangam* of T. V. Gopalkrishnan. As the cheering died down, Harrison took the microphone, wide-eyed with delight: "I'm so happy that you should like it!"

This good mood infected the rest of the show. The first half closed with the supposedly lugubrious star inviting the audience to buy a concert program to benefit an ailing hospital, with a deadpan flourish: "In fact we don't come back on for the second half until you've all bought one!" These gauche asides to the audience are testimony to how little Harrison acted a part while onstage. He seems to have had no concept of projecting an image, or of how his words might be interpreted. It's hard to imagine Bob Dylan introducing his costar as "Someone who affected my life to such a degree that I now have a life worth living."

The second half of the show provided cameos for Harrison's new band. "For You Blue," for instance, became a jam track, with solos for the extravagantly gifted Willie Weeks and jazz percussion master Emil Richards. A straight "Give Me Love" was greeted with ecstasy and, seldom reported, the Harrison version of "In My Life" had the crowd breaking into applause after the newly arranged tension-and-release buildup to the line, "In my life, I love you more." They applaud again the second time around, when he changed it to "In my life, I love God more." From this point, aside from a well-received "Dark Horse" (Harrison: "also a hoarse horse"), the date turns R&B revue, with his own bottleneck showcase "Maya Love" and Scott's "Tom Cat."

Although "Tom Cat" was a snappy piece of light jazz-rock, it was completely eclipsed by the return of Billy Preston for a second set of hits. Some commentators crowed that Preston's showmanship had saved George's bacon, but that isn't how Andy Newmark saw it: "It was always a great moment when Billy came on—he represented up, gospel, tambourine values. He would light the fuckin' place up, and get 20,000 people all of a sudden on their feet. George didn't have that effect, it wasn't his style. He was just grateful to get through his songs and play his guitar parts. He wasn't trying to be charismatic."

The hordes expected Preston to put on a show, and he delivered with a vengeance. During "Outta-Space" or "Nothing from Nothing," he'd launch into one of his legendary dance routines. On a good night Harrison would be there, arms around Billy's shoulders, trying to cop Preston's smart moves. To Newmark, it was part of the man's appeal: "Billy Preston would dance across the stage on one leg and get the crowd going. George joined in with Billy, but he was really making fun of the fact that he was so white, so unblack and unfunky. It was almost a piss-take of himself, and he did it to accentuate his total whiteness and Billy's beautiful blackness. In fact, he was totally aware he was the opposite of that—he meant it as a joke."

Even though reviewers carped that Preston's exuberant funk had "saved the day" for Harrison, it was all part of a well-paced show. Preston's second set piece was used to raise the temperature toward the close, "What Is Life," which at Fort Worth was greeted with a reception that matched anything the New York audience at the Bangla Desh concerts expressed. This raised George's spirits further and he left the stage with the showbiz mantra: "You're beautiful people—I love you." It sounded like he meant it.

The encore was "My Sweet Lord," and the show closed with the sound of an ecstatic crowd. Some reviewers were discontented that Harrison used the gospel arrangement of the song from Billy Preston's *Encouraging Words* album. Reviews also stressed that the star's attempt to encourage some "ragged but rowdy" communal chanting was out of place. But this was what "My Sweet Lord" was about, and chanting the names of the Lord was hardly a new concept for Harrison fans. Still, George was obviously trying to re-create the gospel feeling of "Oh Happy Day"—this is why he chose the *Encouraging Words* arrangement, which had featured Edwin Hawkins.

While Harrison worked tirelessly to distance himself from his Beatle past, by presenting such an innovative show, he was operating within his old band's pioneering tradition. His 1976 explanation of the idea behind the tour confirms this:"I think that's one reason I went on tour with all those people, to do something which was not done every week, you know, the whole idea of having such a whole different bunch of people, different attitudes and different types of music, and just a broader type of show. Another point in the show, fifteen Indian musicians joined the rock band, so you had a band of over thirty people playing some compositions which were written especially for that combination of musicians. The whole band played with Billy Preston and Tom Scott, and guitar solos and *veena* solos and sitars. A lot of musicians were just blown out, they just loved it. Apart from that, people should have something different occasionally, because they can see Led Zeppelin anytime they like, but you're never gonna see something like that again. Actually the audience reaction was great. Every show was standing ovations."[13]

If the scant surviving video evidence is any indication, he seemed satisfied with the tour's last show at Madison Square Garden. The entire Indian troupe joined the Western musicians on stage for the "My Sweet Lord" chanting as the audience behind the stage swayed from side to side. Viewing all this, George Harrison jumped up and down, waving gleefully to the crowd. For a man who hated touring, he looked very happy.

This community spirit was the goal of the Dark Horse Tour, but what is rarely considered is that the venture was groundbreaking in its presentation of music. It was as if Harrison had taken to the road with a rolling revue based on Bill Graham's Fillmore West concept. In his mid-1960s heyday, Graham had put Miles Davis and Steve Miller on the same bill. Now George Harrison presented a show consisting of pop, rock, folk, soul, R&B, funk, and Indian music. He was rightly criticized for the condition of his voice and the immolation of his best-known love song, but in an era before world music and its mass marketing by the ECM label, the Indian section of the Dark Horse Tour was pioneering. Ravi Shankar's skills as an arranger were tested as he organized half an hour's worth of mixed, melodious, and rhythmically exciting music. It took the unique ensemble approach of his *Music Festival from India* to the rock audience. The idea of presenting an Indian music orchestra was new in itself, but to do so in rock arenas was daring. The musicians recognized this, as Emil Richards recalled:

---

[13] From a BBC-Radio interview with Harrison by Anne Nightingale, November 1976.

"The mixing of Indian music, jazz, and rock was great. Both Tom Scott and I played in both groups with George and Ravi. It was a great tour—all first-rate musicians and great friends."[14]

The camaraderie of the trip is also fondly remembered by Andy Newmark, a man who has sat for Sly Stone, John Lennon, Roxy Music, David Bowie, and Ron Wood. He recounts that the star was very interested in how the boys in the band viewed life on the Dark Horse Tour: "He would look you in the eyes and wanted to know, 'Do you like this? Are you having fun?' He cared, he wondered how everyone was doing, and he wanted to know, 'Are you happy on this tour, is this fun for you? This isn't just a job, is it?' You see, George was never relaxed, he was a worrier, and he was often preoccupied with worry. If something was wrong, he was always thinking, 'Someone's unhappy, what have I done wrong?'"

The reception given Harrison's 1974 tour is one of the stranger episodes in rock music. While the majority of reviews were positive, in some cases ecstatic, the "given" view of the tour comes from the *Rolling Stone* articles. The essence is that this was the most calamitous road show in the history of the genre, and it showed Harrison as the talentless, boring also-ran they always suspected him to be. Testimony comes from the *Rolling Stone* review of the *Dark Horse* album and tour: "Yet it is only in the wake of his disastrous tour and *Dark Horse*, his disastrous album, that George Harrison finally stands naked. For his new record, Harrison hired a band of merely competent studio pros, saddled himself with preachy lyrics and then cut the album hoarse, his voice whining offensively, turning each idiot phrase into a prickly barb. Harrison's modest skills suddenly dwindle, overshadowed by the misplaced pride that permitted him to release such a shoddy piece of work. His guitar playing, adequate for fills within precise arrangements, has always been rudimentary and even graceless in an affecting sort of way."[15]

The effect of these reviews was to destroy Harrison's reputation as an artist until he released *Cloud 9* in 1987—he received the biggest and most persistent share of the anti ex-Beatle sentiment that pre-

[14] Richards, Emil. E-mail correspondence with author, August 2001.

[15] Miller, Jim. "George Harrison: Dark Horse (LP Review)." *Rolling Stone*: February 13, 1975, 180.

vailed in the early 1970s. And he reacted to them as personal attacks, which is hardly surprising. They were.

In 1974 Harrison had crossed a line that caused the counterculture's music press to react to his tour and album not just negatively, but as if they were acts of heresy. It wasn't just that his voice was in bad shape, which it was at the start of the tour; this went deeper. The case for the prosecution was put by *Rolling Stone*: "While *Living in the Material World* parceled out more of the same, the formula already showed strains. Harrison continued to snake his guitar through inspirational verse, but his conceits, despite airtight musical support, were beginning to ring hollow: In rock & roll, a little piety goes a long way."[16]

The root of Harrison's treachery is that he had committed the cardinal counterculture sin—he had rejected "rock 'n' roll." There were waves of revulsion underpinning reports that at one of the early dates of the tour Harrison had pointed to his Les Paul guitar—itself a gift from Eric Clapton and steeped in rock 'n' roll mythology—and said, "I would die for Indian music, but not for this." How dare he do that? Rock 'n' roll had saved Harrison from a life of working-class drudgery as an electrician in Liverpool. Why wouldn't he just play his allotted role? After all, he still looked the same as when he was a Beatle: "Here was Harrison himself, with his shag-blown hair and bell bottoms billowing, looking like a picture-perfect Beatle. *It was only natural to imagine* the guitarist ten years younger, bobbing with John, Paul and Ringo, smiling at the crowds and drinking in their adoration."[17] Was it?

The fact was that Harrison *had* rejected rock 'n' roll and moved on. He no longer saw himself as an "entertainer," and hadn't since 1967. His view of music and his role in it was now shaped by the philosophy he'd learned from Ravi Shankar: music is inextricably linked to spiritual practice—a view that was diametrically at odds with rock 'n' roll. This "religious" aspect of Harrison's approach was what most irritated the press. How could one of the leaders of the rock 'n' roll counterculture, and a working-class, first-generation Irish Catholic from Liverpool to boot, so comprehensively embrace the Hindu tradition that appeared to demand greater spiritual discipline than Western faiths? The answer lies in the fact that Hindu thought is centered on unity, not separateness—"religion" is not just for Sunday, and the

---

[16]Ibid.

[17]Ibid. Emphasis added.

music reflects this. It is a different way of thinking, neatly atomized by a leading authority, Dr. Rupert Snell, here referring to Hindu devotional songs: "To place these songs entirely within the Western category of 'religious' is to tell only half the story: in fact they reflect a culture in which 'religiousness' is not separate from everyday life, but is part and parcel of every living moment."[18]

Harrison had also embraced another aspect of Indian thinking that was at odds with the demands of being a "rock star." To a large extent art in the Indian setting is a collective act, as described by Dr. Snell in this observation about the authorship of Hindi religious poetry: "Poets composed their works within a kind of creative co-operation in which phrases and formulae were available for sharing by one and all; when the point of poetry was to describe the transcendent and to celebrate the ultimate unity of all things, claims of individuality would in any case make little sense." It is obvious that on the Dark Horse Tour Harrison reveled in the collective creative experience of working with the Western and Indian musicians. That attitude also explains why he was so reluctant to "play the star" and gave equal billing to Ravi Shankar, Billy Preston, and Tom Scott.

George Harrison's reluctance to take the limelight provoked criticism, but also was entirely predictable given the evidence of his role in the Beatles and at the Concert for Bangla Desh. There he greeted Shankar with a *pranam*, a respectful gesture of greeting made to a teacher. It involves pressing the palms together, and often bending to touch the other person's feet. Pranam is a fundamental part of the teacher-pupil relationship in India, and as Shankar was Harrison's guru, the greeting was appropriate. And while his 1971 pranam at Madison Square Garden had passed unnoticed, the sight of the "rock star" making this gesture to Shankar in 1974 was too much for some. It was interpreted as an act of hypocrisy worthy of Uriah Heep.

Little by little, piece by piece, Harrison was dismantling the image of George the ex-Beatle rock star and presenting himself just as he was. This was a characteristically daring thing to do, using his name to expose Indian music to a wide audience. But his motivations were completely and wilfully misunderstood by certain sections of the music press, unable to forgive Harrison's divergence from the rock 'n' roll myth, and the fact that he spoke and wrote songs in his native working-class idiom. Harrison was being deliberately goaded, and his

---

[18]From liner notes to Lakshmi Shankar's CD *Amrut Ras* (Audiorec, 2003). Dr. Rupert Snell is Reader in Hindi, and head of the Department of the Languages and Cultures of South Asia at the School of Oriental and African Studies (SOAS), University of London.

reaction was true to his roots:"While you attack, create offense, I'll put it down to your ignorance."[19] And falling into the trap, he was castigated further for such intemperance.

Paradoxically, while Harrison and the other Beatles had been lionized as working-class heroes, in the era of "serious rock journalism" they were equally castigated for not meeting middle-class expectations. Fortunately, some understood the Beatles' roots in Liverpool—discussing reactions to Ringo Starr's perceived mawkishness on pieces like "Good Night," Paul Du Noyer tellingly points out that, "Contempt for sentimentality is a privilege of the affluent, not the poor."[20]

Ironically, the root of this journalistic arrogance was Harrison's own friend and favorite, Bob Dylan, for it was he who unwittingly gave license for ersatz literary criticism to displace *music* criticism. And after the Dark Horse Tour, it was open season on Harrison—witness a review of his 1981 album in which one writer exposed the guitarist's clearly crippling lack of syntactical erudition:

> Throughout *Somewhere in England*, he's apt to throttle an attractive melody with mouthfuls of excess verbiage or stretch a word several syllables out of recognition to meet the demands of a tune. A really good lyricist would summon phrases that flow naturally with the music, would find a way to use the word "*hon*-est-y" without rendering it as "hon-est-*ee*-ee-ee."[21]

Much of the criticism of the Dark Horse Tour was in the same vein, to the extent that the whole escapade is better remembered for the reviews than for the music. But in retrospect, the tour was revolutionary in its presentation of Indian music, and for Harrison's refusal to pander to his own ego as a performer. Inexplicably to many, Harrison did not take himself too seriously—to close the last night at Madison Square Garden he simply said, "It'll all come out in the wash."

---

[19]Lyrics from Harrison's song "This Guitar."

[20]Du Noyer, *Liverpool: Wondrous Place*, 239.

[21]Thomas, Harry, "George Harrison: Somewhere in England (LP review)." *Rolling Stone:* August 6, 1981.

Extra Texture—Read All About It
(recorded Los Angeles, April–June 1975;
released September 1975)

Left reeling by the barbarous reaction to the *Dark Horse* album and
tour, George Harrison was back in the studio within five months of
the final Madison Square Garden concert. The haste was almost
unseemly and the choice of A&M studios in Los Angeles plain odd.
George didn't much care for the facility and its sound. Why would he
choose to cut a rehabilitation disc there?

The answer was expediency and prebooked studio time—
George wanted to cut a new album as soon as possible, to extricate
himself from the Capitol/EMI contract so that he could move on to
Dark Horse. A&M obviously wanted to get a product out under his
name to support the label, because the only money-spinner to date
was Splinter. The singing duo had been booked at A&M in early summer to cut a new album. Bob Purvis was suffering from hay fever, a
singer's nemesis, and so couldn't make the May sessions. As the cost of
cancellation would have been punitive, the solution was for George to
move in and record an album in double-quick time. All he needed was
a band.

In 1975, the Dark Horse Records roster grew to embrace four new signings: ex-Wings guitarist Henry McCullough; soulsters Stairsteps; and two troupes of Californian session men, Attitudes and Jiva. Attitudes was a neat sideline for Jim Keltner, a stalwart Harrison drummer-cum-friend, singing bass player Paul Stallworth, and pianist-arranger David Foster, who went on to write a string of hits throughout the 1970s, 1980s, and 1990s. Attitudes only managed one minor U.S. hit; A&M didn't seem too bothered with pushing George's acts. The man who ran Dark Horse for Harrison at the start, Dino Airali, thinks it was all part of the Beatle tag problem: "I felt that A&M funded to distribute a 'Beatle' on his 'Dark Horse' records label, and George wanted to do more with the label."[22] Even if the distributor was napping, George wasn't, and he was much in evidence in Los Angeles overseeing the Attitudes album. The timing was perfect, as this latest signing to Dark Horse provided a ready-made backup band, close at hand.

But during Harrison's immersion in the Los Angeles scene, with his increasing work on Dark Horse Records and this recording, some of his oldest musical partners detected some distinctly bad vibes. "I think he wasn't up for it really," muses Klaus Voormann, who played his final sessions for Harrison on *Extra Texture*. "It was a terrible time because I think there was a lot of cocaine going around, and that's when I got out of the picture. I didn't want to get into that. I didn't like his frame of mind when he was doing this album—I don't play on it too much. The whole L.A. scene turned me off playing sessions. I realised that it was the whole Hollywood thing—the problem was that if you wanted to stay in that scene, you had to hang out with those people, and go and do the clubs. It wasn't me at all. George was in it too far at the time and it was a good step of his to get out of it."

Partly due to the setting and local support for this new offering—but mostly as a reaction to the *Dark Horse* experience—Harrison completely ditched the rough-and-ready feel of that album for a slick Californian production. The commercial sound encased some hastily written ballads and catchy, pop-soul workouts. However, the bitterness and dismay weren't under control and surfaced on a number of tracks. He was clearly targeting the mainstream U.S. audience, with his least electric record to date. Replacing the slightly jarring rock sounds of *Dark Horse* were layers of keyboards, new gener-

---

[22]Airali, Dino. E-mail correspondence with the author, April 2002.

ation synthesizers, and string arrangements. There were few spiritual lyrics and absolutely no references to Krishna, while his much-criticized vocals were stronger, but recorded at a low level, as if the goal was to create a Harrison soul album for lovers.

[56] **You (3:30)** *(Harrison)*
Harrison guitar, vocal; **Ronnie Spector** vocal; **Jim Gordon** drums; **Jim Keltner** drums; **Carl Radle** bass; **Leon Russell** piano; **Gary Wright** electric piano; **David Foster** organ, synthesizer; **Jim Horn** saxophone

After *Dark Horse*, Harrison needed to produce something that generated "George Is Back" headlines, so the vaults were prised open for this ready-made hit. The most obvious of Harrison's Motown tributes, "You" was written as early as 1970 and early demos laid down at the time of *All Things Must Pass*. George tried to cut a version of it with Ronnie Spector as they were recording "Try Some Buy Some." As with that track, he dusted it off, removed her vocals, and recorded it himself.

The presence of Ronnie still looms large as Harrison tackles a vocal at the edge of his range and honors her with his version of her style.[23] "You" has the same surging spirit as "Dancing in the Street" or "Heatwave" and, as the lyrics are full of boy-meets-girl triteness, the groove is what carries it. The song was a good-sized hit and is a convincing tribute in pastiche to a much-loved style and a great pop record.

[57] **The Answer's at the End (5:30)** *(Harrison)*
Harrison guitar, vocal; **Jim Keltner** drums; **Gary Wright** organ; **David Foster** piano, string arrangement; **Paul Stallworth** bass; **Norm Kinney** percussion

Quickly dispensing with the demands of hit making, *Extra Texture* moves into a mellow, reflective soul mood with this ballad, and remains there. Although lambasted at the time for its cool tempo, "The Answer's at the End" is an interesting song. It ponders the nature of relationships in much the same way as Dylan's *Blood on the Tracks*, except that Harrison has reached a more conciliatory frame of mind than is suggested by Dylan's "Tangled up in Blue."

---

[23]Madinger and Easter (page 452) rightly point out that Harrison left a snippet of Ronnie Spector's original vocal on the final track.

However, by reducing his quest for philosophical certainty to a plea for tolerance, Harrison appears to be retrenching, setting out less fervently than he did on *All Things Must Pass* and *Living in the Material World*. It's a defeated, or wiser, George who begs indulgence for his "foibles" and attenuates the search for universal solutions to a simpler, earthbound observation: "Don't be so hard on the ones that you love, it's the ones that you love, we think so little of." This attitude represents a deliberate tempering of tone rather than a change in fundamental beliefs.

But the old, bold George is no more. The certainties of "The Lord Loves the One" seem to have dissipated. A battered Harrison sounds like he has no answers. The passionate searcher of "Hear Me Lord" sounds defeated, asking for a little "live and let live."

These paradoxes are tracked by warm sonic scenes. On an album of soul influences, here George takes just one look back to the Doris Troy session for some rising gospel inflections and a pair of smoochy codas. For these, George performed semiscats, gospel style, over sundown jazz piano. Such seductive grooves did not impress the critics. But for Doris Troy, Harrison's vocals are a partner to his personality: "It was just his style. Some people blast it out, but he had a mellow sound, because he was mellow. The music was just like how he was."

[58] **This Guitar (Can't Keep from Crying) (4:11)** *(Harrison)*
Harrison guitars, vocal, bass synthesizer; **Jim Keltner** drums;
Gary Wright synthesizer; **David Foster** piano, string arrangement;
Jesse Ed Davis guitar

One of the features of *Dark Horse* that most incensed the music press was the desiderata that appeared on the border of the album's inside cover. This was seen as a plea for critical indulgence from an artist who knew that he was releasing a substandard product (it was actually a desiderata from a Victorian map of Friar Park's gardens). Against that background, the lyrics of "This Guitar" were bound to cause more gnashing of journalistic teeth.

In his usual, painfully open way, Harrison uses "This Guitar" to ask his detractors to remember that behind the savaged performer at Madison Square Garden in December 1974 was a real human being. George had never been an actor, and this honesty was what had given *All Things Must Pass* such great power. But it also meant that he was bound to fight back against what he saw as unfair, malicious criticism.

This harrowing song attempts to present a George Harrison with a split personality, the private man versus the musician—the latter personified by his guitar. The inner man is "happier than he's ever been," but the musician, in six-string shape, is wounded and nearly beaten by the hammering of 1974. However, a lyricist as honest as Harrison cannot sustain this artifice for long. It's clear that the pain is his personally, and he flays his detractors with accusations of "ignorance" and "hate." Harrison's candor in his lyrics, which almost form an open diary, always left him vulnerable—ditto Neil Young on his "Ambulance Blues" from the previous year.[24]

George's vocal is unusually passionate and powerful, while on the guitar track he picks Pete Drake stylings against his more familiar glissandos, with one section in particular recalling the raga microtones. But naming and shaming music papers was no recipe for good reviews and the song was inevitably trashed.

[59] Ooh Baby (You Know That I Love You) (3:50) *(Harrison)*
Harrison guitar, vocal; **Klaus Voormann** bass; **Jim Keltner** drums; **Gary Wright** electric piano; **Jesse Ed Davis** guitar; **Tom Scott** horns; **Chuck Findley** horns

One of the brighter moments of Harrison's Los Angeles press conference to launch the Dark Horse Tour came when he was asked to name his favorite pop musician. He answered with wild enthusiasm: Smokey Robinson. Hence, "Ooh Baby," a spiritual brother to Robinson's own "Ooh Baby Baby."

George's interest in soul was hardly a secret; "Far East Man" had already seen him traversing the soul road. Cushioned by Gary Wright's chiffon electric piano and Tom Scott's balmy horn charts, George turns out his best Smokey impersonation, almost going falsetto. All manner of subtle chord voices are used—elegant, jazzy thirteenths and major ninths add a little chiaroscuro to the musical seduction. However, the main point of "Ooh Baby" was that it would not offend anybody and perhaps have crossover appeal to the R&B audience.

[60] World of Stone (4:46) *(Harrison)*
Harrison guitar, vocal; **Klaus Voormann** bass; **Jim Keltner** drums; **Gary Wright** organ; **Jesse Ed Davis** guitar; **David Foster** piano, synthesizer

---

[24]A song from *On the Beach* that dismisses his detractors for being "no better than me" and includes the lines: "I never knew a man could tell so many lies, he had a different story for every set of eyes. How can he remember who he's talking to, 'cos I know it ain't me and I hope it isn't you."

When the Beatles hit it big around 1963, one of the many aspects of fame they were unprepared for was their reincarnation as healers. In extraordinarily bizarre scenes, they were presented with children suffering terrible disabilities, in the hope that just being in the presence of the Beatles would effect some Lourdes-style miracle cure. It was a new peak of fanaticism.

Once Timothy Leary had pulled himself out of his purple haze to describe the Fab Four as the "avatars" of the age, they were recast as the bearers of fundamental spiritual truths. If religion, capitalism, or communism could provide no answers, the Beatles were a no-lose option. The record companies hardly complained. The mythmaking added to the magic and, hardly coincidentally, the sales.

However, in the 1970s, there were spiritually minded musicians who went so far as to bless their audiences, as if they were gurus. Three years before *Extra Texture*, Joni Mitchell was forced to ask: "All this talk about holiness now, is it just the latest style, do you really feel it?" "World of Stone" contains George's answer to this question: "Don't follow me." For anyone listening, this was as clear a statement of ordinariness as was possible. Harrison was gently pointing out that rock stars have no cure for the world's spiritual malaise. As the song goes on to reveal, he even doubted his own epiphanies. The lines "the wiser you can be, the harder it can be to see" contain the usual Harrison ambiguity. It's either another play on the blind seer idea or a complete rejection of the insights of "The Inner Light," namely that knowledge is the key to enlightenment. Alternatively, it might just have been another dig at smartass rock journalists. Again, as he did with "The Answer's at the End," Harrison makes a plea for tolerance: "We all have the right to be" in the world of stone. Of course, that world is the material world under another guise.

Musically, "World of Stone" continues Harrison's walk along the soulful path, not least through the gospel flourishes from Gary Wright's Hammond. The song uses the "Bangla Desh" formula—a slow explanatory introduction followed by a stomping rocker—except that "World of Stone" is more softshoe shuffle than stomp, a piece that once again runs into the smooth, arrhythmic zones that are a feature of *Extra Texture*.

[61] **A Bit More of You (0:45)** *(Harrison)*
Harrison guitar; **Jim Gordon** drums; **Jim Keltner** drums;
Carl Radle bass; **Leon Russell** piano; **Gary Wright** electric piano;
David Foster organ, synthesizer; **Jim Horn** saxophone

Little more than a minute's filler of a saxophone solo from "You," this cut does nothing other than fashion a soul mood for the next song.

[62] **Can't Stop Thinking About You (4:30)** *(Harrison)*
Harrison guitar, vocal; **Jim Keltner** drums; **Klaus Voormann** bass; **Nicky Hopkins** piano; **David Foster** electric piano, string arrangement; **Gary Wright** synthesizer; **Jesse Ed Davis** guitar; **Paul Stallworth** backup vocal

No song on *Extra Texture* speaks more of the need to be commercially acceptable, to forget the ragged rock of *Dark Horse*, than "Can't Stop Thinking About You," Harrison's most obvious new pop cut since "Don't Let Me Wait Too Long." Here he is positively desperate to reach for insignificance, endlessly repeating the simple mantra over a soul-pop backing. This repetition makes the number very much a part of the period: War had a massive U.S. hit the same year with "Why Can't We Be Friends," a funk groove that mostly repeated the title over and over again. The source for this 1970s slogan-shouting was Sly Stone, with his family of chanted hook lines: "Dance to the Music" and "I Want to Take You Higher."

The arrangement aped the currently fashionable Philly Soul sound; hence the lush strings, pop-gospel chord sequences, and richly worked backup vocals. The latter featured Attitudes' bass man Paul Stallworth and were the most intricate Harrison had produced since *The Place I Love*. The overall effect was pop-soul fluff, which is all it was meant to be. The song was obviously written to be a single, which makes it doubly puzzling that it wasn't released as one.

[63] **Tired of Midnight Blue (4:50)** *(Harrison)*
Harrison guitar, vocal; **Jim Keltner** drums; **Paul Stallworth** bass; **Leon Russell** piano

An introvert's rejection of the "rock 'n' roll" life, this swampy mood piece makes clear that Harrison was not about to make the tabloids' day by being seen dispatching televisions from hotel bedroom windows. Not for him the drunken brawls in swimming pools or prodigious feats of sexual athleticism that force names and pictures on the front pages of newspapers—and boost album sales.

It would be the height of naïveté to assume that George Harrison was never compromised by the temptations on offer. *Dark Horse* had partly catalogued Harrison's bad-boy year of 1974, "Simply Shady" in particular being a tale of "booze and birds." "Tired of Midnight Blue," the best song on *Extra Texture*, is the reaction, and it summarizes

George's intention to head back to his English garden and the comfort of family life. Its general similarity to "Bangla Desh" might be explained by Leon Russell's tumbleweed piano. But, as a more soulful develop-ment of his early 1970s Southern rock, the track explores new avenues for Harrison. The smoky, bluesy mood is largely created by the heavy use of strong seventh chords as the root. A simple, effective arrangement, "Tired of Midnight Blue" is the only *Extra Texture* cut with a live feel. Had Harrison not been cast into the critical wilder-ness, the song might have met a better reception.

[64] **Grey Cloudy Lies (3:41)** *(Harrison)*
Harrison guitar, vocal, bass synthesizer; **Jim Keltner** drums;
David Foster piano; **Jesse Ed Davis** guitar

Acknowledging his critical unpopularity, Harrison dubbed himself OHNOTHIMAGEN[25] on the *Extra Texture* inner sleeve. Releasing slow-tempo compositions like "Grey Cloudy Lies" hardly helped, espe-cially as its subject matter was depression. This miserable song opens with the same chord sequence as Billy Preston's Apple hit "That's the Way God Planned It" but is emotionally a million miles away from that stirring gospel mood.

The ambience here is simple despair. It's George's "Not Waving but Drowning," where would-be musical drama is unable to cover for slurred vocals and disturbing candor. Images of life as a "battlefield" and an apparent courting of death through a desire to "padlock the night" make for an uncomfortable few minutes. Even though Leonard Cohen and, later, the Smiths made a living from songs about depres-sion, the justification for recording a piece like this on what was ostensibly an entertainment product is questionable. This is one of the few Harrisongs that would have been better left in the can.

[65] **His Name Is Legs (Ladies & Gentlemen) (5:45)** *(Harrison)*
Harrison vocal, guitars, piano; **Billy Preston** electric piano;
David Foster piano; **Tom Scott** horns; **Chuck Findley** horns;
Willie Weeks bass; **Andy Newmark** drums; **Legs Larry "Smith"**
guest vocal

Every show on Harrison's Dark Horse Tour opened with the strains of Monty Python's Flying Circus yomping out of the loudspeakers. "The Lumberjack Song" subverted image and reality in a way that must have appealed to the star of the show, who was forever struggling to fend

---

[25]Oh, not him again.

off his Beatle George cipher. The Lumberjack is the archetypal all-action hard man. This one actually favors transvestism and the gay bar scene, while George Harrison is a supposed "mop top" who just wanted to be left alone to record his gospel-bhajans.

It was George himself who produced the Python recording of "The Lumberjack Song"—and eventually bailed the team out with the money to make the epochal *Life of Brian*. So it's no surprise to discover that he is an exponent of nonsense word games, Python's stock in trade. Hence: "His Name Is Legs." Curiously, for all the Krishna invocations (and there are actually fewer than fifteen in his entire catalogue), this is the most self-indulgent of George Harrison's songs. Written as a tribute to friend and ex-Bonzo Dog, "Legs" Larry Smith, it's a six-minute in joke, set in the funk-rock sound of the Dark Horse Tour. Its failure is that it engenders no reaction of any sort.

The truth about *Extra Texture* is that it's a largely one-paced, unsatisfactory muddle. It aims to please with the soul-pop workouts "You," "Ooh Baby," and "Can't Stop Thinking About You"—songs designed to rehabilitate Harrison's pop status—while it takes rock writers to task for their negative reaction to his recent music. This was an era when musicians publicly pondered the universe and their careers with the music press, as if they were all part of an artistic "community." It explains the savagely personal nature of the attack on Harrison that *Rolling Stone* ran in the guise of a review of *Dark Horse*. It would have taken the patience of a saint to have suffered this treatment in silence! John Lennon was known for his dialogue with the music press, as were Joni Mitchell and Neil Young, so it was not especially unusual for *Extra Texture* to include two tracks giving Harrison's response to his critics, "This Guitar" and "World of Stone." Sandwiched between these two extremes were a personal joke ("His Name Is Legs") and two slabs of introspection ("The Answer's at the End" and "Grey Cloudy Lies") that were part calls for tolerance and part expression of downright despair. The only piece that really worked from every angle was "Tired of Midnight Blue."

Unlike the scattershot sessions that populated *Dark Horse*, the arrangements on *Extra Texture* were cohesive, the record had a "sound": it tended toward moody, piano-driven soul-jazz, with little room for guitar narrative. Needless to say, George's voice was restored, and in "The Answer's at the End" he tried his hand for the first time at evocative, soul-bar scat singing. The downside was that the engineering produced an unusual, muffled sound that deepened the slightly downcast atmosphere.

Setting aside the welcome hit status for "You" and a return to the British album charts, the response to *Extra Texture* was only slightly less vituperative than the one *Dark Horse* had received. George was declared plain "boring" and the LP certainly suffered by comparison with Dylan's *Blood on the Tracks,* hailed as an instant classic. George's disc was certainly no landmark, but it was the first of his releases to lack passion. Even though some of the melodies were stirring, it sounded like Harrison was punch drunk.

Although *Extra Texture* made #8 on *Billboard*, the inescapable conclusion was that a mood of gloom surrounded the entire venture. Harrison probably had more pleasure resuming his life as a session player. A cameo for Tom Scott's smooth urban-jazz *New York Connection* album set the tone for *Thirty-three & 1/3,* which was also partially presaged by Billy Preston's soft-funk, *It's My Pleasure.* Harrison plays the Wah-Wah Watson role on "That's Life," a song that might have been Preston's words of consolation for his friend's 1974 traumas.[26]

Harrison and Preston also teamed up for the release—at last—of the Splinter number that first captured the guitarist's ear, "Lonely Man." This classic pop melody was sung beautifully on the Dark Horse album *Harder to Live,* which appeared in November along with a rush of other products from Harrison's label. George had enlisted Tom Scott to produce and arrange. Featuring more quality writing, notably "Which Way Will I Get Home," a song that Harrison thought was a sure-fire hit, *Harder to Live* isn't as successful as *The Place I Love,* partly because Scott's arrangements were geared toward period studio funk. "Lonely Man" benefited from a top-notch Harrison production and went on to achieve cult status in Japan—eventually the Splinter guys delivered a version in Japanese. But the U.S. promotion of *Harder to Live* didn't quite work, and the obvious hit potential of the gorgeous "Which Way Will I Get Home" was not realized. Still, "Lonely Man" retains a charm that should make it indispensable for Harrison fans.

---

[26]Wah-Wah Watson is a legendary R&B rhythm guitar player.

The moderate melancholy of his last Apple album was still hanging over Harrison as he devoted time to his Dark Horse record label at its base within A&M's studios in smog-ridden Los Angeles. Running Dark Horse on a daily basis was Dino Airali, who was also connected to Leon Russell's Shelter label. Harrison was working with a new Dark Horse signing, the soul group Stairsteps, marshalled by hit-writing legend Keni Burke,[27] when Airali introduced him to a Californian singer-songwriter with a talent for witty wordsmithing. Airali had the idea after a conversation with the star that revealed Harrison's frustrations with his image: "George told me, 'I just want to be a guitarist and do record gigs and not have people hold me up as a Beatle.' So I asked George to play on an album I was producing for Shelter Records—the artist was Larry Hosford. George sang harmonies and played his signature guitar licks. What a treat!"

Larry Hosford hailed from Salinas (the hometown of another slightly more famous American scribe, John Steinbeck), and his music was steeped in American folk and country traditions but not bound by them. As the media flak for *Extra Texture* was still warm on the walls, Hosford was cutting his second album, *Cross Words*. Harrison liked what he heard and asked to add some slide to "Direct Me," a cat-gets-mouse barroom romance, and backing vocals to "Wishing I Could." Almost thirty years later, Hosford still has a strong recollection of Harrison's studio demeanor: "George is pretty–laid back, played sitting down. Absorbed? Oh, yes, and very focused on getting his stuff right, very intent, not in any way nervous. He knew what he was doing, was prepared. Experience showed. A take-one guy. In the 'stu' he did a slide thing for me, yes, wasn't playing conventionally, but I elsewhere enjoyed watching the serpentine finger work that most great guitarists possess. Smooth moves. George is not a herky-jerky player. Vocally, on 'Wishing I Could,' I was most impressed with how much he seemed to enjoy the sport. I tell folks straight-faced: 'Three-part harmony didn't seem to hold much mystery for him.'"[28]

The result was a shimmering dobro dialogue throughout "Direct Me" that Hosford stills muses on: "He doesn't clone himself tune to tune. But the licks are recognizably within the scope of what we've come to know and expect of him musically: tasty, confident, toneworthy, original, apt, well rendered—those things are, to me, his 'signa-

---

[27]Stairsteps were the renamed Five Stairsteps, who had a million-selling 1970 hit, "O-o-h Child," and were introduced to Harrison by Billy Preston. Their first Dark Horse album, *2nd Resurrection*, produced a Top 10 hit on the R&B charts, "From Us to You."

[28]Hosford, Larry. E-mail correspondence with author, November 2001.

ture.' Nobody I know has ever heard 'Direct Me' and said, 'That doesn't sound like George Harrison.' They say, 'That's him, all right.'"

Like many others, Hosford was struck by the star's contradictory Piscean nature, a mixture of charisma and unassuming ordinariness. "He was 'aurafied.' I have met many, many celebrities, and it wasn't that—not just a star-struck moment. And it wasn't like some colorful-haze-all-about-his-head-and-shoulders, fortune-teller deal either. Maybe it was born of arcane cosmic or psychic phenomenon on his part (or mine), but I did in fact perceive a glow, a shimmer, a something.... It wasn't there every time I looked, yet it was recurrent. Yet, he seemed to be the only one around who wasn't aware he was a superstar of unprecedented magnitude, though I am sure we can assume he was. Everything I know about him defines a bona fide, good-natured human."

[66] **The Pirate Song (2:17)** *(Harrison) (Rutland Weekend TV)* **Harrison** guitar, vocal; **Neil Innes** guitar; **Billy Bremner** guitar; **Roger Rettig** pedal steel; **Brian Hodgson** bass; **John Halsey** drums[29]

When he wasn't called on to play "George Harrison," the guitarist's innate humor flourished. The good nature of the man who dubbed himself OHNOTHIMAGEN, was also in evidence in a cameo appearance for a Monty Python offshoot. Shortly before he created the Rutles, Eric Idle hosted a television comedy show, *Rutland Weekend Television*. For the closing piece of an episode in December 1975, George Harrison sent up his dour media image by turning what looked like a star turn singing "My Sweet Lord" into a sea shanty. Where "The Lumberjack Song" had expressed a yearning to be a "girly," in "The Pirate Song" Harrison just wants to sail away, as he did on "Sunshine Life for Me." Eric Idle, as the greasy host of *Rutland Weekend Television*, tries to eject Harrison for refusing to play the part of George Harrison. As with the Rutles, there was great resonance within these gags.

---

[29]In the *Rutland Weekend Television* series these musicians were collectively known as "Fatso." John Halsey went on to Rutles fame.

Thirty-three & 1/3
(recorded Friar Park, May–September 1976;
released November 1976)

The background to one of Harrison's sunniest albums was, ironically, one of his most turbulent years. But, unlike in 1974, he rode out the storm and produced a fine work.

Already enthusiastic about the "new start" promised by his move from Apple to Dark Horse, he was hard at work on Friar Park sessions with regulars Tom Scott, Billy Preston, Emil Richards, Gary Wright, and Willie Weeks. Added to these were the tough, urban grooves of electric keys man Richard Tee and drummer Alvin Taylor. It was a strong dose of New York street power. Unfortunately, in the middle of the sessions Harrison experienced another strong dose, this time of hepatitis. Months were knocked off the schedule. A&M, who'd bankrolled Dark Horse Records for two years waiting for a Harrison product, ran out of patience and pulled the plug on the star and his label—and launched a $10 million lawsuit. The matter was settled out of court and Harrison relocated along the strip to the tender arms of Mo Ostin at Warner Brothers.

But Harrison wasn't out of the lawyers' clutches yet. September also found him in court, to hear judgment passed on whether "My Sweet Lord" had been plagiarized from an early 1960s pop-soul hit, "He's So Fine." Delaney Bramlett had been called to give evidence, to relate how the song was born in Scandinavia during the Clapton tour. He couldn't make it and Bonnie Bramlett's evidence was deemed inadmissible, so Harrison was on his own and lost the case. According to Delaney, being found guilty of subconscious plagiarism was a terrible blow to Harrison: "It killed him."

Despite these travails, and with Tom Scott's help in the control booth encouraging Harrison to play long guitar solos, George's career on his own label was launched with verve and panache.

[67] **Woman Don't You Cry for Me (3:15)** *(Harrison)*
Harrison vocal, guitars; **Willie Weeks** bass; **Alvin Taylor** drums;
David Foster clavinet; **Richard Tee** keyboards; **Tom Scott** horns

The first seconds of *Thirty-three & 1/3* reveal a renewed George Harrison. The murky sound of *Extra Texture* is replaced with a flowing, open production, and the slapped-bass sound that begins "Woman Don't You Cry for Me" recalls Larry Graham, Stanley Clark, and The Brothers Johnson. With the patented Stevie Wonder stabbing Clavinet, a contemporary sound is born.

The song is actually a throwback to Harrison's days with Don Nix and Delaney & Bonnie; harmonically, the track's monochord simplicity returns to the days of skiffle, when one chord really was all you needed to get rocking. The neutral lyric tends a little toward impersonal macho swagger, but the main point here is Harrison's extravagant Southern-inflected slide that lets rip on a series of blues-shaped licks.

After the turbulence of *Dark Horse* and *Extra Texture*, the cheery slickness of "Woman Don't You Cry for Me" was very welcome. Coupled with a standard-setting guitar showcase, it announced that Harrison was back.

[68] **Dear One (5:08)** *(Harrison)*
Harrison vocal, guitars, synthesiser; **Willie Weeks** bass;
Alvin Taylor drums; **Richard Tee** organ

Harrison's admiration for Joni Mitchell drew him to her famous London concerts as he was recording the flawed *Dark Horse* album in April 1974. Mitchell is an underrated and innovative guitarist who routinely uses open guitar tunings to achieve different resonances within chord voices.[30] For the happy "Dear One," Harrison follows the Mitchell tradition, with an open A tuning that is partly the reason for the ringing sound of the piece.

The subject matter, Indian yogi Paramhansa Yogananda,[31] is esoteric by Western standards but delivered with enough honest joy to recall Harrison's early '70s gospel period. Fittingly, Billy Preston's Hammond is prominent in the mix. The bouncy chorus, reminiscent of the Kashmiri party atmosphere of "It Is He," is set to a calypso rhythm, complete with Emil Richards' mellow steel drums.

One of Yogananda's teachings was on the role of the musician in India: "Indian music is a subjective, spiritual and individualistic art, aiming not at symphonic brilliance but at personal harmony with God. The Sanskrit word for musician is *bhagavathar*, 'he who sings the praises of God.'"[32] "Dear One" is the result of George Harrison's close identification with that philosophy of music.

[69] **Beautiful Girl (3:38)** *(Harrison)*
Harrison vocal, guitars; **Billy Preston** organ; **Willie Weeks** bass; **Alvin Taylor** drums; **Richard Tee** piano

The positive mood of *Thirty-three & 1/3* continues with a pretty guitar ballad that could have appeared on a Beatles album—unlike most of Harrison's solo work. "Beautiful Girl" is full of guitar arpeggios[33] and vocal harmonies that might have come straight from *Rubber Soul*, albeit updated with a 1970s production and the singer's own beguiling guitar statements.

The song has no particular meaning or importance, it just creates the general pleasantness that would also characterize the *George Harrison* album. Most interestingly, it is another of George's songs in search of a chorus. To an extent, this characterises his approach to songwriting. Many of his best pieces—"Isn't It a Pity," "Beware of

---

[30]Open tuning means that the guitar strings are not left in the standard tuning (E, A, D, G, B, E) but tuned so that when they are strummed without any fingering, a complete chord is heard. Mitchell also used the technique to make it more difficult for her imitators to copy her style.

[31]Yogananda's book *Autobiography of a Yogi* was the first to emerge from the subcontinent that recorded in detail the spiritual life of India, from a Hindu perspective. Paramhansa Yogananda was the first Indian yogi to travel to the West spreading Indian yoga techniques.

[32] Yogananda, Paramhansa. *Autobiography of a Yogi*.

[33]The rolling guitar chords that open the song recall "So Far" from the *Doris Tory* album—indeed, "Beautiful Girl" was written during the making of that LP.

Darkness," and "Give Me Love" to name three—have no radio-friendly "we can work it out" or "the night they drove old Dixie down" refrain. In all these songs, the verse *is* the primary melodic foundation.

On "Beautiful Girl," the main musical hook comes with the first line of the piece, and all the musical themes head back inexorably to that resolution. So the attractive, rising middle eight leads not to a catchy chorus but to a clever descending series of guitar runs that return to the verse. In that sense, this is an obvious album track, never destined for chart success. The song is boosted by two excellent countermelody guitar breaks which, in the coda, even run at a counterpoint to the countermelody. Harrison's melodic gifts have rarely been better showcased.

[70] **This Song (4:11)** *(Harrison)*
Harrison vocal, guitars, percussion; **Billy Preston** keyboards;
Tom Scott saxophone; **Willie Weeks** bass; **Alvin Taylor** drums;
Richard Tee piano; **Eric Idle** cameo voices

On "Dark Horse," Harrison dubbed himself the loner who couldn't be controlled—an elusive, cheeky maverick who was never quite what people thought. The same Dark Horse is back on *Thirty-three & 1/3*, with a song that makes light of his travails in court with "My Sweet Lord." With puns, word games, and even a pair of Eric Idle's silly voices, George satirizes the whole legal process in a less aggressive fashion than he did on "Sue Me, Sue You Blues." He sounds like he's having fun, and the supporting video clip borders on the riotous.

Musically, the track is tight, with George back in his 1974 funk groove. An infectious R&B riff (Paul Simon used it in "Gone at Last"), honky-tonk piano, stabbing horns, and the odd burst from Billy Preston's swirling Hammond put the funky chicken into George's gospel-rock. Tom Scott is prominent here, not just through his "perfect as usual" solo but also in the arrangement, which transplants Harrison to New York and surrounds him with hard groovers like Richard Tee and Willie Weeks. Harrison's guitar break underlines his own ability to create short, memorable, infinitely "hummable" solos. As if to underline the point, Harrison sings the first bars of his break.

"This Song" shows George working hard to keep in fashion Stateside. The fact that his *Thirty-three & 1/3* band was almost entirely composed of African Americans created a funky sound in keeping with the increasing commercial potency of War and Earth, Wind and Fire. Sometimes referred to as a comeback hit, the song actually missed the British charts entirely and stalled at #15 on *Billboard*. Certainly a neat piece of gospel-rock, but as on "Beautiful Girl" the hook was not quite catchy enough to produce a major success.

[71] **See Yourself (2:48)** *(Harrison)*
Harrison vocal, guitars, percussion; **Gary Wright** keyboards;
Billy Preston keyboards; **Willie Weeks** bass; **Alvin Taylor** drums;
Richard Tee keyboards

The synthesizer's inexorable rise to prominence was given a major boost by one of George Harrison's best friends, Gary Wright, with his 1975 megahit "Dream Weaver." After twenty-five years, it is hard to imagine a time when synths did not exist. But when Wright put out *The Dream Weaver*, recorded with just electronic keyboards and drums, it was a minor musical revolution. The future started to look bad for guitar heroes—from Moroder's diva disco all the way to the bizarre world of Kraftwerk, the synthesizer was king and guitars were dead. This was not alien territory for Harrison, though. Seven years earlier, he'd kindly shared a full forty minutes of Moog doodlings on the execrable *Electronic Sound* and far more pleasant efforts on "Here Comes the Sun."

Gary Wright's influence had been a strong feature of *Extra Texture*, which was awash with Arp Moog textures. However, "See Yourself" was the first Harrisong basically arranged for synthesizers. Even though a repeating synthesizer line provides the song's hook, this is the least interesting track on *Thirty-three & 1/3*. The arrangement is too ponderous and can't save a mostly bland melody. The lyrics, too, retrace familiar Harrison themes of individual choice versus responsibility ("Run of the Mill"), selfishness, false words, and false friends ("Isn't It a Pity"). Rhythmically, it's quite adventurous, flitting between standard rock 4/4 time and stuttering, staccato 9/8, a time signature fit for the Mahavishnu Orchestra!

[72] **It's What You Value (5:05)** *(Harrison)*
Harrison vocal, guitars, percussion; **Tom Scott** horns; **Willie Weeks** bass; **Alvin Taylor** drums; **Richard Tee** piano; **Emil Richards** marimba

Another of the failed hits on *Thirty-three & 1/3* is this upbeat effort, in the same groove as "This Song." The influence of Tom Scott's arrangement is particularly strong—the mood is very similar to his own *New York Connection* album, on which Harrison played and which, as the title suggests, is an archetype of the urban, New York studio sound. Harrison's album had a little of that flavor, not least because it featured another key mover on the New York studio scene, Richard Tee, veteran of hundreds of recordings. His lithe piano riff opens "It's What You Value." For once, George sings about generalities rather than himself on this "good-time" workout. Unfortunately, his snappy reflection on relativity was never going to trouble the charts.

[73] **True Love (2:43)** *(Cole Porter)*
Harrison vocal, guitars; **Willie Weeks** bass; **Alvin Taylor** drums;
David Foster electric piano; **Richard Tee** organ

George Harrison as "crooner" is some way from the introvert of *Living in the Material World* and *Dark Horse*. So the inclusion of an up-tempo version of a Hollywood standard can only have been a little personal joke, akin to "His Name Is Legs." This cover took Harrison back to the Beatles' days in Hamburg; it was one of the film tunes they thrashed out, in the eclectic approach that eventually set the group apart. Not only did it demonstrate their incredible versatility, it also gave the Beatles a richer knowledge of harmony than the competition. Freed from the simple patterns of basic rhythm and blues, young George Harrison soon knew more than the requisite three rock 'n' roll chords. This Bing Crosby standard was part of the young guitarist's education.

Years away from Hamburg, in 1976 Harrison and Scott treat "True Love" to a dense arrangement, crammed with slide riffs and multiple keyboards, while George just about manages to keep a straight face on a decent vocal. Warner decided to put this out as a single in the U.K., where it inevitably failed to chart. But at least it gave George the chance to ham it up for the cameras in another comical video shoot.

[74] **Pure Smokey (3:52)** *(Harrison)*
Harrison vocal, guitars; **Tom Scott** horns; **Willie Weeks** bass;
Alvin Taylor drums; **David Foster** keyboards; **Richard Tee** keyboards

This attractive exemplar of George Harrison's soul style is the most successful, and succinct, summation of his attachment to the genre. "Pure Smokey" resonates with the warmth of Harrison's affection for Smokey Robinson, in a late-night smooch cushioned by Tee's electric piano and some empathetic horn arrangements. Emerging from the same period as "Far East Man" and "Ooh Baby," the track reflected many years' flipping of Atlantic and Stax classics, as well as his late 1960s work with Billy Preston and Doris Troy.

George is at his best as a guitarist, and his guitar rings very true on "Pure Smokey." Two fine solos summarize his understated, melodic approach. Putting his bottleneck aside, he shows that he knows how to milk bent blues notes to great effect, in a nod to Eric Clapton, but with added Carl Perkins twang.

A fact often overlooked is that none of the other Beatles came close to offering convincing soul moods, whereas they were a fundamental part of the Dark Horse's musical vocabulary. In any context, "Pure Smokey" is one of its author's most appealing songs.

[75] **Crackerbox Palace (3:52)** *(Harrison)*
Harrison vocal, guitars; **Willie Weeks** bass; **Alvin Taylor** drums; **Tom Scott** lyricon, horns; **Richard Tee** keyboards; **Emil Richards** marimba

This jaunty curiosity was the biggest American hit delivered by *Thirty-three & 1/3*. To promote it, Harrison constructed a cheery video set in his own Friar Park home to emphasize the song's "house as the world" metaphor.

This film underscores some of the contradictions and tensions in the guitarist's life as a celebrity. He was fiercely, but understandably, protective of his privacy. Nevertheless, here he puts out a video that is virtually a guided tour of his home and garden. The viewer is shown the main entrance hall, the ballroom, and a bedroom complete with four-poster bed. Moving outside, the camera pans over lakes, woods, and grounds to such a degree that it becomes almost a promotional film for day trips to the "George Harrison Theme Park," complete with the *All Things Must Pass* gnomes. This was the celluloid realization of the "Let It Roll" script. After all, Friar Park was a ready-made movie set.

The explanation might be that Harrison related so strongly to Friar Park that it had become inextricably intertwined with his own identity. The house was primarily his refuge, and its past was also caught up in the same Pisces paradox as its owner. It had been constructed by an eccentric Victorian lawyer with a taste for word games but had passed into the hands of Catholic nuns before George moved in. So "Sue Me, Sue You Blues" and "Hear Me Lord" were both equally at home in the house. Friar Park was also literally a monument to English eccentricity and the nation's general obsession with gardening. It was as if Friar Park were part of the creative act.

[76] **Learning How to Love You (4:15)** *(Harrison)*
Harrison vocal, guitars; **Tom Scott** horns, flute; **Willie Weeks** bass;
Alvin Taylor drums; **David Foster** keyboards; **Richard Tee**
keyboards

Harrison's ballad writing reached a new peak of sophistication with a
composition he considered his best since "Something." Like the *Abbey
Road* classic, the main theme is constructed around a chord pattern
that, every bar, steps down one semitone within the root chord. But
the melody here is longer and subtler than its predecessor's. The middle eight reflects the writer's musical erudition, with subtle musical
colors invoked by chic major ninth chords, supported by a neat jazz
arrangement from Scott.

"Learning How to Love You" captures George Harrison in confident and refined form. Musically, lyrically, and vocally polished, it also
features a rare, beautifully flowing and technically accomplished
acoustic guitar solo. Unfortunately, by 1976 the critics were simply
uninterested in Harrison's music, so the song has not received the
plaudits it deserves. Nevertheless, Paul McCartney might have been
listening. If he was, he might have experienced a twinge of envy.

George Harrison approached *Thirty-three & 1/3* with as much energy
as he'd put into *All Things Must Pass*. It was a renewal: Harrison
almost regarded it as the launch of a new career with new partners
Warner Brothers. The escape from the clutches of Capitol was very
welcome, as he'd found the label increasingly constricting. The result
was the last Harrison album to ape prevailing trends in the U.S. market, which explains the wide variety of its arrangements. Despite the
calculated musical references to soul, Southern rock, funk, a jazzy ballad, reggae, funk, and synth pop, the album is one of Harrison's best.
The mood is upbeat, the songs generally strong, the vocals "on," and
the guitar playing restored to its rightful prominence. Had it been
released in 1974, his career might have taken a different path.

As far as the critics were concerned, it wasn't quite good
enough. Harrison had virtually axed philosophical musings from the
disc, and the rebuke was that *Thirty-three & 1/3* was lightweight. This
was the same problem Joni Mitchell faced when she released *Wild
Things Run Fast* (also the first album on a new label) in 1982. While
its studio predecessor, *Mingus,* was considered too "jazz," it was too
"pop." Harrison in 1976 was also struggling with the tension between

creating a product that would move units and being true to his inspiration. Having been pilloried for letting his philosophical muse run off the leash on *Living in the Material World*, he naturally reined it in for this new album.

Thirty-three & 1/3 certainly lacks the emotional clout of *Material World* and *All Things Must Pass*: it is simply a statement of Harrison's ability to create well-played, well-sung, and well-written, upbeat music. It was an album in the tradition of his great pop-rock songs "What Is Life" and "Don't Let Me Wait Too Long"—a companion piece to Dylan's *Planet Waves* or Paul Simon's *Still Crazy After All These Years*. It also had, in "Learning How to Love You," one of Harrison's finest love songs. Another finally emerged from a six-year hibernation in September 1976, when Ringo Starr delivered his last chart album to date, *Ringo's Rotogravure*.

[77] **I'll Still Love You (2:55)** *(Harrison) (recorded by Ringo Starr)*
Ringo Starr vocals; *Harrison not present on recording*

Also known as "When Every Song Is Sung," this piece was written on the piano during a session to routine songs for *All Things Must Pass*. Its genesis explains the harmonic similarity to "Something"—this song has the same descending semitone pattern. The harsher, dramatic middle eight is also in the *Abbey Road* song's mold, while the basic melody has the same circularity found on "The Light That Has Lighted the World."

Unfortunately, Mr. Starkey's voice is not really suited to delivering an emotionally complex lyric that ponders how love will even survive, "when every soul is free." The sub-Spector production is designed to bury his voice, but the massed strings almost submerge the song too. It deserved better.

George Harrison
plays the dobro for John
Lennon in 1971. *Original art
by Klaus Voormann, especially
commissioned for this book.*
© *Klaus Voorman*

Classic portrait
of the young
Harrison and
Lennon in
Germany, 1961.
*Ulf Kruger/
Redferns*

Waiting for the band, Harrison with his Gretsch in 1963.
Jane Bown/Retna

Right: Harrison and Lennon harmonizing in 1964.
© *David Redfern/Redferns*

The Beatles at the height of their international fame in 1964.
Courtesy of Photofest

Engrossed in his Ramirez Spanish guitar, 1964. *Max Scheler/Redferns*

The Beatles meet Ed Sullivan, 1964. *Courtesy of Photofest*

Harrison leads the Beatles
into the U.S. for another tour.
Courtesy of Photofest

When fame was sweet.
Courtesy of Photofest

Left: Harrison with Ravi Shankar, one of the major influences in his life. *Courtesy of Redferns*

Finding someone to relate to in 1968 as the dream started to turn sour. *CAMERA PRESS/Christopher Simon Sykes. Courtesy of Retna*

Left: As a serious student of the sitar in 1966, Harrison took his first course in musical theory. His understanding of the Indian genre fundamentally changed his approach to music and the guitar. *CAMERA PRESS/Thomas Picton. Courtesy of Retna*

Harrison steps out as leader at the Concert for Bangla Desh, July 1971.
Courtesy of Photofest

Right: Harrison jams on "It Is He" with Bob Purvis of Splinter
at Friar Park in 1974. Splinter was the first signing to Dark
Horse Records, and the main commercial success other than
Harrison. *Photo by Terry O'Neil. Courtesy of Bob Purvis*

Working on a solo in the studio, 1970. *GAB Archives/Redferns*

Contemplating some time off in
Cannes, France, 1976.
Michael Putland/Retna

Hamming it up for the "Crackerbox
Palace" video. *Courtesy of Photofest*

Promoting *Thirty-Three & 1/3* on
Saturday Night Live, 1977.
Richard E. Aaron/Redferns

Harrison and resident of Friar Park's
lakes in 1976. *Courtesy of Photofest*

With the Beatles all but finished, George takes to the road with Delaney and Bonnie. Eric Clapton helpfully took the limelight. *Jan Perssons/Redferns*

Enjoying a performance during the 1974 Dark Horse Tour of North America.
Courtesy of Photofest

Relaxing after a busy year, Harrison in 1977. *Ellen Poppingka/Redferns*

Harrison and Ringo Starr at Starr's wedding in 1981. *CAMERA PRESS/Terry O'Neill. Courtesy of Retna*

Harrison appears in Monty Python's *Life of Brian*. After all, he did pay for the film... *Courtesy of Photofest*

George with the man he called his "guitarist–in–law," Eric Clapton. *Courtesy of Photofest*

Smoothing troubled waters for Madonna in 1986. *Courtesy of Photofest*

George Harrison's final major concert appearance at the Bob Dylan Thirtieth Anniversary Tribute at Madison Square Garden, 1992. *Courtesy of Photofest*

With the working band for "Cloud Nine," 1987. *Peter Stills/Redferns*

Harrison with his original guitar hero, Carl Perkins *(center)*, and Jeff Lynne. *All Action/Redferns*

The Traveling Wilburys at the time of their first album. *Clockwise from bottom left:* Roy Orbison, Jeff Lynne, Bob Dylan, Tom Petty, and Harrison. *Courtesy of Photofest*

8

Working from Home, England

(1979-1982)

George Harrison
**(recorded at Friar Park, March–October 1978;
released February 1979)**

The year after *Thirty-three & 1/3*, punk rock was born, and with it a
new middle-class iconoclasm aimed at the old guard, among them
Harrison and Dylan. A return to "true" rock 'n' roll was proposed,
although the absence of any black following for the music was rarely
mentioned. The metropolitan music press pushed punk hard in
London (soul and heavy metal were the predominant trends in northern England), but it was ignored in the United States. Expert media
manipulation from Malcolm McClaren appeared to create a revolu-

tion. It looked bad for George Harrison, whose work was prone to being dismissed as "music for housewives" and utterly irrelevant to "the kids." Harrison was also no heavy rocker and not authentic enough for the northern soul clubbers.

Back in the recording studio after a virtual year off, Harrison sailed against the prevailing wind, producing his most lush and melodic album to date against the background of some significant life events: the death of his father and the birth of his son in quick succession. Taking the advice of Warner Brothers producer Russ Titleman and the considerable talents of Steve Winwood, Harrison went for beauty—and succeeded. He would have noted the success of the eminently melodic album *Steve Winwood,* released in 1977, also trashed as passé in the punk-crazed spirit of the day.

In retrospect, *Thirty-three & 1/3* is clearly Harrison's last effort at playing rock star, until *Cloud Nine* more than ten years later. The music he released from 1979 to 1982 had little to do with satisfying the demands of the music business, being more of a private musical diary that fans were invited to share. By chance, he had a major hit single, but that wasn't his goal as an artist. His aim was just to express himself. It's refreshing that he wasn't ostentatiously trying to be fashionable; he had the good grace to accept that he wasn't and acted accordingly.

The "Harrison sound" was substantially changed for the new album. The crazy horses of *All Things Must Pass* were tamed, as were the rock tones of *Dark Horse,* the soul of *Extra Texture,* and the cosmopolitan grooves of *Thirty-three & 1/3.* Two more big changes were noticeable. First, rock elements are reduced to near zero and lush acoustic guitars dominate the sound instead. Second, this is his first album to feature minimal horns, perhaps an indication that the American influence was waning and Harrison was settling into a more "English" mode of expression. Witness the percussion sounds of Englishman Ray Cooper, used for the first time on this album. When Cooper plays conga on "Soft Touch," he sounds English, not Cuban; like Cooper, not Armando Peraza.

But Harrison retained the services of the *Dark Horse* rhythm section. Team Newmark-Weeks made a return trip to Friar Park for the first time since 1974. There Andy Newmark found a "new George": "He was more relaxed than when I knew him in 1974; everything seemed more intense for him at that time. When I saw him in 1979, nothing was quite as traumatic, he wasn't quite as worried, fidgeting, and frantic. He only got mellower from 1974 onwards."

For this session, the drummer and bass men eschewed the hospitality at Friar Park for the comforts of the Red Lion Inn on the banks of the River Thames in Henley. They felt George needed space. A studio in the house could mean a suspension of normal life while recording was going on, with troupes of musicians wandering about needing to be watered and fed. But, as Newmark muses, some things about working with Harrison had not changed. Even on the edge of the digital age, *George Harrison* was based on live cuts: "We were playing live, sitting in the room and playing.... He was a traditional, folksy singer-songwriter. His tunes all stood up just on acoustic guitar. He just liked to get the vibe going and was never nitpicking about how people played. It all seemed very easygoing, the song was the song. It was all *au naturel.*"

The appealing sound of the final product may have had something to do with the presence of Russ Titleman as coproducer. He not only took the songwriter-performer-producer pressure off Harrison but also ensured the album would match the American public's mood. After all, the United States was a consistently strong market for George: none of his albums had charted any lower than #11 there. Luckily, Titleman was to George's taste—he'd produced Ry Cooder, Harrison's latest guitar hero, on his classic 1976 *Chicken Skin Music*. More crucially for the sound of the new album, Titleman had recently completed sessions for a new voice on the L.A. scene. Rickie Lee Jones had a mix of talents that inevitably led to her being dubbed "the new Joni Mitchell" when her first album appeared in March 1979. She wrote songs for piano and guitar, had a powerful, idiosyncratic voice, and moved among folk, rock, and jazz inflections. Her platinum debut set, *Rickie Lee Jones*, is a mellow fellow traveler with *George Harrison*. This was hardly surprising, as Jones's core rhythm aces were Newmark and Weeks. Russ Titleman brought keyboards man Neil Larsen with him to Friar Park straight from the Rickie Lee session.

The relaxed mood of the album was partly due to the Friar Park backdrop. Even for a top session drummer like Andy Newmark, the private studio, set on the top floor of the mansion, was breathtaking: "It was unbelievable, absolutely beyond Planet Earth. There was beautiful furniture in there, it wasn't just a studio, it was done up with impeccable taste and integrity. It was so English and tasteful—I sat there and looked over the grounds and it was just, 'Oh my God, this is unbelievable!' What a setting."

Given the choice between such domestic serenity and life on the road, by 1979 it was clear that Harrison was not going to embark on a major tour in support of an album, as nearly every other act would. He was operating outside the normal music business model. Warner would have to rely on a hit single, and the Harrison name, to drive sales of *George Harrison*. In all probability, they were not too disappointed with the results.

[78] **Love Comes to Everyone (4:33)** *(Harrison)*
Harrison vocal, guitars; **Eric Clapton** guitar intro; **Willie Weeks** bass; **Andy Newmark** drums; **Neil Larsen** keyboards; **Steve Winwood** minimoog solo, backup vocal

With its harmonic similarity to the equally mellow "Far East Man," this sophisticated chart makes clear George's intention for his last musical statement of the 1970s. This is not a rock 'n' roll record. The electric guitars aren't screaming axes, they're smooth, ringing purveyors of elegance. George's time off seemed to have regenerated his melodic gifts. All three parts of the song (the verse, the hook, and the middle eight) are harmonically strong—the middle eight especially charming.

The song is supported by fine instrumental backing—Willie Weeks plays beautifully, Eric Clapton picks a few notes for the introduction, and collaborator Steve Winwood delivers a characteristically positive moog passage. Harrison scats along with his own guitar licks in a longish coda, revealing how he composes his guitar solos. He performs them as if they were songs, which they are: songs within songs.

Aside from no longer being angry, George Harrison's worldview remained the same as ever, but he intentionally tempered the presentation of his ideas for the tastes of the listening public. The casual listener may not have detected any spiritual or Krishna references in the grooves of *George Harrison*. But they were rife, only hidden by a deliberately ambiguous lyrical sheen. Hence, the "love" that comes to everyone in this song is, of course, God's.

"Love Comes to Everyone" was the singer's choice for the record's first single, but when it eventually emerged after the catchier "Blow Away," it died a lonely death. This fine example of Harrison's pop style hardly deserved such a fate.

[79] **Not Guilty (3:36)** *(Harrison)*
Harrison vocal, guitars; **Willie Weeks** bass; **Andy Newmark** drums; **Neil Larsen** electric piano; **Steve Winwood** keyboards; **Ray Cooper** conga

There is no better illustration of the difference between George Harrison's music in 1968 and in 1979 than "Not Guilty." Finally released on the *Anthology 3* album in the 1990s, the Beatles' version of the song might have passed for grunge. It sounds like a period piece, with phased vocals and McCartney's pseudo-harpsichord under attack from George's heavily distorted guitars and fierce riff. A tricky change of time signature revives the fairground mood of "Being for the Benefit of Mr. Kite," while the lead guitar track is spiky-rough in a way Harrison would rarely approach again.

In complete contrast, the 1979 reproduction is all shimmering cool and acoustic sea spray—here is a man looking back on events rather than being caught up in their heat. At its inception, the song was a self-parody of his paranoia, a litany of the supposed transgressions of Beatle George, and a denial of each one. The arrangement is a loose version of the Rickie Lee Jones or Paul Simon jazz-pop sound, dominated by phased electric piano and breathy vocals. This kind of mellow moodiness was guaranteed to incense the music press of the era. Harrison's groove had nothing to do with the fashions and trends of 1979, which is probably why it doesn't sound especially dated today.

Above all, this "Not Guilty" speaks loudly of how distant the Beatles era was by 1979. The passion that created "the dream" sounds like a distant spirit, as Harrison looks back, not in anger but with middle-aged acceptance.

[80] Here Comes the Moon (4:46) *(Harrison)*
Harrison vocal, guitars; **Willie Weeks** bass; **Andy Newmark** drums; **Neil Larsen** electric piano; **Steve Winwood** keyboards, backup vocal

A frequent theme in Harrison's songs is the power of nature to reflect and influence his emotions. This lunar ritual was the first in his solo career to recall the psychedelic days of 1967. There's more than a hint of the Beatles' old ADT[1] trick here, although by 1979 the dreamy, swirling effect was generated by phase shifters and other off-the-shelf technical gadgets.

There is much of Harrison's Beatles heritage here, particularly the verdant backup vocals that are worked in three or four parts. In one passage, the "moon" sweeps across the soundscape, almost a cap-

---

[1]Automatic Double Tracking—a tape loop effect that creates a phased sound.

pella, invoking the majesty of "Because," the Beatles' greatest recorded collective vocal exercise.

But George must have known he was tempting fate by calling a track "Here Comes the Moon"; unfavorable comparisons were inevitable. Little of this ditty has any reference to its titular progenitor, except that the basic theme is one of escape: in "Here Comes the Sun," release from the Beatles; in 1979, release from the world itself. Hence "Here Comes the Moon" carries George off to a mystical never-never land of natural purity in the first of the album's little glimpses of heaven. It's a return to the realm promised by "The Ballad of Sir Frank Crisp." The song could not have been further from the prevailing musical trend if it tried.

[81] **Soft-Hearted Hana (4:03)** *(Harrison)*
Harrison vocal, guitars, dobro; **Willie Weeks** bass; **Andy Newmark** drums; **Neil Larsen** piano; **Steve Winwood** backup vocal; **Del Newman** horn arrangement

The time machine stops at 1967, with Harrison's first obvious drug song since "It's All Too Much." This is a trip back to the distorted, parallel reality of LSD and magic mushrooms. He employs some vintage sound effects to create the mood and some instrumentation that looks back to the "anything goes" ambience of the *Sgt. Pepper* era. Introduced for the first time here is a brass band tuba, an indication of increasing eccentricity in Harrison's arrangements, as is the barroom piano that just cries out for a smiling Jelly Roll Morton.

Filled with schoolboy humor and gags, "Soft-Hearted Hana" rivals Cheech and Chong at their peak for multiple drug allusions. The reference to swimming in the midst of a "Richard III" shows the millionaire had not lost touch with the toilet humor on which the British Empire was built.[2] The second of the "I'm still smiling" middle-eights is the longest string of deliberate non sequiturs George Harrison ever managed. The song revisits a world where transient images took over the brain and a bewildered smile was all the narrator could convey. Sadly, many of Harrison's music industry contemporaries never escaped that condition.

Fittingly, Steve Winwood's voice is quite prominent in the backup vocal, as the music shares a mood with Traffic's "Hole in My Shoe." This quirky, drug-infused narrative is in the bluegrass, Band mode of certain songs from *All Things Must Pass*, complete with a

---

[2] "Richard III" is British slang for "turd."

snakey, sinuous dobro workout. There's a certain charm to "Soft-Hearted Hana" that recaptures the mood of an era long gone.

[82] Blow Away (3:59) *(Harrison)*
Harrison vocal, guitars; **Willie Weeks** bass; **Andy Newmark** drums; **Neil Larsen** electric piano; **Steve Winwood** harmonium, synthesizer; **Ray Cooper** conga, cow bell

As he emerged from his musical hibernation, George Harrison listened to *All Things Must Pass* for inspiration. Now, at the end of the 1970s, he looked back over his first decade as a solo artist in the emollient single "Blow Away." In the space of nine years, he'd been emancipated from the Beatles and achieved unimagined solo success with a string of #1 singles and albums. After being sued innumerable times mid-decade, he was cast into the critical wilderness—before even having the chance to be trashed by the self-appointed punk police. To his credit, his public stance in 1979 was this uplifting tribute to the power of positive thinking.

In one sense, "Blow Away" neatly brings Harrison's decade to a close with a subconscious revision of his original nature anthem, "All Things Must Pass." The same cast of characters appears—the wind, cloudburst, the sun, moon, and sky—but here Harrison's mind does "blow those clouds away." He faces the new day reinvigorated by the love he could not be sure of in the 1970 piece.

The music matches the positive mood, and this latest installment in George's long series of U.S. Top 20 hits is built on a chiming guitar riff and a swinging, pop-gospel mood. The main harmonic interest comes when F natural is paired with a C chord on the "be happy" phrase, the musical half-step resonating with the psychological emancipation.[3]

A little saccharine, perhaps, for the "rock" fan, "Blow Away"—and the whole album—saw Harrison move to a soft-rock mode. While that would not satisfy the heavy metal or stadium rock aficionados, who continued to worship at the feet of ego-sodden guitar slingers, the Oxfordshire gentleman presents one of his most gorgeous harmonized slide guitar sequences for the introduction.

[83] Faster (4:40) *(Harrison)*
Harrison vocal, guitars, bass; **Andy Newmark** drums; **Ray Cooper** tambourine; **Del Newman** string arrangement

---

[3]The song's home key of D calls for F-sharp.

Few artists were better qualified to comment on the nature of fame than Mr. Harrison. As he later pointed out in song, his only ambition was to play the guitar; the madness that distorted his life forever was not of his doing. So, on "Faster," he writes about a generic "star"—the sound effects and some of the images imply a Formula 1 motor racing driver, but the experience is personal.[4]

The fame inflicted on the Beatles is only matched by that heaped on British royalty. Both share the distinction of not being able to do most of the activities that everyone else takes for granted. Worst of all, they don't know who their friends are, having been used and abused too many times by hangers-on. "Faster" is about all of this, and it gives a little glimpse of Harrison's experience. He talks about the "friends" who suddenly appear, the vicarious appetites of the public to build up and then knock down celebrities, and the feeling of being constantly on the edge of madness and disaster.

This sense of being trapped was something that Harrison shared with Badfinger in the early 1970s, when the new Apple group was about to head for Pacific bliss. "We were going to Hawaii to represent Apple at a Capitol Records convention," Joey Molland recalls. "So we're down in the Apple offices one day, George comes down the stairs and says hello. He says, 'So, you fellas are going to Hawaii,' and he was talking about how fantastic it was. But he said, 'You guys will have a great time—of course, when I went there, I had to stay in the hotel. I never went out. We could look out at the place, but we couldn't go out.'"

The reluctant celebrity clearly had big plans for "Faster." He unleashes a big sound on what he obviously conceived as an anthem. Neither the multilayered backup vocals nor the chiming "My Sweet Lord" twelve-string guitars can mask the fact that the hook isn't particularly memorable, and the single bombed. "Faster" didn't quite make it off the starting block.

[84] **Dark Sweet Lady (3:20)** *(Harrison)*
Harrison vocal, guitars, mandolin; **Willie Weeks** bass;
Andy Newmark drums; **Steve Winwood** harmonium; **Ray Cooper**
conga, marimba, maracas; **Gayle Levant** harp

The music on *George Harrison* is part aural seduction, and for his first unambiguous love song in years, "Dark Sweet Lady," George conjures a mood of intimacy and sunset cool. For the listener of a nostalgic bent, it strongly recalls "Till There Was You" and one of the young Harrison's

---

[4]Harrison was well known for his interest in Formula 1 racing.

finest guitar cameos. There's another lithe Spanish guitar passage in this touching tribute to his new love for being everything that the false friends of "Faster" and "Run of the Mill" were not.[5]

"Dark Sweet Lady" is another of *George Harrison*'s songs that suggest that the endless wanderer had finally found somewhere to lay his head. Like "Blow Away," it marks the end of a cycle that started in the early 1970s, culminating in the sheer unhappiness of "So Sad," "Bye Bye, Love" and "Grey Cloudy Lies." Ever the honest wordsmith, Harrison accepts that his new love, Olivia Arias, brought him back from the brink after the mad days of 1974. Another overlooked Harrison creation, "Dark Sweet Lady" ranks as one of his most affecting and genuine love songs.

[85] **Your Love Is Forever (3:45)** *(Harrison)*
Harrison vocal, guitars; **Willie Weeks** bass; **Andy Newmark** drums; **Steve Winwood** synthesizer

"To me, atonality is against nature. There is a center to everything that exists. The planets have the sun, the moon, the earth."[6] This statement of the great American composer Alan Hovhaness was partly a defense of his determination to swim against the prevailing tide of twentieth-century music and stick to melody as his musical aesthetic. George Harrison is clearly no Hovhaness, but there are parallels: they both had strong spiritual experiences and both looked to the East for musical inspiration. Above all, both men believed in melody as the highest form of musical expression. No song in Harrison's catalogue better exemplifies this than "Your Love Is Forever."

This captivating composition is pure melody and is almost arrhythmic—the concept is of beauty and contentment, and the love in question is God's. Setting his guitar to an open D tuning and coloring the tone with a heavily phased chorus effect, George serves up one of his most delicious melodies and chord sequences. The opening guitar passage is unique in Harrison's canon, partly honoring the Chet Atkins tradition of guitar instrumentals while simultaneously mirroring the tonal stillness of Indian music.

The guitar solo reveals exquisite lyricism, and is yet another example of Harrison's craftsmanship in creating guitar melodies that are counterpoints to the main melody. While it certainly wasn't rock

---

[5]Those interested in how Harrison's guitar style developed will note that his 1963 solo was played without any vibrato, whereas this passage made notable use of it.

[6]From the liner notes to the Delos CD of Hovhaness's *Mysterious Mountain/And God Created Great Whales* (1994).

'n' roll, this spiritual ballad revealed the closest marriage to date between his musical expression and his inner beliefs. So, although he would never have conceived of the comparison himself, the song expresses sincere emotion and grasps for expression of the spiritual, as Hovhaness's work did. "Your Love Is Forever" is George Harrison's musical image of heaven.

[86] **Soft Touch (4:00)** *(Harrison)*
Harrison vocal, guitars; **Willie Weeks** bass; **Andy Newmark** drums; **Neil Larsen** organ; **Steve Winwood** synthesizer; **Ray Cooper** conga

One of the few musical sidelines George Harrison interested himself with during his "year off" from the business was the final Splinter album for Dark Horse, the patchy *Two Man Band*. The great feeling that produced *The Place I Love* was a distant memory as Bob Purvis and Bill Elliot assembled, for the last time, at FPSHOT. Now that Dark Horse Records had moved over to Warner Brothers, Harrison was aware of the need for this album to be a commercial success. So he introduced American songwriter-guitarist Parker McGee to proceedings with two would-be hits, "Round and Round" and "Motions of Love." Harrison added his lead guitar to both, but that couldn't mask the fact that Splinter's heart was not in these songs. As the mood grew darker, Harrison sought to soothe matters by suggesting that Purvis and Elliot cut a version of his own "Don't Let Me Wait Too Long." This single-that-never-was from *Living in the Material World* was a track Purvis "loved" and would have happily released, even though he still had some strong pieces to offer ("I Apologize," "New York City," "Love Is Not Enough"). Unfortunately, on the finished product the "Splinter sound" was lost in a thick fog of FM-friendly violins and misplaced synthesizers that destroyed melodies like "Silver" (Harrison thought this one was reminiscent of "Do You Want to Know a Secret"). The Geordie duo began to lose heart, and Warner Brothers also seemed to have little appetite for the LP, offering almost classically cheap and nasty packaging, and a slavishly derivative *Sgt. Pepper*-clone cover.

For all the bad vibes around *Two Man Band*, it did have a profound effect on its executive producer, evidence of which can be found on "Soft Touch." For this further installment of South Seas bliss, Harrison replicated the guitar sound, mood, and production of "Round and Round." Indeed, one of the most telling features of the *George Harrison* album is that it sounds like Splinter in places.

Offerings like "Soft Touch" were never to find favor with rock critics. They were too "light"—there was no hint of the turmoil that was generally accepted as a necessary precursor to great art. "Soft Touch" had no pretension to be art of any kind, really, and by 1979, Harrison had no concept of his audience or the music audience in general. Aside from the advice of Russ Titleman, the only thing George had to go on was his Formula 1 friends' desire for some "nice, relaxing music." "Soft Touch" delivers just that.

[87] **If You Believe (2:53)** *(Harrison-Wright)*
Harrison vocal, guitars; **Willie Weeks** bass; **Andy Newmark** drums; **Neil Larsen** piano; **Gary Wright** synthesizer; **Del Newman** string arrangement

Apart from Splinter, the only other music Harrison was involved with in his year off was a guitar cameo on an album by retro soulsters Hall & Oates. Their 1978 release *Along the Red Ledge* was produced by Attitudes keys player David Foster. The sound of "The Last Time" revived early 1960s production values, and might have been Phil Spector's work. The track must have stuck in the slideman's mind, as the mood is recaptured with this finale to *George Harrison*, cowritten by Gary Wright, a close Harrison friend.

The pair's friendship extended to shared spiritual beliefs, making "If You Believe" an apposite title for their first published collaboration. But the song doesn't completely convince; it sounds a little too much like it was produced to a formula. Harrison's biggest hits had come with chanted three-word phrases in "My Sweet Lord" and "Give Me Love"; here he and his cowriter try their luck with a slightly gospel-infused hook. Other nods to past glories are repeating slide riffs designed to stick in the mind, like their forebears on "My Sweet Lord," and synthesized horns and a full string section that are an updated version of the *All Things Must Pass* sound.

Other elements of the arrangement are even more clearly derivative. The syncopation between bass and drums on the first verse is lifted straight from the Hall & Oates piece, itself a throwback to "Leader of the Pack." "If You Believe" sounds like it was conceived to be a hit single, but in the final analysis, it wasn't quite catchy enough.

The release of this album was greeted with muted interest because in 1979 it sounded to many ears like a 1960s throwback. In fact, *George Harrison* actually signaled the start of the musician's retreat into an internal musical dialogue, set amid the woods and gardens of Friar Park. It was the return to nature predicted by "All Things Must Pass" and "Let It Roll." The difference was that Harrison cut the vocals for this new work in the Friar Park studio, where the singer had a panoramic view of "the beauty that surrounds them."

The album was also his growing-up set. Harrison had lived at the speed of light during the '60s, to the extent that he had started tackling the "big" philosophical questions before he'd reached his mid-twenties. Between 1969 and 1976, he'd maintained a relentless schedule of making albums, producing new acts, and touring that took him through the intensity of the Beatles years again as a solo artist. The group's rise to fame in 1963–64 was repeated for George by the initial euphoria and coronation that came with *All Things Must Pass* and the Concert for Bangla Desh. But he found himself on the other side of the coin with *Dark Horse* and *Extra Texture*. In 1974 and 1975, he could do no right: it was as if he'd just been quoted as declaring he was "bigger than Christ."[7]

George Harrison came from a period in which he'd rediscovered life away from the business for the first time in nearly twenty years. He'd also experience two major events, the death of his father in May and the birth of his son in August. The peaceful mood of the new music was the work of a man who had lived the rock 'n' roll dream twice over and was now embracing domestic as well as spiritual bliss. This decidedly melodic and lush album was a deliberate signal that Harrison had no desire to be a part of the current musical fashion that would assuredly pass away. He probably calculated that the value of *George Harrison* would last a little longer. But, as ever with this guitarist's career, turbulence was just around the corner.

---

[7] A comment about the Beatles attributed to John Lennon in 1966, which caused an unprecedented media storm.

George Harrison *Somewhere In England*

Somewhere in England
(recorded at Friar Park, March–October 1980 and November 1980–February 1981; original version almost released October 1980; final version released June 1981)

The 1980s were the graveyard decade for a bewildering array of musicians who had made their names in the 1960s and enjoyed the 1970s. With punk all but dead and New Wave appearing in its place, George Harrison's contemporaries largely went into hibernation. They would return when enough time had passed for their rebirth as "legends." Long to be remembered as the decade of self-immolating right-wing social destruction, the 1980s left many of the previous decade's artistic pacesetters stunned and wasted. Bob Dylan was in the middle of a trio of gospel-inflected religious albums and suffering the same critical browbeating for his pains that Harrison had experienced five years earlier. It's notable that the gospel chorus he used was similar to Harrison's *All Things Must Pass* style. Dylan's 1981 *A Shot of Love* did include one of his most telling songs, "Every Grain of Sand." Harrison's other Concert for Bangla Desh friends were faring less well. Eric Clapton produced light country-rock on *Another Ticket* (1981); Leon Russell had no major releases at all.

Most of the singer-songwriters were in a lull. Paul Simon had ventured into filmmaking with the forgotten *One Trick Pony* (1980), and when he returned three years later with a major release, *Hearts and*

Bones (1983), it received little attention. Neil Young was preoccupied with his disabled son and produced slight, poorly received platters like *Hawks and Doves* (1980) and *Re-Ac-Tor* (1981). It seems that only Joni Mitchell was still trying to push the boundaries as late as 1979, with her fascinating *Mingus* LP, a bona fide jazz record that the rock critics just didn't get. She retrenched with a jazz-tinged "greatest hits live" album, the pleasing *Shadows and Light* (1980), then made a tilt at contemporary acceptance with *Wild Things Run Fast* in 1982. Mitchell took three years off but returned in 1985 with the scathing *Dog Eat Dog*, a social document that set at the 1980s' finance-driven mores with precision vehemence.

These musicians were in the classic dilemma of the bald man: to be bold and bald, or to comb over from the side? They were too old to be contemporary, but would suffer greater scorn for attempts to ape modern styles; Paul McCartney discovered this with *McCartney II,* which was desperate to be on the cutting edge. Hardly surprising then that a number of them simply retired to their mansions and took an extended nap.

This was nothing new for George Harrison, who had tried to retire quite frequently since 1966, and in retrospect he suffered relatively light bruising in the 1980s. Of his releases that decade, only *Gone Troppo* was a complete commercial failure, but even that was a success compared to the travails of Ringo Starr. The London sales of his 1981 effort *Stop and Smell the Roses* were numbered in the tens (of tens). By 1983 and *Old Wave*, Starr could not secure a distributor in the United Kingdom or the United States. Commercially viable rock at the time was epitomized by the brand of anodyne Californian whimsy served up by Fleetwood Mac—a group that was completely unrecognizable from the earthy, powerful late 1960s blues group led by the understated guitar genius Peter Green. Now Green was trying to rebuild his career after an acid-induced mental collapse. Drummer Mick Fleetwood dropped in from Sunset Boulevard to offer help. He was also cutting his own disc, *The Visitor*, and coaxed Harrison into springing some licks for the pleasant "Walk a Thin Line," a title that was about to resonate with the Henley guitarist.

This aside, the decade started badly for George. The saga of *Somewhere in England* pushed him ever further into his shell. It was a classic 1980s vignette of the market taking on the artist and winning. This was the decade that saw entire towns sacrificed to the mantra of "market forces" and job losses in the hundreds of thousands. It hardly seemed important that Warner Brothers had rejected a new

George Harrison project at the last minute on the grounds that it contained no hits. The #13 chart placing of the previous effort was satisfactory, but hardly a stunning return on their investment. They demanded more—and fate intervened to give them just that.

The whole affair was framed by a tendency toward isolation and Anglicization in George Harrison's music. He was partly influenced by the do-it-yourself approach of Steve Winwood, but more particularly by British percussionist Ray Cooper, who'd first worked with Harrison on that long-forgotten 1973 Nicky Hopkins set, and was trusted enough to be offered a job as a director of a Harrison company. Cooper's musical pedigree was faultless, with his Stones and Elton John experience, and he became a sounding board for Harrison as he tried to come to terms with having his record rejected. "George rang me and said he needed some help producing his next album, *Somewhere in England.* So I coproduced the recut version, which really involved the recording of about four alternative tracks," Cooper later recalled. "I think that at that time, George's musical isolationist policy was beginning to have an effect. I think all artists need to feed off other artists' talents. It was a great joy for me, as coproducer, to put him in touch with some new faces. So there was some new blood coming in and new conversation." The new faces were all British musicians and included drummer Dave Mattacks, pianist Mike Moran, and bass man Herbie Flowers.[8]

The original *Somewhere in England* came very close to being released in October 1980. Test pressings were made before the project was ditched, and some found their way into the sweaty hands of collectors. What they had was a cohesive statement from Harrison, who observed the 1980s upheaval with scorn. It's somewhat better than the 1981 version, which is loaded with obvious pop songs and takes the prize as Harrison's worst recording. Four selections from the original were axed ("Flying Hour," "Tears of the World," "Lay His Head," and "Sat Singing"), and all were superior to the ditties that replaced them. Strangely, "Flying Hour" sounds more like a hit than any of the efforts that remained.

[88] **Tears of the World (3:48)** *(Harrison)*
Harrison vocal, guitars; **Tom Scott** saxophone; **Jim Keltner** drums; **Willie Weeks** bass; **Neil Larsen** keyboards; **Ray Cooper** percussion; **Gary Brooker** synthesizer

---

[8]Harrison, *Live in Japan*, 161–62.

Suspicion of "the establishment" fueled the protest songs of the 1960s, and in 1980 was still alive and well in George Harrison's heart. The *George Harrison* album had documented the "beauty that surrounds them"; the yin-yang pendulum now moved him to a place where he could only see the negative, "because of all their tears." The picture created by this caustic exercise is of Harrison sitting in his Henley garden, observing the decay of the 1980s with despair. Instead of feeling helpless, he did what many others did in the era—he joined CND (Campaign for Nuclear Disarmament) and supported Greenpeace. Unlike the majority of activists, Harrison had a public status that he used to get his message across. It was his version of Bob Dylan's "Hurricane" escapade, the "star" moved by an injustice to speak out. Harrison's targets were warmongers—for which read "government"—and big business, the unholy alliance that was leading humankind to a polluted hell on earth, or nuclear holocaust. Unfortunately for him, Warner Brothers didn't like the sound of such damning lyrics and cut the track.

As ever, there was ambiguity in George's words—he asked the listener if they felt their life was worth saving, in either the here and now or the hereafter. A bleak picture was on the cards: either man-made nuclear hell or spiritual hell. Take your pick. Over a stabbing horn section, Harrison tells us that "Each one pays his debt"—this is the old enemy karma again, but also the instant karma of industrial pollution. There wasn't much of an appetite for protest songs in 1980, and this moody piece was not released for twelve years, when it finally emerged on the *Songs by George Harrison II* package.

[89] Flying Hour (4:32) *(Harrison-Ralphs)*
Harrison vocal, guitars; **Jim Keltner** drums; **Willie Weeks** bass; **Neil Larsen** keyboards; **Ray Cooper** percussion; **Gary Brooker** synthesizer

As this determined track was also recorded during the *George Harrison* album sessions, it is moderately bizarre that it missed the cut for two albums. The song's purpose is to remind its author to continue moving ahead rather than be caught in nostalgia for the past. In 1970s Britain, "the past" even had its own television show called *The Good All Days,* celebrating the "golden age" of the Edwardian music hall. This is what Harrison sings about in the opening line of this collaboration with Bad Company guitar hero Mick Ralphs. For him, of course, the "good old days" centered on the Beatles, his albatross.

Nevertheless, the song is a jaunty affair that may have been one of his best compositions of the 1980s—but for Warner boss Mo Ostin, what would have been a sure-fire hit in 1973 wasn't sufficiently attractive in 1980. And Ostin's focus groups had told him that the way to sell records was to write songs about teenagers falling in and out of love. Harrison's lyrics about living in the present with spiritual eyes were hardly in this category, despite the attractive melody and upbeat mood to which they were set. In being true to himself, Harrison was clearly at odds with the mores of the music business. *Songs by George Harrison* finally emancipated "Flying Hour" in a remixed version, minus some natty guitar licks. That would not quell Harrison's natural iconoclasm. Soon he would find a way to stop people from telling him what to sing about: he wouldn't try to release his songs at all.

[90] **Sat Singing (4:30)** *(Harrison)*
Harrison vocal, guitars; **Jim Keltner** drums; **Willie Weeks** bass; **Neil Larsen** keyboards; **Ray Cooper** percussion; **Gary Brooker** synthesizer

A pivotal composition in George Harrison's career, "Sat Singing" is a companion piece to "Tomorrow Never Knows," with the key difference being that it sings of attainment, not just the vision of an abstract idea. The startling *Revolver* cut, one of the last and greatest meetings of minds between Lennon and Harrison, wheels and rolls, dervish style, as it contemplates the philosophy of *The Tibetan Book of the Dead*. George Harrison always made it clear that his own grasp of Hindu philosophy followed the basic ideas set out in "Tomorrow Never Knows."[9] Here he records his experience of meditation.

Lost during the *Somewhere in England* debacle and eventually released on the superexpensive *Songs by George Harrison*, "Sat Singing" traces what is effectively the musician's retreat from the world we all know into a meditative trance. He loses all memories of the past and his own identity—"the moment I lose my mind," the realization of "turn off your mind, relax and float downstream." The singer "surrenders to the void" and loses his identity in the superconsciousness that some term God. The result for Harrison is joy and bliss, "every atom of your body is buzzing," exceeding anything he has experienced from his life on earth. This state is more enriching than all the platinum albums, millions of dollars. He'd "gladly kiss it all good-

---

[9]Beatles, *Anthology,* 210.

bye" to stay there. This song, from this songwriter, has to be the result of direct experience. Any listener familiar with Harrison's music cannot doubt his sincerity in writing these lyrics.

On another level, "Sat Singing" raises a number of questions. If George would be glad to "kiss it all good-bye" and merge with the infinite, does "all" include family ties, children, and relationships? One of the books on Hindu philosophical thought that Harrison knew well spells out what he must leave behind: "We think our love is the only lasting love. How can that be? Even love is selfish; and the yogi says that in the end we shall find that even the love of husbands and wives and children and friends slowly decays. It is only by giving up this world that the other is seen—never holding on to this one."[10]

For this revelation, the music matches the serene mood with a melody of some beauty, colored by warming, golden slide guitar licks. As a musical essay on serenity and joy, it is one of Harrison's best, but it also documents his desire to completely remove himself from any sense of the world as we know it. More than that, it records his desire to shake off his ego and identity and disappear into infinity. Not too many rock stars would have that as their primary ambition.

[91] **Lay His Head (3:50)** *(Harrison)*
Harrison vocal, guitars; **Jim Keltner** drums; **Willie Weeks** bass; **Neil Larsen** keyboards; **Ray Cooper** percussion; **Gary Brooker** synthesizer

Finding a place of refuge had figured in George Harrison's music since "Don't Bother Me," where he imagined the need for solitude after a teenage love spat. As that age of innocence rapidly disappeared with the onslaught of the mania that surrounded the Beatles, the archetypal ordinary man found himself living his life in public. Moreover, he was subjected to the kind of collective lunacy catalogued by playwright Arthur Miller in *The Crucible*. For the Beatles themselves, the psychological impact of their fame became the "collateral damage" of the period. Whether they were killed, assaulted, or just roughed up in Manila in 1966, it was the same bounty for the media—a screaming headline. If they became deranged as a result, all the better; it was another banner.

So "Lay His Head" is not about male wanderlust, as in "Wherever I Lay My Hat"; it's more akin to The Band's "The Weight": "I just need some place where I can lay my head." The meat of the song is a gentle

---

[10]Swami Vivekananda, *Raja-Yoga*, 157.

reminder of what a man loses when he becomes a media entity: a connection with other people that everyone else takes for granted. Celebrities like Harrison are so used to wondering if anyone is actually interested in them as a person rather than as what they symbolize (or for what can be got out of them) that they end up living in a bubble, not knowing whom to trust. Here Harrison declares that if he had a "true friend" on whom he could rely, he would be relieved. The concept is part of George's ongoing search for peace, refuge, and solace—physical, emotional, and spiritual.[11]

"Lay His Head" emerged from a seven-year incubation in 1987, as the B-side to "Got My Mind Set on You," and was the first of the *Somewhere in England* dropouts to see the light of day. Vaguely reminiscent of the country style used by Splinter, replete with fine harmony vocals and another pretty melody, it is one of his most quietly affecting works. The real sadness is that, even during his subsequent fight against the real horror of cancer, his plight was just more bait for the watching world. That makes "Lay His Head" yet more poignant.

It is impossible to speak of the final *Somewhere in England* album without mentioning John Lennon's murder on December 8, 1980. As the catalyst for a temporary surge in Beatles interest, it turned a weak pop ditty into a major hit. The album grazed the fringes of the Top 10 charts around the world—proof that the world obsession with the Beatles could still benefit its ex-members.

Lennon's estate benefited too, as the speed with which the reception of *Double Fantasy* turned from chronic to classic was breathtaking. Upon its release in November 1980, one of the still-powerful British weekly music magazines had welcomed it with the headline, "Get Down Lazarus." The single "Starting Over" was scorned for its hackneyed 1950s sound, and there were many lined up to point out the cloying quality of "Beautiful Boy," as McCartneyesque a tear-jerker as anyone could wish for. Lennon's death soon became a virtual martyrdom. "Starting Over" shot to #1 in all territories, followed by an indecently hasty re-release of "Imagine." In time, sympathy would even be expressed for Yoko Ono's efforts as a "major artist"—but not to the extent of listening to *Sometime in New York City*. Harrison was rarely

---

[11]From Beatles, *Anthology*, 223: "We got in the car and drove off, and they were all on little scooters, with the Sikhs in turbans all going, 'Oh, Beatles, Beatles!' I thought, 'Oh no! Foxes have holes and birds nests, but Beatles have nowhere to lay their heads.'"

seen in New York in 1980: he preferred to stay at home in England. That his sad, and partly bitter, English record went gold is due not to its quality but to the reawakening of the ever-latent Beatlemania that Harrison so abhorred.

[92] **Blood from a Clone (3:58)** *(Harrison)*
Harrison vocal, guitars; **Herbie Flowers** bass; **Dave Mattacks** drums, percussion; **Mike Moran** keyboards[12]

George Harrison had always been wary of the perils of ego, and his beliefs taught him that its dissolution was a way to reach God. He had already catalogued his concerns with self-indulgence on "I Me Mine." Sadly for him, the soap opera of *Somewhere in England* is very much about bruised egos. "Blood from a Clone" is that same battered self, hitting back at its persecutors (for which read "the music business").

Becoming the first ex-Beatle to have an album rejected outright by a record company must have hit Harrison hard. Such things just did not happen to the royalty of rock. As the 1980s progressed, squadrons of 1960s and 1970s vintage rock stars faced the same trauma and documented their ire on vinyl. Harrison was one of the first and one of the most bitter. His angst caught the mood of the day.

When Mo Ostin rejected the first pass at *Somewhere in England* because it contained no hits, it was another way of saying that Harrison was out of touch. That may be why the opening track on the new disc began with a fashionable ska rhythm and a major rant. "Blood from a Clone" was Harrison's answer to the music business, cataloguing his chagrin at having his LP rejected, but it verges on being a throwaway tune.

George vents his opprobrium on his tormentors, as he likens them to Nazis in one of his more extreme images: record company executives in jackboots along the highways and byways of Britain. Harrison uses distorting effects to get his point across. The ska is satisfactory, but the drums are deliberately played out of time on the rhythmic instrumental break. It was a depressing opener for a new album, but at least showed that Harrison shared in the general nihilism of the age.

---

[12]*General note regarding player annotations*: The performers on *Somewhere in England* were not listed on a track-by-track basis. However, it is obvious that there were three groups of players involved: the Keltner, Weeks, Scott, Larsen, Brooker unit on the original sessions; a one-off group put together for the Ringo Starr sessions that became "All Those Years Ago"; and the wholly British team who recorded the three "new" songs for the revised version (confirmed by Dave Mattacks in an e-mail communication to the author in September 2002).

[93] **Unconsciousness Rules (3:04)** *(Harrison)*
Harrison vocal, guitars; **Tom Scott** saxophone; **Jim Keltner** drums;
Willie Weeks bass; **Neil Larsen** keyboards; **Ray Cooper**
percussion; **Gary Brooker** synthesizer

It's inevitable that rock stars lose touch with the "real world"—the demands of "the public" forces them. *Hello* magazine would not sell many copies looking through the doors of terraced houses in Blackburn. The detachment makes the story and the celebrity, as it offers a glimpse of the unattainable. At the same time, such wealth and celebrity irk some readers of those same celebrity magazines. But these are the Frankenstein's monsters created by the age. Little wonder, considering George Harrison's fantastic story, that he lost touch in his Friar Park hideaway and became prone to writing tirades like "Unconsciousness Rules."

Any unsuspecting teen tempted by the fluke success of "All Those Years Ago" into buying this album would have found themselves subjected to an all-out harangue about the perils of nightclubs. Hitherto seemingly long estranged from his Lancastrian roots, here Harrison assumes the role of "plain-speaking northerner" and speaks his mind. He turns his gaze upon the disco craze engendered by *Saturday Night Fever* and trashes it. By British standards, he verges on rudeness. Harrison saw discos as havens for puffed-up egos, where the blind lead the blind into degradation and despair—an opinion that says much for his worldview in 1980.

Curiously, the song itself is quite danceable in a *Thirty-three & 1/3* way, with its happy-go-lucky sound and Tom Scott's superprofessional solo, disguising the lyrical sting in the tail. Unfortunately, as a commentator on late 1970s pop culture, Harrison sounded way off.

[94] **Life Itself (4:24)** *(Harrison)*
Harrison vocal, guitars; **Neil Larsen** keyboards; **Ray Cooper**
drums, percussion; **Gary Brooker** organ

Like "My Sweet Lord," "Hear Me Lord," and "Your Love Is Forever," this painstakingly created ballad comes close to the heart of George Harrison's musical life. It explores the same ground as Bob Dylan's pivotal "Every Grain of Sand," also released in 1981 on *Shot of Love*.

Harrison's piece is a love song to his God, a concept hardly likely to endear him to critics, who were wont to liken these songs to musical chloroform. But there is a touching simplicity of expression here, as the superstar again adopts a childlike stance to express his feelings. Unlike with Dylan, there is no narrative exposition of a spiritual journey. "Life Itself" is the work of a man who has arrived at his destination. Harrison is not "hanging in the balance of the reality of man"— he's making an offering.[13]

It is the offering of a man who lavished all he knew on the song, starting with a demo version that itself represented many hours' effort. This private work features four guitar tracks, three backup vocals, and a little ukulele. George introduces a new, clean-and-clear electric guitar sound to the song, picking out the melody as an acoustic David Bromberg would. This is supplemented by two slide guitars and Harrison's vocal, which give collective exposition to a simple refrain, similar in construction to "Don't Let Me Down."

The first completed version appeared on the original *Somewhere in England*, with an added rhythm section, while the final version installed the finishing touch—gospel Hammond organ, similar to "Sing One for the Lord," with the George O'Hara Smith singers returning to provide sweeping, multilayered backup vocals. This, combined with George's guitar choir, represents his attempt to convey his spiritual vision in music. Such meticulous craftsmanship typifies George Harrison's best art. Although the song is lyrically naïve compared with the sheer poetry of "Every Grain of Sand," George reaches the same depth of expression in his music. *His* poetry is contained within the elegance of his guitar idiom, coupled with the finely etched span of the vocal chorus.

Inevitably, the critics hated "Life Itself." The man could surely have expected nothing else in 1981—what place did the music of belief have in a new age of reason, economic utilitarianism, and cultural iconoclasm? His problem was that his belief system was not born from the fads of the 1960s; it had deeper roots and was something he maintained until the end of his life. Even if the zeitgeist of the day had changed, he was unable to change his core values.

"Life Itself" is a Harrisong that touches the heart of George Harrison's musical aesthetic, which John Barham, one of his closest musical allies, thinks derives from Indian music:

> George felt music as deeply as any musician that I have ever known. I met George through Indian music, which we both believed to be a music that can put the player and the listener in close contact with a spiritual dimension. I know that George did not want this merely for himself, but also to be able to influence others to reach the same point.

---

[13]"I am hanging in the balance of the reality of man, like every sparrow falling, like every grain of sand," was one of Dylan's observations in "Every Grain of Sand" from the *Shot Of Love* album.

He wasn't dogmatic that everybody should listen to Indian music or practice any particular religion. But, as he was primarily a musician, he continued throughout his life to express in some of his songs his own longing for spiritual fulfillment. In as far as he wanted to move his listeners in his spiritual songs, I think he had a vision of what he wanted his music to be for.

[95] **All Those Years Ago (3:43)** *(Harrison)*

Harrison vocal, guitars; **Ringo Starr** drums; **Paul McCartney** backup vocal; **Linda McCartney** backup vocal; **Denny Laine** backup vocal; **Al Kooper** keyboards; **Herbie Flowers** bass; **Ray Cooper** synthesizer, percussion

In the midst of a distorted album, "All Those Years Ago" is a microcosm of the contradictions and angst that often characterized George Harrison's music.

Locked into a facile, nursery-rhyme chorus line, it presents a picture of a man at odds with the world—a world that had just taken away a friend whose murder "All Those Years Ago" turns into a metaphor for the death of "the dream." The song's purview presents two distinct camps, in a classification straight out of the 1960s: those seeking truth and to be "free of the lies," namely Lennon and Harrison and the few who "had ears"; and Harrison's negative ions, those he consistently calls "they" or "them" in his lyrics.

Somewhere in England in its various guises is full of dire warnings about "them." In "Blood from a Clone," "they" are the music business, distorting the beauty of music by demanding formula hits that infect the listening public with their mediocrity. "Save the World" and "Tears of the World" are concerned with politicians, warmongers, and big business leading the innocent masses to a polluted Armageddon, while "Unconsciousness Rules" is an uncomfortable rant about disco junkies who've fallen for the plastic music predicted in "Blood from a Clone."

"All Those Years Ago" is more bitter still. The "bad guys" have forgotten about "God" and "mankind," leaving only enlightened artists to "shout about love" and point the way to "the truth." The punishment "they" have in store for the "good guys," personified in the song by Lennon, is to be treated "like a dog" and ultimately destroyed. Love means nothing to "them" because they are dishonest charlatans.

The paradox is that this embittered declamation is matched with a winsome pop tune and became a major hit amid the general mythmaking that surrounded Lennon's murder. Its success was the product of the fantasy world of Beatlemania that George so despised.

Another irony is that Al Kooper, a man who burst onto the rock scene when he added organ to Bob Dylan's cataclysmic "Like a Rolling Stone," plays on the track. *Highway 61 Revisited* and that particular cut almost invented the "serious" rock genre, and the cult of celebrity around Dylan spread to other carriers of the rock torch, such as John Lennon. So, as fate would have it, Kooper was "in the room" at the start of the rock era, and he was at Friar Park when John Lennon was killed in New York. Lennon was the victim of an obsessed fan, as Harrison would almost become in 1999. Of course, Paul McCartney and Ringo Starr also play on the track to complete the circle.

Had "All Those Years Ago" found its way onto yet another forgotten Ringo Starr album, under a different name, it would have been ignored and lost in the sands of time. That would have been preferable to its status as one of Harrison's most famous hits, when it is actually one of his most agonized.

[96] **Baltimore Oriole (3:57)** *(Hoagy Carmichael)*
Harrison vocal, guitars; **Tom Scott** saxophone; **Jim Keltner** drums; **Willie Weeks** bass; **Neil Larsen** keyboards; **Ray Cooper** percussion; **Gary Brooker** synthesizer

Approaching middle age, George Harrison began reflecting on his musical roots. One of the quiet coincidences of his career is that he chose to record two Hoagy Carmichael classics in 1980. As fate had it, they were released a year later, the same year that the songwriter passed away.

Carmichael was one of a group of white tunesmiths who crossed over into black jazz. He was also an early friend and collaborator of legendary white cornet player Bix Beiderbecke, who encouraged the pianist to write his own songs. The history of jazz is tainted by record companies preferring to promote white, rather than black, jazz musicians. This built a strain of resentment that is easily found in the biographies of black jazz legends like Miles Davis and Charles Mingus. Nevertheless, Carmichael proved that music can transcend color: his pieces "Georgia on My Mind" and "Stardust" became standards for all races.

The original "Baltimore Oriole" was reputedly Carmichael's favorite of all his songs. The 1956 recording on *Hoagy Sings Carmichael* is a languid-tempo semiblues, framed by an arrangement clearly influenced by Gil Evans's orchestrations for classic Miles Davis albums such as *Birth of the Cool*. When George Harrison recorded the song in 1980, he was fortunate to have Tom Scott as a collaborator.

Although not quite in the Gil Evans league, he's an accomplished composer and arranger. The *Somewhere in England* version of "Baltimore Oriole" heavily features Scott's tenor saxophone, and the song's key is swapped to G minor from its original D-sharp minor for a better fit with Harrison's vocal.

The Harrisonization of this classic involved an increased tempo to steady pop, sweeping Beatlesque backup vocals, and more guitar— although the final 1981 cut excised the running bottleneck commentary of the 1980 version. As he did with Dylan's "If Not for You," Harrison sings the piece straight, searching for a fixed melody, while the original is characterized by Carmichael's deliberately lazy slurring and tonal ambiguity. Clearly, Harrison had no desire to be a crooner.

Recording this song was a treat to himself for Harrison, a short detour to his roots and a comfortable place to be. Mo Ostin and his marketing men at Warner Brothers must have been wracking their brains to identify the target audience for this one. But after "All Those Years Ago" hit the charts, they probably didn't care.

[97] **Teardrops (4:04)** *(Harrison)*
Harrison vocal, guitars; **Herbie Flowers** bass; **Ray Cooper** percussion; **Dave Mattacks** drums; **Mike Moran** keyboards

There are two ways to look at a number like "Teardrops." On the one hand, it is a perfectly pleasant four minutes, a well-produced power-pop tune with a catchy hook and attractive bridge; on the other hand, it is one of the very few George productions that sound like hack work. Mo Ostin wanted hits; Harrison went away to write some. This exercise in sub-Elton John pop sounds like something he put together in half an hour.

The song was obviously recorded without the singer's heart within the grounds of Friar Park; somewhat surprisingly, its catchy vapidity didn't send it up the charts in the post-Lennon glare. That would have been unfair, as "Teardrops" doesn't mean anything, add anything to the disc, or really amount to anything. It's the kind of forgettable pop fluff that Harrison had been trying to escape for years.

[98] **That Which I Have Lost (3:42)** *(Harrison)*
Harrison vocal, guitars; **Herbie Flowers** bass, tuba; **Ray Cooper** percussion; **Dave Mattacks** drums; **Mike Moran** keyboards

The four new songs for the New Improved [*sic*] *Somewhere in England* were written to order: they had to be up-tempo and cover the subject of boy-meets-girl. The last of the quartet wasn't quite what

Warner had in mind; it was another slightly belligerent third-person rant about the need for spiritual enlightenment, but at least "That Which I Have Lost" just about meets the up-tempo criterion. Harrison revives his Dylanesque strumming circa "Apple Scruffs" but goes one step further, sounding like the archetypal one-man band, banging out a two-beat message.

It's a rather eccentric recording, as Harrison seems to turn back to skiffle simplicity and lays down neat guitar tracks that re-create Carl Perkins as Albert Lee. Musically, with Herbie Flowers's tuba prominent, the song is slightly whimsical; lyrically, it's another turn around the old salvation wheel that gets close to being hectoring. In retrospect, it sounds like a precursor to the Traveling Wilburys sound. Otherwise, it's just not memorable, and far inferior to "Flying Hour," "Lay His Head," "Sat Singing," and "Tears of the World"—the more noticeable losses from the album.

[99] **Writing's on the Wall (3:57)** *(Harrison)*
Harrison vocal, guitars, gubgubbi; **Jim Keltner** drums;
Willie Weeks bass; **Neil Larsen** keyboards; **Alla Rakha** tabla;
Ray Cooper tambourine, conga; **Gary Brooker** synthesizer

By the time George came to write and record "Writing's on the Wall," his work had almost no reference point in popular music, nothing to be compared with. It is so totally out of kilter with the musical values of the period as to be in a genus all its own. The *George Harrison* and *Thirty-three & 1/3* albums had been extremely accessible, full of classy melodies, but pieces like this one took George's idiosyncrasy to new levels. It was the ultimate expression of his introverted music in an extroverted age.

"Writing's on the Wall" is cast in the same moderate, dreamy tempo as "Be Here Now" and "Long, Long, Long," and is a meditation on the nature of existence, nothing more and nothing less. George considers lost friends and the futility of material considerations, as "death holds onto us with every passing hour." Who else would dare to write such a lyric and present it to a multinational corporation like Warner Brothers and suggest its release to the public?

Interestingly, "Writing's on the Wall"—which features a tabla cameo from the late, great Allah Rakha—is the first Harrisong to equate music with spirituality. George invokes the Nada Brahma belief and casts music itself as a healing force for good. Hopelessly unfashionable in all aspects, this song is, along with "Life Itself," about the only reason to look into the 1981 *Somewhere in England*.

[100] **Hong Kong Blues (2:54)** *(Hoagy Carmichael)*
Harrison vocal, guitars; **Jim Keltner** drums; **Willie Weeks** bass;
Neil Larsen keyboards; **Ray Cooper** percussion, gong, timbales;
Gary Brooker synthesizer

The music of the postwar period into which George Harrison was born is characterized by one quality above all: melody. In the days before mass domestic use of television and video, the wireless was king, as Woody Allen showed in his nostalgic *Radio Days.* The scenes of American families huddled around Bakerlites were replicated on the other side of the Atlantic, and it was through this medium that the young George Harrison first absorbed music. In the era before rock 'n' roll, he would have heard the great American dance bands and their British equivalents like Henry Hall and the uniquely British George Formby. But the radio also released music from far afield into English homes: European jazz through Django Rheinhardt and Stefan Grappelli, along with the American composer Hoagy Carmichael.

This recording is clearly about nostalgia, as "Hong Kong Blues" was the first song Harrison remembers hearing on the radio as a five-year-old child. More than thirty years later, it returned to the front of his mind and he recorded it. As if his brain were an onion, the layers of memory peeled away, and somewhere near the center was this song. It was a standard of the period, having been featured in the 1944 Hollywood classic *To Have and Have Not*, a film that featured the legendary pairing of Humphrey Bogart and Lauren Bacall.

Harrison's version also sounds like a soundtrack piece, although it's more Henley than Burbank. For one thing, where Carmichael's take was utterly deadpan, he completely ditches the pseudo-Chinese motif of the original and delivers a vocal full of character. The Englishness of Harrison's cover is also due to the increasing influence of percussionist Ray Cooper, who introduces the sound of the Cuban timbales. There's also a tendency toward honky-tonk, rather than jazz swing, in the middle eight.

The other Beatles had already traveled this reflective road, creating pastiches of the music they'd heard as children. The results were songs like "Honey Pie" and "Your Mother Should Know." The fact that Harrison chose to record this and "Baltimore Oriole" shows that, even in 1980, he occasionally worked on the premise that an ex-Beatle had total license to record whatever he chose, to satisfy whatever whims he had. Those who were of his generation would have known Hoagy Carmichael; the rest would probably have wondered why Harrison was singing about a "colored man," using language of the segregationist era.

[101] **Save the World (4:56)** *(Harrison)*
Harrison vocal, guitars; **Tom Scott** horns; **Jim Keltner** drums;
Willie Weeks bass; **Neil Larsen** keyboards; **Ray Cooper**
percussion; **Gary Brooker** synthesizer

This quirky protest song is another chunk of Harrison's 1980s disillu-
sionment, and his idiom for expressing his concerns is peculiarly
British. Harrison was renowned for his fanaticism for Monty Python's
Flying Circus, to the extent that he mortgaged Friar Park in order to
bail out their successful *Life of Brian,* which hit cinema screens in
1979. He often mused that the madness of Palin and company held up
a mirror to the insanity of world events. Little surprise then that, for
his first try at ecological protest songwriting, he produced a musical
vignette that sounds like a Python outtake. With its quirky march
rhythm and "looney" sound effects, "Save the World" has more in common with "Eric the Half a Bee" than with "Mercy Mercy Me (The
Ecology)." It is the culmination of the Pythonization of Harrison's
music that began with "Soft-Hearted Hana."

In five years, he managed to record three different versions of
the cut, which reflects his general rejection of modern society in
much the same way as "Tears of the World" did. George must have
enjoyed a splendid time in the studio, conjuring up a plethora of
sound effects for the tune over a groove vaguely related to "His Name
Is Legs." The horn charts and moog riffs are straight out of 1975.

But he digs back further to get his message through as "Save the
World" fades out, by using an excerpt from "Crying," a *Wonderwall*
oldie. It's a snippet of music played on the esraj, a bowed Indian
instrument. To Harrison, the Indian music emphasized the pain, but
also pointed to the solution.[14] Ethnomusicology aside, "Save the
World" is about George Harrison's 1980s worldview as revealed in an
almost hidden aside on the 1985 remix: "You greedy bastards."

It is of course ironic that *Somewhere in England* became a hit album
for the very reasons that Harrison should have hated. He had railed
against the marketing tactics of the music business in "Blood from a
Clone," but the burst of Beatlemania engendered by Lennon's death
was what paved the way for this music to trouble the Top 10. The sad

---

[14]For Harrison it was: "It's very simple knowing that God in your heart lives."

fact is that the album wasn't a hit because of its quality—*Somewhere in England* is Harrison's weakest LP by some distance. Though the 1980 version probably would not have been as successful, it was much better and truer to its creator. As it stands, *Somewhere in England* is a sad episode in Harrison's career.

The real angst of *Somewhere in England* was what it represented for Harrison and the 1960s generation. If anything signaled the end of the counterculture dream, this was it. The bitterness of the album was a recognition that the dream was dead, the new generation didn't care about the hopes of a bygone era. Bob Dylan changed the world forever by delivering artistic freedom to the pop musicians of the '60s, but by the time Harrison delivered *Somewhere in England* to Mo Ostin, songs about ecology and spirituality were definitely passé. Ostin wanted teenage love drivel of the sort that ruled pop music before Bob Dylan turned matters on their head. To George Harrison, it must have seemed as if all the hard-won freedoms of the 1960s amounted to nothing in the face of the corporate rush for profits.

Not only that, but the media-induced cult of celebrity that had plagued Harrison for years had done for his friend, John Lennon. As George pointed out on "All Those Years Ago," he was still shouting about love, but no one was listening. The musical heroes of the 1960s and early 1970s found themselves in a parallel universe, living out their own legends and playing to an audience that was aging with them. Lennon's murder stood for the death of the values that led those musicians to think they could change the world "with our love." By 1980, they knew they couldn't, and the realization was hard to stomach.

George Harrison did not readily bow to corporate mission statements about the subjects of his songs. His reaction to the *Somewhere in England* soap opera was to complete his contractual obligations as soon as possible and declare his independence. No conglomerate could tell him what to record if he simply stopped offering his songs for release. Because he had his own studio, he didn't need a record label to buy studio time for him. He could record his private music for his own ears, and his friends'.

In 1981, Ringo Starr may have innocently wondered if the revived interest in all things Beatles would extend to his new offering, *Stop and Smell the Roses.* Trying as hard as possible to put the awfulness of *Ringo the 4th* and *Bad Boy* behind him, the drummer returned to the *Ringo* formula and sought help from his friends. The album was a commercial disaster, but George Harrison offered a new song that gave Starr his last U.S. Top 40 hit.

[102] **Wrack My Brain (2:20)** *(Harrison) (recorded by Ringo Starr)*
Harrison guitars, backup vocal; **Ringo Starr** drums, vocal;
Al Kooper keyboards; **Herbie Flowers** bass; **Ray Cooper**
synthesizer, percussion, backup vocal

Probably written as a reaction to the *Somewhere in England* episode, this minor hit for Ringo Starr is a work of piercing self-analysis from his guitarist chum. Never able to conceal his feelings, not devious enough to try, Harrison declares himself artistically "dried up" and "out of touch." Realizing that he's no longer the lad from Liverpool but a wealthy mansion-dweller, he notes that he has no idea how people live these days; using the British vernacular "you and yours" leaves no doubt as to his meaning. Worse still, he fears creative block, especially when the challenge is to get people away from their televisions.

This is a companion piece to "Grey Cloudy Lies," his other song of despair, on which he also talks about "going insane." The soul-affirming blue skies of "Blow Away" are gone after little more than a year; now the sky is pouring rain. Such a level of self-exposure hardly makes for comfortable listening, which may be why the song was given to Starr, so Harrison could keep a little distance from it. Starr's typically jaunty vocal distracts from a lyric that documents something close to despair.

Gone Troppo
(recorded at Friar Park May–August 1982;
released November 1982)

George Harrison didn't much like the 1980s and accepted his status
as a rock dinosaur with good grace. The twelve years since *All Things
Must Pass* were akin to light years for Harrison's critical status—by
1982, even punk, the would-be salvation of "rock 'n' roll," had come
and gone. The music industry descended into a twenty-year cycle of
repeating old styles fronted by young faces. Harrison would still
oblige old pals like Gary Brooker by adding his guitar signature to an
album track,[15] but in general, his interest in the business was waning
fast.

   Gone Troppo was the first Harrison release that sounded like it
was recorded to pass the time with a few friends. Most of those mates
were now English musicians who were either suggested by Ray
Cooper (drummer Henry Spinetti, pianist Mike Moran, and Herbie
Flowers) or old and trusted pals (Deep Purple neighbor Jon Lord,
1960s rocker Joe Brown and his wife Vicki). Only one track was
recorded with a primarily American band ("Unknown Delight") and,

---

[15] "Mineral Man" from *Lead Me to the Water*.

aside from the trio of backup singers from Ry Cooder's touring band, the American presence was downsized to cameos from Billy Preston and Jim Keltner. The sense was that George would keep on recording songs at home in his old meticulous way, and if anyone else liked them, that was fine. He wasn't going to try too hard to be liked. He actually didn't care.

The fact was he had other fish to fry. George's main line of business at this time was films: his Handmade company was growing exponentially, heading for its 1987 peak with the cult classic *Withnail and I*. The financial risk he'd taken by establishing Handmade to bankroll *The Life of Brian* had paid off. Harrison made his money back and more. Handmade Films was credited in some circles as the single-handed savior of the British film industry. By contrast, the music on *Gone Troppo* suggested a man recording music as a hobby, rather than to be part of an business.

[103] **Wake Up My Love** (3:33) *(Harrison)*
Harrison vocal, guitars, bass; **Ray Cooper** percussion; **Mike Moran** keyboards; **Henry Spinetti** drums

The opening bars of "Wake up My Love" sound like a reinvigorated George Harrison. A loud, rocking piano/guitar riff recalls a similar one on "It's What You Value," but the upbeat start masks a malaise of artifice. Essentially a rewrite of "Teardrops," "Wake up My Love" is a contrived, deliberate tilt at the charts. After "All Those Years Ago," George might have reckoned his chances of scoring another hit. His game plan seems to have been to ape Elton John again, as evidenced by the prominent piano riffs, layers of period synthesizers, and heavily studio-managed vocals delivering a demand for spiritual reconnection.

With a little promotion, this might have been a bigger hit, but despite its foot-tapping power-pop groove, "Wake up My Love" contains too much fluff to be a serious contender.

[104] **That's the Way It Goes** (3:32) *(Harrison)*
Harrison vocal, guitars, synthesizer; **Herbie Flowers** bass; **Ray Cooper** percussion; **Mike Moran** keyboards; **Henry Spinetti** drums; **Willie Greene** bass vocal

Harrison turns social commentator on this, the highlight of the LP. His target is the money madness of the 1980s, the decade when "society" was declared dead by Margaret Thatcher. Observing the insanity, the song marks George's further withdrawal—the phrase "that's the way it goes" is a typically British term for passive acceptance of unfairness or failure. Harrison is saying that he doesn't want any part of society at all if "that's the way it is." He can only help himself by sticking to his inner spiritual life. The old urge to share the vision ("The Lord Loves the One") is gone; he's settled for being misunderstood. To some, this worldview verges on misanthropy; to others, it's a form of realism.

In contrast to the lyrical angst, musically "That's the Way It Goes" is richly positive. At the time Harrison was keen on the music of musical archaeologist and guitar maestro Ry Cooder, both for his slide guitar work and for the fine posse of black vocalists he featured on his biggest hit album, *Bop 'Til You Drop*. A classic African-American doo-wop formation, the trio of Bobby King, Pico Pena, and Willie Greene produced close, tight, rich harmonies. Harrison wasted no time in recruiting them to appear on *Gone Troppo*, and Willie Greene, the diminutive man with the deep bass voice, is featured on "That's the Way It Goes."

Other than this, the arrangement is Harrison's standard—layers of acoustic guitars topped by picking light electrics, understated keyboards, and lots of slide riffs. An instrumental break comes after each verse, and each is the product of meticulous craftsmanship and varied nuances of sound. The second segment has George picking in his pseudo-country style while a duetting slide tracks him exactly; another doubles with a synthesizer and uses obvious inflections from Indian music in the shape of microtonal vibrato (gamaks).

Harrison's slide playing remained innovative throughout his career, albeit largely overlooked. Ironically, it was Ry Cooder who underlined the obvious proximity between Harrison's slide sound and Indian phrasing. If there's one instrumental album George Harrison may have dreamed of recording, it is probably Cooder's *Meeting by the River*, a collaboration with Indian slide maestro V. M. Bhatt. A series of long, ragalike pieces allows Bhatt to demonstrate how he adapted the guitar (and specifically acoustic slide guitar) to the demands of Indian music. That was a 1993 disc—with "That's the Way It Goes," Harrison had shown that he was the true pioneer of honestly incorporating Indian music into Western rock.

[105] **I Really Love You (2:53)** *(Swearingen)*
Harrison vocal; **Herbie Flowers** bass; **Ray Cooper** feet, Fender Rhodes, glockenspiel; **Mike Moran** keyboards; **Henry Spinetti** drums; **Willie Greene** vocal; **Bobby King** vocal; **Pico Pena** vocal

The postwar generation grew up to the sounds of tightly harmonizing black American vocal groups like The Volumes and The Marcels who transferred the highly structured choral standards of church choirs to popular music. Although doo-wop never had the industry backing needed to crack the charts, the music heavily influenced Harrison and his contemporaries; by the 1980s, they were acknowledging it. Joni Mitchell took the Persuasions onstage with her in 1980 for a flip take on "Why Do Fools Fall in Love," while Paul Simon invited modern doo-woppers the Harptones to cut a track with him on *Hearts and Bones* in 1983.[16]

A year before that, George Harrison cut this jolly tribute to the genre with the Ry Cooder vocal ensemble of Greene, King, and Pena. "I Really Love You" was a hit for the Stereos in 1961, and Harrison creates a faithful rendition of the original. The opening footsteps weren't a Starr innovation, as some reports have suggested; they are heard on the 1961 cut—but here they cunningly merge into drums for a good-time session that recalls the days of the George O'Hara Smith singers of *All Things Must Pass*. At least ten separate voices are recorded and mixed with great clarity. With no guitars, this is a unique item in Harrison's body of work, and a charming return trip to more innocent days.

[106] **Greece (3:57)** *(Harrison)*
Harrison vocal, guitars; **Herbie Flowers** bass; **Billy Preston** keyboards; **Mike Moran** keyboards; **Henry Spinetti** drums; **Willie Greene** bass vocal

"Pisces Fish" is a song George Harrison recorded in the 1990s and finally released on *Brainwashed* in 2002. The title is a reference to his own zodiac sign, and the guitarist lived out an abundance of change in his professional life. This oscillation between extremes was part of his musical character, a fact never better illustrated than by the entire *Gone Troppo* project and "Greece" in particular.

Less than one year after the release of the bitter songs "Blood from a Clone" and "Unconsciousness Rules" and deeply introspective meditation pieces like "Writing's on the Wall," George produced this whimsical instrumental. Even within the *Gone Troppo* context, it contrasts wildly with the fuguelike keyboard parts of "Circles."

Melodically simple, "Greece" is based on one childlike seven-note theme, surrounded by a collection of blink-and-they're-gone guitar riffs. Here George's guitar orchestra is led by his trusty dobro, and a host of palm-fringed six-string parts that range in style from Hawaiian

---

[16]"Rene and Georgette Magritte with Their Dog After the War."

to fast-picking *bouzouki*. Only the Python-pastiche word games break the mood of the *Gone Troppo* hammock swaying in the sun, kissed by warm winds, with waves gently lapping the beach.

[107] **Gone Troppo (4:27)** *(Harrison)*
Harrison vocal, guitars, marimba, *jal tarang*; **Herbie Flowers** bass; **Ray Cooper** percussion, marimba; **Mike Moran** keyboards; **Henry Spinetti** drums; **Jim Keltner** percussion; **Joe Brown** backup vocals; **Vicki Brown** backup vocals

After twenty years of almost constant music-making, George Harrison finally succumbed to the demands of hedonism and made clear that his manifesto for 1982 was to "go on holiday." As "Gone Troppo" testifies, he was quite contented with this virtual relocation to Hawaii, including a chorus peppered by swaying marimba and tinkling percussion. He even tried his hand at playing the Indian jal tarang instrument, a series of bowls filled with water to give different tones.

The acoustic guitar arpeggios, especially his pseudo-mandolin picking, suggest a past Harrison era. "Gone Troppo" takes the knowing listener back to "Deep Blue" and his Band fixation; the song's musical roots go way back to 1971 and George's work with Dylan and David Bromberg. Indeed, the main musical hook is virtually identical to that of "The Hold Up," an overlooked Harrison-Bromberg composition.

"Gone Troppo" is one of George's most exotic offerings, a virtual South Sea shuffle. But Harrison was not the first star to turn travel agent—Bob Dylan had already offered such a vision with his equally sunny "Mozambique," on a much darker album, *Desire*.

[108] **Mystical One (3:43)** *(Harrison)*
Harrison vocal, guitars, mandolin, synthesizer; **Herbie Flowers** bass; **Ray Cooper** percussion, synthesizer; **Mike Moran** keyboards; **Henry Spinetti** drums; **Joe Brown** mandolin

An album track so obscure that it is rarely even overlooked, "Mystical One" quietly summarizes Harrison's life story as a celebrity. When he sings "they say I'm not what I used to be," he's referring to his legend, not necessarily himself. The song seems to acknowledge that he relates to the "media me" as well as the "real me." It's a tacit acceptance of how abnormal his life has become.

The accompanying psychological pressure can only be imagined. The Harrison solution is retreat from this world, into his self-contained spiritual alternative. The language he uses to record his emotions in this state is a heady mix of nature metaphors that recall "All

Things Must Pass" ("shine or rain, sitting here by a stream") and swooning romantic hyperbole ("melting my heart," "lulling me"), backed by mandolins plucked straight out of Venice. The net effect of this meditation is that he becomes "more real," suggesting that there are three Harrisons—the man, the media figure, and the ego-free meditator!

Interestingly, "Mystical One" builds on the hints in "Writing's on the Wall" that link music with his state of meditative bliss, a neat way of saying that words cannot convey his feelings but music can. Lines like "You answer my deepest prayer, in a song" clearly indicate the importance of music in George Harrison's life, and give a partial clue as to why he dropped out of the business in the 1990s. Music was so personal to him that he didn't need to make it public. Commercialization is a potential distortion of the musical-spiritual axis.

All this heady revelation is contained in a very pleasant musical package that allows listeners the option of just enjoying the sound of multiple guitars and mandolins, recalling George's past trysts with The Band and David Bromberg.[17]

[109] **Unknown Delight (4:14)** *(Harrison)*
Harrison vocal, guitars, synthesizer; **Jim Keltner** drums;
Willie Weeks bass; **Neil Larsen** piano; **Ray Cooper** percussion;
Gary Brooker synthesizer; **Willie Greene** backup vocal;
Bobby King backup vocal; **Pico Pena** backup vocal

Like "Learning How to Love You," this ballad is based on the same circular structure as "Something," but here the sense is of a deliberate return, on a love song from father to son. As if to make the point, Harrison even quotes the first phrase from his famed "Something" guitar solo at the start of the break.

Less sugary than Lennon's 1980 "Beautiful Boy" but not as powerful as Pete Ham's overlooked "Dennis,"[18] "Unknown Delight" is filled with harmony, from the lullaby backup vocals of the Cooder team to Harrison's own resonant guitar. It also demonstrates that, as a producer, George had learned to let the song speak for itself rather than fall into "Try Some Buy Some" bombast. In Phil Spector's hands, this ballad would have been overwhelmed with a million mandolins,

---

[17]The Band's "Rockin' Chair" was filled with the sound of mandolins.

[18]A song from Badfinger's *Wish You Were Here* album, released only months before Ham's suicide.

boastful trumpets, and banks of strings. Not groundbreaking in any way, the mix of vocal and six-string elegance nevertheless makes it a charming diversion.

[110] Baby Don't Run Away (3:57) *(Harrison)*
Harrison vocals, synthesizer; **Jim Keltner** drums; **Mike Moran** bass synthesizer, keyboards; **Ray Cooper** percussion; **Billy Preston** backup vocal; **Rodina Sloan** backup vocal

The synthesizer pop of Soft Cell and Depeche Mode was *de rigueur* in 1982, but while those groups had ditched guitars, they retained a sense of melody that may have appealed to George Harrison. "Baby Don't Run Away" sounds as if it should be Harrison's attempt to answer the synth-popsters, and his line of attack is a dramatic melody and plenty of period-piece vocoder effects and pseudo-drama à la Phil Spector, but on synths. Marking the first appearance of Billy Preston on a Harrison album in years, the song should have worked, but it fails simply because it's too turgid. The overblown production casts it as a love song from a Disney cartoon.

[111] Dream Away (4:27) *(Harrison)*
Harrison guitars, vocal; **Dave Mattacks** drums; **Alan Jones** bass; **Mike Moran** keyboards; **Ray Cooper** percussion; **Billy Preston** backup vocal; **Syreeta** backup vocal; **Sarah Ricor** backup vocal

George's first venture into film music since *Wonderwall* was this ditty, which closed *Time Bandits,* another success for Handmade Films. An enjoyable sub-Python epic, the film matched some pointed, but very good, jokes with a pseudo-spiritual mood of distorted realities, and a struggle between good and evil that probably appealed to Harrison. *Time Bandits* abounds with yin-yang contradictions and, aside from quickly summarizing the plot, Harrison returns to his favorite theme of duality in the final verse, which he concludes with the thought that life itself is just a dream.

"Dream Away" has no pretension to be anything other than another pop blast with a suitably exaggerated cinematic arrangement. Very similar to "Faster," it earned single status in Japan. Although a relative throwaway, it's faultless within its context.

[112] Circles (3:45) *(Harrison)*
Harrison vocal, guitars, bass, synthesizer; **Ray Cooper** percussion, synthesizer; **Mike Moran** keyboards; **Henry Spinetti** drums; **Jon Lord** synthesizer; **Billy Preston** organ, piano

A throwback to the Beatles' 1968 Rishikesh foray, "Circles" took the idiosyncrasies of Harrison's oeuvre to new heights when he finally recorded it in 1982. It seems at least partly to be Warner Brothers' payback for *Somewhere in England*, as if George were challenging Mo Ostin's men to achieve the impossible and market a song about reincarnation. Warner simply didn't bother to try.[19]

Few listened, but this is one of the composer's most complex pieces. A bootleg of the Beatles running through the song at the 1968 Esher session illustrates that the song was written on the organ and gives prominence to the almost Bach-like bass figures that characterize the chorus. In final form on *Gone Troppo* "Circles," Harrison spins a chromatic melodic web that matches the lyric's story of repetition and entrapment—like "Beware of Darkness," it is a study in Harrison's unique harmonic sense. Very few songwriters would conceive a D minor–B-flat–B minor progression ("I go round in circles"), and fewer still would set a piece in F major but write a melody that yearned for a resolution on E minor. But Harrison was writing music that perfectly matched his theme, revolving in dissonance like a lost soul awaiting its place in the reincarnation checkout line.

For all the quaintness, some of the elements are strictly earthbound: while at face value Deep Purple's Jon Lord is an odd musical partner on "Circles" for Harrison, they were close friends. In tandem with Billy Preston's gospel flourishes and Harrison's unique guitar tones, rich instrumentation frames this most unusual song, here cast as Harrison's first Hindustani blues. At this point, there was no doubt at all that George Harrison was recording music purely as a form of self-expression, without the slightest interest in its market suitability.

Gone Troppo is an enjoyable, if unusual record, and it certainly has more going for it than its reputation would suggest. For one thing, George's guitar stylings are excellent. He shows a versatility that is a rare gift and commits to vinyl some of the most revealing Indian inflections of his career. He hasn't lost the knack of carving out fine melodies, as evidenced by "Mystical One" and "Unknown Delight." The mood of the release is, on the whole, highly positive and infectiously happy.

---

[19]*Gone Troppo* failed to crack the *Billboard* Top 100.

The addition of the Ry Cooder vocalists is very effective. They not only enabled George to re-create the doo-wop groups he admired but also gave him the feeling of being in a band and harmonizing as a team. Normally, Harrison performed overdub upon overdub in his solitary role as both lead and backup singers.

Above it all sits "Circles," a throwback to the early days of enlightenment in the 1960s. Its ponderous, stuttering, meditative pace and bizarre, circular melodic structure give the feeling of being transported to one of the parallel realities of *Time Bandits*. "Circles" was so personal and eccentric that it seemed to close the book on George's recording career. It felt like he was making music only for himself.

9

On Holiday in the Armani Age
(1985-1987)

As far as the public was concerned, George Harrison was musically silent between 1983 and 1984, except for a surprise appearance with Deep Purple in Australia in 1984, during their reunion tour. Encouraged by his friend and neighbor Jon Lord, he rendered a version of "Lucille"—but this was not the only time he performed live with Lord. According to legend, they played occasional impromptu gigs in the Henley area, as a duo cunningly named the Pishill Artists.[1]

Meanwhile, another "Henley Mafia" friend, Alvin Lee, was coaxing Harrison to cut a demo of a joint composition called "Shelter in Your Love," on which the guitarist almost casually summoned catchy soul-pop hooks. Another widely bootlegged demo from this period is a full mix of a Dylan *Desire* outtake, "Abandoned Love." Here Harrison gives Bob's work an upbeat, jaunty treatment, stuffed full of country picking, making it a cousin to "That Which I Have Lost."

Aside from Harrison's private music-making, his main efforts were concentrated on supporting his Handmade Films company, which was premiering a would-be blockbuster in January 1985. *Water* starred Michael Caine and had a large budget but made no impression at all at the box office, despite Harrison's appearance in a concert sequence. This was filmed in one day at Shepperton Studios, and Harrison enlisted Ringo Starr, Jon Lord, and Eric Clapton to support the Scottish comedian-actor Billy Connolly's delivery of the ham-reggae "Freedom." As Robert Sellers reveals in his history of Handmade Films, *Very Naughty Boys*, they were paid in cash: "Producer David Wimbury remembers it well. 'We paid these stars the musician's mini-

---

[1]Pishill is a small village close to Henley.

mum rate for a playback session on set. At lunchtime, I gave them the little brown envelopes of cash, not much, I think about forty quid, and they had to sign for it. They were well pleased.... It was the first real wages they'd seen in a brown envelope for many years I guess. They got a big kick out of it.'"[2]

Aside from the concert, Harrison contributed to two songs on the film, both of which appeared on a soundtrack album.

[113] **Celebration (3:43)** *(Moran, Harrison) (recorded for the* Water *soundtrack)*
Jimmy Helms vocal; *Harrison not present on recording*

Both of George's contributions to the *Water* soundtrack were cowritten with *Gone Troppo* synthesizer standard-bearer Mike Moran, and both are formula 1980s pop. The only notable feature of the pseudo-gospel "Celebration" is that it predicts the sound of 1990s British pop-soul act M People—the respective lead vocalists sound nearly identical.

[114] **Focus of Attention (2:10)** *(Moran, Clement, Harrison)* *(recorded for the* Water *soundtrack)*
Jimmy Helms vocal; *Harrison not present on recording*

This is a predictably bland film score piece that matches Moran's harmonic precision with another Harrison lyric about being famous. He runs through a litany of intrusion, noting that a celebrity can be seen on television and in newspapers, worn on a T-shirt, and heard on the radio. In humorous exasperation, he lapses into the colloquial, advising that fans can even "put it in your pipe and smoke it."

Porky's Revenge
(soundtrack album—Harrison contribution recorded in Los Angeles, November 1984; released May 1985)

[115] **I Don't Want to Do It (2:51)** *(Bob Dylan)*
Harrison guitar, vocal; **Chuck Leavell** keyboards; **Michael Shrieve** drums; **Kenny Aaronson** bass; **Jimmy Vaughan** guitar

This unreleased Bob Dylan piece was first given the demo treatment by Harrison during the *All Things Must Pass* sessions. It lay dormant

---

[2]Sellers, *Very Naughty Boys*, 158.

for nearly fifteen years before being resurrected for inclusion on the soundtrack to the teenage flick *Porky's Revenge,* an unlikely home for a George song. He was talked into contributing it by English rocker Dave Edmunds, who shared Harrison's admiration of Carl Perkins.

"I Don't Want to Do It" certainly sounds as if it would have fitted well with the country-tinged parts of *All Things Must Pass,* although the reflective lyric makes it more apposite to Harrison in 1985 than 1970. The instrumentation used follows the "basic" Dylan model of guitar, bass, drums, and organ, which makes the effective multipart harmonies of George's backup vocals the main feature. Indeed, there is no instrumental solo in the song; it is replaced with a sinuous line from the Harrison chorus. An unexpected phoenix from the Dylan-Harrison 1968 Woodstock gathering, this "bound to fail" single marked the official start of Harrison's return to public gaze.

Porky's Revenge caused little excitement, but the work with Dave Edmunds did lead to the climax of Harrison's musical year, when he agreed to appear at a session with his original hero, Carl Perkins. The entire "Blue Suede Shoes"[3] video venture was the brainchild of Edmunds, who'd assembled a cast including Harrison, Ringo Starr, Rosanne Cash, and Eric Clapton. Within the limited musical vocabulary of rockabilly, the results taped at a small London television studio in October 1985 were spectacular, and contained a revelatory performance from Harrison, who looked like he was reliving his teenage years.

The point of the date was that it gave Harrison the chance to again combine playing music with friendship, as he had when he first played Carl Perkins's tunes in the early 1960s. The warmth of the show struck Rosanne Cash, who'd been drafted on the insistence of Perkins. Her father, Johnny Cash, was one of his oldest friends. Although she'd emerged from the giant shadow cast by her father to establish her own career, Rosanne felt intimidated by the reality of Harrison, Starr, and Clapton. She recalled that, stepping straight from a transatlantic jet into rehearsals, she "walked into a room and saw Eric Clapton and George playing on this little stage in a cramped, cold room. I stood stock still and watched them. I remember feeling that I

---

[3] The video's full title was the snappy "Blue Suede Shoes: A Rockabilly Session with Carl Perkins and Friends." The shooting date was Monday, October 21.

had stepped into an alternate universe, one populated by my heroes. I was as quiet and unobtrusive as I could be, and they were all very polite and welcoming to me."[4]

The Harrison welcome extended to bringing all the performers to Friar Park for dinner, the night before the taping. Cash's nerves weren't soothed by the surreal Henley estate; thrust into a setting that contained artifacts of the Beatles years, she had the same sense of wonder that Bob Purvis had felt more than ten years earlier. As with Purvis, there was one guitar in particular that caught the singer's eye: "After a lovely dinner, we all went to a room where George's guitars were kept. One wall was hung with guitars and I walked the length of it, admiring his instruments. George came alongside me and commented on a couple of guitars. I pointed out a wildly decorated Stratocaster and asked him about it. He very modestly said that he had painted it himself, 'for a movie.' Later I realized it was the guitar he had used in *Magical Mystery Tour.*"

The real purpose of the adjournment to the guitar room was for "the boys to sit around and play," just as if it were George's mother's house in Liverpool, where John, Paul, and George would gather to play Carl Perkins tunes and to be fed. Now, jamming in his own mansion with the real Perkins, George was enjoying the simple pleasures of life as a guitar player, but he hadn't forgotten his quiet guest. "Carl and Dave and George sat on the floor and played for hours, and I sat in a chair behind them, listening. The three of them were into some deep guitar stuff that was way out of my depth. I do remember George turning around at some point, long into the night, and saying, 'Oh, poor Rosanne,' referring to the fact that I had not slept since leaving the United States the day before."

The following day, Harrison sang "Everybody's Trying to Be My Baby" and "Glad All Over," and gleefully admired Perkins's exuberant guitar solos, presenting the most animated George Harrison ever captured on film. This was the guitarist who loved to play music just for the thrill of it and for the sheer delight of mastering his hero's licks— in short, it was a glimpse of George Harrison before fame, and the music business, intervened. But honoring Perkins was as daunting for Harrison as it was for Rosanne Cash, she recalls: "I had a moment with George. We stood in the wings waiting to go on, as he was going on right after me. He was nervous. When I noticed that he was nervous, I almost stopped being nervous myself. He wished me luck as I went

---

[4]From Rosanne Cash's web site.

on. I went out and did my two songs, and came off. George gave me a little hug, said I was great. I lamented that I had not been as good as at rehearsal and he said, 'It's always that way. Rehearsal is always better.'"

Shanghai Surprise
(film soundtrack—recorded at Friar Park and Abbey Road, May and July 1986)

Harrison had been finding the film business far more congenial than the music equivalent, and having written songs for two Handmade ventures, his main musical project in 1986 was writing a soundtrack for a new film, *Shanghai Surprise*. One of the pleasing aspects of Handmade Films for George was that it was a British company, producing movies largely shot in England, using British actors and crew. That definitely suited his easygoing temperament. It's perhaps too easy to suggest that as soon as Handmade wandered into Hollywood territory, things went awry, but *Shanghai Surprise* was certainly a bumpy ride for all concerned.

Harrison's trip, as executive producer, to Hong Kong to settle matters between the film's stars, Madonna and Sean Penn, is well documented. The Henley impresario also reported that he had to smooth severely ruffled feathers among the crew, who were not used to waiting on superstar egos. The shooting was just about jolted back on track and the picture finished. This was a disappointment to many, as the final result was, at best, boring. George's varied soundtrack was one of the few reasons to be cheerful. He created the title music, two ballads ("Someplace Else" and "Breath Away from Heaven"), one Cab Calloway pastiche ("Hottest Gong in Town"), and a big band instrumental ("Zig Zag"). These pieces were released over a period of six years.[5]

---

[5]The ballads appeared on *Cloud Nine*, "Zig Zag" was the B-side to the 12" version of the "Got My Mind Set on You" single, and "Hottest Gong in Town" was featured on the *Songs by George Harrison II* EP in 1992. "Shanghai Surprise" was finally released as a bonus track on the reissue of *Cloud Nine* in 2004.

[116] **Shanghai Surprise (5:07)** *(Harrison)*
Harrison guitar, vocal; **Vicki Brown** vocal; **Bruce Gary** drums;
Prescott Niles bass; *uncredited keyboards and strings*[6]

This merry workout, bursting with sardonic Harrison jocularity, is based on a simple melodic fragment, twisted and turned through verse and chorus, over a cinematic production full of strings and tympani. Writing to order, George delivers just enough musical drama to meet the needs of the silver screen. Unfortunately, the song was written for a grade A celluloid turkey.

It was the first, and only, recorded duet between Harrison and a female vocalist, Vicki Brown. Oddly, the two work well together, Brown gliding through effortlessly, in comparison to George's anxious vocal. Otherwise, the main point of interest about "Shanghai Surprise" is that its arrangement suggests the Electric Light Orchestra, and therefore provides a pointer to Harrison's subsequent new album.

[117] **Hottest Gong in Town (3:37)** *(Harrison)*
Harrison banjo, guitar, vocal; **"Gaslight Orchestra"** remaining instruments

One of the attractions of scoring the soundtrack for a film set in the 1930s was that Harrison could indulge his passion for prewar music and honor heroes like Cab Calloway.

Recalling the Ellington era, "The Hottest Gong in Town" opens with Harrison's banjo, period Jelly Roll piano, and heavily syncopated drums. And for the first time since "The Answer's at the End," Harrison is heard scat singing with some spirit. He took this performance into *Shanghai Surprise*, where he made a cameo appearance as a slick hotel crooner. It's a testament to Harrison's flexibility as a songwriter that he could produce this convincing tribute to "Minnie the Moocher" and her creator.

---

[6]Gary and Niles were members of the U.S. pop band the Knack.

Cloud Nine
(recorded at Friar Park January–August 1987; released November 1987)

The year 1986 was the apogee of rock's Armani age, when the stars of the 1960s and 1970s had been rehabilitated by the media and filled their days recording challenge-free music and playing at "establishment" charity concerts. It was an era that cast Phil Collins as the cutting edge of musical creativity. Images of middle-aged rock stars sporting Armani suits with jauntily rolled-up sleeves became a photographic rash. It was a little surprising that Harrison should perform at these turgid events, but in the mid-'80s he played two: a summer 1986 date in Birmingham and a June 1987 appearance for the British royal family, for which he went back into the Beatle time machine, playing "While My Guitar Gently Weeps" and "Here Comes the Sun" with a band that included Ringo Starr. These were faithful recreations of the Beatles' recordings. Hence for the guitar showcase, Elton John replicated Paul McCartney's piano intro, and Eric Clapton skirted close to his original solo.

These two concerts featured most of the musicians who were to play on the first new Harrison album in five years, and the Birmingham show brought George face to face with the onetime leader of the Electric Light Orchestra, Jeff Lynne. It seemed that Harrison was beginning to associate playing the guitar with having fun, and soon he was planning a new album. In between cutting solos for Alvin Lee and a theatrical concept album, George was reunited with his old guru, Ravi Shankar, for their first musical encounter in more than ten years. Shankar had kept his musical distance from the rock star in reaction to the critical opprobrium their collaborations had spawned in the conservative Indian music press.[7]

After this, it was time for Harrison to get to work on his new disc, which would be radically different from its predecessors. But the distinction came from the people involved, not a shift in the guitarist's basic concept. The key agent of change was Jeff Lynne, whom Harrison invited to coproduce the album and cowrite some tunes. Lynne was the strongest personality George had used in the control room since Phil Spector, and as he was an established artist and producer in his own right, his presence was bound to have an impact. But at the time, it was an extra pair of hands that George welcomed. Harrison had long bemoaned the life of the "one-man band" recording artist that he had endured on a number of his works. The pressure of writing, playing, and then producing an album was huge; using Jeff Lynne reduced the burden on him and, crucially, provided a sounding board. Lynne was no "yes man," and he provided the kind of honest appraisal that was so obviously lacking on *Dark Horse*. George's career might have been very different had someone suggested keeping that one in the can, until his voice was in better shape. The two other keys to Lynne's role on *Cloud Nine* were his monumental love of the Beatles and his admiration for Harrison's slide guitar sound. These elements hugely influenced the album.

The other new feature of *Cloud Nine* was that, unlike every other Harrison production, there was a smack of showbiz about it. Donning their Armani casuals, Eric Clapton and Elton John joined the session; it seemed that George was teetering on the brink of the Live Aid rent-a-star formula. Fortunately, the steady professionalism of dyed-in-the-wool Harrison session players Jim Keltner and Jim Horn kept the glitz under control. What also remained the same was the convivial atmosphere of recording at Friar Park. Jim Horn's recollections

---

[7]Lee's album was *Detroit Diesel;* the other session was for Wombles creator Mike Batt on his *Hunting of the Snark* release. The Shankar album was *Tana Mana*.

paint a picture of bucolic serenity that is just not rock 'n' roll:"George made you feel at home, in his home, and I'd see him at breakfast, discuss the day's news, have tea in the garden, and go up to his studio whenever we felt like working. He once had me sit on the toilet and play my soprano sax, and they miked it at the end of the hall for a distant sound. I thought they were kidding—we all had a good laugh on that one. Another time he stopped me in the middle of a sax solo and brought my 3 p.m. tea—again I thought he was kidding."

Clearly, at forty-four years of age, Harrison was no longer the jester who left Delaney Bramlett running down a London street with no pants, but his audience had grown up with him, and the retrospective mood of *Cloud Nine* fully met their expectations. More surprisingly, perhaps, it found him an entirely new audience of listeners, who hadn't even been born when he first sang "Do You Want to Know a Secret."

[118] **Cloud 9 (3:14)** *(Harrison)*
Harrison vocal, guitars; **Jeff Lynne** bass; **Elton John** electric piano; **Jim Keltner** drums; **Eric Clapton** guitar; **Jim Horn** saxophone; **Ray Cooper** percussion

When Mo Ostin received George's demo for *Cloud Nine*, he was delighted, and this eponymous opening track shows why—"Cloud 9" is the closest Harrison has ever come to cutting "Prince's Trust" rock. Here was a track that would appeal to the mass, anesthetised audience for Dire Straits, Chris Rea, and the like. It was made for FM radio.

The song had the hallmarks of stadium rock nothingness—it was harmonically simple (a three-chord trick, no less); featured nonthreatening, meaningless lyrics; and was driven by a pounding rock beat. Jeff Lynne mixed the bass drum and electric bass high, to emphasize the basic rock rhythm. Without the slide guitar and vocal, it could have been anybody, even Bryan Adams. The difference between this and "Circles," the closing number of Harrison's last LP, *Gone Troppo*, was intergalactic.

The good news is that in the midst of all this rock dullness, the personality of George Harrison survives. Not unlike "Maya Love" and "Woman Don't You Cry for Me," this piece is a guitar showcase with lyrics appended out of necessity. And the gentle sparring between Harrison's slide and Clapton's thick-toned Stratocaster is worth hearing—it is the best-recorded duet between the two. It felt like they had come full circle in their twenty-year musical relationship—what started with Clapton's solo on "While My Guitar Gently Weeps" and passed through "Badge" reached a mature conclusion here. It lacks the slightly chaotic passion of the *Concert for Bangla Desh* "Gently Weeps" closing bout and it speaks of empathy, not gun-slinging competitiveness.

Aside from Jim Horn's "Savoy Truffle" baritone sax charts, Beatles fans would have noted that Harrison's voice had become noticeably deeper with the passing of time. Even though the urgent, compelling musician of the early 1970s was nowhere to be seen on this exercise in blandness, as far as the music business was concerned, "Cloud 9" gave notice that George Harrison was back as a force to be reckoned with.

[119] That's What It Takes (3:58) *(Harrison–Lynne–Wright)*
Harrison vocal, guitar, first guitar solo; **Jeff Lynne** bass, guitar, keyboards; **Jim Keltner** drums; **Eric Clapton** second guitar solo; **Ray Cooper** percussion

Calculated planning turns rock to finely crafted pop for the second cut, the collective work of Harrison, Lynne, and Gary Wright. In effect, "That's What It Takes" is a version of the Harrison-Beatles sound for the late 1980s. Melodically strong, especially in the rising gospel chorus, the track is arranged for banks of chiming twelve-string guitars, à la "My Sweet Lord." The clock turns back even further when a series of tumbling guitar arpeggios straight out of *Help!* appears, before one of George's patented "odd" chord changes (G to A-flat) introduces the middle eight. By the time he'd taken his solo, one minute and forty seconds of Harrison pop perfection had been crafted.

It sounds contrived, but the whole thing works so well, the guitars ring so true, the backup vocals are so engaging and the melodies so full of catchy uplift, that the song prevails. Even though George had finally gone back in the time machine, "That's What It Takes" is a very good pop-rock song. It wasn't anything new, but as the 1990s proved, after nearly thirty years, old Beatles values were back in fashion.

[120] Fish on the Sand (3:20) *(Harrison)*
Harrison vocal, guitars; **Jeff Lynne** bass, keyboards; **Ringo Starr** drums

Not content with reviving Beatles pop heaven on the preceding piece, Harrison and Lynne turn in the most Beatlesque sound in decades with "Fish on the Sand." As soon as the Beatle fan hears that opening riff from the dusted-down twelve-string Rickenbacker, the collarless suits come to mind. But there's more—not just the *Rubber Soul* twang, but some old Elvis Presley wobble too. Only the synthesized bass and drum machines speak of 1987 (too much)—the guitar hook is straight out of 1965 and the backup vocals circa "We Can Work It Out."

Curiously, all this nostalgia conceals a mental struggle as, amazingly, against this musical candy the song lyrics describe the writer's moments of spiritual crisis, when he feels alienated from the Creator. How many of the millions who bought *Cloud Nine* realized that? They didn't care—it sounded like the Beatles.

[121] Just for Today (4:04) *(Harrison)*
Harrison vocal, guitars; **Jeff Lynne** bass, guitar, keyboards;
Jim Keltner drums; **Gary Wright** piano

In commercial terms, *Cloud Nine* would become one of the great comebacks in popular music history, and soon Harrison was recognized as one of the main survivors of the rock era. Others were not as lucky, due to either external forces or their own inherent lack of self-control. Even as early as 1969 and the Rolling Stones' notorious Altamont concert, the rock dream was going off the rails. By the time of *Cloud Nine*, the casualties of rock numbered in the hundreds. In that sense, this hearse-paced ballad is an elegy for the "rock 'n' roll life."

At face value, the song is about drying out. For those who lived to tell the tale of the 1960s and 1970s addiction boom, here was a survivor's manual. George only briefly plumbed the depths of addiction himself in the crazed 1973–74 period; many more of the *Cloud Nine* cast would have had more reason to relate to "Just for Today." A roomful of Ringo Starr, Elton John, and Eric Clapton amounted to many thousands of dollars spent with the likes of Betty Ford and her professional helpers.

"Just for Today" was conceived for the patrons of Alcoholics Anonymous, but really touches on all the addicts Harrison would have come across in the music and film businesses, which are littered with the corpses of people driven to find fame but unable to handle the consequences. The song commemorates those who didn't survive (Hendrix, Joplin, Morrison), those on whom excess crept up (Jesse Ed Davis, Carl Radle, Rick Grech) and those who survived relatively unscathed and were trying to avoid relapse. One of these was Elton John, whose own mournful "Song for Guy" this *Cloud Nine* track closely resembles.

The funereal tempo gives plenty of time to note that the man who sang "Within You Without You" now has a vocal range that dips down to G below middle C, and two exquisite solo guitar passages that try to offer some comfort to the confused and bewildered fame addicts. Here is evidence that Jeff Lynne was working on the ex-Beatle's sound, adding plenty of delay and a touch of reverb to alter the presentation of Harrison's guitar, which in his own hands as producer generally sounded the same.

Beautiful as the guitars of "Just for Today" are, this is a song about sadness, and the fact that many of the people who want to be "stars" are driven by deep-seated psychological problems that fame just exacerbates. As Harrison had shown in the five years between *Gone Troppo* and *Cloud Nine*, he had long ceased to crave one more swig of the fame brandy.

[122] **This Is Love (3:45)** *(Harrison–Lynne)*
Harrison vocal, guitars; **Jeff Lynne** bass, guitar, keyboards; **Jim Keltner** drums; **Ray Cooper** tambourine

When hits came easily to ex-Beatles in the early 1970s, there was no thought of the songs as "products." Not until *Extra Texture* did George Harrison deliberately set out to create a record that would be palatable in the marketplace. As he rapidly and brutally discovered at the turn of the 1980s, ex-Beatles had to move units like anyone else. The result was a certain amount of soulless hack work ("Teardrops"). With "This Is Love," Harrison managed to fulfill the need for strong product and express his own musical identity.

Lynne's presence is heavily felt here in the rising melody for the "may appear from way out of the blue" line—pure ELO. On what is generally a very fine pop mood, the chugging acoustic guitar rhythm also recalls Lynne's old style, although it most closely resembles "Don't Let Me Wait Too Long."

On the positive side, Lynne was a great advocate of Harrison's guitar skills, and as "This Is Love" demonstrates, encouraged greater freedom and tone variation. So for this upbeat single the maestro's bottleneck is tinged with a little hint of wah-wah. This makes another fine performance grab the attention more. Tellingly, it is introduced by more obvious Beatles references, in the shape of a heavily echoed piano vamp. George the guitarist was also abundantly featured in a cheerful video that accompanied the song. First singing to the ocean, then moving among Hawaiian foliage, friends, and family, Harrison appears contented. "This Is Love" may have been product, but it was also happy product.

[123] **When We Was Fab (3:58)** *(Harrison–Lynne)*
Harrison vocal, guitars; **Ringo Starr** drums; **Jeff Lynne** guitar, bass, keyboards; **Ray Cooper** percussion; **Bobby Kok** cello

The paradox of George Harrison's musical career has received no better summation than this tired exercise in self-consciousness. For once, Harrison's sense of comedy cannot save what amounts to a capitulation to all the artifice and iconic Beatles imagery that had haunted him for decades. Based on "I Am the Walrus," this effort gave Jeff Lynne the chance to live out his Beatles fantasies from the Friar Park control room. The "Walrus" model accounts for the cellos, whooping "oohs," timpani, backward tape loops, and sitars, but of course there was more. Dredged from the "make your own Beatles song" kit came Ringo Starr's judiciously "wrong" drum fills, echoed piano from "While My Guitar Gently Weeps," and "All You Need Is Love" horns. For Lynne, this was only the prelude to the "Free As a Bird" affair, when his dream was fully realized.

Harrison's detached lyrical stance leaves doubt as to whether he is celebrating, or reviewing with hindsightful despair, all the clichés and myths of Beatles lore. Hence, the whole affair threatens to crash as self-parody verges on self-mockery and name checks for Bob Dylan ("It's All Over Now Baby Blue") and Smokey Robinson ("You Really Got a Hold on Me") provide no succor. In one very rare instance, George Harrison's music sounds insincere. "When We Was Fab" is a little too coy for comfort.

[124] **Devil's Radio (3:52)** *(Harrison)*
Harrison vocal, guitar; **Jeff Lynne** bass, keyboards; **Ringo Starr** drums; **Eric Clapton** guitar solos; **Elton John** piano; **Ray Cooper** percussion

It had been a very long time since George Harrison used the rock 'n' roll idiom to exorcise negativity. Not since "Wah-Wah" had he adopted an aggressive musical style to convey a confrontational stance. Some would characterize *Cloud Nine* as the music of self-satisfied, middle-aged decadence, but this track brings the guitarist's gentle rebelliousness back to life.

Cloud Nine, and the Traveling Wilburys project that followed, would probably never have happened had Carl Perkins not persuaded Harrison to play on his 1985 *Rockabilly Session* video. That gig rekindled Harrison's self-identity as a musician and reminded him how much fun it could be to play music. It also made him wonder if he should start writing rockabilly songs, acknowledging that that was what he was good at. In a direct way, "Devil's Radio" proves the point, with its Chuck Berry opening, Harrison's strong vocal, and the fine Clapton counterpoint.

As Harrison's first major attack on the media, "Devil's Radio" unearths all manner of contradictions. When the *Cloud Nine* band-wagon began to roll, Harrison was much in evidence, playing the media game to sell his product—yet the media were his main tormen-tors. Setting out a worldview in which the artist adopted a clearly superior moral stance, George was openly calling journalism the devil's work.

His position would be that of the "ordinary man," emerging from the shadow of the "star" to bluntly ask his listeners how they would feel if they suffered the same media attention he did: "You wonder why I don't hang out much, I wonder how you can't see." The Beatles were no royal family, they weren't trained in the art of being public figures, so they had to learn on the job. But worse, they could remem-ber what it was like to be able to go unmolested for a quiet night out.

As usual with George Harrison, he employs no Dylanesque alle-gory but tells it from the heart. Nevertheless, Dylan's "Restless Farewell" may have provided a lyrical template—on that piece from *The Times They Are A-Changin'*, Dylan mulls over "the dirt of gossip" that blows into his face and "the dust of rumors" that covers him. Harrison's 1987 rocker covers the same ground, and it would be a use-ful document for any future historian investigating the celebrity's experience of fame in the twentieth century.

[125] **Someplace Else (3:51)** *(Harrison)*
Harrison vocal, guitars; **Jeff Lynne** bass; **Ray Cooper** drums, percussion

The Western music that George created for *Wonderwall* now seems to be trapped within the context of the film: it's hard to imagine it having a life outside the cinema. This went slightly against the grain for a Beatles-related celluloid soundtrack, as the group were masters at creating songs that stood alone but also fitted into a film setting. The same could be said for "Someplace Else," one of the first tunes to be emancipated from the wreckage of bruised superstar egos and weak plots that comprised *Shanghai Surprise*. The slight hint of dramatic overkill does not drown a strong melody characterized by the sweet, but unfulfilled A major seventh root. Harrison shows how to change the mood of a song by taking an abrupt turn to E major for the chorus, giving it a more purposeful temperament.

The song is lifted by a passionate guitar passage with all the Harrison trademarks. One of the spin-offs from the success of *Cloud Nine* was a feature on Harrison's six-string skills in *Guitar Player* magazine. At last, some long-overdue credit was coming his way. While the media have been slow to recognize his playing abilities, other musicians have long held him in high esteem. Singer-guitarist Larry Hosford puts it very neatly: "Let's say that, noteswise, he is more profound than prolific. I think first and foremost that he is a very original slide man. Very unique approach; what he hears and what he seeks out doesn't derive of standard bluegrass or blues or rock approaches. It derives of his own head, heart, and soul. I have heard the word 'elegant' used here, and endorse it wholeheartedly."

[126] **Wreck of the Hesperus (3:30)** *(Harrison)*
Harrison vocal, guitar; **Jeff Lynne** bass; **Ringo Starr** drums;
Eric Clapton guitar solos; **Elton John** piano; **Ray Cooper**
percussion; **Jim Horn** horns

Procol Harum had already celebrated Longfellow's morbid poem in popular song by the time George Harrison recorded this blues-rock highlight of *Cloud Nine*. Harrison's good spirits and humor shine through as he casts his media self as a kind of musical tourist attraction, like the Eiffel Tower or the Great Wall of China. Never one to be concerned about the demands of fashion, the star is happy to declare that he's no "spring chicken" in one of his funniest lines. When he says he's been "plucked," it's safe to assume that he meant a homonym that might not have passed the censors.

The other side of his story as Beatle George is his old adversary, the media, and that honorable profession comes in for a significant assault from Harrison's pen. His targets are the rotten "poison pen men" of the tabloid press—particularly the British version. The slight awkwardness is that the public buy the tabloids—they are Harrison's "other heads as dense as they is." Unfortunately, these same people are, in theory, his audience.

Still, in the cool light of day, a beguiling Harrison emerges from "Wreck of the Hesperus," a man who is "All By Myself," just like his blues hero Big Bill Broonzy. As if in tribute to Broonzy, the track is based around a riff that Lightnin' Hopkins would have enjoyed, and plenty of Clapton's Stratocaster. The song, and Harrison, sweep off into the distance with the repeated words of reassurance "But it's all right, it's all right"—the same comfort he offered to close "Here Comes the Sun" and that characterized the "message" of *All Things Must Pass*.

This song has much better claims to a *Best of George Harrison* album placing than "All Those Years Ago," and the crack about Broonzy is one of his finest ever.[8] Unlike the futile "When We Was Fab," this is one of the best-humored exercises in self-effacement that any semiretired rock star ever conjured.

[127] **Breath Away from Heaven (3:35)** *(Harrison)*
Harrison vocal, keyboards; **Jeff Lynne** keyboards; **Ray Cooper** tambourine, percussion

The fact that this piece was another leftover from the ill-fated *Shanghai Surprise* venture gave Harrison license to let his imagination run free. It isn't a song expressing his feelings, so he creates a Dylanesque "I" to narrate the story—a rare event for the guitarist.

The result is the most consciously poetic lyric in his songbook, with lines like "as the morning light was painting whispers of a sigh," using rich adjectives such as "iridescent." He displays great skill and a definite ability to conjure pathos—"like an opalescent moon all alone in the sky of a foreign land" suggests more than a passing acquaintance with the techniques of poetry.

Musically, Harrison cleverly suspends the melody in a still sea of time, as if it were the soundtrack to the graceful yogic morning exercises seen in Chinese communities the world over.

[128] **Got My Mind Set on You (3:51)** *(R Clark)*
Harrison vocal, guitars; **Jeff Lynne** bass, keyboards; **Jim Keltner** drums; **Jim Horn** saxophone; **Ray Cooper** percussion

James Ray was just one American R&B singer whose career was wrecked by the Beatles' 1964 arrival. Record buyers suddenly lost interest in his classy, brassy charts like "If You Gotta Make a Fool of Somebody," a 1962 hit. Another effort from Ray had the elaborate title "I've Got My Mind Set on You (Parts 1 & 2)," which suggests that it was an early progressive rock, concept single. This was actually a horn-driven session that caught R&B on the cusp of rock 'n' roll—it still has the strings and jazz band drumming style of older 1940s recordings by T-Bone Walker or Saunders King. There are no guitars on the cut, but banjos and a choir of falsetto female voices support Ray's voice, which owes much to blues star Bobby Bland.

---

[8]"I'm not the wreck of the Hesperus, feel more like Big Bill Broonzy."

George Harrison's take of the song for *Cloud Nine* replicated the Beatles' approach to covering early 1960s pop soul—he re-created it as a rock 'n' roll session, arranged for guitars. The new version swings the original melody into a strongly rhythmic setting—both vocally, where George's strong performance contrasts with Ray's laid-back smoothness, and with Jim Keltner's forceful backbeat. It's a tribute to Keltner's panache that he manages to inject some vestige of humanity into drum synthesizers. Back in the studio with old friends and a partner full of ideas, Harrison could let the good times roll. "Jeff Lynne coproduced the song with George," recalls sax player Jim Horn. "We stacked twelve to fourteen saxophones and came up with some great sounds. George called it 'being stung by saxophones.'"

As few but dedicated collectors would have remembered James Ray, Harrison's work was virtually a new song and a surefire success. Megahit status was secured by a brutal Warner Brothers marketing campaign that George fully embraced—this was to be no *Gone Troppo*. There were two separate videos to accompany the single and a variety of promotional or collector's release formats. Naturally, all that would have counted for nothing if the song hadn't got people up on their feet dancing—but, as it was a success in that way too, it came up to the mark on all counts.

Single (B-side, 1988)

[129] **Zig Zag (2:40)** *(Harrison–Lynne)*
Harrison guitar, banjo, vocal; **"Gaslight Orchestra"** remaining instruments

As a longtime fan of Cab Calloway, Harrison had no difficulty in creating a pastiche of 1930s dance hall jazz. Little more than a chord sequence spiced with period saxophone and cornet solos, "Zig Zag" conveys the era well, but is no more than film music. The main noteworthy point is that it's a rare recording of George's banjo picking.

The *Cloud Nine* experience is generally positive. The songs are strong, the vocals good, and the guitar stylings outstanding. Good grace and humor bound out from pieces like "Wreck of the Hesperus," and in "That's What It Takes" and "This Is Love," Harrison released two of his most charming pop-rock charts yet. The return to rock 'n' roll roots depicted by "Devil's Radio" and "Got My Mind Set on You" is a powerful reminder of why this man became a rock star and not an electrician. But this collection is clearly removed from the confessional Harrison of nearly all his previous albums, where his basic musical model was the Dylan-legacy acoustic template. The very fact that most of *Cloud Nine* is played on electric guitars signals its retrenchment to the days before the Fab Four heard *Bringing It All Back Home*.

A slight uneasiness emerges from concerns that Harrison's innately powerful and emotionally compelling musical personality have been diluted like wedding beer. Jeff Lynne's fanaticism for the Beatles resurrected all manner of arrangement references to Harrison's old group and generally cast him back into that mold. There seems no musical logic to the H. G. Wells exercise "When We Was Fab," and "Cloud 9" itself verges on being trapped in the designer rock of the time. *Cloud Nine* is fun, but it lacks the old Harrison passion of *All Things Must Pass* and *Living in the Material World*. Ultimately it's a very good album, but not a gripping one.

Naturally, the music press welcomed this watering down, on the grounds that it "curbed the excess" that, in their view, was inherent in the guitarist's approach. The public embraced it too and, on the massive success of "Got My Mind Set on You," which made Harrison the first, and to date last, solo Beatle to have a U.S. #1 single, sales of the LP soared. As usual, Harrison did not tour in support of *Cloud Nine*—if he had, the sales would have been outrageous. Not too many artists sell a million with no tour.

A lesser-known result of the *Cloud Nine* sessions at Friar Park was a companion to the Carl Perkins video—this time a project that sought to bring another original Harrison guitar hero, Duane Eddy, back to the public gaze. Not just George but also Steve Cropper, John Fogerty, James Burton, and Paul McCartney, as well as Ry Cooder, supported the *Duane Eddy* release. This set produced the first and last album to showcase two great slide guitar stylists, Harrison and Cooder. Harrison had long admired and wanted to emulate the American's style. As Klaus Voormann recalls, his struggles caused the star frustration, but ultimately fulfillment in finding his own voice: "George tried and tried again to play slide finger-style like Ry Cooder, but he could not get it together. He said himself that he does not have the control over the instrument that he would like. He did the best he could, so he developed his own style—every time he does a solo, it's like writing a piece of music."

One of the most exotic features of the *Duane Eddy* album is one of the Harrison collaborations, "The Trembler," based on a fragment of Ravi Shankar melody once heard by Harrison. Given a soupçon of Duane, the world's most unlikely writing credit was born—"Shankar-Eddy." That "The Trembler" mixed Carnatic (a school or style of south Indian classical music) tones and Eddy's chunky-tremelo sound with an archetypal Jim Horn rock 'n' roll solo was curious enough. With the raga tone of Harrison's slide added, the result is a notable concoction.

One of the other side effects of *Cloud Nine* was that Harrison owed some favors to the musicians who played on it, and shortly afterward found himself participating from a safe distance in the slightly bizarre world of Elton John. The singer's sometime wife, Renate, had decided to launch a new career as a record producer on Elton's Rocket label. The object of her plans was a friend of hers who had been lead singer for the curiously named Kissing the Pink. Nepotism being what it is, Sylvia Griffin soon found herself working with the Elton John camp on an album for which the diva himself would provide a song, and George Harrison would grace another on guitar. The result was "Love's a State of Mind," a lively pop single that charted nowhere, but still featured Harrison's playful slide high in the mix. There was, however, no sign of Renate engineering at Friar Park.

In 1988, Harrison was fully immersed in promotional activities for *Cloud Nine*, which rapidly sold a million. He still found time to cut guitar tracks for his less colorful friends, Jim Capaldi and Gary Wright, on their new releases, and it seems that the Harrison pendulum had swung very much toward a period of being wholly engaged in the music business again—so much so that, in his most unlikely guest appearance ever, he grafted a notably exciting solo onto a massive hit for the warbling Californian pop-chanteuse Belinda Carlisle.[9] When he guested on these record dates, there were none of the old 1970s studio gatherings—Harrison received tapes and cut solos in private at his Friar Park studio. Nevertheless, with *Cloud Nine* a massive success, he was spending more and more time in California. This relocation led, by chance, to the formation of a new band and time away from the cocoon of home.

---

[9]"Leave a Light on for Me."

10

Good Times with Old Friends

(1988–2001)

"It feels so good to just, you know, be a part of such a good band. It feels great just to be able to melt into a band—more than people might want me to, but I'm gonna melt into this band." This statement of intent from Harrison at the Fort Worth show in 1974 is not the testimony of a "star." This was a man who wanted to be in a good-time band, like Delaney & Bonnie, or the Beatles circa 1962. Late in his career, he was presented with one more chance, The Traveling Wilburys.

Born entirely through luck and coincidence, this most unlikely of all "supergroups" might have been more accurately named The Accidental Wilburys. It started with a Los Angeles conversation between Harrison and Lynne about putting together a B-side for "When We Was Fab." As Lynne was producing a new album by Roy Orbison,[1] the veteran friend of the Beatles[2] offered to sing on the tune. To save money, Harrison arranged to use Bob Dylan's home studio in Santa Monica to cut the track that did not yet have a title. But his guitar was at the home of another local musician, Tom Petty, who naturally joined the session. Harrison had a few guitar riffs and, having challenged Dylan to "give us some lyrics," found inspiration on a label on a packing case that announced, "Handle with Care." A song was created on the spot, in Dylan's garden, with Harrison writing a part specifically to suit Orbison's voice, which he loved. It wasn't the first time he'd written with the Texan in mind—"Who Can See It" from *Living in the Material World* was conceived with an Orbison vocal.

---

[1] *Mystery Girl.*

[2] Orbison toured the U.K. with the Beatles in 1963 and knew them socially.

The next day, Harrison took the tape to Warner Brothers, who pronounced the song too good to be buried on a B-side. Inspired by the muse known as beer, the two main *Cloud Nine* protagonists then hatched the idea of an entire album. When Dylan, Orbison, and Petty agreed to play along, a new band was born. The whole album was recorded over ten days, in the summer of 1988, and became a spontaneous gift from God for Warner Brothers, who soon fitted the million-selling product into the pre-Christmas schedule.

For Harrison, clearly the Wilburys' leader, the group achieved a number of ambitions. Most importantly, it taught him that the music business could be fun; it allowed him to play in a proper band, by far his most natural setting; and it gave him the chance to deflate the pomposity of rock. It also marked the culmination of his friendship with Bob Dylan, a relationship that underlines Harrison's unique position—it is simply impossible to imagine Lennon or McCartney forming an impromptu band with Dylan. By contrast, Harrison and Dylan had been musical partners off and on since 1968. Twenty years later, they were in the same band.

The musical aspects of the Wilburys are less significant in Harrison's story than what the group said about his attitude to stardom. Without a doubt, this was his most obvious attempt to shed his alter ego, the "George Harrison, rock star" cipher. The Wilburys were a phantom band, where Harrison and Dylan in particular could hide beneath pseudonyms and find liberation from themselves. Hence the semiserious Wilbury anthropology, from the pen of Michael Palin, that parodied the Beatles lore continually pored over and revived the world over. This constant mythologizing of the Beatles threatened to turn the group into objects of historical curiosity. Eric Idle and Neil Innes had satirized this obsessive approach with the Rutles; Harrison did it with the Wilburys.

The Traveling Wilburys: Vol. 1 (recorded Los Angeles and Friar Park, April and May 1988; released November 1988)

The mood of the first Wilburys album is of a bunch of guys on a busman's holiday, having fun, raking over their formative musical influences and, for Harrison and Dylan, escaping their media personas. There was nothing innovative or significant about music that ranged from knockabout skiffle love songs to a classic American pop theme (the cars of "Dirty World"), through rockabilly ("Rattled"), to pure

Orbison microdrama ("Not Alone Any More")."Handle with Care" was a worthy hit, working through three contrasting but equally catchy sections that showcased the very different styles of the vocalists—Harrison's Scouse strivings, Orbison's soaring vibrato and Dylan's compelling, nasal whine.The song closes with two of the most famous instrumental signatures in popular music in tandem, Dylan's harmonica and Harrison's slide.

The pair are more dominant on the second side of the album, Dylan with his classic tall tale ("Tweeter and the Monkey Man") and the archetypal Dylan-Harrison slow-tempo ballad, "Congratulations." There is some throwaway filler (i.e., "Margarita"), but all the pieces revel in excellent and imaginative four- or five-part harmonies that must have taken Harrison back to the happy memories of this greatest of Beatle skills.

Harrison's guitar ranges far and wide on the album, as he runs through most of his rock 'n' roll influences,[3] but his bottleneck is in short supply. Maybe the idea was to keep instrumental identities under wraps.[4] Nevertheless, a nod to his Beatle past slips through on the merry skiffle of "End of the Line," which opens with a replay of the guitar intro to "I'm Looking Through You" from *Rubber Soul*. And there is also one obvious Harrisong.

[130] **Heading for the Light (3:37)** *(Harrison-Lynne)*[5]
Harrison guitar, vocals; **Jeff Lynne** bass, guitar, backup vocal; **Roy Orbison** backup vocal; **Tom Petty** guitar, backup vocal; **Bob Dylan** guitar, backup vocal; **Jim Horn** horns; **Jim Keltner** drums; **Ray Cooper** tambourine

George Harrison produced his most uplifting account of his spiritual search with this upbeat rocker, similar in construction to "All Those Years Ago" but far better. On *Cloud Nine* he had matured sufficiently to mask his meditative musings with lyrical ambiguity. "Heading for the Light," on the other hand, is quite explicit in its meaning, but so spirited that most listeners wouldn't have cared.

Surrounded by riffing guitars, Jim Horn's rock 'n' roll sax, and an ethereal Orbison backup vocal, Harrison recounts his travails as a star, the ennui of fame and fortune ("nothing more than time on my

---

[3]There are some notable deep Duane Eddy riffs during "Congratulations."

[4]Dylan too plays almost none of his trademark harmonica parts.

[5]All the Wilburys' songs were credited to the "group," but this song was actually written by Harrison and Lynne.

hands"), and the ups and downs of his career ("my hands were tied, jokers and fools on either side"). As he had cautioned himself years before on "The Lord Loves the One," transformation can only come from within. That is why on "Heading for the Light" he sings of the world remaining the same as he gets back on the road to enlightenment. The message was constant; it was only the medium that had changed. Still, this would have been a worthy *Cloud Nine* track.

[131] Run So Far (4:06) *(Harrison) (recorded by Eric Clapton)*
Harrison guitar, harmony vocal; **Eric Clapton** guitar, vocal;
Rob Mounsey synthesizer; **Greg Phillinganes** synthesizer;
Alan Clark synthesizer; **Darryl Jones** bass; **Jim Keltner** drums;
Carol Steele percussion

A minor diversion of the Wilburys escapade was speculation about who could ever be a Wilbury and who never would. A case in point is Eric Clapton, who, like Harrison and Dylan, had certainly spent years escaping his own image. But did the band really need a virtuoso?

Like those of the two leading Wilburys, Clapton's career was constantly in the shadow of 1960s glories, but as the 1980s progressed he benefited from one of the fashion reincarnations that feed the music industry. Clapton's mainstream blues-rock suddenly regained its 1970s popularity, and a 1989 work, *Journeyman*, almost hit the top of the British album charts.

Nevertheless, the spirit of the age did take a new Harrison tune into the mainstream, in the shape of "Run So Far." In fact, in return for his *Cloud Nine* cameos, George offered Clapton three songs for the album; the others were "Cheer Down" and "That Kind of Woman." Clapton chose a poignant acoustic offering over the harder rock numbers. "Run So Far" could be read as "Behind That Locked Door" for Clapton, an open letter from one friend to another. In the opening lines Harrison writes of the star escaping on a plane, leaving behind a false, fixed smile for the press, and facing the reality of emotional turmoil. "Run So Far" is about the loneliness of stardom and the fact that when the star, "the product," sees past all the demands and veneer of the business, they have to face up to themselves. Musically attractive, this is a song with a tough message for the millionaire rock-star fraternity. It obviously had great significance for Harrison, as his version was later released on the *Brainwashed* set.

Best of Dark Horse 1976–1989
(new songs recorded at Friar Park, July 1989;
released October 1989)

The purpose of this compilation album was to close Harrison's contractual obligations to Warner Brothers, hardly a situation conducive
to the creation of new music. After the massive successes of *Cloud
Nine* and the Wilburys album, George's stock was higher than at any
time since 1974. *Best of Dark Horse* may have reminded some that
the guitarist had not disappeared completely after "You." Harrison was
still writing and recording his songs at Friar Park, largely for his own
gratification. Three of them were tacked onto this "best of" release.

[132] **Poor Little Girl (4:31)** *(Harrison)*
Harrison vocal, guitars, banjo; **Jeff Lynne** bass, keyboards;
Ian Paice drums; **Jim Horn** saxophone; **Richard Tandy** piano

On the evidence of "Poor Little Girl," the success of *Cloud Nine* and
the Wilburys had not fundamentally altered George Harrison's worldview. Still relying on a Jeff Lynne sound, George manages to concoct a
catchy Beatle-ish track (more tumbling guitar arpeggios and "Savoy
Truffle" horn charts) that was never really going to cause any chart
action. There is a pop pseudo-drama to the middle eight that is a little
too reminiscent of the Electric Light Orchestra, or of a producer looking to mimic the Spector sound.[6]

   Still, at least Harrison's sense of humor continued to prevail.
Perhaps remembering that Warner Brothers had told him almost ten
years earlier to record music about teenage love, he uses the
metaphor of horny teenagers looking for love (masquerading as sex)
to highlight their lack of spiritual enlightenment. At this point in his
career, the singer seems to have been acknowledging that his feelings
were far from mainstream, and confessing that he was trying to understand why he had them. He also couldn't fully understand his need to
share feelings with others. As ever with Harrison, the search went on.

---

[6]The ELO inflections were hardly surprising, as Jeff Lynne had enlisted ex-ELO man
Richard Tandy to handle keyboards on this three-song session. During this period Tandy co-wrote
"Take Away the Sadness" with Jim Horn, a cameo for Harrison's slide guitar that came out on
Horn's 1990 *Work It Out* album.

[133] **Cockamamie Business (5:14)** *(Harrison)*
Harrison vocal, guitars, banjo **Jeff Lynne** bass, keyboards;
Ian Paice drums; **Jim Horn** saxophone; **Richard Tandy** piano

This moderate, bluesy rocker features enough tasty riffs and licks to keep George's fans happy, but the track has the mood of a valedictory address. As the 1990s would prove, it wasn't far from the truth. Through a series of "Cloud 9" couplets, he reviews his career with a despairing humor. Full of hindsight, he rejects it through the now customary association with ecological trauma.

Initially name-checking some key points in his career (Ed Sullivan, the Marquee Club, etc.) and music business friends like Bad Company, Harrison parodies his own marital tribulations, as previously described in darker times on "Simply Shady." He quickly shifts gear into a "Run of the Mill" mood, reflecting on the imbalance between resources and demand, but, well buried in nearly six minutes of word games and in-jokes, George Harrison sums up his life: "Didn't want to be a star, wanted just to play guitar."

[134] **Cheer Down (4:08)** *(Harrison–Petty)*
Harrison vocal, guitar; **Jeff Lynne** bass, guitar, keyboards, backup vocal; **Ian Paice** drums; **Ray Cooper** percussion; **Richard Tandy** piano

Of all the designer rock numbers George Harrison released after *Cloud Nine*, this bottleneck bonanza is easily the finest. It first appeared in the unlikeliest setting ever for a Harrisong, the soundtrack of *Lethal Weapon 2*, through a number of Eric Clapton–inspired hoops. "Cheer Down" could have been buried on *Journeyman*, or on *Lethal Weapon* as a Clapton performance.

With steady-rocking humor and melodic twists, this chugging workout summons the spirit of "Old Brown Shoe": with Deep Purple drummer Ian Paice, Harrison creates one of his more effective rock songs. The closing guitar passages are fitting epitaphs to George's extravagant slide skills—he runs the gamut from Indian blues chops to two-part countermelodies and sweeping Pete Drake jaunts through the octaves. In the mold of "Woman Don't You Cry for Me," "Maya Love," and "Cloud Nine," "Cheer Down" is the last bottleneck showcase George Harrison played live, and one of his most accomplished. This is the sort of performance that drew praise from real guitar heroes, among them Eric Clapton: "I like the way he bends strings, too. He's a great slide player, most of all he's a fantastic slide player."[7]

[7]From press conference in Tokyo, Japan, at the start of the Harrison tour.

Nobody's Child
(various artists compilation; released April 1990)

Proving that the altruism of the Bangla Desh concerts remained, Harrison used his muscle to put together this album in support of his wife's charity for Romanian orphans abandoned by a brutal but recently deposed dictatorship. Enlisting such heavy-hitters as Stevie Wonder, Clapton, and Guns 'n' Roses, George cut a new track with the Wilburys, dug out an old television appearance with Paul Simon, and released a Clapton–Harrison outtake from the *Journeyman* sessions.

The Wilburys charity single didn't match the power of "Bangla Desh," but took Harrison back to his pre-Beatles days, with a straightforward take of "Nobody's Child," once sung by skiffle king Lonnie Donegan—and the Beatles. The "new" Harrison composition presented a throwback to the days when women were known as "chicks."

[135] **That Kind of Woman (3:56)** *(Harrison) (recorded by both Eric Clapton and Gary Moore)*
Harrison guitar, harmony vocal; **Eric Clapton** guitar, vocal; **Rob Mounsey** synthesizer; **Nathan East** bass; **Jim Keltner** drums; **Robbie Kondor** synthesizer[8]

This unusually lecherous Harrison lyric was cut by two of his virtuoso guitar buddies in the space of a few months, but seems marooned in late 1980s safeness. Clapton's version has less spontaneity than a roomful of insurance salesman, even though Harrison produces a neat riff that would have been suited to *Cloud Nine*, and the same chugging rhythm of "Cheer Down."

The rendering released by Harrison's new guitar chum, Gary Moore, in April 1990 is looser than Clapton's and pitches the songwriter's bottleneck next to the Irishman's heavily overdriven Les Paul. Featured on Moore's *Still Got the Blues* venture, "That Kind of Woman" reached the ears of more than three million hard rock fans. Nevertheless, it's obvious that Harrison was writing to a formula, which makes "That Kind of Woman" largely irrelevant.

---

[8]These credits refer to the Eric Clapton recording.

[136] **Homeward Bound (2:38)** *(Simon)*
Harrison guitar, vocal; **Paul Simon** guitar, vocal

This cheerful, folksy duet was exhumed from a 1976 *Saturday Night Live* television session during George's gargantuan efforts to promote *Thirty-three & 1/3*. Predating the "unplugged" formula by decades, this upbeat performance by two legendary harmonizers was suitably crowd pleasing, but hardly essential.

As the Wilburys were reconvening, their manager was flexing his guitar muscles in a notably varied series of musical settings. In March he was heard in an instrumental setting, coupling with the soprano saxophone of Jim Horn on a rare solo album, *Work It Out.* The melancholy aspect of "Take Away the Sadness" is that it's the only guitar ballad Harrison ever recorded. His ability to convey emotion with the simple melody is striking, but any careful listener can detect that his technique had slightly changed. Rather than picking every note, he was now letting the bottleneck fly through a stream of notes with one stroke of the plectrum, in the manner of an Indian *vichitra veena* player.[9] The effect was musical liberation. Horn was also on a new solo set from George's fellow Wilbury Jeff Lynne, whose *Armchair Theatre* is surprisingly introspective—its decidedly noncommercial setting suggests that the recent Wilburys payoff had given Lynne sufficient latitude to exercise his muse. Along with rock 'n' roll throwbacks like "Every Little Thing," there are companion pieces to Harrison's Hoagy Carmichael covers, "Stormy Weather" and "September Song," both standards of such weight that they could only be approached with caution. For connoisseurs of George Harrison the guitarist, these two pieces are a treat, as Lynne's dedication to recording him well provides an outstanding opportunity to hear the full, delicate precision of Harrison's technique. The unaccompanied intro for "September Song" is a testament to Harrison's six-string craft, and to Lynne's desire to tape it properly.

As if to emphasize his flexibility, George's next session slots were with different guitar voices—his job for Vicki Brown on her last album

---

[9]Also known as the *chitravina* in South India, the *vichitra veena* is a development of the classic Indian stringed instrument, the veena. The vichitra veena is played with a slide to create perfect intonation and vibrato. Harrison was an expert on all forms of Indian music and would have been very familiar with this instrument.

before succumbing to cancer, *About Love and Life*, was to play Hawaiian slide guitar. Hearing "Lu Le La," the listener would be hard pressed to tell this Liverpudlian apart from a 1990s Sol Hoopii. Finally Harrison turned back to the country inflections of *New Morning* for Bob Dylan's latest offering, the perplexing *Under the Red Sky*. The title piece is a distorted Brothers Grimm tale of baked children, men in the moon, and failed regeneration, the kind of curveball lyric that Dylan has been pitching at his fans for years. The desperate scramble for meaning and allegory digs up precisely nothing. Maybe Dylan just liked the way the words sounded, strung together. The song itself has the mood of a rocking nursery rhyme, and Harrison's part is a little fragment of innocence.

The Traveling Wilburys: Vol. 3 (recorded in Bel Air, California, March–May 1990; released October 1990)

Of course Dylan and Harrison joined again for the second Traveling Wilburys album, a more straightforward affair than its predecessor. It suffered fundamentally from the loss of Roy Orbison's vocals and sheer presence, and lacked the carefree atmosphere of *Vol. 1*. Like many young bands, The Wilburys soon discovered the pressure of following a big-hit first album. To offset it, they went for a virtually live recording at an estate in Coldwater Canyon. They worked very quickly, producing multiple songs in a single session, sometimes using the first vocal recorded ("If You Belonged to Me"). Overall, George Harrison's production work is far more pronounced on *Vol. 3*, possibly because he had virtually become the Wilburys manager. Handling all the tedium of rock business administration may have taken the shine off his escape-hatch band for Harrison, but he still worked hard with Lynne to create a polished product.

As if to emphasize the artifice of the Wilburys, Harrison is now Spike rather than Nelson Wilbury. But unlike on the first album, there's no "Heading for the Light" or "Handle with Care," no obvious Harrisongs. George, the songwriter, had a hand in "She's My Baby," "Inside Out," "You Took My Breath Away," and the beautiful "New Blue Moon." Dylan was obviously the main force behind "If You Belonged to Me" and "Where Were You Last Night?", the latter reviving a faster take on the descending riff from "So Sad."

There are two uninteresting tracks to grapple with: the opener, "She's My Baby," is a disappointment, sounding like a formula, flash-rock track of the ELO type. It's too much of an obvious "rocking" first track, retracing the steps of "Back in the USSR." The closer is obviously a Harrison-inspired joke: "The Wilbury Twist" does provide interest in hearing Dylan and Harrison going over the top, but is ultimately a throwaway.

"You Took My Breath Away" is the album's strongest and cleanest melody, sounding like a *Cloud Nine* outtake, while "7 Deadly Sins" is the best gag, with angelic choruses intoning luxuriant Everly Brothers harmonies while keeping a tally of sins committed. The best moment comes with "New Blue Moon," a gorgeous revival of the Beatles' rich 1950s vocal harmonies—long, languid notes richly sung in two parts by Harrison and Lynne, accompanied by chiming slide flights of fancy. A middle eight that has Bob Dylan singing, "you, you, yahoo," is surely worthy of note.

The Harrison guitar is also far more prominent than on *Vol. 1,* and alongside the mix of slide and Carl Perkins served up on "Poor House," there is "The Devil's Been Busy," a track that uncovers the roots of George's guitar style. For the first time since 1967, he unpacks his sitar in anger and plays a "solo" on it. The difference is that he doubles the sitar track with a slide guitar, as if to emphasize the shared vocabulary he took from one to the other. Stuck away on a nuthin' fancy album track, this is an important footnote to George Harrison's development as a musician.

Another interesting aside is a Harrisong developed for the sessions but ultimately rejected. "Maxine," with its almost Andean mood, probably wasn't up to par, but is fascinating because it has George narrating a typically Dylanish tale about a lady who once passed through an imaginary town in an imaginary time. Harrison seldom wrote lines like, "I bought a tabloid paper she was rumoured to be in, there was photo of a woman on a llama, but she never came through here again." [10]

The Traveling Wilburys: Vol. 3 was released as the Gulf War exacerbated another sales-denting transatlantic economic recession. The hard fact was the Wilburys joke had enough appeal for one album and was stretched too far for a second—the novelty of hearing these players in tandem had worn off. Nevertheless, Harrison was rightly identified as the power behind Spike, and all the other Wilburys, and he started to receive plenty of favorable coverage. In retrospect, the

---

[10]One "extra" from these sessions that was released as a bonus on a 12" single was a version of the Del Shannon hit "Runaway."

group was an interlude for Dylan and Harrison, a chance to escape their assumed and/or inherited performing personas. Very much "retro," these discs' grooves show no musical growth or innovation, but there's plenty of good-time music. Both Harrison and Dylan benefited from the looser images the venture fabricated and, from a song-writing stance, "Heading for the Light" and "New Blue Moon" were welcome additions to the Harrison canon. The Wilburys were good news, but they would never replace the power and passion of the real George Harrison's music. Sadly, years would pass before any new Harrison work was heard.

Part of the reason for Harrison's retreat from public affairs was that he had been very badly burned in the business world again with the collapse of Handmade Films. Between 1988 and the final hearing in a Los Angles court ten years later, Harrison was embroiled in a serious dose of the "Sue Me Sue You Blues" with his former business partner Dennis O'Brien. Harrison alleged, and the courts agreed, that O'Brien had mismanaged Handmade and Harrison's finances (the two were the same) to such an extent that Harrison had liabilities of £25 million, well in excess of his liquid assets. It was a shattering blow to George, who had only formed Handmade out of artistic altruism. Even worse, it was the actions of a close friend that had caused the destruction of yet another dream. As Eric Idle told Robert Sellers, "I know George never forgave Dennis. He hated him with an intensity that was quite rare for George. He felt bitter, betrayed, angry and let down. In fact, he wrote a song called 'Lying O'Brien' which he played me."[11]

Live in Japan
(recorded in Japan, December 1991; released July 1992)

During the late 1970s and 1980s, George Harrison worked in cycles. He took a long sabbatical between *Thirty-three & 1/3* and *George Harrison*, and almost five years as an interlude between *Gone Troppo* and *Cloud Nine*. The success of that album, and the accidental Traveling Wilburys ventures, gave George another solid three years in the limelight. As 1990 slipped away, another "off" cycle was clearly imminent. In the past, the guitarist had just switched off unannounced, but this time he'd go with a medium-sized bang.

---

[11]Sellers, *Very Naughty Boys*, 271.

In October 1991, under pressure from Eric Clapton, Harrison suddenly announced a series of megaconcerts in Japan. The attractions of the venture were obvious—big revenue and well-behaved crowds (George wouldn't have to break up any fights in Osaka).[12] The other main factor was Clapton, who put himself, his band, and his crew at Harrison's disposal, thus ensuring a stress-free experience for the reluctant star. All George had to do was turn up and play.

Eric's offering included two keyboards (Chuck Leavell and Greg Phillinganes), a taut rhythm section (Nathan East and Steve Ferrone), and a pair of backup singers (Tessa Niles and Katie Kissoon). As Ray Cooper was a "must have," the only addition Harrison made was Andy Fairweather Low, to add even more guitar cover. Low was stunned to learn that George wanted him to play his own slide guitar parts. As ever, there was little prospect of the Henley resident turning dictator.

The results of the seven-city, thirteen-date jaunt were recorded and unleashed on the public, with only a whimper of publicity, on the *Live in Japan* album. The set offered a half-and-half mix of Beatles and solo hits, all delivered with note-perfect precision, within the five-minute egg-timer song length limit. There was no fault or flaw to the album, but a more accurate title would have been *Safe in Japan*. The double set was strangely passionless, the reason probably being the layers of sonic insulation in which George was wrapped. Clapton's band was superslick, boasting top professionals on each instrument. The results were supremely tight, but ultimately the group was not as interesting musically as the *Dark Horse* band, with its more unpredictable flair.

The opener, "I Want to Tell You," loses nearly everything without Ringo Starr's eccentric touch—Steve Ferrone is a fine drummer, but he's not Starr. Nonetheless, the recordings convey the impression that, despite the energy castration, the fact of George Harrison's singing his classic songs live was enough to satisfy the audience. The same steady, note-for-note re-creations serve "Taxman," "Old Brown Shoe," "Piggies," "Here Comes the Sun," and even "If I Needed Someone." To some, the duet of female backup voices and Eric Clapton's unchanging solos would have skewed the songs a little too far, but George was in good voice and evidently having fun. But on the live bow of "Isn't It a Pity," the talents of this band finally reach full bloom, supporting Harrison's committed, fiery vocal with a sweeping accompaniment that skims the original's grandeur.

---

[12]On the 1974 Dark Horse Tour, Harrison played boxing referee as he intervened to separate two pugilists in Providence, Rhode Island: "Krishna, Krishna, Krishna, Stop the fighting! We didn't come here for a fight, you can get one of them anywhere."

Of the solo songs, "Dark Horse," rendered in full voice, is the only real surprise. Synthesizers replicate the original flutes of Scott, Horn, and Findley—Eric's band could produce every note of every original. But that's as adventurous as it gets, and some of the more interesting song choices didn't even make the release, notably "Love Comes to Everyone" and "Fish on the Sand." Eric Clapton's nightly half-hour segment was completely axed to keep the contract managers happy.

The stadium formula does work well for some of the later pieces: "Cloud 9" and "Cheer Down" rock with spirit, spotlighting fine signature slide from the star. Strangely, on three of George's most famous guitar tracks,[13] he strums acoustic guitar, while Clapton and Andy Fairweather Low try to re-create his bottleneck sound. The fact that the attempts fail states the obvious: only George plays like Harrison.

Another guitar highlight is "Something," to which George adds a characteristically expressive solo passage as an overture, setting the scene for Harrison and Clapton solos where both find real emotion, making this one of the more convincing performances of the set. Happily, with no repeat of the "When there's something in the way, we move it" gaff, it seems that George had made peace with his own legacy. On these dates George's rock 'n' roll time machine careered through his own life, closing with some power on the perennial "While My Guitar Gently Weeps" before taking one last turn around the Harrison block for "Roll Over Beethoven." But this was Fukuoka 1991, not Hamburg 1961, and George Harrison was nearer fifty than twenty.

Live in Japan does not present George Harrison as the same committed firebrand who sang "My Sweet Lord" with passion at the Concert for Bangla Desh twenty years earlier. Too much had changed—he didn't need to take a three-man horn section on the road with him, synthesizers could reproduce an orchestra, and a ragged but rowdy gospel choir was hard to find in 1991. And as the star of the show was nearing his fifth decade, this live collection was not about breaking new ground or making a grand statement to the music business. The whole affair was internationally low-key and the album, almost an afterthought, released with less publicity than *Gone Troppo* had enjoyed. The recordings simply represent a string of fine songs, sung well and brought to life by excellent musicians, to produce a good package. The Dark Horse Tour had lived on the edge; *Live in Japan* caused its main turn no sleepless nights.

---

[13]"My Sweet Lord," "Isn't It a Pity," and "Give Me Love."

Shortly before the live album's release, Harrison took to the boards in London for his first, and last, solo British concert. The show was a rougher, edgier version of the Japanese one, less slick and more risky. Seemingly at peace with his past and his present, the star of the show looked nervous but ultimately exhilarated by the tumultuous reception from the Albert Hall crowd. This was probably the most challenging concert of his career, facing a British audience who could, if pressed, match his own levels of cynicism and grumpiness.

But the fact that the concert was a benefit for the Maharishi Mahesh Yogi's "Natural Law Party" stirred up the well-worn suggestions that Harrison was more than a little eccentric. Of course, the opposite was true—the man remained true to his convictions, unmoved by fashion or zeitgeist. For many, the very fact of George Harrison playing live in London was a near miracle in itself, one that few expected would ever be repeated.

Bunbury Tails
(television soundtrack album—Harrison contribution recorded at Friar Park and London, March 1988; released October 1992)

[137] **Ride Rajbun (4:59)** *(Harrison)*
Harrison vocal, sitar; **Dhani Harrison** backup vocal; **Ravi Shankar** sitar introduction; **David English** cameo vocal; *uncredited tabla, shenhai, and flute*

The game of cricket may well be the most popular sport in the world, given the fanaticism it engenders in India, Pakistan, Sri Lanka, and Bangladesh. It is also the world's most notably postcolonial pastime— the countries that play the game at the international level are all past members of the British Empire.[14] For all of them, the most important goal is to beat England on their home soil; for the rest of the world, and the many who hate cricket, it's an extreme, bewildering, and tedious example of English eccentricity. However, the sport is deeply embedded in English culture and most villages still have a cricket team, often with a field in the center of the community.

---

[14]Apart from England and the subcontinent states, the main cricketing nations are Australia, South Africa, the West Indies, New Zealand, and Zimbabwe.

For most of his life, George Harrison would have counted himself as a cricket hater, and no sport seems less imbued with the sheen of rock-life cool. However, once he fell into company with Elton John and Jeff Lynne for *Cloud Nine*, the guitarist was passing time with cricket lovers and soon found himself whiling away a day in time-honored, beer-quaffing fashion at English cricket grounds.

So it was not completely inexplicable that the only new Harrison composition written and released between 1992 and 2001 was a ditty for a children's cartoon series about a troupe of cricket-playing rabbits: *The Bunbury Tails*. Of course, he was not the first of the ex-Beatles to work on children's projects—Starr was already better known among the United Kingdom's under-tens as the voice of the avuncular steam train Thomas the Tank Engine.

"Ride Rajbun" will never be regarded as a Harrison classic, but it is still noteworthy, being the first piece of purely Indian music issued under his name since "The Inner Light." Rajbun was the Indian member of the Bunbury cricket team, and once the guitarist got involved, he enlisted no less a figure than Ravi Shankar to play a characteristically precious short *alap*. The remaining sitar parts were played by George himself.

It seems that deep subconscious memories were stirred through the "Ride Rajbun" concept—the evidence being a childlike chorus. This brings to mind the British children's song "London's Burning" that generations of U.K. schoolchildren (almost certainly including Harrison) have grown up singing in rounds. The "rounds" on "Ride Rajbun" are sung by George and Dhani Harrison. Given the media attention the father had suffered, it is a little surprising that he introduced his son to the limelight, even in this modest way.

In response to George's early 1990s Japanese and British shows, a few planeloads of American fans traversed the time zones, east or west, to see him play live. The Dark Horse Tour still lingered in the Harrison memory, and it would take a lot for George to appear again Stateside. As ever with George Harrison, the main motivation was friendship, and as 1992 was the thirtieth anniversary of the first Bob Dylan album, his commitment to a friend landed this most reticent of performers in New York. The venue for the October concert was Madison Square Garden, where George had cajoled Dylan into breaking *his* performing sabbatical in 1971. The Garden held good memories for

George. Not only was it the setting for the Concert for Bangla Desh, but it had even lifted his spirits in 1974: such was the demand from the city to see the Dark Horse perform that a third concert had been added on short notice that December, almost twenty years earlier.

As with the Dark Horse Tour, a drop or two of controversy attended the Thirtieth Anniversary Concert Celebration, provided by a young Irish firebrand, Sinead O'Connor. In truth, Sinead was a welcome jolt to the senses at a concert that cast Dylan's masterly songbook in a formula, house-band setting and allowed a few distinctly subpar performances to slip through the net. Fortunately, George Harrison was not among these, and he was captured on tape offering an intense reading of "Absolutely Sweet Marie" and a nod to a shared past with "If Not for You."

It's fitting that the final appearance Harrison made at a major concert was to honor Bob Dylan. That was in keeping with his tendency to shun the limelight and honor others, and Dylan had been a major influence and collaborator over more than twenty years. In retrospect, the concert provided the perfect moment to review how the two had bounced around the music business, and each other's careers, like a pair of slightly grumpy comics whose orbits occasionally crossed—a musical "Odd Couple."

To many artists, the greatest gift that Bob Dylan gave them was the freedom to express and, by extension, discover themselves. For a man like George Harrison, his identity twisted and bent by the madness of Beatlemania, hearing Dylan's songs of free articulation, combined with the promised spiritual emancipation of Indian philosophy and music, was doubly liberating. Even as George immersed himself almost exclusively in Indian music, he remained engaged with Dylan's—he later revealed that when the Beatles traveled to Rishikesh in 1968, the only non-Indian music he took with him was the bard's *Blonde on Blonde*. Putting the two together gave Harrison a truth to hold on to, and a vehicle for its expression.

Dylan provided the key for legions of artists, even if the memory of his initial impact fades after nearly forty years under his influence. Another musician of the period, David Bromberg, offers a neat summation: "Dylan's impact cannot be overstated and people who weren't there can't get it, because he changed things so radically that it's hard to envisage what it was like before. He invented the electric light."

Once let loose, Dylan's filament was at the mercy of myriad muses, some inspired, some redundant. But in George Harrison it found a simple, honest search for truth, as Delaney Bramlett saw for himself: "He had more love to give than you could ever imagine, he was such a gentle soul. He was just a beautiful, beautiful person, who wanted to be close to God." Harrison's uncomplicated view of life was partly fueled by 1960s mores that tended to group people and concepts as representatives of either the problem ("Taxman," "Piggies," "Blood from a Clone") or the solution ("Life Itself," "My Sweet Lord," "Pure Smokey"). This struggle between two extremes is best expressed in his greatest song, "Isn't It a Pity," where the solution is within touching distance ("the beauty that surrounds them"), if only he can see past the problem ("how we break each other's hearts").

So Dylan had provided the means, but Harrison's essentially internal dialogue didn't call for Bob's obvious intellectual clout. To David Bromberg, Dylan had tapped a deep well of inspiration: "Dylan's expression is subverbal in a way. It's also complex, not in an intellectual way, but he's found some path from his brain to his mouth that gets things much more directly and not filtered. It's very high art. He's able to say things I wouldn't know how to describe."

In Harrison's case, he was trying to describe emotions and concepts that were literally beyond words. He occasionally presented a convincing verbal picture, but his most powerfully expressive weapons were his musical representations and guitar statements. This skill, which contrasted with Dylan's, also draws Bromberg's admiration: "He got a tone, a voice, and it worked perfectly with his melodic sense; it was a voice and he used it beautifully. It was completely different from anyone else's use, it was completely unique."

Dylan's essentially poetic approach was entirely different. In a poetic setting, the writer creates a complex web of narrators and viewpoints, which partly frees him from identifying with the polemic. With Dylan, it doesn't matter if he, Robert Zimmerman, is the narrator of "Sad-Eyed Lady of the Lowlands" or "Every Grain of Sand." Whatever truths or resonances there are in these songs do not depend on how closely the author identifies with them. Very few Harrisongs are neutral in this way; it is usually clear that George is presenting his feeling of the moment, directly. This has produced some uncomfortably blunt and even unsophisticated observations, where Dylan's early satire damned its targets with sophistry. But it's Harrison's directness that offers an insight into the impact of fame on an ordinary man.

If Zimmerman did create Dylan, at least he was in control at some point. George Harrison was never in control of his own Frankenstein's monster. The Beatles had started life as a decent rock band with few pretensions. Their transition to "product" swiftly meta-morphosed them into the "media-fantasy" Beatles, which effectively left Harrison three steps removed from himself as the artist. Looked at from a safe distance, and taking into account the preposterous intru-sions into his personal life, this is a surreal state of affairs. In the end, Harrison shrugged his shoulders and invented his own counterbluff with the Traveling Wilburys, in recognition of the reality that he was not this product.

The neatest summation of the different approaches is "Every Grain of Sand," the Dylan song closest to Harrison's brand of spiritual universalism. Dylan's work depicts a spiritual journey that swings between certainty and alienation, skirting the same subject matter as "Hear Me Lord," "Life Itself," and "Fish on the Sand." But Dylan's muse is poetic, built on allegory and metaphor, dealing not with feelings but with intellectual contemplation. Harrison's work, on the other hand, is all feeling—heartfelt pleas for truth, answered by sweeping, musical visions of certainty ("Sat Singing").

Occasionally, the pair's muses worked in the same direction, a case in point being the key song from Dylan's tumultuously contro-versial 1979 album, *Slow Train Coming*. "Gotta Serve Somebody" was received with a mixture of confusion and hostility. John Lennon in particular seemed to be incensed by its content and committed a sav-age parody to tape, calling it "Serve Yourself." "Gotta Serve Somebody" certainly covers almost identical subject matter to two songs from *Living in the Material World*, "The Lord Loves the One" and "The Day the World Gets 'Round." Dylan's song is a more sophisticated warning about the dangers of hubris than Harrison's pair, but there isn't as much as a cigarette paper's thickness between Bob's "you might be a rock 'n' roll addict prancing on the stage" and George's "we all fool around, with objectives in mind, to become rich or famous with our reputations signed." And "it may be the devil or it may be the Lord" from "Gotta Serve Somebody" makes the same point as "but Lord there are just a few who bow before you" from "The Day the World Gets 'Round." Like George's had before, Dylan's "inspirational" counsel drew naked fire, and during this period in Bob's career their respec-tive orbits drew closer than they'd ever been.

The Dylan–Harrison relationship was characterized by an equal mix of similarity and diversity that made them well matched. Harrison obviously did not have Dylan's poetic genius, but his musical vocabu-lary was broader, and his near-perfect ability as a guitarist to "play the song" made him an ideal foil for Dylan. While the real Bob Dylan remains as elusive now as he did in 1962, the "real" George Harrison was virtually inescapable on his albums. In retrospect, Dylan's genius and Harrison's deeply musical and expressive approach verged on a true synergy.

Mo's Songs
(promotional release—Harrison contribution recorded at Friar Park, spring 1977; released December 1994)

[138] **Mo**[15] **(4:52)** *(Harrison)*
Harrison guitar, vocal, bass synthesizer; *uncredited drums, organ and electric piano*

Although humor and goodwill radiate from Harrison on this song, in hindsight its creation is full of irony. George recorded "Mo" in 1977, to celebrate the fiftieth birthday of Warner Brothers grandee Mo Ostin. The warmth of the lyrics shows the loyalty the guitarist accorded his friends. But a year after delivering this most unique birthday present, he presented the finished demos for *Somewhere in England,* and Mr. Ostin showed him that sentiment does not accord with the music business by discarding the album.

This most rare of Harrison releases finally emerged during Ostin's retirement bash in 1994. Modesty forbade any ostentatious self-congratulation, with the exception of an unassumingly lavish six-CD boxed set of Warner hits given to each of the 600 guests, an instant collector's item. Harrison's birthday tribute to the business-man was the first cut on the set.

Comprehensively bootlegged, this reverse version of the "Faster" chord sequence is worth hearing for its strong, rising melody, banks of acoustic guitars, and soaring guitar solos. It was the only new Harrison material released between 1992 and 2001, although his guitar was still employed on behalf of trusted friends. The highlight of a batch of sessions for Alvin Lee, which included George's participation on a cover version of "I Want You," is a beautifully expressive passage on a 1993 minor blues, "The Bluest Blues." Harrison could surprise guests with

---

[15]Madinger and Easter note that the song was registered for copyright purposes in June 1977.

an encyclopedic knowledge of the blues, but when he played in a strict electric blues idiom, his musical manifesto remained melodic essaying.[16]

One of the barriers to new George Harrison music reaching the public in the mid-1990s was the revival of the Beatles, under the catchall title of *Anthology*. By 1999 that had included a book, a television miniseries, and three double-CD sets of studio or live outtakes and foul-ups. The third of these discs gave legal release to many high-quality Harrison demos from the 1968–69 period. Outstanding among these are plaintive, affecting solo takes of "While My Guitar Gently Weeps" and "All Things Must Pass." Just voice and guitar, they reach close to the heart of the real George Harrison, a man who saw music as an expression of his inner search.

The various *Anthology* projects were boosted by the media to the extent that the Beatles ghost rose again and was spotted on music charts, tabloids, and talk shows around the globe. All that was fine. The more challenging aspect was the release of two "new" Beatles songs. The idea of creating these by dubbing the three remaining members of the group onto rather tatty Lennon demos was perhaps overoptimistic. There were other dangers too: would the professional differences between Harrison and McCartney that had been festering since 1969 bring the whole project to a halt?

It was in early 1969 that Lennon and McCartney had a public discussion questioning the guitarist's "competence." Now, more than twenty-five years later, no one would feel empowered to mention it. So much had changed—Harrison was a long-established artist in his own right, a world-renowned guitar stylist and expert producer. The evidence of the new order was that Harrison's preferred producer, Jeff Lynne, was used, and his signature *solo* guitar sound dominated the first single. A comment from Paul McCartney to the press indicates his stance: "I was worried because it was going to be George on slide. When Jeff suggested slide guitar I thought, 'Oh it's "My Sweet Lord" again,' it's George's trademark."[17] But after the session was complete, it was obvious that Harrison's solos were the highlight of the track, so

[16]The song appears on Lee's *I Hear You Rockin'* CD. Harrison also cut a solo for Lee on a 1992 disc, *Zoom*, and all his work with the ex-Ten Years After leader is caught on a compilation set, *Pure Blues*.

[17]Quoted in Du Noyer, "But Now They're Really Important."

much so that Paul McCartney was singing its praises. Longtime Beatle buddy Klaus Voormann was one of the first to hear about it: "Paul came up and told me, 'George played a fantastic guitar solo on "Free as a Bird."'" And he himself has been deeply affected by this modest musician's guitar skills. "To me, George's guitar playing is outstanding on emotional, musical, lyrical, and personal levels." These are sentiments shared by Badfinger's Joey Molland: "I think it surprised everybody just how good he was playing slide. I don't know if I've ever heard anyone better. Not even Duane Allman had the touch that George had. I mean, the slide guitar on 'Free as a Bird' is just stunning."

The guitar Harrison used on "Free as a Bird" was a graphite model, often seen in the back of the guitarist's personal McClaren F1 Supercar, a £540,000 machine that even had a built-in amplifier! But there were more than just guitar antics—the single even offered a little taste of Harrison's talents on the ukulele as a coda. The passage was the solo from a George Formby classic, "When I'm Cleaning Windows," a song as deeply embedded in the British psyche as the national anthem. For 1940s children like the Beatles, Formby and his ukulele were ubiquitous on radio, at the movies, and in music halls. The Lancastrian was strongly identified with the British war effort, as he'd toured the world to entertain the troops and gained a medal for his efforts. Formby was so famous that the Hawaiian ukulele was as common a household instrument in the 1940s as the guitar would become after the Beatles' entrance twenty years later. John Lennon's mother and Paul McCartney's father both played the ukulele. The Fab Four themselves were known to break into Formby jams, as they did during the *Let It Be* sessions.[18]

But Harrison was the most public ukulele plucker of the Beatles, and a member of the Ukulele Society of Great Britain to boot. It was an instrument he associated with pleasure—the owner of a holiday resort in Fiji later recounted how a vacationing George spontaneously joined in a ukulele session with villagers in the late 1990s. Noting the ragged state of the locals' ukes and guitars, Harrison shipped them a large box of new instruments after his visit. Harrison also produced a ukelele to cover a Cab Calloway song, "Between the Devil and the Deep Blue Sea," for a television show in 1991, the same year he actually played live at a George Formby convention.[19] This annual event

---

[18]Harrison even worked on an arrangement of Formby's "Leaning on a Lamppost" with Delaney Bramlett in the late 1960s.

[19]A version of the song made it onto the 2002 *Brainwashed* album, which represented the music George was working on toward the end of his life.

was held in Blackpool, a Lancashire seaside town, and George turned in a performance of his fellow Lancastrian's "In My Little Snapshot Album" to general acclaim. Indeed, contemporary Formby scholars highly rate Harrison's melodic skills on the instrument, which he used to introduce his unreleased "Dehra Dhun" to the world during the *Anthology* films.

However, the creation of "Free as a Bird" was less easily accomplished, and Jeff Lynne's labors with the Lennon demo tape were Herculean. Unfortunately, the basic problem was that the song was simply not that strong and sold largely through nostalgia, or for novelty value. The second "new" song, "Real Love," is better, and its strong pop-melodic qualities are obviously closer to George's own muse. Once again Harrison's guitar is prominent and, unexpectedly, his Stratocaster unveils a completely new tone that has more in common with Eric Clapton than Carl Perkins. On "Real Love," his notes swoop and soar with a new vitality, and reveal an almost subconscious empathy with Lennon's music. It is a vital, powerful performance.

After the Threetles, the Henley Fab dropped out of the media spotlight again, but continued to work on musical projects with old and trusted friends and heroes. Carl Perkins's final music was recorded on *Go Cat Go*, shortly before his death. On the Harrison collaboration, "Distance Makes No Difference with Love," it sounds like the guitarist knows it. For a straightforward pop-rock song, the depth of emotion is startling, and Harrison's guitar literally weeps in sympathy.

As he approached the second millennium, and the fourth decade of his career, George Harrison continued to find the private solace of music as a spiritual force his primary interest. Over the years he had gone some way to create musical expression of his spiritual life ("Sat Singing," "Your Love Is Forever"), but he always looked to the great musicians of India to best express his yogic aspirations. The late 1990s saw a flurry of releases from Ravi Shankar under Harrison's gaze, which were infused with Harrison's true love for the music. He toiled over two major Ravi Shankar projects, one of which saw the resurrection of Dark Horse Records for a lavish four-disc retrospective, *In Celebration*, which showcases his musical guru in a bewildering range of settings and styles. The sheer, stunning virtuosity of the boxed set is in stark contrast to a 1997 release that captured the spiritual essence at the heart of Indian music. *Chants of India*, marketed as a Shankar-Harrison collaboration, took George back to the roots of his 1969 Krishna chants, "My Sweet Lord" and "It Is He," by presenting a series of sacred Hindu prayers and texts in short, listener-friendly packages. Indian philosophy teaches that religious chants are the root of all music; here Shankar and Harrison presented them for the modern age.

The recording of this set was a return to the days of *Wonderwall* and Shankar's Dark Horse albums of the mid-1970s. The first session took Harrison to Chennai from January to April 1986, but ironically, the atmosphere in the South Indian city was not conducive to the spiritual nature of the project, so in July, they reconvened at Friar Park. Back in the old ballroom, set in the gardens that George had lovingly created to frame his refuge, the old Harrison energy returned with a vengeance as he oversaw the production and played a huge range of instruments.

One piece in particular recalls the days, almost thirty years earlier, when Harrison first recorded Vedic chants. "Prabhujee" is a cut designed for Western ears, with an evocative melody cast with Harrison's simply strummed acoustic guitars at his "Life Itself" tempo. Harrison's deep voice is heard throughout, intoning Shankar's newly written plea for God-realization. It was the closing of a circle that had begun with "Hare Krishna Mantra," "Oh Happy Day," *Encouraging Words*, and "My Sweet Lord."

It was fitting then that for this recording Harrison was reunited with John Barham, the classical musician who had been his original partner on his voyage of discovery into Indian music. Barham was delighted to be recalled: "The *Chants of India* recording was somewhat complicated by the fact that the record company wanted to release an album of 'spiritual' music that would go to number one. They got the idea from an album of Gregorian chants with a rhythm section which sold very well. Neither George nor Ravi intended to commercialize it to anything like that extent. Apart from one song where George adds some acoustic guitar, the album is strictly a Ravi Shankar classical Indian record. George and Ravi were very relaxed, and it was a pleasure working on this beautiful record."

Chants of India, the final Shankar-Harrison work, was intended to produce a profound emotional response in the listener. George Harrison's own reaction reveals the depth of his attachment: "After the final mixing of the first four numbers, he played them back for me and they sounded fantastic, giving me goose bumps and a deep spiritual awareness. That evening he came and embraced me with tears in his eyes and simply said, 'Thank you, Ravi, for this music.'"[20]

[139] **Any Road (1997 version)** *(Harrison)*[21]
Harrison guitar, vocal

As part of the promotional activity to support *Chants of India* Harrison made a highly unlikely appearance on the cable rock channel VH-1. As well as discussing his view of life with great candor, he was persuaded to busk a few tunes in what became his final public performance. He stunned the awestruck presenter with off-the-cuff renditions of "All Things Must Pass" and the Wilburys' "If You Belonged to Me," but managed to top even that by quickly busking a piece that he later finished as "Any Road," thus an entirely new song. It was not broadcast at the time, but VH-1 later emancipated this unique offering as part of the tributes after the guitarist's death.

Playing in the simple "folky" style that was his basic mode, George introduces a Dylanish travelogue that reviews the journey of his life. As with so many of his songs, and "Heading for the Light" in particular, on "Any Road" Harrison sticks to his path of spiritual enlightenment and pondering the "Circles" of karma. As he pointed out during the accompanying interview, he was aware by 1997 that his musings on spiritual matters placed him "out on a limb" in the music business. This is probably why he hadn't released a solo album since 1987—he expected to be misunderstood. It was another sign that he felt his musical paradigm could not fit within the prevailing mores of the industry.

This private performance coincided with the first news of George's cancer diagnosis, which began to fill the newspapers in 1997. And reports continued to leak out that the Henley star was working on new music. His second favorite drummer, Jim Keltner, told the press that he had visited Friar Park to help finish songs that Harrison was unearthing from his vaults. One writer was treated to a listening session of tracks that included versions of old material ("Run So Far," plus covers of Dylan's "Abandoned Love"—reportedly a duet with Bob—and "Every Grain of Sand") and new songs, among them "Valentine,"

---

[20]Shankar, *Raga Mala*, 308.

[21]The song was finished for the 2002 *Brainwashed* album.

"Rising Sun," "Pisces Fish," and "Brainwashed." A retrospective was planned, with the working title *Portrait of a Leg End*, plus a rumored Traveling Wilburys retrospective, possibly titled *Maximum Traveling*.[22] Fate intervened to keep this new music under wraps for future construction.

All the same, in 1998, Ringo Starr was still going up and down memory lane and, as well as hitting the "legends" concert circuit, planned one last effort at a major album, *Vertical Man*. Here was a disc that was never going to attract many plaudits, sales, or critical acclaim, as the drummer must have known—the music is self-referential, but honest nevertheless. One highlight is a rehash of the "Photograph" formula. "King of Broken Hearts" comes complete with "I Am the Walrus" cellos, and a powerfully emotive guitar segment from Harrison. Naturally, despite this, the album sank, stone fashion.

The translucent beauty of Harrison's guitar on "King of Broken Hearts" speaks again of the private musical craftsman sharing a little of his soul from his bucolic refuge, a million miles removed from the music business. This moving musical statement speaks of the musician's inner peace, a peace that was brutally shattered on December 30, 1999, when the madness of Beatlemania revisited Friar Park.

In the years following John Lennon's murder, there were attempts to characterize George Harrison as an eccentric recluse, hiding monklike in his Friar Park lair. Why, they pondered, was Harrison so obsessed with his personal security? That early December morning provided the answer—the depersonalization of the man into a celebrity, shrouded in myth, had made him the target for attempted murder. That anyone even questioned Harrison's need to protect himself and his family shows how utterly disconnected from reality the tabloid media really is. Why would a "star" have any less need to protect himself than anyone else? Even way back in 1967, he'd scored *Wonderwall*, a film that urged the audience to realize that behind every celebrity photo is a real human being.

Once again, in grotesque distortion of an ordinary man, the tabloids feasted royally on the attack and subsequent trial. George Harrison must have looked in despair at what had almost become a self-fulfilling prophecy, as all the concerns he documented on "Writing's on the Wall," "Devil's Radio," and "Wreck of the Hesperus" were played out before his eyes, with himself as the leading man.

---

[22]One source reported that this included contributions from Del Shannon and a cover of Paul Simon's "Run That Body Down."

Happily, Harrison quickly bounced back, and was soon reveling in the critical rehabilitation that came with the thirtieth-anniversary reissue of *All Things Must Pass*. As the "good enough" sound of compact discs swept the globe in the 1980s, the record companies were delighted to sell baby boomers a supposedly improved version of the same product they'd bought ten or fifteen years earlier. By the 1990s, as those same children of the 1960s and 1970s hit middle age and deeper pockets, the boxed set phenomenon was born. Usually tied in with a real or artificially created anniversary of some sort, the same product was repackaged and presented for a third time. The carrot on offer was a smattering of maybe one or two unreleased songs that were often too tempting to pass over.

At least George Harrison was honest enough to declare that the *All Things Must Pass* reissue on his new Gnome Records label was inspired by the truly boggling success of the Beatles' *One* hits compilation. Nevertheless, the Gnome product was tastefully created with good humor and some genuine musical nuggets, even if the sound offered no real improvement over the original vinyl!

The Harrison gnomes were generous enough to offer five bonus cuts for this set. The weakest was a mix of "What Is Life," different only for a "Penny Lane" trumpet part, while the inclusion of the first airing of "Beware of Darkness" in front of Phil Spector seemed to be in answer to the happy bootleggers who'd had these tapes for years. A demo of "Let It Down" from the same session was embellished with a taste of fluid, jazzy, Harrison guitar circa-2000, but the real interest came with two "new" offerings.

[140] **I Live for You** (3:36) *(Harrison)*
Harrison guitar, vocal; **Klaus Voormann** bass; **Alan White** drums;
Bobby Whitlock piano; **Pete Drake** pedal steel guitar;
Dhani Harrison Fender Rhodes, backup vocal

An unreleased gem from *All Things Must Pass*, this balmy ballad owes much to "Lay Lady Lay," but also indicates that Harrison's gift for melody was growing. The self-contained main melodic couplet is one of his most effective.

A companion to "Behind That Locked Door," it also features the late Pete Drake high in the mix. But where the former piece counsels Dylan to confide in his friends, "I Live for You" describes its singer's sense of isolation and an early desire for detachment from the world. At the time Harrison was not satisfied with the final mix, feeling that only Drake's efforts hit par; from the perspective of thirty years on, it would have been preferred to "I Dig Love" or the second "Isn't It a Pity."

[141] My Sweet Lord 2000 (4:58) *(Harrison)*
Harrison slide guitar, vocal; **Eric Clapton** guitar; **Bobby Whitlock** piano; **Klaus Voormann** bass; **Gary Wright** electric piano; **Badfinger**[23] acoustic rhythm guitars; **John Barham** string arrangement; **Ringo Starr** drums; **Jim Gordon** drums; **Mike Gibbins** tambourine; *uncredited harmonium*; **Dhani Harrison** acoustic guitar; **Ray Cooper** tambourine; **Sam Brown** lead and backup vocals

Few will ever know if George Harrison was aware of the gravity of his medical condition when he refreshed his most famous hit. Since he died just a few months after this piece was released, it seems even more poignant that he produced such a passionate reworking of his signature song.

In truth, he only retained the basic rhythm track of the original, recutting his vocal and guitar parts, adding some sonic memory joggers, and replacing the George O'Hara Smith singers with the single, soaring voice of Sam Brown.

So much of George Harrison's musical journey is covered in the five-minute piece that it becomes a microcosm of his career. The track opens with a snippet of sitar to emphasize its spiritual roots, while the simple, Dylanesque acoustic strumming is still the basis of the song. But Harrison also looked back to Delaney Bramlett, Billy Preston, and *Encouraging Words* to emphasize the song's gospel genesis, especially in the piano-led coda. And more telling than any other part of the cut, for the second half, he stops singing and gives the floor to his second voice, his guitar. He had never made so clear a musical statement that his signature bottleneck sound was as much his tool for self-expression as his vocal cords.

Mostly dismissed as a disappointment on release, "My Sweet Lord 2000" updates—yet also recaptures—the passion of the original and reminds his audience that the man's musical and spiritual values had not changed in over thirty years. Recording this song, with the built-in Hare Krishna mantra, was a statement from Harrison that his funda-

---

[23]Pete Ham, Tom Evans, and Joey Molland; the band's drummer, Mike Gibbins, played percussion.

mental spiritual beliefs had remained constant. Even at the time of his death, the tabloids struggled to come to terms with Hindu custom, oblivious to the fact that in 2001, hundreds of thousands of Hindus lived in Britain and the United States. For a press more used to dealing with soap opera stars and microwave-ready boy bands, Harrison's steadfast belief was beyond their ken. "My Sweet Lord 2000" is a testament to George Harrison's honest, sometimes reckless, sincerity.

But the new millennium also found George supporting fresh talent. There was some circularity to the fact that he'd been played some demos of a new Irish band who had just set off to Boston to try to "make it," but who also had a melodic, Beatle-ish sound. Rubyhorse attracted Harrison's ear and, almost incredibly, his bottleneck is heard on a retro-rock track, "Punch Drunk," on an album[24] that was sold almost exclusively at the band's shows or through their Web site. Maybe Rubyhorse reminded the guitarist of another group of melodic rockers with Irish roots.

Slowly but surely, as the newspapers filled with often lurid and blatantly offensive stories about his health in 2001, George Harrison the musician reappeared. He started with a series of slide cameos and culminated with his first newly recorded composition since 1992's "Ride Rajbun." Harrison was once again an in-demand session guitarist, cutting solos on new tracks by friends from the 1960s (Bill Wyman and Jim Capaldi) and the 1980s (Jeff Lynne, masquerading as ELO). He sounds strong on Wyman's straightforward reading of the staple "Love Letters," tracking the melody in his trademark style. He is less prominent on two of Lynne's chilly pop-rockers, but is back on home ground with Capaldi's notably Beatle-ish version of a classic Brazilian pop song, "Anna Julia." Besides Harrison's guitar, Capaldi recorded Beatles harmonies direct from 1964, and his own startling vocal was ersatz John Lennon. "I thought that 'Anna Julia' had a Beatles connection. That *ou-ou-ou* [the backing vocals of the song] reminded me of 'I Should Have Know Better.' I took the recording to George; he listened and loved it. Then I suggested to him that he record a guitar solo using a slide guitar. Two weeks later, he called me to say he wanted to finish the recording soon. A short time later, George traveled to the United States, where he passed away."[25]

---

[24]*How Far Have You Come?*

[25]"Jim Capaldi Interview." *O Globo* (Brazil), February 2002.

Throughout this period, reports about George Harrison's health continued to leak out, like half-formed, chilling stage whispers. In the final months of his life, Harrison spent his time avoiding the media circus that now speculated on every minute personal detail of his condition. Even Swiss medics could not contain themselves and broke their professional code of confidentiality about the guitarist's brain tumor. To many, it was a disgusting spectacle. It seemed that the press would stop at nothing to pursue a dying man, almost as if they felt George Harrison owed it to the world to breathe his last live on cable television. In the midst of this madness, the musician came out fighting with one of his most powerful songs in years.

[142] **Horse to the Water (5:00)** *(Harrison–D. Harrison)*
(recorded in London and Switzerland, September–October 2001)
Harrison vocal; **Jools Holland** piano; **Gilson Lavis** drums;
Mark Flanagan guitar; **Sam Brown** backup vocal[26]

English pianist Jools Holland has made a substantial career in the music business, from happy pop days with Squeeze through a television presenter sideline to parallel solo work, championing good-time R&B. The amiable Holland was trusted to conduct the *Anthology* interviews. For all that, never in his wildest dreams did he expect to host the final George Harrison recording.

The only fitting description for the man who recorded the "Horse to the Water" vocal on October 2, 2001, is "courageous." A close ear to the track confirms a straining shortness of breath that suggests the personal effort needed to cut this song.

Musically reminiscent of "Cockamamie Business" and "Cheer Down," this valedictory song has a vocal that recalls Bob Dylan in his *Slow Train Coming* period, but saves most of its fascination for its stanzas. Here is more Dylan checkpoint, as Harrison assumes ambiguous narrative voices that appear to shift. One interpretation could cast "Horse to the Water" as George's personal life review: the dead-end feeling of empty fame in the first verse gives way to the "Simply Shady" spirits guzzler of the second. The final verse replays a rejection of organized religion, first heard in "Awaiting on You All"—the truth seeker needs to reach "God," but is held back by religious civil servants for whom the organization and the rules have become more important than the message.

---

[26]The other musicians from Holland's band on this track were: Phil Veacock, Michael Rose, Leo Green, Lisa Walsingham, and Peter Long, saxophone; Jason McDermid and Jon Scott, trumpet; Winston Rollins, trombone; Rita Campbell and Claudia Fontaine, backup vocals.

A second view could be that the song recounts real events and real people, and a third could say that it doesn't matter, it's all Dylanesque allegory. Whatever, the song does contain a message, the one that remained constant in Harrison's music: the truth that is "all laid out in front of you" is spiritual revelation, the "God-realization" sought in the final section.

There's an urgency underlying "Horse to the Water," a throwback to the roseate days of "Within You Without You," when the artist felt an overwhelming desire to show the way. A statement released by Harrison's family about his passing in November 2001 told the world, once and for all, that Harrison's spiritual quest was no psychedelic fad: "He left this world as he lived in it, conscious of God, fearless of death, and at peace, surrounded by family and friends. He often said, 'Everything else can wait but the search for God cannot wait, and love one another.'"

In the months between "My Sweet Lord 2000" and George Harrison's death, work was being completed for the release of his retrospective album, which would include the host of unheard songs he'd written throughout the 1990s. By the time of his passing, preparations were at an advanced stage, and his old friend John Barham had been drafted to consider an orchestration for a track. George had asked Barham to work on the music in a chance meeting in August 2000, when Barham was conducting a work by Deep Purple's Jon Lord. The title, "From Darkness to Light," suggests bonds between the two musicians that were more than musical, especially as it was so unusual for Harrison to travel even the four miles to St. Mary the Virgin Church in Hambleden, where the concert was staged.

Finally, in September 2002, the news came that the posthumous George Harrison album would be released in November with the title *Brainwashed*.

11

And in the End
(2001–2003)

When George Harrison was first diagnosed with cancer in 1997, his reaction to being given six months to live was typically defiant. But according to those closest to him spiritually, he had also reached a point of profound tranquility. He maintained his links with the Krishna Consciousness movement, being especially close to a number of the devotees he had first met in 1968. One of the adherents, Syamasundara Dasa, who was among the troupe who cut the "Hare Krishna Mantra" with Harrison, reflected on the star's state of mind as he approached the end of his life: "In 1999 when I visited him, he was becoming so serene, so transcendental in his every action. His outlook on the world was resigned to, 'Whatever Krishna wants, I'm ready.'"[1]

Brainwashed
(recorded at Friar Park, "Swiss Army Studios," Montagnola, Switzerland and "on the road" July 1999–October 2001; released November 2002)

Between 1997 and 1999, Harrison finally decided to prepare an album of new material for release, and contrary to expectation and myth, Jeff Lynne was involved from the start. "We started working on the album in 1999," Lynne said. "George would come 'round my house and he'd always have a new song with him. He would strum them on a guitar or ukulele. The songs just knocked me out. George talked about how he wanted the album to sound. He told Dhani a lot of things he would like to have done to the songs and left us little clues. There was always

---

[1]*Hare Krishna Tribute to George Harrison*, released by ITV Productions in 2001.

that spiritual energy that went into the lyrics as well as the music."[2] Of course, Harrison had never stopped recording his songs at Friar Park, and he'd carried the majority of what became *Brainwashed* around on tape for years. As is evident from the genesis of "Life Itself" (see 94), George spent his time creating live or multitracked tapes of his work, just for its own sake. The Harrisons even had a portable recording unit that they used for taping while traveling the globe. Some elements of *Brainwashed* were cut this way.

By June 1999, he had completed painstaking twenty-four-track working demos of most of the compositions that would eventually form *Brainwashed*, with all the instruments played by himself or Dhani Harrison, with the exception of drum tracks cut by stalwart friend and Sidebury[3], Jim Keltner.[4] The recording of what would be in retrospect a critical Harrison album was characterized by typical George casualness, as Keltner later reported: "He would call me and ask, 'What are you doing in February? Can you come over?' I'd say, 'What have you got?' and he'd say, 'I've got some new ones and some of the ones you've heard over the years.' It was always such a thrill when I'd first hear them. Sometimes he would say, 'Um…I don't know about this one,' but I'd be like, 'God, I love that one, George. Let me put

---

[2]From the official EMI press release about the album, September 9, 2002.

[3]A nickname Harrison gave to the sidemen who played on the Wilburys' albums.

[4]Keltner's parts were recorded before summer 1999, and not overdubbed after Harrison's death. It is also important to note that Dhani Harrison's acoustic guitar was part of the original demos.

drums on it,' and he'd say, 'Okay.' So we'd put drums on it, but then I'd never be sure whether he was going to use it."[5]

Harrison's search for a place in a band of friends had been realized with a core father-and-son team. All he needed was a tape operator to record music; if no engineer was on hand, Dhani pressed the "record" and "stop" buttons. George would overdub his vocals and guitar solos onto the basic track in the control room at Friar Park. Harrison had freed himself from studio trickery, and "the industry." He wouldn't be targeting his music at a particular audience—he listened to no focus groups and made no more promo films to encourage the Warner Brothers sales team to hit the streets and move units. He'd taken back ownership of his entire non-Apple back catalogue and, in 1999, was considering what record label would release his music without interfering.

Musically, all the signs were that Harrison was planning a set that eschewed most of the technological developments in recording that the Beatles themselves had pioneered with George Martin. This was to be a largely acoustic package, with electric guitars unleashed for solos only, and a minimum of keyboards. Of the original prototypes, only one song ("Marwa Blues") had any keyboards at all. The whole thing was recorded "the old way," on analogue tape (i.e., reel to reel), and his instructions to the musicians, such as they were, called for a return to the fundamentals: "George had a lot of set ideas, so he would tell me pretty much what he would want," recalls Jim Keltner. "Basically he would tell me what he *didn't* want. He didn't want fancy fills and he didn't want too much quirkiness. It was hard to do that sometimes, because he would always talk to me about Ry Cooder and how he loved Ry's records, which I played on. And he loved the quirky side of my playing, which he always got a kick out of. But when it came down to playing on *his* songs, it wouldn't work for him, so he would always have me kind of straighten out things, and play more conventional and basic."[6]

The development of this distilled musical approach really started in earnest with the Traveling Wilburys' albums from 1988 and 1990, which were almost entirely based on acoustic guitar workouts, with minimal ornamentation. Even the "new" Beatles recordings for "Free as a Bird" and "Real Love" were essentially acoustic, with electric guitars used only for Harrison's potent solos. And the casual session held at

[5]www.moderndrummer.com.

[6]*Modern Drummer Magazine*, November 4, 2003.

Friar Park in summer 1994, at which George and Paul McCartney played together for the first time since 1970, were either ukulele-driven or, as the 2003 *Anthology* DVDs showed, led simply by acoustic guitars, with Ringo Starr's drums. Indeed, the relative warmth of the Threetles' 1994 jams at Friar Park gives a clear indication of how *Brainwashed* was recorded. It seems that George was stripping away the layers of complexity and just getting to the heart of the matter—the song.

Nevertheless, he was unsure whether he wanted to step back into the music business, as he told Klaus Voormann: "George talked to me about his intentions to make another product, and how hesitant and split-minded he was about actually doing it." George's friends knew he had plenty of songs in the can and were well used to hearing a selection played among all the Hawaiian or Hoagy Carmichael tunes rendered on the ever-present ukulele, and they tried to persuade him to make an album to capture them. The material had been available for years—one of the pieces ("Rocking Chair in Hawaii") started life during sessions for *All Things Must Pass*, and another four dated from the period between *Cloud Nine* and *Live in Japan*.

In a rare 1997 interview, the reluctant star candidly described his problem with releasing music and its ultimate solution: "Musically I'm not really that good. I'm nowhere near any level that's worth talking about. What I can do is like somebody who can make a cake. I can mix things together and make something that is quite nice. But if you take it all apart I don't believe I have great musical or great lyrical ability, and I have a bigger problem than that—which is, because of my influence from Indian music and that whole spiritual thing, I don't see the point of writing songs. I could write hundreds of songs, you know, 'Hey baby, whatcha gonna do,' I could churn them out, but I don't want to. If I'm going to say something, I'd like it to have some kind of value." [7]

So, thinking that he still had something to say and that the world was in need of some 1960s good sense, he was persuaded to record again. Naturally, the success of the *One* album of Beatles hit singles may have appealed to his more secular business considerations.

But almost as soon as he'd decided to record again, work halted after the attempt on his life in December 1999. Having recovered from this trauma and completed work on remastering *All Things Must Pass* in the spring of the following year, he turned his attention back

---

[7] *Hare Krishna Tribute to George Harrison.*

to his "new" album. Despite a mischievous remark to a reporter in late 2000 that he would not work with Jeff Lynne again, plans were already afoot to complete the disc at Lynne's Los Angeles studio in March 2001. This was suspended for a year because Lynne became ill, but the two Harrisons continued working on the tracks in a studio in their new home in Montagnola, Switzerland. Harrison kept recording there until he left for his final journey to America in October 2001.

The decision to complete *Brainwashed* posthumously had been made by the spring of 2002, and the time booked at Jeff Lynne's studio in March was used for an examination of the tapes, to see what the guitarist had left. The issue of completing posthumous works has been raising temperatures for centuries in the world of classical music. Controversy has raged for nearly half a century around the unfinished Tenth Symphony of Gustav Mahler, which had two fully orchestrated movements and three that were complete in terms of main thematic content, but was hardly scored at all. A British musicologist prepared a full "working version" of the symphony; it is regularly performed by a coterie of Mahlerian conductors, and considered a blasphemous aberration by the remainder.

No such problems faced Lynne and Harrison junior. What they had before them was close to a finished product—the basic tracks were mostly finalized, and the guitarist had left taped or written instructions for the finishing touches. For instance, George had sung the string quartet orchestration for "Rising Sun" onto tape—it just had to be transcribed, played, and recorded. In fact, Mike Moran had worked with him to record the string arrangements on synthesizer, and Marc Mann had been hired to score them for strings. So, contrary to some Lynne-bashing copy, Harrison had planned the vast majority of the project before his death.

He'd also cut multiple takes of his guitar solos for many of the tunes, thus presenting Lynne with what turned out to be an embarrassment of six-string riches. Some of the takes just needed "tidying up"—Harrison had played bass himself on some of the cuts, but on others he'd given up halfway through, or changed the progression. The job was to finalize consistent bass parts. So, technically Lynne had a much less taxing challenge than those he'd overcome to produce "Free as a Bird" and "Real Love" for the Beatles *Anthology* project.

The final product was surely better than anyone outside Harrison's circle could have expected. Although the late star had had no input into the eventual running order, his son selected the sequence with great care, creating an intimate emotional travelogue. Whether by accident or design, the songs included constantly have the effect of a life review, either directly or by reviving distant reverberations. The net result is one of the most compelling and convincing recordings of Harrison's career.

[143] **Any Road (3:50)** *(Harrison)*
Harrison vocal, guitars, banjulele; **Dhani Harrison** electric guitar, backup vocal; **Jeff Lynne** bass, piano, backup vocal; **Jim Keltner** drums

In spirit the recording of "Any Road" is a higher-tech version of the nascent Beatles sitting in Paul McCartney's Liverpool front room in 1960, singing "Hallelujah, I Love Her So" into a single microphone, fed into a tea chest-sized reel-to-reel tape machine. That group of guitarists, with no drummer but a novice bass owner, was recording music for their own amusement.[8] Rock 'n' roll was their shared passion, but they were also steeped in the music of their parents—country and western, folk blues, jazz, Tin Pan Alley, movie and show songs, and the ukulele of national hero George Formby.

So while the opening track on Harrison's first album of new material in fourteen years isn't quite as rough and ready as the early Beatle recordings, it revels in the same direct simplicity. "Any Road" features George playing acoustic guitar and banjulele,[9] rendering a country blues shindig in full voice. His slide guitar boasts a thick bluesy tone, with just a hint of Pete Drake's lithe "Behind That Locked Door" pedal steel excursions. The song also smacks heavily of the Traveling Wilburys' style, notably "The End of the Line," but it had quite a long gestation, unlike the Wilburys' one-take wonders. The song had been worked on during the final summer 1996 *Chants of India* sessions at Friar Park—initially it was over five minutes long and included a string arrangement. It also received an impromptu, skiffle airing in a 1997 appearance on VH-1 (see 139).

In its final state, "Any Road" sets the scene thematically for *Brainwashed*. It's a powerfully sung, jaunty reflection on life's jour-

---

[8]Stuart Sutcliffe was persuaded to use a £75 art prize to buy a Hofner bass, which he didn't know how to play.

[9]The banjulele is a hybrid between a ukulele and a banjo.

ney, Harrison's words flowing with a new ease in the endless search for the antidote to ignorance: "You may not know where you came from, you may not know who you are." And even toward the end, and separated by thousands of miles, he was still traveling the same road as his poetic mentor, Bob Dylan, who was musing, "Where do you come from, where do you go?" on "Summer Days," a track from his excellent, seminostalgic travelogue album, *Love and Theft*, also released in 2001.

On "Any Road," perhaps contrary to expectation, Harrison sounds refreshed and exuberant, as he updates his travel diary from 1973 and "Living in the Material World," where he observed that he would "use my body like a car." The renewed directness convinces, as does an uncluttered production that allows George's voice and stringed alter egos room to breathe.

Finally, in May 2003, "Any Road" was put out as a single in the United Kingdom. Backed by "Marwa Blues," it crept into the Top 40 singles chart for one week. The CD-single package included a joyous "Free as a Bird" style video, which welded together footage from nearly every stage of George's career, including tantalizing glimpses of the Dark Horse Tour film. It felt like a parting gift to Harrison's fans, one that would be treasured.

[144] **P2 Vatican Blues (Last Saturday Night) (2:37)** *(Harrison)*
Harrison vocal, guitars, ukulele; **Dhani Harrison** acoustic guitar, backup vocal; **Jeff Lynne** guitars, bass, Wurlitzer organ, backup vocal; **Jim Keltner** drums

A powerful account of the self-evident appeal of the Beatles was served in April 2003 with the DVD release of the *Anthology*. Memories were jogged worldwide with footage that made it clear why the group conquered the planet in two years and remained preeminent forty years later. One of the nonmusical traits that may have been lost to collective recollection was the sheer unaffected wittiness of the band, natural perhaps for Liverpudlians. The media hyperbole of the day had tagged them the "new Marx Brothers." "P2 Vatican Blues (Last Saturday Night)" is a reminder of just how genuinely funny Harrison and the other Beatles were; it contains one of the guitarist's most droll assaults. The targets are the excesses of 1950s Catholicism and the financial shenanigans of a certain Cardinal Paul Marchinkus.

Harrison's childhood immersed in the Irish Catholicism of 1950s Liverpool provides the backdrop to his hilarious mimicry of priests going door-to-door for cash, and the Saturday night ritual of confession in preparation for Sunday mass. This shameless effrontery provides a partial sequel to "Awaiting on You All," which had also targeted Rome back in 1970.

It all prolongs the bubbling start to *Brainwashed*, which could be a function of the fact that like "Any Road," this was another cut from 1987—a buoyant R&B chart first taped for possible inclusion on *Cloud Nine*, filled with the kind of Claptonesque blues guitar licks that Harrison hadn't played since the 1974 Dark Horse Tour.[10] George also adopts a radically different vocal style, consciously "putting on" a thick Liverpool accent, as if to emphasize this journey back to his youth and home city. Although conveying a serious message from an "ex-Catholic," at heart, this was meant to be two and a half minutes of gentle rib tickling, and underlines the natural humor that was always a part of Harrison's solo work, although not part of the George of media cliché.

[145] **Pisces Fish** (4:50) *(Harrison)*
Harrison vocal, guitars, ukulele, bass; **Dhani Harrison** electric guitar; **Jeff Lynne** electric guitar, keyboards, percussion; **Jim Keltner** drums; **Mike Moran** keyboards; **Marc Mann** keyboards

The album's travel metaphor proceeds unimpeded with this first song on *Brainwashed* of relatively recent vintage (the lyrical references to the mad cow disease mass cull suggest 1996).

"Pisces Fish" presents one of Harrison's most accomplished, impressionistic lyrics, in which he observes the world of activity bustling along his "eternal river" but remains detached from it, as he contemplates his personal spiritual journey.

It is the first of three songs that form a distinct movement within the album (the others are "Looking for My Life" and "Rising Sun"). They are a reflective trio, a life review. In this first installment, Harrison reflects with humor on his yin-yang personality and fantastic life story, but his true goal is to join his gods in perfect silence, which is why the song's hook flows down into oblivion. Nevertheless, at this late stage of his career, George Harrison seems to have tapped into a new strain of lyrical inspiration, with a series of verses literally bursting with sophisticated metaphors.

---

[10]Witness the tour versions of "For You Blue" released on *Songs by George Harrison*, and the comprehensively bootlegged "While My Guitar Gently Weeps."

George examines quite complex concepts here; he's traveling along the river of life, but also the river of spiritual enlightenment is flowing through him and waiting to be explored. It all depends, he suggests, on the coxswain; he'd already established on "Any Road" that "If you don't know where you're going, any road will take you there." And decades of devotion to Bob Dylan's linguistic contortions and conundrums pay off with images of the Catholic Church as a fetid brewery.

The crux of the song, "I'm a Pisces Fish and the river runs through my soul," recalls the "Hare Krishna Mantra" chant as it tumbles down through an octave, neatly mirroring the river's passage from mountain to sea. The aquatic preoccupation comes directly from the final words of *Raja Yoga*, a key tome in the guitarist's spiritual life: "Thus [nature] is working, without beginning and without end; and thus, through pleasure and pain, through good and evil, the infinite river of souls is flowing into the ocean of perfection, of Self-realisation."[11]

Musically, Jeff Lynne and Dhani Harrison barely sully George's bucolic incantation, strummed on fat acoustics that recall the earlier eco-etchings "All Things Must Pass" and "The Ballad of Sir Frankie Crisp." George was partly on a mission to reacquaint the listening public with the merits of "just acoustic guitars, played by *people*, into microphones."[12] Naturally, the music's emotional intimacy and complete lack of artifice had nothing at all to do with contemporary popular musical values. So while those looking for innovation on *Brainwashed* might have been disappointed, by 2003 Harrison's "human music" expressing genuine emotion was a radical departure from the norm.

[146] **Looking for My Life** (3:49) *(Harrison)*
Harrison vocal, guitars; **Dhani Harrison** acoustic and electric guitars, backup vocal; **Jeff Lynne** acoustic and twelve-string guitars, piano, bass, backup vocal; *uncredited drums*

Jangling, almost Rickenbacker chord melodies provide a sprightly sonic framework for an intimate, informal chat with an ailing superstar facing the abyss. But, although this song appears to be a reaction to being diagnosed with terminal illness, it was written before 1997 and records an earlier "dark night of the soul."

---

[11]*Raja Yoga*, 221.

[12]From the Electronic Press Kit released at the time of the album's release.

"Looking for My Life" is infused with genuine pathos, a feeling of almost childlike bewilderment at life's vicissitudes experienced by a mind that was constantly seeking answers. Hence the naïve innocence revealed by "I never knew that life was loaded" and "I never knew that things exploded," and the anguish of losing the spiritual certainty grasped in "Your Love Is Forever" and "Sat Singing."

There are also some startling reverberations from childhood that drift up to trouble the singer in his darkest moment—the old wounds of British class-consciousness still haunt him. Why else would a wealthy man in his fifties reflect that he "never got any GCEs"? These were the old examinations for sixteen-year-olds in Britain, the first step on the road to higher education and "establishment" values.

In contrast to the lyrics, the music is light and breezy, with a melody more inscrutable than immediately catchy—but Phil Spector would surely have enjoyed deluging this stripped-down, power pop with reverb and timpani. At its heart, "Looking for My Life" is about lyrical disclosure, a frank portrayal of mental distress. Few Harrisongs have been as brutally touching.

[147] **Rising Sun (5:26)** *(Harrison)*
Harrison vocal, guitars, ukulele; **Dhani Harrison** Wurlitzer organ; **Jeff Lynne** electric guitar, bass, piano; **Jim Keltner** drums

The third of the contemplative triptych, "Rising Sun" is among the most powerful songs of Harrison's career. It was written during the 1991 tour in "the land of the rising sun," a typically mixed period in his life. While the tour was a great success for the stage-shy Harrison, the risk of financial oblivion and more litigation concerning the troubled Handmade Films tempered the joy.

So the verses of "Rising Sun" swing between two dissonant chords (D and G minor). Here Harrison the musician examines the tension between the notes in the chords. It becomes a mirror of his own struggle to overcome the symptoms of business betrayal, feelings of despair and psychological stress ("'til your nervous system starts to tilt"), with Tin Pan Alley and its successors renamed "the avenue of sinners."

But while "Looking for My Life" only catalogues desolation, "Rising Sun" provides overall balance with a chorus that advocates classic Vedic self-realization. As these songs were written without any prospect of being released commercially, the clichés about Harrison preaching to his audience cannot apply—he's talking to himself. However, now that the work has been made public, the listener is offered a unique firsthand experience. It's like having George Harrison sitting beside you, sharing his feelings, *sotto voce.*

The expressive climax comes with an intense guitar solo at the end of the song. The power of emotion articulated by this passage even evokes some of saxophonist John Coltrane's spiritually inspired musical eruptions. Dhani Harrison recalled listeners at the session for this song being awestruck by this raga-blues performance.[13]

The spellbinding outburst at 3:59–4:05 is an object lesson in less being more. Never had Harrison's matchless slide guitar voice sounded better—until the following track.

[148] **Marwa Blues (3:40)** *(Harrison)*
Harrison guitar, keyboards, finger cymbals; **Dhani Harrison** acoustic guitar; **Jeff Lynne** acoustic guitar, keyboards; **Ray Cooper** percussion; **Marc Mann** string arrangement

Toward the end of his life, George Harrison reportedly told a visitor to Friar Park's gardens, "Sometimes I wish I could just turn into a light beam and go away."[14] "Marwa Blues" captures that feeling in music.

The genesis of this exquisite offering was in the mid-1960s, when Harrison first immersed himself in the majestic ragas of Indian music, and met Ravi Shankar and one of his English pupils, John Barham. The evening "Raga Marwa" was among Harrison's favorite pieces of music, and at that time there were legendary recordings of it by Ravi Shankar and by Ali Akbar Khan (on the famous 1968 album *The Forty Minute Raga*). George also had a never-released piano interpretation of the raga by Barham, which had a significant impact on Harrison and Lennon. This slide guitar interpretation of the raga, set in Western harmony and with a blues subtext, closes the circle, thirty-five years later.

Completing four cycles around a gently undulating harmonic framework that pivots on a major-to-minor variation, Harrison presents the most personal and emotionally resonant guitar performance of his career, beautifully recorded. Every nuance of vibrato can be discerned, and the elegant, crystalline purity of his tone is fully exposed. The passages at 2:20–2:27 and 2:41–2:55 are potent cries from the heart, which convey more of Harrison's struggle for spiritual fulfillment than lyrics ever could. It is the sound of a man crying "Hear me Lord" through a musical instrument.

---

[13]*Le Journal du Dimanche*, November 2002.

[14]See Tom Petty's recollection in Fine, *Harrison*, 225.

In "Marwa Blues," Harrison reaches beyond mere entertainment toward art. His playing is at once almost unbearably touching and spiritually enraptured, offering a multidimensional emotional experience. It is one of his most important accomplishments. Inevitably a man who doubted the veracity of language throughout his life would only reach this level of sophisticated expression in an instrumental setting. George always found the greatest "truth" in the music of India, and with this piece he fulfilled his search for a musical voice that embraced his devotion to the ancient Indian tradition. Harrison's finest hour as a guitarist, in a career packed with six-string highlights, was recognized with a Grammy in 2004—public recognition of his unique instrumental talents.

[149] **Stuck Inside a Cloud (4:03)** *(Harrison)*
Harrison vocal, guitars; **Dhani Harrison** Wurlitzer organ;
Jeff Lynne bass, electric guitar, piano; **Jim Keltner** drums

At first "Stuck Inside a Cloud" seems to be a uniquely candid reaction to illness and mortality, and the narrative certainly causes deep discomfort. However, the 1975 *Extra Texture* contains "Grey Cloudy Lies," a downbeat lament that covers similar ground. Lyrically, the two songs are blood brothers—where "Grey Cloudy Lies" cried out, "at times it gets so lonely, could go insane," the *Brainwashed* piece reflects, "only I can hear me…talking to myself…never been so crazy."

But there is a key difference: whereas "Grey Cloudy Lies" is locked in the vaguely ponderous groove of *Extra Texture*, "Stuck Inside a Cloud" happily skips along. Gorgeous guitar fills, even tinged with the Chinese violin, the *er-hu*, dance playfully in juxtaposition to the crisis-point lyrics, and Harrison is in fine melodic form, tapping into lilting soul inflections.

This kind of split personality between lyrics and music is evident in previous Harrisongs ("Isn't It a Pity" and "This Guitar"), but never quite as starkly presented as here. The guitarist frequently mused that it was far easier for him to express his true feelings in music than through the tangle of lyrics. But "Stuck Inside a Cloud" provides more questions than answers. In past creations like "Isn't It a Pity," the musical and guitar content often embodied the struggle between the "spiritual sky" light and verbal darkness. But, except in the most extreme cases of depression—like "Grey Cloudy Lies"—there was always a glimmer of poetic hope ("The beauty that surrounds them"). There is no hint of a way out in "Stuck Inside a Cloud," which matches the

Extra Texture song as a depiction of sheer despair. So while musically Harrison has presented four minutes of crisp, concise, upbeat pop rock, lyrically he's created harrowing company.

[150] **Run So Far (4:05)** *(Harrison)*
Harrison vocal, guitars; **Dhani Harrison** acoustic guitar, backup vocal; **Jeff Lynne** acoustic guitar, keyboards, acoustic bass, backup vocal; *uncredited drums*

Harrison's decision to find a slot on his new album for this homespun version of a song already recorded by Eric Clapton in 1989 (see 131) was made as late as 1999. In the summer he played his old demo to a visiting *Billboard* journalist and suddenly realized how well it matched the mood of his newer material.

In some respects this recording gets to the heart of what George Harrison was about as a musician—naked, affecting simplicity. He told *Guitar Player* in 1987 that all he played was "posh skiffle," which perfectly characterizes this take of "Run So Far." While the Clapton version is a little overcooked with studio precision, the *Brainwashed* take is chastely organic, just acoustic guitars, rudimentary drums (played by Harrison himself?), and bass. George's natural abilities as a rhythm guitar player who kept near perfect time have rarely been given a better airing. Its two- or three-chord assembly recalls Dylan's early folk directness but also draws attention to a convincing melody that is part lullaby, an effect emphasized by a consoling, wistful vocal.

As "Run So Far" ousted some entirely unreleased Harrisongs for a slot on *Brainwashed*, it might be viewed as a lesser choice for inclusion on the set. Nevertheless, it amply demonstrates that Harrison's "posh skiffle" had the potency to express considerable personal depth.

[151] **Never Get Over You (3:25)** *(Harrison)*
Harrison vocal, guitars; **Jeff Lynne** bass, piano; **Jim Keltner** drums

In the midst of the *American Idol* era, populated by instant pop sensations, the Harrisons' peripatetic recording studio bore witness to the homemade taping of a love song that could take its place easily alongside "Something" and "Learning How to Love You."

The song is introduced and characterized by graceful bottleneck counterpoint. Harrison again explores the D to G minor chord change heard previously on "Rising Sun." This sequence emphasizes the modulation of F-sharp to G and A to B-flat, each a musical half step.

Individually and collectively, these changes create a hesitant mood of imperfection, used by Harrison to suggest simultaneously feelings of love and loss through the juxtaposition of a beguiling, positive melody with harmonic tension. The conflicting emotions of life are concealed in what appears at first sight to be a simple love song.

In every respect, "Never Get Over You" underlines the sheer quality of George Harrison as a songwriter, musician, and arranger. Harrison is setting his own standards here, and he is not found wanting, notably in his singing, which has often been considered his key weakness. For a highlight of the track is his warm and soulful vocal, which was an entirely new turn for him, but wholly convincing. The realization that this fine Harrison love song might never have been heard is another of the bittersweet facets of *Brainwashed*.

[152] Between the Devil and the Deep Blue Sea (2:33)
(Harold Arlen and Ted Koehler)
Harrison vocal, ukulele; **Jools Holland** piano; **Mark Flanagan** acoustic lead guitar; **Joe Brown** acoustic rhythm guitar; **Herbie Flowers** bass, tuba; **Ray Cooper** drums

Of all the music presented on *Brainwashed*, this carefree cover of a 1930s New York show tune probably best embodies George Harrison's private music-making in the last decade of his life. After his interest in 1940s British entertainer George Formby was reignited in the late 1980s, Harrison was rarely to be seen without a ukulele, the instrument Formby made famous, in his hand. Throughout the 1991 *Live in Japan* tour, George held after-show ukulele sessions in his private suite, and the Friar Park Threetles get-together in the summer of 1994, captured at length on the *Anthology* DVD, gives ample evidence of his dedication to the four-string instrument. Dhani Harrison provided the most succinct recollection: "That's really what he was like around the house—all day, just playing the ukulele."[15]

In the context of this album, the piece harkens back to Harrison's formative childhood years listening to the prewar standards of Cab Calloway, Django Reinhardt, and Hoagy Carmichael. Harold Arlen and Ted Koehler penned "Between the Devil and the Deep Blue Sea" in 1930, for a show called *Rhythm-Mania*, and the tune quickly became a standard. For George Harrison it was a taste of an era of music that epitomized high-quality songwriting and musi-

---

[15]From the *Brainwashed* press kit.

cianship; he would later wonder whether the popular music of the 1990s would still be potent after seventy years.

The actual recording on *Brainwashed* is a stereo remix of a 1991 television appearance for Jools Holland that would have fitted snugly in the holiday mood of Harrison's *Gone Troppo* set.[16] Here is Harrison in strong voice, performing with a group of friends in an ultrarelaxed spirit. It is one of the most contented-sounding releases in his catalogue.

[153] **Rocking Chair in Hawaii (3:04)** *(Harrison)*
Harrison vocal, dobro, acoustic guitar, ukulele, keyboards;
Jeff Lynne bass; **Jim Keltner** drums

The sense of a life review is strong on this stylistic sequel to "Deep Blue," which was initially taped as impromptu merriment during the sessions for *All Things Must Pass* in 1970. "Rocking Chair in Hawaii" is a celebration of the first guitar music that the preteen George Harrison heard, before he was even aware of rock 'n' roll—the country blues of tragic figures Jimmie Rodgers and Hank Williams. Harrison recalled in his autobiography, "The 'old' Jimmie Rodgers and Hank Williams…they were good for me until I was about twelve."[17] It was Rodgers's "Waiting for a Train" that first inspired him to pick up a guitar, and George honors "The Singing Brakeman" with his version of Rodgers's yodel-moan, a technique picked up by Hank Williams, a country singer who lived the archetypal rock 'n' roll life. And Williams was the main inspiration—George makes the point by forming the recurring dobro hook of the song around guitar licks from two of Hank Williams's postwar hits, "Love Sick Blues" and "Long Gone Lonesome Blues." The second of these leads off with a line that echoes Harrison's "Pisces Fish" spiritual aspirations, and his preference for passing his days immersed in nature: "I went down to the river to watch the fish swim by."

The original tongue-in-cheek take during *All Things Must Pass* was a straight pastiche of the Williams track. It opens with a yodel but soon breaks down into chaos, as testified to by one of Harrison's bluntest lyrical observations: "I'm going down to the river, take me my fishing hook, I'm going down to the river, so fucking what."

---

[16]Holland hosted a television special called *Mr. Roadrunner*, for which Harrison surprisingly taped a slot.

[17]*I Me Mine*, 53.

By the time George cleaned things up for another Friar Park demo, he'd modified Williams's opening line to, "I'm going down to the river, going to take me my rocking chair." It was almost as if in memory of the proto-recliners honored in song by Harrison heroes Hoagy Carmichael and Big Bill Broonzy,[18] although this remains an obvious Hank Williams cover at heart. The sassy, sensuous lyrics mix a celebration of feminine wiles with a taste of the old Harrison "Krishna or woman" ambiguity, all delivered in a completely new singing style: a lazy, moody vocal that mixes Hoagy Carmichael's precisely lethargic drawl with the Williams yodel, the latter doubled with dulcet dobro. For the first time in his career, Harrison sounds sexy on what is a charming, stress-free time-out from the emotional turmoil that surrounds it.

[154] **Brainwashed (4:02)** *(Harrison)*
Harrison vocal, guitars, bass; **Dhani Harrison** acoustic guitar, backup vocal; **Jeff Lynne** electric guitar, twelve-string guitar, keyboards, backup vocal; **Jim Keltner** drums; **Bikram Ghosh** tabla; **Jon Lord** piano; **Sam Brown** backup vocal; **Jane Lister** harp; **Isabella Borzymowska** narration

Drawing on the spirit of Dylan's "Like a Rolling Stone," and with a startling structural similarity to "Living in the Material World," "Brainwashed" is the climax of an emotionally taut album. It captures a pervasive antiestablishment feeling that swept the West in the late 1990s and the first years of the new millennium and climaxed in 2003 with widespread antiwar protests that almost rekindled the spirit of revolution pondered by the Beatles in 1968.

Harrison's targets in his newly fashionable, classic 1960s protest lyrics are the denizens of politics, big business, the press, and most of the mass communications media developed by baby boomers like himself. In another throwback to his mildly rebellious youth, George sets these feelings of alienation in a rock 'n' roll idiom, adopting a Dylanish vocal style that rattles off a litany of establishment infamy with increasing desperation.

The listener is left in no doubt of the star's worldview on one of the newest songs on the disc, and there's also no ambiguity about his solution—"God, God, God." This literal spelling out of the word was significant for a man who was taken aback by the occasionally hostile

---

[18]Carmichael's "Rockin' Chair" and Broonzy's "Rockin' Chair Blues," which may have been the original template for the oft-claimed blues classic "Rock Me Baby."

reception his use of the word "Lord" received in 1970, and who often used all manner of poetic artifice to mask the spiritual nature of his lyrics. To make his point, he employs a serene middle section, as on "Living in the Material World," to evoke the spiritual goal. Fittingly, this interlude was initially recorded in the summer of 1996 using musicians booked for Ravi Shankar's *Chants of India* album.

Although few contemporary antiwar marchers would have turned to Patanjali's *How to Know God* for their answer as Harrison had, "Brainwashed" perfectly captured the general feeling of being duped and doomed that characterized public spirit in 2003.

[155] **Namah Parvati (2:02)** *(traditional Sanskrit prayer, arranged Harrison)*
Harrison vocal, harmonium; **Dhani Harrison** vocal;
Bikram Ghosh tabla

In 1968 George Harrison closed *Wonderwall*, his first solo project, with the simplest of the Vedic chants, "Singing Om," a recording of just voices and harmonium. In the inextricably wedded relationship between music and philosophy in Hindu culture, the constant monochord drone of the harmonium (or tamboura) that sits behind all musical expression represents the unchanging, eternal nature of the soul.

It was entirely appropriate then that Dhani Harrison chose to add a recording his father had made of another Sanskrit prayer, "Namah Parvati," as the true finale of his last album, and, in effect, public life. So Harrison's final statement is one of devotion to God:

Namah parvati pataye hara hara mahadev
Shiva shiva shankara mahadeva
Hara hara hara mahadev
Shiva Shiva shankara mahadeva.

Surrender to Shiva, Parvathi's Lord, Shiva is the destroyer
of ignorance, the Great Lord, the Eternal Lord.

The extreme contrast between the final, angry rock 'n' roll chord of "Brainwashed" and the serenity of "Namah Parvati" rather sums up Harrison's "Pisces Fish" life, which, from 1966 until his death, contrasted his desire for the spiritual with his on-and-off professional life as a mostly hesitant rock superstar.

Harrison often strove to represent his spiritual aspirations in the rock idiom, in songs like "Life Itself," "Your Love Is Forever," "My Sweet Lord," and "It Is He," and he garnered plenty of criticism for his efforts.

Consequently, this emotive home taping of a genuine bhajan is a fitting culmination to his quest, and to *Brainwashed*.

Introducing his segment at the Concert for Bangla Desh in 1971, Ravi Shankar noted that Indian music was an art form that required a "little concentrated listening" on the part of the audience. To some extent the same could be said of *Brainwashed*, an album that appears deceptively simple in conception. But the bare bones, "guitar-voice-song" setting is the backdrop to music of some depth.

As ever with Harrison's music, the album operates on a largely emotional basis and evokes an emotional response. There is a strong sense of letting go, partly from elements of life review (the preteen musical influences, thoughts on the failure to achieve academic qualifications, and being raised as a Catholic), and partly from the open window into the anguish of facing up to disease and mortality. The result is a brutally frank album in a career full of them—the product was not conceived to target any part of the market and is "just what it is." The music captures spiritual aspiration, humor, depression and a withdrawal from life. Perhaps the reality of his death had freed Harrison further to be more himself in his work. This sense of emancipation through mortality was contemplated by an American psychotherapist, Sheldon Kopp, when facing up to his own certain death: "Nothing is done in order to achieve something else. No energy is wasted in maintaining the illusions. My image does not matter. I do not worry about how I am doing. I do what I do, am what I am." [19]

And the George Harrison captured on *Brainwashed* is an outstanding guitarist, accomplished songwriter, and moving vocalist, entirely comfortable in his own skin. Paradoxically, amid all the emotion a calm Harrison emerges—so at ease that we hear him assuming vocal personas to match the mood or message of the songs. So "P2 Vatican Blues" is delivered in his native Liverpool brogue, "Rocking Chair in Hawaii" with a lazy, seductive burr, and "Never Get Over You" in close, soul intimacy. He hadn't done this since the Beatles' "live act" period as captured on *Live at the BBC*, notably his take of "Youngblood." With *Brainwashed* Harrison was consciously using his voice as an instrument for the first time in his solo career. He was well served in this by Jeff Lynne's treatment of his vocals, which is a feature

---

[19] From Kopp's book, *If You Meet the Buddha on the Road, Kill Him.*

of the album. Whether by close miking or mixing-desk wizardry, the expression in George's voice has never been captured better.

However, when the album finally emerged in November 2002 it seemed to be only targeted at Harrison's fans, those who knew it was coming. Although *Brainwashed* debuted at #18 on *Billboard*, it plummeted to #57 in the second week, while the U.K. chart performance was more moderate still. The impulse buyer was not a target—the futuristic cover art had no picture of the artist, and even his name was tucked away, bottom right in notably small type. No single was released, although "Stuck Inside a Cloud" was a promotional release. Could the casual music buyer ever have known that this was a new George Harrison album?

For all that, the album was certified Gold by *Billboard* by December 2002, but it was clear that more could have been done. So it was no real surprise when the set was effectively repackaged for the British market in May 2003 on the back of the "Any Road" single and video. The new visuals for the CD included an "in your face" picture of George, and his name in beefy print. For many, this was the first they had heard of *Brainwashed*, and by the end of May 2003 it was at #29 on the U.K. album chart, where it settled for a one-week run. However, any lingering disappointment with the promotion of this music should be set against the fact that it was released at all.

Brainwashed was frequently, and favourably, compared with *All Things Must Pass*, the album that started George Harrison's solo vocation in earnest. But while there are similarities, the overall mood and arrangements are closer to the early Friar Park home studio recordings "So Sad," "I Don't Care Anymore," and "Miss O'Dell." Arguably the strongest precedent for the *Brainwashed* approach was the deeply unfortunate "Bye Bye, Love." This sorry effort had Harrison overdubbing himself playing all the instruments, while the more successful, original Friar Park demo of "Dark Horse" was created in exactly the same way as songs on the new set, just guitar, bass, and drums.

Nevertheless, the album was similar to the 1970 classic in that it "Hoovered up" songs that had been stockpiled for years. The key difference was that by and large, the sonority of *Brainwashed* wasn't the product of another's vision. The vast sound of a fair chunk of *All Things Must Pass* emerged from Phil Spector's imagination, whereas the songs on the 2002 disc are dressed in little more than their birthday suits. And while Jeff Lynne has been the whipping boy of many a Beatles and Harrison fanatic, his personality is almost invisible on *Brainwashed*, save for some extraneous tympani on "Looking for My Life." Overall, Lynne deserves great credit for his efforts.

Essentially, this product is about Harrison's quest for freedom, artistic and personal. His musical freedom is evident from the natural instrumentation and arrangements, which provide the scaffolding for songs that chart a personal journey to spiritual fulfillment. A case in point is "P2 Vatican Blues," which is partly a rough-and-tumble joke at the expense of the Catholic Church, but has a more serious undertone about going from "home" to "Rome" as a spiritual seeker and rejecting the Vatican, ultimately for the direction of "Namah Parvati." So Harrison is describing which of the many directions alluded to on "Any Road" he is going to take.

This travelogue provides many poignant moments and no little pain, but the profound honesty is wrapped in musical serenity. The pathos results from more than George's struggle with cancer; it's also a function of his life as a reluctant superstar. He joined a band to escape life as an apprentice electrician in the days before skilled tradesmen could name their price. Did the band that first recorded *Please, Please Me* really understand what "making it" would mean? The track that best epitomizes this struggle to escape contradiction is "Marwa Blues," a work of pure expression, created with no thought of who might be listening. It is Harrison freed from the constraints of language, revealing his deepest emotions.

Such self-revelation is nothing new for Harrison—all his releases have exhibited unstinting openness—and in that respect *Brainwashed* is part of the continuum started with *All Things Must Pass*. George Harrison here is the same man who cried out "Hear Me Lord" and "Give Me Love," still reaching out for the answer amid no little personal distress. And Harrison's answer remained the same philosophical support he'd embraced in 1966, and a return to earlier musical values.

It was telling that the album was released in 2002 and virtually relaunched with the release of "Any Road" as a single in 2003, as this was the apogee of a new era of artifice in the music business. Stars were manufactured, literally in front of the public, who had an open view of the processing plant through their televisions with shows like *Pop Idol* and *American Idol*. This grotesque form of puppetry made the appeal of "serious" contemporary acts like Coldplay ever more potent, and they were lauded for being honest and unaffected. The fact is that the same qualities are found in abundance on *Brainwashed*, which in time will come to be recognized as a remarkable recording by a great musician who went down fighting, but also knowing, as Jim Keltner reflects, "He gave it his best shot. He knew he was leaving, he knew he was getting out of here. I had a hard time believing that. But I think he was so prepared, and everything just fell into place the way he wanted it."

It will never be known if George Harrison would have wanted a concert held in his memory by his friends and family. He would clearly have enjoyed hearing a troupe of Indian master musicians playing in his honor, and he might have been pleased with how credible his songbook sounded.

The Concert for George was held a year to the day of his passing, at the Albert Hall, the only British venue ever to host a solo Harrison concert ten years earlier. The event had the potential to be a disastrous example of rock 'n' roll sanctimony.[[[flWhat does this mean?]]] [SL—I've changed it but for the record the phrase derives from Mr. Pecksniff, a famously hypocritical character in the Charles Dickens novel 'Martin Chuzzlewit']That it avoided this fate is a tribute to the organizers, who kept the focus on the matter at hand—the music. And like that 1992 date, this show underlined the sheer quality of Harrison's songs to anyone who'd forgotten. Although the lineup was based largely on the *Live in Japan* set, the assembled cast threw in some unexpected but welcome offerings, like "That's the Way It Goes," "Handle with Care," "I Need You," and, most startlingly, "The Inner Light," now a wonderfully eloquent duet between Anoushka Shankar and Jeff Lynne.

It was Anoushka who started the performance with fitting dignity on a solo sitar recital, seemingly handed the mantle by her father, Ravi, in much the same way that Dhani Harrison appeared to have assumed his father's responsibilities. The venerable sitar master was much in evidence as composer on "Arpan," the delightfully rich Indian piece that closed the first half of the night's festivities. Here was a 2002 realization of Harrison's *Wonderwall* concept, and the old Dark Horse Records *Music Festival from India* album. That the attendees were so receptive to this great music speaks volumes for how much Harrison and Ravi Shankar achieved in bringing it to a mass audience.

"Arpan" wanders and wheels through myriad moods, from the Hare Krishna mantra to celebrations led by the swaggering shenhai to the deeply felt lamentation of the sarangi. The music at once celebrates a life and mourns its loss. It was fitting too that V. M. Bhatt of *Meeting by the River* legend was featured on his "Indian slide guitar," as was an Indian mandolin soloist. This was an instrument that had made a star of youngster U. Srinivas, a player frequently praised by Harrison in public. "Arpan" was the musical highlight of the evening.

When the vast rock band led by Eric Clapton took to the boards after a suitably riotous Python interlude, it was as if the old "cowboys and Indians" gag from the Dark Horse Tour had returned. That tour mixed large casts of Indian and Western performers, and the 2002 cast included a number from the original lineup, with Jim Horn, Tom Scott, Jim Keltner, Emil Richards, and Billy Preston present. They formed part of an enormous sound marshalled with consummate ease by Eric Clapton, whose complete lack of showboating set the tone for the evening. The theme for the Western half of the performance was deference to the songs, not the performers' egos, and in that they all matched Harrison's own musical dictum.

On those terms Paul McCartney might have surprised some of his detractors by playing it absolutely straight with a stunning ukulele rendition of "Something" and a warm "For You Blue." There might have been irony in McCartney rendering "All Things Must Pass," but not in a performance that showcased the timeless quality of the classic song, perhaps the greatest solo Beatle composition. Other powerful turns were given by Sam Brown, Gary Brooker, and Ringo Starr, who demonstrated stagecraft and some of his old insecurities: "I loved George, George loved me." It was left to Billy Preston to reflect the gospel grounding of "My Sweet Lord" with an entrancing reading of the classic.

In retrospect, the concert served as a testament to the friendship that George Harrison inspired, and it was a rare showbiz event in that it revealed the basic ordinariness and vulnerability of George's cadre of multimillionaire pals. Certainly fame is prized and fantastic wealth is still as fantastic as it ever was, but the basic human experience is the same for all. The musicians on the stage, in "all the magazines," and on the "Devil's Radio" aren't gods from Olympus, they are just people. That somehow was the message of the show, and Harrison's message too. After all, this man wrote: "Wise men you won't be to follow the like of me in this world made of stone." So, fittingly, the Albert Hall that night saw a number of George's friends gathering to simply say good-bye, minus any celebrity excess. Another of George's lifelong friends, Joe Brown, produced the most poignant moment of the night with his ukulele on "I'll See You in My Dreams," a song that Harrison often asked the Londoner to play for him.

The simplest music of the date proved the most touching, because it was about friendship Brown and Harrison shared. The story of George Harrison's solo recordings is framed by friendships—very rarely did the guitarist ever cut a track with faceless session men who weren't his pals. *The Concert for George* was a very palpable demonstration of the affection he inspired among his friends, but naturally little of what he did to inspire such devotion will be told. However, one of Harrison's oldest musical chums, drummer Jim Keltner, has offered a glimpse: "Now, George had this tremendous living room, which was like three stories high, with a balcony overlooking it. My bedroom was on the third floor—"the loft," they used to call it. It was a beautiful place with a kitchen and den and everything. I used to come down in the morning and stand on this part of the balcony that extends out over the room a little bit. A few times over the years I'd snap my fingers to hear the sound, and I'd say to George, 'It would be great to have the drums here,' and he'd just laugh, because he had a major studio built in another part of the house; why would he want to put drums there? But when I arrived for this recording, I walked in and the drums were set up right in that space. I was so knocked out. He did that for me."

The Concert for George was offered to the public in the standard CD and DVD formats, but also as a limited-run cinematic offering, and the modest publicity generated was the forerunner to a host of posthumous Harrison happenings in 2004. Not only was he inducted into the Rock and Roll Hall of Fame as a solo artist, but he also won a Grammy for the brilliant "Marwa Blues," long overdue public recognition of his outstanding skills as an instrumentalist. Perhaps it was now safe to describe him as slide guitar master.

Besides the fact that these awards and the ceremonies that framed them were very much not to Mr. Harrison's taste, the other irony was that by and large the music press establishment had dismissed his work as a solo artist since 1973. Indeed, by 1975, to paraphrase another Harrison observer,[20] the release of a new Harrison set was the cue for the hacks to outdo each other in finding inventive new ways to describe just how bad George's music was. Despite the

---

[20]Peter Doggett.

awards, to many critics these failings were still evident, and the rerelease on CD in spring 2004 of George's Dark Horse Records catalogue after more than ten years saw this body of work summarily hung, drawn, and quartered again.

As ever with boxed sets, there were trivial quibbles about remixes and bonus tracks. Then again, an expensive package calling itself *The Dark Horse Years 1976–1992* was hardly entirely credible without the three "new" songs from the 1989 *Best of Dark Horse* package ("Cheer Down," "Poor Little Girl," and "Cockamamie Business"). And, while the original cover of *Somewhere in England* was restored, along with the first, longer take of "Unconsciousness Rules," the original song lineup was not. One of the pieces, "Tears of the World," was tacked onto *Thirty-three & 1/3* as an add-on with more than a hint of top-notch Politburo revisionism. Some also noted that "Tears of the World" had already been released on one of the *Songs by George Harrison* packages; another of the "bonus" cuts, "Zig Zag," had also seen previous life as the B-side of "When We Was Fab." Add to this that nothing extra at all was offered on *Live in Japan* when it was well known that "Love Comes to Everyone" and "Fish on the Sand" had been recorded during the tour, and a feeling of lost opportunity was inescapable. While the boxed set's DVD featured priceless footage of Harrison's peerless slide from Japan, it strangely omitted some promo videos ("Blow Away" in particular), which it surely would have been easier to include. On these grounds, the *Dark Horse Years* set was a little disappointing.

The package was salvaged by the welcome inclusion of "Shanghai Surprise," with its sumptuous Vickie Brown vocal, and three charming demos of "Here Comes the Moon," "Save the World" and "Mystical One." The latter two certainly sounded far more convincing as acoustic guitar home brews than they did on their eventual release, and both underscore Harrison's unique harmonic approach, which verges on twelve-tone freedom. They also reveal how Harrison wrote songs initially by finding chord patterns, then eking out the melody contained within the chords. The acoustic simplicity of these demos was probably where Harrison's heart lay, as *Brainwashed* amply highlighted. "Save the World" in particular now sounds horribly overproduced on *Somewhere in England*, in comparison to the demo, which is more Dylan than Monty Python.

It seemed that Harrison's post-1971 solo music was always destined to be regarded as failure in the orthodox doctrine of the music press, and the release of the Dark Horse back catalogue evoked what amounted to another strangely damp response. But maybe that was what George Harrison expected—after all, he had personally selected the bonus tracks. And in the twilight of his career, the guitarist did say that he'd rather play to an audience of twenty-five who knew and cared for his music than a soccer stadium of casual thrill seekers. The Harrison yin-yang legacy of the reluctant superstar remains intact. That's the way it goes.

Conclusion

Joni Mitchell once sang that her life had been a search for love and music. The same could be said of George Harrison, with the caveat that in his case the search extended to finding his true self as a musician and as a man.

There is a certain poignancy to the fact that as he was no self-publicist, Harrison's achievements have often been overlooked, partly because they are to be found in details, not headlines. His role in the Beatles is a case a point.

Even his original role as lead guitarist developed into a kind of rock 'n' roll conductor, holding the structure of the songs together while the front men put on a show for the public. In this setting, his mix of country and rock lead styles gave him unparalleled versatility—it seemed he could produce a memorably melodic riff or solo to suit any song. Harrison was different, because he played the song, not his own self-importance. This was evident even in the Hamburg years to an early observer, Tony Sheridan: "George was not a guy who was using music to impress the word. He was trying to express something. He is one of the most important figures in early rock 'n' roll history—he left his ego out of it. He was the 'Egoless Beatle.'"[1]

And once the group made it into the studio, Harrison was a prominent harmony vocalist, an equal player in their unerring ability to deliver exquisite three-part harmonies. But above all, it was as an arranger for electric guitar that Harrison had the biggest single impact on the Beatles. Over the years it has proven less taxing to celebrate Lennon and McCartney's unassailable songwriting skills than to recognize Harrison's critical role in turning songs from ideas to finished recordings. It is a fact, and one especially true for John Lennon's compositions, that without Harrison's guitar arrangements, *obbligati*, and solos, many Beatles songs could never have emerged as they are now known. The equation is very simple indeed: no Harrison = no Beatles.

Perhaps ironically, the final evidence for this comes from the early solo releases of the ex-Beatles. Paul McCartney's first solo albums were obviously not designed to sound like the Beatles, but the absence of notable guitar arrangements on them is glaring. And Harrison's playing on Lennon's *Imagine* album provides more indications of the effect he could have on a recording. A case in point is his

---

[1] Sheridan, Tony. Interview with author, August 2004.

beautiful introduction for "Oh My Love," which recalls a similarly understated contribution to "In My Life." But the most compelling example is found on the opening track of the 1973 *Ringo* album. John Lennon wrote "I'm the Greatest" on the piano in 1970, but happenstance brought Harrison into the studio for the Starr version. In this case McCartney's absence is notable, as in the course of little more than four minutes Harrison commits to tape a summary of the guitar parts he brought to so many Beatles songs. He opens with stabbing "Get Back" rhythms, flows through a classic "Help!" arpeggio, and fills the track with riffs that easily lodge themselves in the listener's head. The denouement comes with a classically understated but fitting solo that gives an unexpected twist to the melody. In a mirror image of his Beatles work, Harrison had produced a guitar arrangement that created an entirely new song. "I'm the Greatest" sounds just like the Beatles, and the main reason is Harrison's guitar arrangement. It's almost a self-conscious statement, reminding the world and himself, "That's what I used to do."

And in a period of such Beatles revisionism that sanctions a project imbued with the sheer, crushing narcissistic pointlessness of *Let It Be...Naked*, Harrison's role as innovator is also forgotten. After all, it was Harrison alone of the Beatles who created a true musical revolution by fusing Indian music with pop-rock to create a new form. "It is a mark of Harrison's sincere involvement with Indian music," writes Indian music authority Gerry Farrell, "that, nearly thirty years on, the Beatles' 'Indian' songs remain among the most imaginative and successful examples of this type of fusion—for example, "Blue Jay Way" and "The Inner Light.""[2] The one flaw in this statement is that the achievement was Harrison's alone, as the rest of the Beatles played no part in the conception and arrangement of Harrison's Indian songs, and with the exception of "Love You To," almost no part in the performance. Working on his own, and virtually inventing world music, Harrison was perhaps the greatest Beatle innovator of them all.[3]

And although he rarely played blues-roots guitar solos, in retrospect Harrison was also a key guitar innovator. The 1960s blues revival and psychedelic detours reshaped the role of guitarist in new ways, none of which were Harrison's forte. The virtuoso guitar revelations of Eric Clapton and Jimi Hendrix left Harrison seemingly off the pace,

---

[2] Farrell, Indian Music and the West, 188.

[3] No other Beatle appears on "Within You Without You," while Lennon and McCartney sang a few seconds' worth of backing vocals on "The Inner Light," and Starr drummed on "Blue Jay Way."

as the guitar hero momentarily became *de rigueur*. In any event, George had virtually abandoned the guitar for the sitar in this period, catalyzing one of the main forces in psychedelia. But for Harrison Indian music wasn't a fad, it was his salvation. Its instrumental virtuosi taught him a depth of expression unknown in Western pop music, and its close spiritual-cultural roots gave him a model of music as a sacred duty.

By the time Harrison swung back to the guitar in 1968, the man who'd invented the guitar hero, Eric Clapton, had grown tired of the idea. Suddenly the song had assumed its original status over the "solo," a switch catalyzed by The Band and *Music from Big Pink*. And Harrison clearly saw Robbie Robertson's understated leads for The Band as a mirror of his own approach: "You know, there are some players who can play ten thousand notes a second, but you know it doesn't mean anything. Sometimes I wish had a little bit of that dexterity, but I don't really want to be that type of player. I always thought Robbie was that type of guitarist who was more concerned with the overall song and structure than his own personal prowess."[4]

This return to melodic values signaled George's discovery of a new voice on the guitar, through which he could give full expression to his melodic instincts and devotion to Indian music. He came to slide guitar through Delaney Bramlett, but George developed something completely new and unique. In his hands the bottleneck was capable of articulating the most exquisite musicality while honouring raga inflections. George Harrison's slide guitar became his musical alter ego, his second voice—with it he could say more with one note than most guitar heroes manage in a lifetime. His extraordinary performances on "Marwa Blues," Jim Horn's "Take Away the Sadness," Lennon's "How Do You Sleep?," and countless other songs are works of expressive virtuosity. But for those who knew him, his musicianship was always inextricably linked to his loyalty to his friends. "I really think he is a great guitarist," says Klaus Voormann. "And he was the best friend I ever had."

That George Harrison developed into a classic songwriter as well as guitarist was the result of the emotional distortion of Beatlemania, spanning 1963 to 1966, and a parallel phenomenon called Bob Dylan. Within a few short years of being a happy, jobbing rock 'n' country guitar boy, Harrison's private life had evaporated, as

---

[4]From the DVD *Album Classics: The Band (Rhino)*, 1997.

he became an unwitting victim of a peak of teenage hysteria. George enjoyed early out-of-body experiences, watching an image of himself walking the high wire in the worldwide Beatles circus. The impact of fame on this private man was immense, a tidal wave of damaging intrusion and danger.

Even as Beatlemania rumbled on unchecked, the Beatles were transformed from teen favorites to cultural icons, once Bob Dylan had emancipated popular music from payola and Tin Pan Alley. Dylan demonstrated that musicians could write songs about any subject and sing them however they liked. For some this was a chance to exorcise deep-seated demons—childhood psychological scars of the sort borne by John Lennon, Paul McCartney, and Eric Clapton. Even though Harrison didn't have any such specters to oust, he did have the psychological stress of fame to expel. George used his Dylan-given freedom of expression to offer a deeper glimpse into the effects of fame than any of his contemporaries would. Over time, he came to link the distortion of his own life with his perception of a world gone wrong.

As George Harrison developed into a singer-songwriter, he discovered the inner peace of Indian philosophy and music. Momentarily inspired by LSD and a growing awareness of their cultural significance, rock musicians felt they could, and should, change the world. In this 1960s period of revelations and epiphanies, Harrison wrote songs that captured his immediate feelings or his response to an event. The world was moving fast, cultural and political upheavals were rife, and a new order beckoned. Unlike Dylan, the only true genius of rock, George Harrison had no use for allegory to express his internal dialogue—he had an urgent need to say what he thought. Later in his career, this honesty would create endless misunderstanding of his intentions.

Musically his manifesto was always obvious—his anchor was melody above everything. When The Band signaled the rebirth of "the song," it coincided with the full flowering of Harrison's innate, postwar ear for melody, which was powerfully manifested in "Something," "Here Comes the Sun," "Long, Long, Long," and "While My Guitar Gently Weeps." His commitment to melody, as both songwriter and guitar player, never faltered on his solo projects. These spanned decades where "the song" was sometimes forgotten. Harrison's work contains a marvelous richness of melodic invention; he used his guitar to create two or three countermelodies within a song. His musical instincts remained constant, and he rightly calculated that, when fads and fashions had faded, quality songwriting and musicianship would survive.

As an artist, Harrison has always been more noted for his guitar than for his vocal skills. But while he could never be described as a "strong" singer, he had the fundamental skill of expressing emotion through his voice. This was because George Harrison rarely sang anything he didn't believe in—his songs documented his commitment. When he felt that the music industry demanded that he dilute his statement, his response was to withdraw completely and record music in private. His retreat from an industry he'd partly created was the only way for Harrison to maintain his integrity. The recollection of the late Doris Troy, who was a veteran of forty years in the music business, suggests a man unwittingly caught up in a dirty world: "George was beautiful, his soul was beautiful, and his mind was beautiful. His attitude was beautiful, he was just a beautiful guy, he was one of a kind. There's not many people like George, I'm telling you, and I've met a lot of people over the years. The man was one of a kind."

Music became even more important to Harrison once he'd been exposed to a philosophy that cast it as a spiritual force. He eventually found a Western equivalent to this Indian axiom in gospel music, and his late 1960s work with Billy Preston, Delaney Bramlett, and Doris Troy squared a musical-philosophical circle that led to his great statement, *All Things Must Pass*. His personal search for spiritual fulfillment led him to Krishna and Hinduism, a path that brought accusations of treachery in some quarters. But those who knew him professionally never doubted the man: "This was not a phony guy, he was put in the middle of so much phony stuff and maintained his integrity through everything." The falseness that David Bromberg is referring to surrounded Harrison in the 1970s, and was still searching for a true identity. As he was freed from the Beatles, George found himself swinging between the asceticism demanded by his sanity-saving spiritual beliefs and the temptations of the rock life.

This struggle produced some turbulent years in the mid-1970s, but eventually his internal search for peace was manifested in gentle, introspective music that made no concerted attempt to be contemporary. In that respect it was a deeply personal *hejira* from the fabricated falseness of contemporary pop.

Throughout this period of discovery, some sniped that he was an obsessive recluse, a cultural tourist who'd soon tire of his bizarre beliefs. But his family's statement after his death points to a powerful belief: "We are deeply touched by the outpouring of love and compassion from people around the world. The profound beauty of the moment of George's passing—of his awakening from this dream—

was no surprise to those of us who knew how he longed to be with God. In that pursuit, he was relentless."

The prying eyes of the world pursued George Harrison to his deathbed—the ultimate invasion, especially for a man who had no desire to be a "star" or to be significant. The paradox of George Harrison is that he *did* change the world, even though he just wanted to change himself. Without doubt, he single-handedly sparked the mass interest in world music and Eastern philosophy that is now taken for granted in the West. His Dark Horse Records was the first label of the 1970s to release innovative world music, and Harrison was the first (and last) popular musician to take Indian music into rock arenas. He lifted occidental eyes from their own myopic, cultural purview and, with the Concert for Bangla Desh, did more than invent the charity rock concert: he also helped terminate the self-indulgences of the 1960s.

George Harrison's musical journey mirrored his personal search for truth and peace. Given that he shared the Hindu belief that music was a conduit to God, it became inevitable that, at its purest, his music would try to depict his spiritual vision. Consequently, his songs "Life Itself" and "Your Love Is Forever" are the closest to his musical "soul," and they are formed from the beauty of melody. On these songs and others, George's meticulous craftsmanship as a singer, guitar player, and arranger was used to create aural replicas of grace. The summation and apogee of this life's work is found on "Marwa Blues."

Essentially, George Harrison's musical aesthetic was split between the music of his youth and the music of his internal philosophical dialogue. The first music that he heard as a 1940s war baby remained a passion throughout his life, and he often celebrated George Formby, Cab Calloway, and Hoagy Carmichael in his work. The arrival of Elvis Presley, Carl Perkins, Eddie Cochran, and Little Richard gave Harrison the music of his teenage years, a sound that spoke of ringing out the old and gentle rebellion. While he deeply loved both these strands of music, he never used them to reflect his own deepest feelings; they remained external. Indeed, he only ever used a rock 'n' roll setting in his solo work to release anger about external events, as on "Wah-Wah" and "Devil's Radio."

The other side of his artistic divide was the music that documented his personal feelings and spiritual search. This was uniquely his: the layered vocal and guitar harmonies, the singing slide guitars and relative harmonic richness all came from a place where music was an offering to a higher power. His models for this approach were

Indian and gospel music, and the conduit for covering this subject matter in popular music was Bob Dylan. In fact, Harrison only ever had two models of songwriting to follow—Lennon and McCartney, and Dylan. Being around John and Paul as they flourished gave him an insight into constructing melodies and songs, while Dylan's emancipation of the language of rock music gave Harrison the artistic "right" to express himself in words, as well as notes.

In George Harrison's interior aesthetic of music, the song was of supreme value, because it was, itself, in the service of God, just like a gospel standard such as "Going Home" or a Hindu bhajan. This is why Harrison never felt the need to play roaring rock guitar solos that would have thrown the spotlight back onto him and his ego. One of his oldest musical friends, Klaus Voormann, reflects, "George did not want to be up there in front of people—he wanted to be in a band with other people, like the Band or the Beatles. He loved to be part of something."

This view of music was that it was necessarily disconnected from the rock 'n' roll vision and was only a part of pop culture in that it cast a different light on it. As his music was largely an internal dialogue, Harrison had no real need for a concept of his relationship with his audience, or even any self-awareness of himself as an "entertainer." So hitting middle age in the 1990s gave him no "My Generation" convulsions; being fifty and an "aging hippie" was irrelevant to his life as an artist—his music was not about fashion. The irony was that, as his original audience aged with him, his "old before his time" songs about death and the meaning of life became more relevant. While some found Harrison's musical vision too self-contained, his songs were essentially about an ordinary man trying to make sense of his extraordinary life as a celebrity, and the truth of his existence as a man.

That the vast majority of George Harrison's albums were commercially potent[5] suggests that his audience understood his search for peace. Similarly, the reaction to his death hints of empathy with his efforts to look beyond the sheen of the music business. His integrity earned him the loyalty and respect of his peers, among them Bob Dylan, unparalleled mentor to the rock generation. Dylan's ability to express the inexpressible with words mirrored Harrison's struggle to reflect the abstraction of personal spiritual experience in

---

[5]Other than *Gone Troppo* and *Live in Japan*, none of Harrison's albums of original material charted at lower than #13 on Billboard. For most artists, this would represent an outstanding hit rate.

music. Dylan's statement after George Harrison's death crystallizes his abilities as a wordsmith, and a great musician's impact: "He was a giant, a great, great soul, with all of the humanity, all of the wit and humor, all the wisdom, the spirituality, the common sense of a man and compassion for people. He inspired love and had the strength of a hundred men. He was like the sun, the flowers, and the moon, and we will miss him enormously. The world is a profoundly emptier place without him."

Epilogue

Sometime in 1975 (the months blend into years), George Harrison made Splinter an offer that might have really broken them into the Los Angeles scene and made them into superstars.

He had arranged a special showcase session for them at The Troubadour, the club where John Lennon and Harry Nilsson were quite well known. All Bob Purvis and Bill Elliot had to do was hang around L.A. for six weeks and then pick the low-hanging fruit Harrison was offering. He'd also arranged for the duo to pass away the days at a luxury hotel frequented by stars, Chateau Marmont on Sunset Boulevard. Although they didn't realize it at the time, it was one of those once-in-a-lifetime moments. Different futures lay mapped out in front of them, depending on which way they chose to go.

It would have been so easy, but both Elliot and Purvis had wives and children to think about, and the pull of South Shields was strong. They were soon at the airport heading back to the place they loved. Splinter made two more albums for Harrison's Dark Horse Records, but neither recaptured the magic of *The Place I Love,* and the duo left Harrison's stable dissatisfied.

Looking back on his time working with George Harrison, Bob Purvis sipped a glass of red wine in a comforting Durham hotel, the city where he boarded the bus for Leeds on "Half Way There," one of his wanderlust songs. While reminiscing warmly about trips to Friar Park to record *The Place I Love,* he recalled how Peter Sellers appeared out of the blue for a photo session. "Did he make you laugh?" I asked. "No," said Purvis, "he was straight as a die."[1]

The cast of characters the songwriter met at Friar Park suggests the *National Enquirer* model of the rock-star lifestyle. But the George Harrison Bob Purvis knew and worked with rarely spoke about himself and always asked after his friend's wife and children. It was as if the superstar had lost sight of his own ego and knew how to touch others: "George was always interested in you and made you feel special."

The Beatles and Splinter may have come from opposite sides of England, but more joins than separates Liverpool and Newcastle in spirit. They shared the cobbled streets of back-to-back houses, and the worlds of hard-working and hard-drinking men, whose escape valves were football and music. As two northern men, George Harrison and

---

[1]Durham, England, November 2001.

Bob Purvis were cast from the same mold. Harrison really broke free from his roots; Purvis was ultimately unable to do so and maybe "kissed it all good-bye."

It was obvious that his time with Harrison had deeply affected this guy who was a family man above all. I asked him what he would say to George Harrison now if he had a blank piece of paper. Purvis sighed, as if Joni Mitchell's "Big Yellow Taxi" had just slipped into view. "We didn't deserve to have someone as nice and kind as George helping us. We were just a couple of naïve kids from Newcastle who didn't realize how lucky we were. I just wish I could have let him know that I was grateful, and sorry for not seeing what he was trying to do for us. He was an absolutely sincere man."

Appendix I

George Harrison
Solo Discography

Albums

Wonderwall Music (Apple, SAPCOR 1—1968)
Electronic Sound (Zapple, 2—1969)
All Things Must Pass (Apple, STCH 639—1970)
Living in the Material World (Apple, PAS 10006—1973)
Dark Horse (Apple, PAS 10008—1974)
Extra Texture—Read All About It (Apple, PAS 10009—1975)
Thirty-three & 1/3 (Dark Horse, DH 56319—1976)
George Harrison (Dark Horse, K 56562—1979)
Somewhere in England (Dark Horse, K 56870—1981)
Gone Troppo (Dark Horse, 923734-1—1982)
Cloud Nine (Dark Horse, WX 123—1987)
Songs by George Harrison EP (Ganga Distributors, SGH 777—1988)[1]
Songs by George Harrison II EP (Ganga Distributors, SGH 778—1992)[2]
Live in Japan (Dark Horse, 7599-26964-1—1992)
All Things Must Pass Thirtieth Anniversary Reissue (Gnome, 7243 530474
    2 9—2001)
Brainwashed (Dark Horse, 5-43246-2—2002)
The Dark Horse Years 1976-1992 (Dark Horse, GHBOX 1—2004)

Traveling Wilburys Albums

The Traveling Wilburys: Vol. 1 (Wilbury Records, WX 224—1988)
The Traveling Wilburys: Vol. 3 (Wilbury Records, WX 224—1990)

Other Albums (Compilations, Promotional and Charity Releases)

The Concert for Bangla Desh (Apple, STCX 385—1972)
The Best of George Harrison (Parlophone, PAS 10011—1976)
Greenpeace (Towerbell/EMI, FUND 1—1985)
Porky's Revenge (CBS, 70265—1985)
The Prince's Trust Concert 1987 (A&M, PTA1987—1987)
George Harrison—Best of Dark Horse (Dark Horse, WX 312—1989)
Nobody's Child (Warner Brothers, WX 353—1990)
Bunbury Tails (Polydor, 515 784-2—1992)
Mo's Songs (Warner Brothers Promotional Release, PRO-MO-1994-)

---

[1]The cuts on this EP were "Sat Singing," "Lay His Head," "Flying Hour," and a live version of "For You Blue" from 1974.

[2]The tracks on this EP were the demo version of "Life Itself," "Tears of the World," "Hottest Gong in Town," and "Hari's on Tour (Express)" from the 1974 tour.

Miscellany

Ageless Body, Timeless Mind—Deepak Chopra (Random House Audio, 1993)[3]

Singles

My Sweet Lord / What Is Life (Apple, 1970)
What Is Life / Apple Scruffs (Apple, 1971) *(US release)*
Bangla Desh / Deep Blue (Apple, 1971)
Give Me Love / Miss O'Dell (Apple, 1973)
Ding Dong Ding Dong / I Don't Care Anymore (Apple, 1974)
Dark Horse / Hari's on Tour (Apple, 1974)
You / World of Stone (Apple, 1975)
This Guitar / Maya Love (Apple, 1975)
This Song / Learning How to Love You (Dark Horse, 1976)
My Sweet Lord / What Is Life (EMI reissue, 1976)
True Love / Pure Smokey (Dark Horse, 1976) *(U.K. release)*
Crackerbox Palace / Learning How to Love You (Dark Horse, 1976)
    (U.S. release)
It's What You Value / Woman Don't You Cry for Me (Dark Horse, 1977)
    (U.K. release)
Blow Away / Soft Touch (Dark Horse, 1979)
Love Comes to Everyone / Soft-Hearted Hana (Dark Horse, 1977)
Faster / Your Love Is Forever (Dark Horse, 1977)
All Those Years Ago / Writing's on the Wall (Dark Horse, 1981)
Teardrops / Save the World (Dark Horse, 1981)
Wake up My Love / Greece (Dark Horse, 1982)
I Really Love You / Circles (Dark Horse, 1983) *(US release)*
I Don't Want to Do It / Queen of the Hop *(Dave Edmunds)*
    (Columbia, 1985)
Got My Mind Set on You / Lay His Head (Dark Horse, 1987)
When We Was Fab / Zig Zag (Dark Horse, 1988)
This Is Love / Breath Away from Heaven (Dark Horse, 1988)
Cheer Down / Poor Little Girl (Dark Horse, 1989)
My Sweet Lord / My Sweet Lord 2000 (Gnome, 2002)
    Any Road / Marwa Blues (Dark Horse, 2003) *(U.K. release)*

Traveling Wilburys Singles

Handle with Care / Margarita (Wilbury Records, 1988)
End of the Line / Congratulations (Wilbury Records, 1989)
Nobody's Child / Lumiere *(Dave Stewart)* (Wilbury Records, 1990)
She's My Baby / New Blue Moon (instrumental) (Wilbury Records, 1990)[4]
Wilbury Twist / New Blue Moon (instrumental) (Wilbury Records, 1990)

[3]In a completely unprecedented move, Harrison allowed three of his songs, "Life Itself," "That Which I Have Lost," and "Writing's on the Wall," to be used as musical accompaniment to a 1993 audio book by his friend Deepak Chopra.

[4]Some 12" and CD-single versions of this release included an additional track, "Runaway," which has otherwise not been released.

Appendix II

George Harrison
Guest Appearances

Is This What You Want?—Jackie Lomax (Apple) 1969*
Goodbye Cream—Cream (Polydor) 1969*
Songs for a Tailor—Jack Bruce (Atco) 1969
Joe Cocker—Joe Cocker (Regal Zonophone) 1969*
That's the Way God Planned It—Billy Preston (Apple) 1969
"Hare Krishna Mantra"/"Prayer to the Spiritual Masters"—The Radha
    Krishna Temple (Apple Single) 1969
"Instant Karma"/"Who Has Seen the Wind" *(Yoko Ono)*—John Lennon/
    Plastic Ono Band (Apple Single) 1970
On Tour—Delaney & Bonnie & Friends with Eric Clapton (Atlantic) 1970
Leon Russell—Leon Russell (Shelter) 1970
Layla and Other Assorted Love Songs—Derek and The Dominoes (Polydor)
    1970
The Worst of…—Ashton, Gardner and Dyke (Capitol) 1970
Encouraging Words—Billy Preston (Apple) 1970*
"Ain't That Cute"/"Vaya Con Dios"—Doris Troy (Apple Single) 1970*
"Jacob's Ladder"/"Get Back"—Doris Troy (Apple Single) 1970
Doris Troy—Doris Troy (Apple) 1970*
"Govinda"/"Govinda Jai Jai"—The Radha Krishna Temple (Apple Single)
    1970
"Try Some Buy Some"/"Tandoori Chicken"—Ronnie Spector (Apple Single)
    1971
"It Don't Come Easy"/"Early 1970"—Ringo Starr (Apple single) 1971
I Wrote a Simple Song—Billy Preston (A&M) 1971
Footprint—Gary Wright (A&M) 1971
David Bromberg—David Bromberg (Columbia) 1971*
Imagine—John Lennon (Apple) 1971
Radha Krsna Temple—Radha Krsna Temple (Apple) 1972
"Back Off Boogaloo"/"Blind Man"—Ringo Starr (Apple single) 1972
Bobby Keys—Bobby Keys (Warner Brothers) 1972
Son of Dracula—Harry Nilsson (RCA) 1972
Straight Up—Badfinger (Apple) 1972
Bobby Whitlock—Bobby Whitlock (Columbia) 1972
Sometime in New York City—John Lennon (Apple) 1972

---

*Indicates that a Harrison composition appears.

On the Road to Freedom—Alvin Lee (Chrysalis) 1973*
The Tin Man Was a Dreamer—Nicky Hopkins (CBS) 1973
It's Like You Never Left—Dave Mason (CBS) 1973
Hobos, Heroes and Street Corner Clowns—Don Nix (P-Vine) 1973
Los Cochinos—Cheech and Chong (Ode) 1973
Ringo—Ringo Starr (Apple) 1973*
"Photograph" / "Down and Out"—Ringo Starr (Apple single) 1973*
I've Got My Own Album to Do—Ron Wood (Warner Brothers) 1974*
The Place I Love—Splinter (Dark Horse) 1974
Shankar Family & Friends—Ravi Shankar (Dark Horse) 1974
Harder to Live—Splinter (Dark Horse) 1975
It's My Pleasure—Billy Preston (A&M) 1975
Blast from Your Past—Ringo Starr (Apple) 1975*
Hard Times—Peter Skellern (Island) 1975
New York Connection—Tom Scott (Ode) 1975
Cross Words—Larry Hosford (Shelter) 1976
Two Man Band—Splinter (Dark Horse) 1977
Along the Red Ledge—Hall and Oates (RCA) 1978
The Visitor—Mick Fleetwood (RCA) 1981
Stop and Smell the Roses—Ringo Starr (Boardwalk) 1981*
Lead Me to the Water—Gary Brooker (Mercury) 1982
Water—Soundtrack (Filmtrax) 1985*
Blue Suede Shoes—Carl Perkins (MCA/Universal) Video 1985
Detroit Diesel—Alvin Lee (US) 1986
Hunting of the Snark—Mike Batt (Adventure) 1986
Blind Faith—Blind Faith (Polydor) 1986
    (Some German and Japanese CD reissues of this album included two
    tracks from a Rick Grech 1969 session, on which Harrison played.)
Tana Mana—Ravi Shankar (Private Music) 1987
His Twangy Guitar and The Rebels—Duane Eddy (Capitol) 1987
Love's a State of Mind—Sylvia Griffin (Rocket) 1988
Some Came Running—Jim Capaldi (Island) 1988
Who I Am—Gary Wright (Sonet) 1988
Crossroads—Eric Clapton (Reprise) 1988
Runaway Horses—Belinda Carlisle (Virgin) 1989
Mystery Girl—Roy Orbison (Virgin) 1989
Journeyman—Eric Clapton (Reprise) 1989*
Full Moon Fever—Tom Petty (MCA) 1989
Work It Out—Jim Horn (Warner Brothers) 1990
Under the Red Sky—Bob Dylan (CBS) 1990
Armchair Theatre—Jeff Lynne (Reprise) 1990
Still Got the Blues—Gary Moore (Virgin) 1990*
About Love and Life—Vicki Brown (Polydor) 1990

Hell to Pay—Jeff Healey (Arista) 1990*
Zoom—Alvin Lee (Sequel) 1992
Growing up in Public—Jimmy Nail (East West) 1992
I Hear You Rockin'—Alvin Lee (Magnum) 1993
The Thirtieth Anniversary Concert Celebration—Bob Dylan (Columbia) 1993
First Signs of Life—Gary Wright (Triloka) 1995
Pure Blues—Alvin Lee (Chrysalis) 1995
    (This compilation includes all Harrison's sessions with Lee.)
Playback-Tom Petty (MCA) 1995
In Celebration—Ravi Shankar (Angel / Dark Horse) 1995
    (This compilation includes most of Harrison's sessions with Ravi Shankar.)
Go Cat Go—Carl Perkins (BMG) 1996
Chants of India—Ravi Shankar (Angel) 1997
The Bootleg Series Volumes 1-3—Bob Dylan (Columbia) 1997
Vertical Man—Ringo Starr (MCA) 1998
Gary Wright: Best of the Dream Weaver—Gary Wright (Rhino) 1998
    (This compilation includes all Harrison's sessions with Wright.)
How Far Have You Come?—Rubyhorse (Horsetrade) 2000
The Very Best of Badfinger—Badfinger (Apple) 2000
    (This compilation includes all Harrison's guitar cameos with Badfinger.)
Double Bill—Bill Wyman's Rhythm Kings (Ripple) 2001
Zoom—Electric Light Orchestra (Epic) 2001
Living on the Outside—Jim Capaldi (Steamhammer) 2001
Small World Big Band—Jools Holland (WSM) 2001*

Bibliography

Amendola, Billy. "Jim Keltner" (WEB Exclusive interview). *www.moderndrummer.com*, April 2003.

Atlas, Jacoba. "Harrison Delights L.A." *Melody Maker* (November 1974).

Badman, Keith. *The Beatles After The Breakup 1970-2000*. London: Omnibus Press, 1999.

Beatles, The. *Anthology*. London: Chronicle Books, 2001.

Beatles, The. *The Beatles Complete*. London: Wise Publications, 1983.

Best, Pete. *Beatle! The Pete Best Story*. London: Plexus Publishing UK, 2001.

Bond, D. P. "Harrison Rocks the Coliseum." *Seattle Post Intelligencer,* November 5, 1974.

Brown, Christine, "Ex-Beatle George Delayed, But Wait Was Worth It." *Detroit Free Press,* December 5, 1974.

"Jim Capaldi Interview." *O Globo* (Brazil), February 2002.

Dawson, Walter. "Harrison Proves Tapes Don't Lie." *The Commercial Appeal,* November 27, 1974.

Dogget, Peter. "The Music of George Harrison" (review). *Record Collector,* April 2003.

Du Noyer, Paul. "But Now They're Really Important." *Q,* December 1995.

Du Noyer, Paul. *Liverpool: Wondrous Place*. London: Virgin Publishing, 2002.

Farrell, Gerry. *Indian Music and the West*. London: Oxford University Press, 1997.

Fine, Jason, ed. *Harrison*. New York: Simon and Schuster, 2002.

Fleischmann, Larry. "Tucson Takes George to Its Heart." *Tucson Citizen,* November 15, 1974.

Fong-Torres, Ben. "Lumbering in the Material World." *Rolling Stone,* December 19, 1974.

Gelzinis, Peter. "Harrison: Less Than Electrifying." *Boston Herald American,* December 11, 1974.

Haacke, Lorraine. "Harrison, Group in Center Show." *Dallas Times Herald,* November 23, 1974.

Harrison, George. *I Me Mine*. London: Genesis Publications, 1980.

———. *Live in Japan*. London: Genesis Publications, 1993.

"Dhani Harrison Interview." *Le Journal du Dimanche* (France), November 2002.

Hart, Richard E. "Remembrance of Music Past: Harrison Concert." *Morning Advocate,* November 1974.

Kemnitz, Robert. "George Harrison at Forum." *Los Angeles Herald,* November 13, 1974.

Kopp, Sheldon. *If You Meet the Buddha on the Road, Kill Him*. London: Sheldon Press, 1974.

Lewishon, Mark. *The Complete Beatles Chronicle*. London: Hamlyn, 2000.

———. *The Complete Beatles Recording Sessions*. London: Hamlyn, 1990.

Leyland, Don. "East Meets West and Georgie Comes Good in Comeback Capital." *Sounds*, December 14, 1974: 7-8.

MacDonald, Ian. *Revolution in the Head*. London: Pimlico, 1994.

McDonough, Jack. "What's in a Weekend." *Pacific Sun,* November 14, 1974

Madinger, Chip and Mark Easter. *Eight Arms to Hold You*. Chesterfield, MO: 44 1 Productions, 2000.

Majid, Professor Farida. "Talibanization of Cyberspace by Crypto-Islamists." *News from Bangla Desh*, December 2001.

Miller, Jim. "George Harrison: Dark Horse" (LP review). *Rolling Stone*, February 13, 1975.

Murawski, Patti. "All Aboard the Hari's on Tour Express!" *The Harrison Alliance* (July–December 1994).

Pleeth, William. *Cello*. London: Kahn & Averil, 1982.

Reck, D. B. "Beatles Orientalis: Influences from Asia in a Popular Song Form." *Asian Music* XVI (1985): 83–150.

Rense, Rip. "There Went The Sun: Reflections on the Passing of George Harrison." *The Rip Post* (website), December 2001

Richmond, Dick. "George Harrison and Company at the Arena." *St. Louis Post-Dispatch,* November 21, 1974.

Rockwell, John. "George Harrison Returns to the Garden." *The New York Times,* December 20, 1974.

Rohter, Larry. "For Harrison, Some Thing Must Pass." *The Washington Post,* December 14, 1974.

Rolly, Paul. "George Harrison Wows Crowd at Salt Palace.*" Salt Lake Tribune*, November 17, 1974.

Rudis, Al. "George Still Has It Together—And How!" *Chicago Sun Times,* December 1, 1974, 100–101.

Sellers, Robert. *Very Naughty Boys*. London: Metro, 2004.

Shankar, Ravi. *My Music My Life.* New York: Simon and Schuster, 1968.

———. *Raga Mala.* London: Genesis Publications, 1997.

Sloman, Larry. "George's Tour Winds Down in New York, and Mr. Harrison Goes to Washington." *Rolling Stone* (January 30, 1975).

Takiff, Jonathan. "A Pleasant Victory for George Harrison." *Philadelphia News,* December 17, 1974, 34.

Thomas, Harry. "George Harrison: Somewhere in England" (LP review). *Rolling Stone,* August 6, 1981.

Turner, Steve. "Eric Clapton Interview." *Rolling Stone*, July 18, 1974.

Vivekananda, Swami. *Raja-Yoga.* New York: Ramakrishna-Vivekananda Center, 1980.

Wenderborn, John. "Opening Concert by ex-Beatle Harrison Left Many Listeners Grumbling." *The Oregonian,* November 2, 1974.

Yogananda, Paramhansa. *Autobiography of a Yogi.* Nevada City, CA: Crystal Clarity Publishers, 1995.

Index